American Ethnicity

The Dynamics and Consequences of Discrimination

SECOND EDITION

Adalberto Aguirre, Jr.
University of California, Riverside

Jonathan H. Turner
University of California, Riverside

Boston, Massachusetts Burr Ridge, Illinois Dubuque, Iowa
Madison, Wisconsin New York, New York San Francisco, California, St. Louis, Missouri

McGraw-Hill

A Division of The McGraw-Hill Companies

AMERICAN ETHNICITY:

The Dynamics and Consequences of Discrimination

Acknowledgments appear on page 307, and on this page by reference.

This book is printed on acid-free paper.

1 2 3 4 5 6 7 8 9 0 FGR FGR 9 0 9 8 7

ISBN 0-07-000627-X

This book was set in New Century Schoolbook by Ruttle, Shaw & Wetherill, Inc.
The editor was Jill S. Gordon;
the production supervisor was Annette Mayeski.
The cover was designed by Karen K. Quigley.
Project supervision was done by The Total Book.
The photo editor was Inge King.
Quebecor Printing/Fairfield was printer and binder.

Library of Congress Cataloging-in-Publication Data

Aguirre, Adalberto.
American ethnicity: the dynamics and consequences of discrimination / Adalberto Aguirre, Jr., Jonathan H. Turner. — 2nd ed.
p. cm.
Includes bibliographical references and index.
ISBN 0–07–000627–X
1. United States—Race relations. 2. United States—Ethnic relations. 3. Discrimination—United States. 4. Ethnicity—United States. I. Turner, Jonathan H. II Title.
E184.A1A38 1998
305.8'00973—dc21

97–10257
CIP

http://www.mhhe.com

About the Authors

ADALBERTO AGUIRRE, JR., is professor of sociology, University of California at Riverside. He is the author of over five books and many articles in professional journals. Among his books related to this effort are *Race, Racism and the Death Penalty in the United States, Perspectives on Race and Ethnicity in American Criminal Justice, Chicanos in Higher Education: Dilemmas for the 21st Century,* and *Chicanos and Intelligence Testing.*

JONATHAN H. TURNER is professor of sociology, University of California at Riverside. He is the author of over twenty-five books and many articles in professional journals. Among his books related to this effort are *Oppression: A Sociohistory of Black-White Relations, American Society: Problems of Structure, Social Problems in America,* and *Inequality: Privilege & Poverty in America.*

To Our Wives,
Carmen Alicia Aguirre
Alexandra Maryanski

Contents in Brief

Contents

Preface

At the close of this century, it is clear that the ethnic composition of the United States is undergoing a profound change. Change always produces tension; and change in the relative distributions of ethnic populations is one of the most volatile forces in human organization. At the core of ethnic tensions are (1) the sense of threat experienced by some ethnic people and (2) discrimination against those who are perceived to pose this threat. Our goal in this book is to understand how these dynamics have played out among the most prominent ethnic subpopulations in America. To this end, we employ a conceptual framework that incorporates the key ideas from existing theories to organize both historical and more recent census data on the situation of an ethnic population. The great virtue of using a unified conceptual framework to organize the data is that such a framework enables us to compare the respective fates of diverse ethnic groups in the United States and, as we explore in a new chapter, of ethnic populations in other parts of the world.

Our analysis of each ethnic group in America begins with simple questions: What share of resources does this ethnic subpopulation receive? How much income, education, health care, housing, and other valued resources does an ethnic group possess, relative to other ethnics? Then, we explore how discrimination in the past and the present can account for inequality in the distribution of resources among various ethnic groups. In examining the dynamics of discrimination, we call attention to other important forces, such as the sense of threat experienced by those who discriminate, the negative stereotypes that are created to legitimize discrimination, the varying degrees of identifiability of people as targets for discrimination, and, most importantly, the institutionalization of discrimination in economic, political, legal, educational, and housing patterns. These forces, as they have fueled and channeled discrimination, have created a system of ethnic stratification which, once in place, reinforces the very discriminatory forces that created this system of stratification in the first place. True, for many ethnics, this system of ethnic stratification is breaking down, but for others, despite active protests, it remains in place. The challenge for the twenty-first century is to mitigate against the discriminatory forces that produce ethnic stratification; and this challenge is doubly difficult because of the rapidly changing ethnic composition of America today and the inevitable sense of threat and ethnic tension that changes in the composition of ethnicity produce.

We have amassed a large number of debts in writing this book. The following reviewers provided many helpful comments and suggestions: E. M. Beck, University of Georgia; Larry Carps, Northwestern Michigan College; Richard M. Cramer, University of North Carolina at Chapel Hill; Timothy Evans, Community College of Allegheny County; Charles Green, CUNY-Hunter College; Meg Wilkes Karraker, University of St. Thomas; Peter Kivista, Augustana College; Peter Melvoin, Bellevue Community College; Ernest Quimby, Howard University; Peter I. Rose, Smith College; Ellen Rosengarten, Sinclair Community College; Sara A. Soule, University of Arizona; and Becky Thompson, Memphis State University. The following individuals were invaluable in assisting us with the research for population statistics: Manuel de la Puente and Edna Paisano at the U.S. Bureau of the Census; Ruth McKay at the U.S. Department of Labor Statistics; Tony Hernandez at the Hispanic Research Center, Arizona State University and Georges Vernez at The Rand. We have also attempted to incorporate into the second edition many of the comments sent to us from instructors using the book and from students who have used the book. Our thanks to David Baker for serving as a sounding board for many of the issues in this book. Our special thanks to Clara for helping us bring coherency to the manuscript. Finally, we give our heartfelt thanks to our families for giving us the space and time to complete this book.

Adalberto Aguirre, Jr.

Jonathan H. Turner

American Ethnicity

The Dynamics and Consequences of Discrimination

CHAPTER 1

Ethnicity and Ethnic Relations

Ethnic strife exists in virtually every part of the world, and it is a force that drives people to kill each other or, at the very least, to treat each other as inferior or dangerous. It is a force that mobilizes the most intense hatreds and animosities, often leading to war among nations and violence within a country. If we look at the world today, the power of ethnicity is clearly evident: In what used to be Yugoslavia, a tense peace exists in the aftermath of the attempted genocide of Muslim Bosnians by Serbians; in the rest of the old Soviet Union and its satellite nations, the remnants of a once powerful empire have collapsed into constituent ethnic populations; in what used to be Czechoslovakia, there are now two nations, divided by their perceived ethnic differences; in what is now Canada, the French-speaking population is prepared to secede from the union; in what is today India and Pakistan was once a larger civilization that was partitioned on the basis of ethnicity; in what was once Palestine, a promising peace process between Arabs and Israelis appears to have taken a step backward; in South Africa, a bloody civil war between whites and blacks was miraculously avoided, although transition to majority rule is far from complete; in what was once colonial central Africa, Hutus and Titsis seek to kill the other on a mass scale; in what is now an emerging European union, ethnic conflicts have surfaced not only among old enemies but also against new immigrants; and in what is supposed to be the **United** States, divisions by ethnicity can be found everywhere.

Indeed, at almost any spot on the globe, ethnic hatreds or, at the very least, ethnic tensions can be found in many forms and guises: Noisy protests and strategic disobedience, long-term patterns of oppression, terrorist bombings, and mass killings. Why does ethnic tension and racial hatred persist in patterns of human organization? Why did the early white settlers in North America, for example, kill so many Native Americans? Why did slavery exist? Why are neo-Nazi hate groups emerging in Germany? Why are churches attended by African Americans arson targets?

Why do Catholics and Protestants in Northern Ireland wall themselves off from each other? Why do ethnic jokes about Pollacks, Whops, Japs, Jews, and others still persist in America at the close of the twentieth century? Why do European-origin Americans so fear Latinos? And so the questions go.

Our goal in this book is to answer these and the many related questions that can be asked about ethnicity. Our emphasis is on American ethnic tensions, but we will also seek to place these tensions in a more global perspective. Indeed, compared to the violence and killings in many parts of the world, the dynamics of ethnicity in America can appear rather muted. This is not to say, however, that tensions among American ethnics are not severe. On the contrary, the existing divisions among ethnics in the United States are at a critical phase; America will either become a viable multiethnic society, or it will degenerate into patterns of hatred and violence so evident in our nation's past and so clear in much of the world today. The task before us, then, is to understand American ethnic antagonisms; and with this understanding, perhaps we can better appreciate what needs to be done in order to reduce the conflicts among ethnic groups in America.

In this chapter, we will get started in this task by clarifying basic concepts. To understand a phenomenon like ethnicity, we need to define key terms that will be used to understand how this phenomenon operates. So let us begin with a conceptual mapping of our subject; and in the next chapter, we can turn to theorizing about the dynamic properties of American ethnic relations in global perspective.

RACE AND ETHNICITY

The term "race" connotes biological differences among peoples—skin color, facial features, stature, and the like—that are transmitted from generation to generation. As such, these biological differences are seen as permanent characteristics of people. The notion of race does not make much sense as a biological concept, however, because the physical characteristics that make people distinctive are trivial. A few alleles on genes are what account for these differences, and, most importantly, these alleles are on genes that are not determinative of basic biological functions. These biological differences are, in essence, superficial. Moreover, they do not mark clear boundaries: Where does "black" end and "white" begin? Is the child of an Asian mother and a European father more Asian or more European?

Even though biological differences are superficial and difficult to use as markers of boundaries between peoples, they are important sociologically. For if people believe that others are biologically distinctive, they tend to respond to them as being different. And, when people associate superficial biological differences with variations in psychological, intellectual, and behavioral makeup, they may feel justified in treating members of a distinctive group in discriminatory ways. For example, if some individuals in a society consider dark skin an important distinction, and this distinction becomes associated in their minds with differences in the behavior of "black people," then this superficial biological difference will influence how those with black skin are treated in that society.

How, then, should we conceptualize the notion of "race" if it does not make much biological sense? Our answer is to subordinate and incorporate the idea of race into a broad definition of *ethnicity*. When a subpopulation of individuals reveals, or is perceived to reveal, shared historical experiences as well as unique organizational, behavioral, and cultural characteristics, it exhibits its ethnicity. For instance, when country of origin, religion, family practices, interpersonal style, language, beliefs, values, and other characteristics are used to demark a population of individuals from others, then ethnicity is operating. The more visible the characteristics marking ethnicity, the more likely it is that those in an ethnic category will be treated differently.

Here is where race or presumptions of biological differences become a part of ethnicity. Physical features like skin color and facial features can be used as highly visible markers of organizational, behavioral, and cultural differences among individuals. When someone is labeled "black," more than skin color is involved; whole clusters of assumptions about historical experiences, behavior, organization, and culture are associated with this label. The same is true for labels such as "white," "Asian," "Mexican," "Jew," and "Indian."

In fact, as we will come to see, labels are often self-fulfilling in creating and sustaining ethnicity. If people are given a label because of their skin color and then discriminated against as if they were different, they will react to such treatment by behaving and organizing in ways that are indeed distinctive. Once behavioral and organizational differences exist and are elaborated culturally into norms, beliefs, and other systems of symbols, they become an additional marker of differences, both justifying the earlier label and the distinctive treatment of these others as somehow "different." So, if biological distinctiveness can become a part of the label for denoting populations, then biology becomes an aspect of the social dynamics producing and sustaining ethnicity. Indeed, racial labels are like turbochargers in ethnic relations: They escalate the heat and power of emotions and tensions.

ETHNIC GROUPS

What is a group? Sociologists generally define a group as a gathering of individuals in face-to-face interaction. According to this definition, an ethnic "group" would be a number of interacting individuals distinguished by their ethnicity. Not every one of these individuals interacts face to face, but they may interact in various social settings. Obviously, when we use the term "ethnic group," we have something much bigger, broader, more inclusive in mind. *Subpopulations* of individuals in a society can be distinguished by their history as well as their distinctive behavior, organization, culture, and, perhaps, superficial biological features. An *ethnic group* is a subpopulation of individuals who are labeled and categorized by the general population and, often, by the members of a group itself as being of a particular type of ethnicity. They reveal a unique history as well as distinctive behavioral, organizational, and cultural characteristics, and, as a result, they often are treated differently by others. In addition to the term "ethnic group," in this text we use the terms *ethnic subpopulation* and *ethnic population*, which more accurately describe the groups that we are discussing.

MINORITY GROUPS

What is a *minority group?* Louis Wirth (1945:347) long ago offered the basic definition, the general thrust of which is still used today: "A group of people who, because of their physical or cultural characteristics, are singled out from others in the society in which they live for differential and unequal treatment and who therefore regard themselves as objects of collective discrimination." There are many problems with this definition, however. First, it is not a group but members of a larger subpopulation who are singled out for unequal treatment. Second, the label "minority" is not always accurate; sometimes it is a majority, as was the case historically in South Africa, that is discriminated against. Thus, we should begin to revise this traditional definition of "minority group" by acknowledging what it really means: an ethnic subpopulation in a society subject to discrimination by members of *more powerful ethnic subpopulations*. Usually the victimized subpopulation is a numerical minority, and the more powerful discriminators are in the majority. Since this is not always true, however, the important issue is this: Which ethnic subpopulation has the power to discriminate? The more powerful subpopulation is the dominant or superordinate ethnic group, and the less powerful ethnic subpopulation is the subordinate group. This latter terminology, which revolves around dominance and subordination, more accurately frames the issues that were once classified as "minority group relations."

ETHNIC DISCRIMINATION

Phrases like "unequal treatment" and "distinctive treatment" have been used rather loosely thus far. These and related terms can be consolidated by one key term: "discrimination." In general, *discrimination* is the process by which an individual, group, or subpopulation of individuals acts in ways that deny another individual, group, or subpopulation access to valued resources. So, in the context of ethnic relations, *ethnic discrimination* is the process by which the members of a more powerful and dominant ethnic subpopulation deny the members of another, less powerful and subordinate ethnic subpopulation full access to valued resources—jobs, income, education, health, prestige, power, or anything that the members of a society value.

Today, the term "reverse discrimination" is often used to emphasize that programs designed to overcome the effects of past discrimination against members of a subordinate subpopulation often deny some members of the dominant subpopulation equal access to valued resources. What makes these programs so controversial is that those denied access to resources—say, particular classes of jobs—are usually not the ones who engaged in discrimination in the past. Thus, they feel cheated and angry—emotions that the victims of discrimination almost always feel. The phrase "reverse discrimination" is pejorative in that it emphasizes the net loss of resources for those who may no longer discriminate but whose forefathers did; and so, they ask: Is this fair? On the other side, those who must live with the legacy of past discrimination ask: How are the effects of past discrimination to be overcome? There is no easy answer to either of these questions, but one thing is clear: The term "discrimination" often becomes the centerpiece of ideological and political debate over ethnic tensions (Kinder and Sanders, 1990; Thomas, 1990; Feagins, 1990; and Ross, 1990).

The process of discrimination is the most important force sustaining ethnicity in a society. Discrimination denies some people access to what is valued, making it a highly volatile process. Because discrimination varies in nature, degree, and form, we need to identify some of its dimensions.

Types of Discrimination

The ways in which discrimination is perpetrated against an ethnic population vary considerably. The most intense form is *genocide,* where members of an ethnic subpopulation are killed or, potentially, an entire ethnic group is exterminated. The Nazi death camps with their gas chambers constituted an effort at genocide; the exposure of Native Americans to diseases and then the carnage of the Indian wars resulted in the virtual genocide of the original population in America. More recently, the "ethnic cleansing" policies of the Serbians in the former Yugoslavia is another example of genocidal behavior.

Expulsion is a somewhat less intense form of discrimination because those who are exiled from a society retain access to at least one highly valued resource: life. Expulsion is a common form of discrimination. For example, during the time of slavery in the United States, several American presidents, including Abraham Lincoln, considered the creation of a black state in Africa to which "free" black people would be sent. Expulsion is usually forced, but it is often the case that one group makes life so miserable for another that the latter leaves "voluntarily." Thus, the concept of expulsion has ambiguity: If we confine its use only to cases in which people are thrown out of a country by direct coercion, the importance of more indirect expulsion, where people's lives are made sufficiently miserable that they pack up and leave, is underemphasized.

Segregation is a process of spatially isolating an ethnic subpopulation in areas where they cannot have the same access to valued resources as those who are not isolated. For instance, as we will see in Chapter 4, most African Americans were confined to the decaying cores of large cities during the post–World War II era by governmental and private housing policies; and as a result, they were denied access to the jobs, schools, and housing enjoyed by white Americans who moved to suburbia. The black townships and various rules of residence in South Africa mark another segregation pattern that historically denied access to resources. The Indian reservations that dot the American landscape are yet another form of segregation.

Exclusion is a pattern of discrimination that denies members of an ethnic group certain positions, independent of the effects of segregation. Slaves were denied basic citizenship rights. Up to just a few decades ago, African

Box 1.1

The Gender Dimension of Discrimination

Discrimination denies people access to valued resources, such as jobs and income. Most of the analyses of ethnic groups in this text emphasize the ethnic subpopulation as a whole, but it is also necessary to emphasize that ethnic discrimination reveals a gender dimension: Men and women of any ethnic population have different degrees of access to many important resources, indicating that women and men are treated differently in American society. For example, examine the figures in the table below. Across the board, in 1990 women received less income than their male counterparts. These differences reflect not only the income discrepancies between men and women in the same occupation but also the disproportionate numbers of women in lower-paying occupations.

Ethnic Population	Male	Female	Proportion of Median Female Earnings to Male Earnings, %
White American	$28,540	$18,920	0.66
African American	20,430	17,390	0.85
Latino	14,047	9,861	0.70
Asian	22,168	14,122	0.63

The table on the next page compares the occupational distribution of men and women in 1990. In the top-paying category—managerial and professional—the proportion of women equals or tops that of men, except within the Asian American population. But in the lower-paying technical, sales, and administrative support jobs (mostly secretarial), the proportion of women nearly doubles that of men. Coupled with the virtual exclusion of minority women from higher-skill, better-paying blue-collar positions such as precision production workers, craft laborers, repair people, operators, fabricators, and laborers (who are often unionized), the reason for the lower incomes of most minority women becomes clear: These women are excluded from most higher-paying occupations.

Selected Occupations by Sex, Race, and Ethnicity, 1990

Occupation	*White Americans, %*		*African Americans, %*		*Latinos, %*		*Asian Americans, %*		*Native Americans, %*	
	Male	Female	Male	Female	Male	Female	Male	Female	Male	Female
Managerial and professional specialty	27.3	27.4	13.4	18.8	10.7	16.0	35.9	27.9	13.5	20.9
Technical, sales, and administrative support	20.8	45.7	16.6	39.7	14.7	38.4	24.3	43.3	13.9	39.1
Service	8.7	16.1	17.5	27.0	16.2	25.1	14.6	15.7	10.0	23.8
Precision production, craft, and repair	19.9	2.1	16.3	2.3	20.6	2.7	12.4	3.0	22.1	3.2
Operations, fabrication, and labor	19.2	7.6	33.4	12.0	29.8	16.7	11.6	10.0	35.1	11.8
Farming, forestry, and fishing	4.1	1.1	2.8	0.2	8.0	1.1	1.2	0.1	5.4	1.2
	100.0	100.0	100.0	100.0	100.0	100.0	100.0	100.0	100.0	100.0

Source: 1990 Census Detailed Occupations EEO File for the United States.

Americans were excluded from most craft unions; even in industrial unions, they were allowed to rise only to certain grade levels and not beyond. For many decades, African Americans and Latinos in the Southwest were excluded from the political arena through poll taxes, literacy tests, gerrymandering of districts, and other exclusionary tactics. Exclusion in the job sphere is especially harmful because it denies members of an ethnic group the money they could use to buy other valued resources—health care, housing, education, and political power. Exclusion from the political arena denies an ethnic group the power to move out of its subordinate position.

Selective inclusion is the process of allowing members of ethnic subpopulations into certain positions, while at the same time excluding them from other positions. For instance, Jews in Europe historically were excluded from most economic, social, and political positions but were included in the world of finance. In the United States, early Asian immigrants were allowed access to some positions—the Chinese were laborers on the railroads and later in small service businesses. According to Takaki (1993), the Japanese were denied access to the industrial labor market in California during the 1920s; as a result, many moved into the agricultural labor market where they used their entrepreneurial skills to become successful farmers and land owners. Today, many Asian immigrants are given easy access to ownership of small retail businesses but are excluded, to some degree, from white- and blue-collar positions in large companies. In the past and still today, Mexican American laborers were included in the low-wage farm labor workforce and, later, in other low-paying jobs in light industry, but they were excluded from better-paying economic positions as well as positions in the political and educational arena. Thus *exclusion* and *selective inclusion* tend to operate simultaneously, in a pincerlike movement that denies access to some positions and opens access only to those areas that are often (though not always) financially unrewarding or lacking in power and prestige.

The intensity of discrimination varies according to its type: from genocide and expulsion to physical segregation to exclusion and selective inclusion. None is pleasant, if you are on the receiving end. Historically, these patterns of discrimination have been implemented in various ways, but the underlying mechanisms of discrimination are much the same, as we explore below.

The Institutionalization of Discrimination

Acts by individuals who seek to deny others access to valued resources are the most salient form of discrimination. When a white refuses to sell a house to an Asian, when a police officer physically abuses a member of a minority group, or when a supervisor refuses to promote an ethnic worker and these actions are taken simply because a person is a member of an ethnic group, discrimination is at work. These examples are isolated acts of discrimination if (1) they are not sanctioned by cultural values, beliefs, and norms; (2) they are not performed as a matter of policy within an organized structure such as a corporation, police department, board of realtors, school, or factory; and (3) they are not frequent and pervasive in the informal contact among people within an organization. In contrast, *institutionalized discrimination* exists when these individual acts are sanctioned by cultural values, beliefs, laws, and norms; when they are part of the way a social structure normally operates; and when they are a pervasive and persistent feature of the contact among people.

The distinction between isolated acts of discrimination and institutionalized discrimination is easier to make in a definition than in practice. For example, when discrimination is institutionalized in one sphere—say, housing practices—it becomes easier to commit acts of discrimination in other arenas, such as schooling, politics, or jobs. If enough people practice such isolated acts of informal discrimination, these acts become institutionalized. In the United States, civil rights laws and cultural beliefs do not condone discrimination as they once did; indeed, they demand that all individuals be given equal access to schools, jobs, housing, and other important resources. They even mandate punishments for those who discriminate, and they have led to the creation of watchdog and enforcement agencies. Yet, individual acts of informal discrimination are so widespread in many

Prejudicial attitudes toward black people created a context in which Africans were auctioned off to the highest bidder.

communities that discrimination is informally institutionalized even in the face of formal prohibitions.

Thus, the process of institutionalized discrimination is subtle and complex. It can operate at formal and informal levels, and these two levels can even be in contradiction. Isolated acts of discrimination can increase in frequency when they constitute a normatively sanctioned and, hence, institutionalized form of discrimination.

The subtlety and complexity of institutionalized discrimination is demonstrated in past patterns of discrimination that are now formally banned and no longer practiced. Yet, the legacy and cumulative effects of past discrimination can be so great that they prevent ethnic subpopulations from gaining equal access to resources. For example, many African Americans today live in urban slums away from decent schools, housing, and jobs because of past patterns of discrimination. In this environment, many blacks do not acquire the education, job skills, or motivation that would enable them to leave the slums and take advantage of new opportunities that were not available even thirty years ago. Thus, sometimes the legacy of the past operates as a barrier in the present and constitutes a pervasive pattern of discrimination. For example, many blacks (Native Americans, Latinos, and others) are systematically denied by their present circumstances the same access to valued resources as whites. Even if we could assume that no employer, realtor, teacher, or police officer currently acts in a discriminatory way, many African Americans would not have the same degree of access to resources as white Americans because of their present location in segregated slums with a long history of exclusion from most spheres of mainstream life in America. The same is true of other ethnic groups, and so we must acknowledge that institutionalized discrimination has a lag effect beyond the period in the past when individuals and organizations practiced discrimination routinely.

Another facet of institutionalized discrimination is that it is often unintentional. This is certainly the case with the holdover effects of past discrimination discussed above, but more is involved. To take the most obvious example in the United States today—schools—it is now clear that the school curriculum, testing procedures, and classroom activities place some ethnic students at a disadvantage in comparison with others. This type of discrimination is not intentional, at least in most instances; and it could be argued (albeit problematically) that schools facilitate the acquisition of the critical skills necessary for success and for overcoming the effects of past discrimination. Yet, if the schools are organized in ways that are, for example, alien to students, that are unresponsive to the problems of poor children or immigrant children, and that are insensitive to the distinctive culture of a minority population, then the schools can become a source of discrimination. Students will have difficulty adjusting and will become discouraged—dropping out and finding themselves with few prospects for jobs and income. The school may not have intended this to occur—indeed, just the opposite—but the very nature of its structure and operation has worked to discourage students and, in so doing, has subtly and inadvertently discriminated against students whose access to resources is dramatically lowered when they drop out (Hilliard, 1988; Medina, 1988; Trueba, 1986; and McCarthy, 1990). In a society that uses educational credentials as a quick and easy way to sort people out in a labor market, the consequences for members of ethnic subpopulations who find the school experience unrewarding extend to all spheres of their life—their job, home, income, and health.

Thus, the institutionalization of discrimination is an important force in ethnic relations. The pattern of institutionalization affects the type of segregation, exclusion, and selective inclusion that a subordinate ethnic subpopulation experiences, if it is not killed off or sent away. As the pattern of institutionalized discrimination changes, so do patterns of segregation, exclusion, and selective inclusion.

ETHNIC STRATIFICATION

Discrimination, as it operates to segregate, exclude, and selectively include members of a subordinate ethnic subpopulation within a society, produces a system of ethnic stratification. Because discrimination determines how many and which types of valued resources the members of an ethnic subpopulation are likely to have, it establishes the location of an ethnic subpopulation within the stratification system of a society. Moreover, discrimination also determines the patterns of mobility, if any, across social class lines.

For our purposes, *ethnic stratification* refers to several interrelated processes:

1. The amount, level, and type of resources—such as jobs, education, health, money, power, and prestige—an ethnic subpopulation typically receives
2. The degree to which these resource shares locate most members of an ethnic subpopulation in various social hierarchies
3. The extent to which these resource shares contribute to those distinctive behaviors, organizations, and cultural systems that provide justification to the dominant group for making them targets of discrimination

We can take almost any ethnic group—Latinos, for example (see Chapter 6)—and determine their average income, their level of political representation, and their average years of education. In performing this exercise, we soon find that, on the whole, many Latinos in America have relatively low incomes, are underrepresented in the halls of political power, and attain less education than Anglo-Americans. The statistics can be determined by simple counts of average income, years of education, and number of political offices held. The numbers show the share of resources that Latinos possess in American society. One often finds, in addition, differences in the shares of resources *within* an ethnic subpopulation. There are affluent Latinos as well as very poor ones; their average level of affluence, power, and prestige tends to vary in terms of which subpopulation—Mexican American, Cuban, Puerto Rican, South or Central American—is being addressed. Yet, when ethnic stratification is in evidence, a majority of a subpopulation does reveal a particular level and configuration of resource shares. On various social hierarchies—power, income and wealth, prestige, and education—a profile of resource shares locates a majority of the ethnic group at a particular place in the broader system of stratification. There are always deviations, of course, but when ethnic stratification is in force, these deviations apply to a minority of cases. Some Latinos, such as Mexican Americans, are located near the bottom of the power, income and wealth, prestige, and education hierarchies, thereby placing them in the lower and working classes. There are middle- and upper-class Mexican Americans, to be sure, but they are a tiny minority of this subpopulation as a whole. This profile of resource shares and the resulting location on various social hierarchies contribute to the distinctiveness of Mexican Americans and, as a consequence, justify new and continuing prejudices and discrimination against them, thereby perpetuating the ethnic dimensions of social stratification.

In general, discrimination causes members of an ethnic subpopulation to be (1) overrepresented in lower and working classes or (2) overrepresented in a narrow range of middle-class positions, usually in small businesses of various kinds. As discrimination lessens, mobility to other classes and positions within classes occurs, but a holdover effect persists that limits such mobility for many.

Thus, institutionalized discrimination, as it segregates, excludes, and selectively includes, determines the kinds and shares of resources received by members of an ethnic subpopulation; these shares locate them on society's hierarchies. By virtue of its pattern of resource shares and location on various social hierarchies, an ethnic subpopulation's distinctiveness is created and sustained. Thus, the principal consequence of ethnic discrimination is to give the broader stratification system in a society an ethnic dimension, one that is often more tension-producing and volatile than the normal antagonisms between members of different social classes.

ETHNIC PREJUDICE

The terms "prejudice" and "discrimination" are often uttered together, for it is presumed that prejudiced people discriminate, and vice versa. *Prejudice* is a set of beliefs and stereotypes about a category of people; hence, *ethnic prejudices* are beliefs and stereotypes about designated subpopulations who share certain identifying characteristics—biological, behavioral, organizational, or cultural—or at least are perceived to share these identifying characteristics. Those prejudices that lead to, and are used to justify, discrimination are negative, emphasizing the undesirable features of a subpopulation.

Does prejudice invariably lead to discrimination? In a classic study in the early 1930s, Richard La Piere (1934) observed in his travels with a Chinese couple that, despite a climate of hostility toward Asians in the United States at that time, the couple was served and treated courteously at hotels, motels, and restaurants. He was puzzled by this observation because all the attitude surveys at that time revealed extreme prejudice by white Americans toward the Chinese. La Piere sent a questionnaire to the owners of the establishments where he and his Asian companions had experienced courteous service, asking if they would "accept members of the Chinese race as guests in your establishment." More than 90 percent said no, thus demonstrating that prejudice and discrimination do not always go together.

Robert Merton (1949) defined four categories of people in his analysis of the relationship between prejudice and discrimination:

1. *All-weather liberals* who are not prejudiced and do not discriminate
2. *Reluctant liberals* who are unprejudiced but will discriminate when it is in their interest to do so
3. *Timid bigots* who are prejudiced but afraid to show it
4. *Active bigots* who are prejudiced and quite willing to discriminate

In La Piere's study of motel owners, then, he encountered timid bigots who, in face-to-face contact with an ethnic group, did not implement their prejudices.

Even though prejudice does not always translate into discrimination, it is an important force in ethnic relations, for several reasons. First, prejudicial beliefs and stereotypes highlight, usually unfairly and inaccurately, certain characteristics of an ethnic subpopulation. By spotlighting these characteristics, they make ethnic group members become more identifiable, alerting others to their existence, separating them from the majority, and potentially making them easier targets for discrimination. Second, prejudices present negative images of an ethnic group, legitimizing discrimination against such "undesirable" persons. Third, prejudices arouse fears about, and anger toward, an ethnic group, placing members of the ethnic group in constant tension with those who are prejudiced and, often, making them vulnerable to unprovoked acts of discrimination. Fourth, prejudice creates a general climate of intolerance for differences not only in a selected ethnic group but in other categories of individuals as well (such as the disabled or the elderly).

Prejudice may generate potential or actual discrimination, but the reverse is also true: Acts of discrimination can generate prejudice or, as is often the case, reinforce existing prejudices. Most people feel they must justify their acts of discrimination; in a society like the United States, where cultural values emphasize equality and freedom, discrimination, which violates these values, has to be rationalized and made to seem appropriate. Prejudice is one mechanism for doing this because it makes the denial of freedom and equality seem acceptable "in this one case" since "after all, these people are so . . . (fill in the prejudice)." Those who are victims of discrimination react in different ways: sometimes passively and other times aggressively. The results of people's reaction against prejudice and discrimination vary—prejudicial stereotypes are sometimes reinforced, other times changed or eliminated.

Thus, prejudicial beliefs based on negative and stereotypical portrayals of an ethnic subpopulation stimulate and sustain ethnic tensions. Such beliefs do not always translate into direct discriminatory action, but they target, highlight the negative, arouse fears and anger, and create a culture of intolerance that can erupt into discriminatory acts or legitimate those that have been practiced in the past. Prejudice provides the rationale for discrimination, either before or after the fact, and is thus central to understanding discrimination and patterns of ethnic stratification.

ADAPTATIONS TO PREJUDICE AND DISCRIMINATION

When confronted with discrimination, members of a subordinate subpopulation respond. Usually, they seek to make the best of a difficult situation. Depending upon the nature and magnitude of discrimination, as well as upon other social conditions, several responses are possible: (1) passive acceptance, (2) marginal participation, (3) assimilation, (4) withdrawal, (5) rebellion, and (6) organized protest. Different segments of a minority population may resort to several of these adaptations at the same time, or a population may pass through different patterns of adaptation.

Passive Acceptance

If the power of an ethnic group is small and the magnitude of the discrimination great, members of the group may have no choice but to accept the discrimination. For example, during the slavery era in the United States, it was virtually impossible for African slaves to do anything but accept subjugation. Yet, even under severely oppressive conditions, populations acquire interpersonal techniques for dealing with their oppressors while maintaining their sense of identity and dignity. The stereotypical slave, as portrayed in Harriet Beecher Stowe's *Uncle Tom's Cabin,* offers a vivid example of such techniques. Uncle Tom's bowing and scraping and repeated use of the phrase "Yes sir, yes sir" allowed him to gain favor with white people and to enjoy some degree of privilege. Passive acceptance, then, is often not passive but, rather, active manipulation of a situation. Some slaves were able to develop their own culture and to enjoy some of the basic pleasures of life through the appearance of "passive acceptance." Of course, such a pattern of adjustment tends to perpetuate itself; the subordinate population does not initiate change, and the majority is not pressured to cease its discriminatory practices.

Marginal Participation

At times, subordinate ethnic subpopulations can find a niche where they can use their creative resources and prosper. In essence, these subpopulations are allowed *marginal participation*. For example, Jews have often been able to find business opportunities and to prosper in societies that actively discriminated against them. At the turn of the century and up to the present, many Chinese Americans were able to prosper in small businesses providing services to the white American majority. Such marginal niches are created when the majority is not inclined to enter a specialized field. Marginal participation tends to be most successful when the minority population is small and does not enter areas dominated by the majority. It is probably for this reason that African Americans and Chicanos have been unable to find specialized niches; their numbers are simply too great.

Assimilation

Assimilation is the process by which the members of an ethnic group become part of the broader culture and society, losing their distinctive character. Minorities that are less identifiable biologically and culturally are more readily assimilated. Ethnic populations that can be easily identified, however, have greater difficulty assimilating. It is for this reason that white ethnic groups in America, such as the Protestant Irish and Germans, have become largely assimilated, although enclaves are thriving in some large eastern cities. Other Caucasian migrants, such as Poles, Italians, and Catholic Irish, have also tended to assimilate, although the East and Midwest have cohesive ethnic cultures of these populations. African Americans, on the other hand, have had a more difficult time assimilating because of their visibility and the resulting ease with which the majority can locate them as targets of discrimination.

Withdrawal and Self-Segregation

Another adaptation to discrimination is withdrawal and the creation of a self-sustaining "society" within the broader society. Such *self-segregation* enables a population to create and support their own communities, businesses, schools, leadership, churches, and other social forms. For example, the early black Muslim movement in America advocated a separate African American community, self-supporting and isolated from "white" institutions. Urban communities as well as rural communes were established and still prosper, although there has been a clear trend away from complete withdrawal and isolation among many black Muslims. Self-segregation is a difficult adaptation to maintain. Opportunities are necessarily limited compared to those in the broader society. As a result, some seek these outside opportunities. Moreover, economic, political, and social isolation is often

Mennonites, like other groups such as the Amish, practice self-segregation in order to sustain their distinct ethnicity. Here Mennonites travel in horse and buggy as a way of avoiding new forms of transportation that could undermine their distinctive community.

difficult to sustain in urban, media-dominated societies, where alternatives and options constantly present themselves.

Revolt and Rebellion

Subordinate ethnic subpopulations do not always accept, assimilate, withdraw, or marginally participate. Frequently they rebel. Such *rebellion* can take a number of forms, one being general hostility and aggressive behavior toward the majority. For example, few white Americans would feel comfortable walking through a black ghetto or a Chicano barrio because they fear that there is some likelihood of intimidation and assault. Another example is rioting, as was the case with the urban riots of the 1960s and the turmoil in Los Angeles in the early 1990s. All forms of rebellion involve minorities "striking back" and venting their frustrations, and at times, these revolts become extremely violent, mobilizing people for mass killings.

Organized Protest

Rebellious outbursts are often part of a larger social movement, and, hence involve *organized protests*. All such protests involve subordinate ethnic

Box 1.2

Where Minorities Are a Majority

When minorities—African Americans, Latinos, and Asians—are all counted together, the 1990 census shows that in the 200 cities with at least 100,000 population, minorities constitute a majority in 51 of them. Most of the increase in such cities comes from Latino and Asian immigration over the last decade. Since 1980, 22 cities have seen minorities become the majority (these are starred). These shifts in the relative numbers of ethnic groups foretell of changes in power and patterns of discrimination.

City	*Percent Minority* 1990	1980	City	*Percent Minority* 1990	1980
Atlanta	69.7	67.9	Los Angeles	62.4	51.0
Baltimore	61.3	56.3	Macon*	53.1	45.3
Birmingham	64.2	56.3	Memphis*	56.3	48.5
Bridgeport*	54.0	39.6	Miami, Fla.	87.7	80.1
Chicago	61.9	56.0	New Haven*	50.8	40.6
Chula Vista*	50.0	31.3	New Orleans	66.8	59.5
Cleveland*	52.1	47.3	New York*	56.5	47.2
Corpus Christi	56.0	52.3	Newark	83.1	76.7
Dallas*	52.2	42.7	Oakland	71.5	64.0
Detroit	79.2	65.9	Ontario*	52.7	32.4
East Los Angeles	97.0	95.7	Oxnard	67.5	56.5
El Monte	84.6	65.1	Pasadena*	53.1	43.9
El Paso	73.5	66.5	Paterson	75.1	62.7
Elizabeth*	60.0	45.6	Pomona	71.6	52.5
Flint*	51.6	44.5	Richmond	57.0	52.3
Fresno*	50.3	36.2	Salinas*	61.0	47.0
Gary, Ind.	85.8	77.8	San Antonio	63.6	61.6
Hartford	69.1	54.5	San Bernardino*	54.2	42.1
Hialeah	89.0	75.8	San Francisco*	53.2	46.2
Honolulu	74.3	69.7	San Jose*	50.2	35.1
Houston*	59.2	47.1	Santa Ana	76.7	53.8
Inglewood	91.1	77.6	Savannah	53.8	50.6
Jackson*	56.6	47.7	Stockton*	56.2	41.2
Jersey City	63.1	50.1	Vallejo	53.7	38.7
Laredo	94.3	93.2	Washington	72.5	73.6
Long Beach	50.2	30.9			

groups' becoming organized to make broad-based and concerted efforts to change patterns of discrimination. The civil rights movement represented one such effort. Beginning with sit-ins and freedom rides in the 1960s, progressing to large-scale demonstrations, teeming over into riots, and culminating in several national organizations that effectively changed many legal and social patterns, African Americans successfully challenged pervasive discriminatory practices. The movement has been far from successful, however, since substantial integration of African Americans into the American mainstream has not occurred. But when an ethnic population is large and organized, it can generate political power and initiate some degree of social change. When minorities become majorities in cities and regions, as has often been the case in the late twentieth century in the United States, they can wield additional power and can force changes in old patterns of discrimination.

SUMMARY

Ethnic antagonism is one of the oldest and most pervasive dimensions of human social organization. To study this phenomenon, it is necessary to define terms and key concepts. The term "race" is of little importance biologically, but it is relevant sociologically. For if people perceive and believe others to be biologically distinctive and different, superficial biological traits become an important consideration in the formation of ethnicity. For our purposes, "ethnicity" refers to the history as well as the behavioral, organization, and cultural features of people that make them distinctive and distinguishable from others. People can be distinguished on the basis of superficial biological traits, but these traits are associated with presumed behavioral, organizational, and cultural features—that is, with ethnicity.

The term "ethnic group" is commonly used, but we prefer the term "ethnic subpopulation." The latter term emphasizes the fact that people who are distinguished on the basis of an interrelated cluster of characteristics—biological, cultural, behavioral, and organizational—constitute a population more than a closed group. They are not all necessarily engaged in face-to-face contact, as the notion of "group" implies. To be sure, people's involvement in local groups and other structures sustains their distinctive patterns of organization, but these do not embrace the population as a whole. Ethnic subpopulations exist, instead, within a larger, more inclusive population. This point is not merely semantic; it is fundamental to an understanding of the dynamics of ethnicity.

The term "minority group" is also limited. Not all ethnic subpopulations subject to discrimination are minorities. They can constitute the majority in a community or in a nation as a whole. The underlying issue is *power*. Which groups have the power to limit the activities of other groups? More accurate terms are "*super*ordinate ethnic subpopulations" and "*sub*ordinate ethnic subpopulations."

Discrimination is the process of denying others access to valued resources. Ethnic discrimination occurs when members of a superordinate ethnic subpopulation are able to limit or deny members of a subordinate ethnic population access to valued resources—jobs, income, education, power, health care, and anything that is valued and prized in a society.

Ethnic discrimination surfaces in several different forms: genocide, or the systematic killing of members in a subordinate ethnic population; expulsion, or the exiling of all or selected members of an ethnic population; segregation, or the spatial confinement or isolation of members of an ethnic group so that they have difficulty gaining access to resources; exclusion, or the denial of rights to positions in a society that provide access to valued resources; and selective inclusion, or the confinement of members of an ethnic subpopulation to a narrow range of positions in the society. These types of discrimination gain effectiveness as discrimination becomes institutionalized. We define "institutionalized discrimination" as individual acts of discrimination that are (1) pervasive; (2) culturally supported in norms, beliefs, and values; and (3) lodged in social structures as matters of policy and practice. The more institutionalized the discrimination is, the more a subordinate ethnic subpopulation is segregated, excluded, and selectively included, while being vulnerable to genocide and expulsion. Discrimination is thus the central process underlying ethnic problems in society.

Institutionalized discrimination produces ethnic stratification. When members of a subordinate ethnic subpopulation receive only certain types and levels of valued resources, it becomes possible to establish their location on the social hierarchies of society. On the basis of this location, the distinctiveness of an ethnic group is retained, thereby making it a target of further prejudice and discrimination.

"Prejudice" refers to negative and stigmatizing beliefs, concepts, and stereotypes about people; "ethnic prejudice" is based on negative beliefs, conceptions, and stereotypes about members of a subpopulation distinguishable in terms of their history and biological, behavioral, cultural, and organizational features. Prejudice and discrimination are not perfectly correlated, but discrimination cannot be easily institutionalized without widespread prejudice among dominant ethnic subpopulations.

Prejudice and discrimination force their targets to respond and adapt. Assimilation, or the elimination of ethnically distinct characteristics and adoption of those of the superordinate ethnic population, is one method of adaptation. At the other extreme are rebellion and revolt against superordinate ethnic groups, the goal being redistribution of power and, hence, the patterns of discrimination. Another response to discrimination is organized protest, often arising out of or even prompting acts of rebellion, in which ethnic groups and their allies organize to change patterns of discrimination. Yet another response is withdrawal and self-segregation of the subordinate ethnic group in order to isolate itself from the discriminatory acts of others. Members of an ethnic group may choose to accept their position passively, or they may participate marginally, finding narrow niches where they can secure resources.

This chapter has presented many useful terms and distinctions that will deepen our understanding of and provide a perspective on ethnic relations in America. These distinctions do not explain ethnic relations; they only describe them. We also need to know *why* people make ethnic distinctions, *why* they discriminate, *why* they hold prejudices, and *why* superordinate populations force subordinate groups to adapt in certain ways. Explaining these "why" issues is the job of theory. Within the framework of definitions and distinctions developed in this chapter, we can now move on to explore the theories that have been used to explain ethnicity, prejudice, discrimination, and other aspects of ethnic relations.

POINTS OF DEBATE

In any society where distinct ethnic subpopulations exist, the issue of ethnicity is a subject of debate and controversy. No society revealing ethnic differences has ever been able to organize itself in ways that avoid the tension and conflict accompanying ethnic identity. The United States is not an exception; indeed, American society is one of the few in history that has sought to integrate so many large and diverse ethnic subpopulations into its cultural core. The problems of ethnicity in the United States have stimulated and continue to create many points of debate. When reading the coming chapters, keep in mind the following controversial issues.

1. The "first American dilemma": How can a society that values equality and freedom engage in systematic discrimination against minority subpopulations? This question is rhetorical because the evidence is irrefutable that discrimination has occurred, and continues to occur, on a massive and long-term scale. Can the accumulated effects of such discrimination be undone?
2. The "second American dilemma": Can the values of freedom and equality be used to justify efforts to compensate the descendants of past discrimination? An affirmative answer to this question has many implications, all of which are debatable: (a) Are Americans willing to spend billions of tax dollars to create jobs, housing, and educational programs to overcome the effects of past discrimination? (b) Is private enterprise willing or able to participate on a massive scale in creating jobs for members of particular ethnic groups who have been the victims of this legacy of discrimination? (c) Are white Americans willing to give up some of their access to valued resources so that disadvantaged minority groups can increase their access, or is such action simply going to encourage accusations of "reverse discrimination"?
3. If Americans are unwilling to meet the challenges posed by the second American dilemma, what is the alternative? Conflict and violence among ethnic groups are escalating; poverty among ethnic groups is on the rise; out-of-wedlock childbearing is reaching epidemic proportions (now 63 percent) among African Americans; substance abuse and other social problems among minority groups are growing; the number of crimes committed by minority group members is increasing; and innu-

merable problems are arising from the accumulated effects of past discrimination. This reality confronts Americans in their daily lives. What is to be done? Nothing? Build more prisons? Hire more police? Actively try to address the problems at enormous cost? What are the viable options? Such questions are ultimately part of any discussion of ethnicity in America.

CHAPTER 2

Explaining Ethnic Relations

A theory tries to explain *why* specific events occur. In the context of ethnic relations, then, theories seek to explain why ethnic distinctions are made in the first place, why they are sustained over time, why some ethnic groups discriminate against others with varying degrees of severity, why prejudice exists, why some ethnic groups remain identifiable, and why others melt into the dominant culture.

Many different theories exist concerning ethnic relations. Our goal in this chapter is to pull these theories together so that we have a coherent framework within which to examine specific ethnic groups in America—African Americans, Latinos, Native Americans, Asian Americans, and European-origin white ethnics. The first step is to review the range of diversity in existing theories; later we can incorporate the strengths of each theory into a more general one that can guide us throughout our review of ethnic relations in America.

THEORIES OF ETHNIC RELATIONS

Assimilation Theories

Part of the early American creed was a belief that successive waves of ethnic immigrants could be incorporated into the mainstream of social life. Robert Park, one of the earliest American theorists on ethnic relations, saw such assimilation as "a process of interpenetration and fusion in which persons and groups acquire the memories, sentiments, and attitudes of other groups, and, by sharing their experience and history, are incorporated with them into a common cultural life" (Park and Burgess, 1924:735).

Park proposed stages of assimilation, beginning with contact among diverse ethnic groups. Out of such contact comes a *competitive phase* in which ethnic populations compete over resources, such as jobs, living space, and political representation. The next stage is an unstable *accommodation* in which immigrants and their descendants are forced to change and adapt to their new environment. During this phase, there is some degree of stabilization of relations between immigrants and those in the host society, even if this accommodation forces migrants into lower social strata. Moreover, once ethnic stratification exists, the pace of assimilation is dramatically reduced, although Park believed that, ultimately, even a lower-class, subordinate ethnic subpopulation could be *assimilated*. It might take hundreds of years, but eventually assimilation would occur. Thus, the last phase in Park's theory is assimilation in which the migrant ethnic merges with other ethnic groups (Park, 1950).

More recent assimilation theories have been more explicit about (1) the nature of the host society and culture to which migrant ethnic groups must adapt and (2) the various types, levels, and degrees of assimilation that can develop. For instance, as Milton Gordon (1964) emphasizes, it is to "the middle class cultural patterns of . . . white, Anglo-Saxon" culture that immigrants to the United States have had to adapt. Various ethnic subpopulations may evidence, however, different degrees of progress in adapting to the dominant Anglo-Saxon culture. *Cultural assimilation* occurs when the values, beliefs, dogmas, ideologies, language, and other systems of symbols of the dominant culture are adopted. Most ethnic groups become, to varying degrees, culturally assimilated. In contrast to cultural assimilation, *structural assimilation* occurs when migrant ethnic groups become members of the primary groups within dominant ethnic subpopulations—their families, close friends, cliques within clubs, and groups within organizations. Gordon emphasizes that structural assimilation is more difficult to achieve than cultural assimilation because it involves penetration into the close interactions and associations of dominant ethnic groups. Even when members of ethnic groups penetrate more secondary and formal organizational structures—schools, workplaces, and political arenas—they may still lack more primary and personal ties with members of dominant ethnic groups.

Other types of assimilation are based on the degree of cultural and structural assimilation an ethnic group is able to achieve: *marital assimilation*, or the emergence of high rates of intermarriage between the migrant and dominant ethnic groups; *identification assimilation*, where individuals no longer see themselves as distinctive and, like members of dominant groups, stake their personal identities to participation and success in the mainstream institutions of a society; *attitude-receptional assimilation*, or the lack of prejudicial attitudes and stereotyping on the part of both dominant and migrant ethnic groups; *behavioral-receptional assimilation*, or the absence of intentional discrimination by dominant ethnic groups against subordinate ethnic groups; and *civic assimilation*, or the reduction of conflict between ethnic groups over basic values and access to the political arena.

According to Gordon, assimilation occurs over generations in the United States. By the third generation, a considerable amount of assimilation has occurred, especially among white ethnic groups. They have become culturally assimilated; they have made inroads into the primary groups or, at the very least, into the organizations of the Anglo-Saxon core; they have begun to intermarry with members of other ethnic groups; they identify with the institutional system; they are victims and perpetrators of fewer prejudices, stereotypes, and acts of discrimination; and they are engaged in less conflict over values and political rights. But what about nonwhite ethnic groups? For them, the assimilation process, Gordon (1981) admits, is slower, but he is optimistic that even the most identifiable subordinate ethnic groups in America—African Americans and Native Americans—are on the path to further assimilation.

Assimilation theories probably paint an overly benign view of ethnic relations, viewing assimilation as inexorable. Yet, they provide us with a way to measure how far an ethnic group has moved into the dominant culture along various dimensions—cultural, structural, marital, identifications, attitudes, beliefs, behavioral, and political. Indeed, the amount and pace of assimilation along these dimensions provide clues about how much and what type of discrimination has been working against an ethnic subpopulation. For example, if we find that, after hundreds of years of coexistence with the dominant Anglo-Saxon society, African Americans and Native Americans are structurally unassimilated and only partially assimilated in terms of culture, reveal low rates of intermarriage with other ethnic groups, identify only partially with the society and its institutions, suffer many prejudicial stereotypes, experience acts of discrimination, and remain partially disenfranchised from the political arena, then it is likely that massive amounts of informal and institutional discrimination exist. Assimilation theories do not explain how these discriminatory forces operate, but they provide a sense of what their consequences are.

Pluralism Theories

Partially in reaction to the "melting pot" assumption underlying most assimilation theories are those that stress the process of maintaining patterns of ethnicity. Indeed, the maintenance of distinctive cultural, organizational, and behavioral characteristics is often a way of coping with discrimination. A distinct ethnic identity provides sources of support and guidance in a sometimes hostile world. When ethnic identity is nurtured, a pluralistic and permanent mosaic of ethnic subpopulations becomes evident.

Most scholars who subscribe to this more pluralistic view do not deny that some assimilation into the dominant segments of a society occurs. Rather, they argue, ethnicity remains a powerful force, even among white ethnic groups who are often presumed to be fully assimilated. Nathan Glazer and Daniel Moynihan (1970) were among the first to emphasize that even as many of their customs are replaced with those of the dominant Anglo-Saxon society, white ethnic groups continue to reveal residential, behavioral, organizational, and cultural patterns that mark their distinctive ethnic identity, one that subtly separates them from the middle-class, Anglo-Saxon Protestant core.

The term *ethnogenesis* is often employed to describe this process of creating a distinctive ethnicity as a means of adapting to discrimination, even as some degree of assimilation occurs. Andrew Greeley (1971, 1974) has been one of the most forceful advocates of this position, arguing that there is considerable ethnic diversity in America that simply cannot be explained by assimilation models. Ethnic groups not only retain elements of their past but they also construct and create new ways of adjusting to discrimination. As generations pass, and ethnic groups come to share many characteristics with the dominant white, Anglo-Saxon Protestant segments of society, they selectively retain elements of their ethnic heritage and they create new elements. For example, third- and even fourth-generation Irish Americans, Poles, and Italians continue to display their ethnic identities; moreover, they often strive to create new symbols to mark with pride their ethnic heritage.

Pluralistic theories offer an important corrective to assimilation theories, but they do not explain adequately the broader social forces that cause and sustain discrimination. If ethnic pluralism is, to some degree, a consequence of discrimination, these theories have little to say about those forces producing such discrimination. They are, instead, concerned with ethnogenesis, per se, rather than the external structures in the society that set ethnogenesis in motion.

Biological Theories

The spectacular rise of sociobiology in recent decades has produced another kind of theory of ethnogenesis. This theory is different from pluralist theories in its emphasis on the biological underpinnings of ethnicity. What are these biological underpinnings? The basic position of early sociobiology was that the units of natural selection are the genes, rather than the individual. The individual is, from a sociobiological point of view, only a temporary house or vessel for genes that seek to survive in the gene pool. Thus, genes are seen as "selfish" and as driven to maximize their fitness, or their capacity to remain in the gene pool. Sociobiological theories of ethnicity, then, start with these assumptions and see them as a driving force operating to produce and sustain ethnicity (Turner and Maryanski, 1993). How do these evolutionary and biological forces operate? Pierre van den Berghe (1981) has provided the most forceful argument from a sociobiological perspective; let us examine his answer to this question.

According to van den Berghe and most sociobiologists, social structures are merely "survival machines" that exist to maintain the fitness of genes. Sociobiologists have introduced two concepts to explain why "selfish genes" create social structures or "survival machines." One concept is *kin selection* or *inclusive fitness,* which holds that family structures are a strategy allowing males and females to maximize their fitness by keeping as much of their genetic material as possible in the gene pool. Moreover, when family members help each other, they are assuring that a portion of their genes remains in the pool (since brothers, sisters, parents, and offspring all share 50 percent of the same genes; grandparents, half siblings, uncles, aunts, nieces, and nephews share 25 percent of their genes; and first cousins, half nephews, great grandchildren share 12 percent of their genes). Thus, familism is simply a strategy that allows genes to stay in the pool. The other concept is *reciprocal altruism,* which was developed to explain why nonfamily members help each other survive; for if maximization of fitness is the goal of genes, an explanation is needed for the fact that people help others with whom they do not share any genes. Reciprocal altruism seeks to provide this explanation: People offer assistance to nonkin because they know that at some future time their acts of altruism will be reciprocated by those they help. Such reciprocation promotes fitness and, thereby, enables individuals to keep their genes in the pool.

Van den Berghe uses these two concepts—kin selection and reciprocal altruism—to explain ethnicity. He extends the idea of kin selection to a larger subpopulation. Historically, larger kin groups (composed of lineages) constituted a breeding population of close and distant kin who sustained trust and solidarity with one another and mistrusted other breeding populations. Van den Berghe coins the term *"ethny"* for "ethnic group." An ethny is an extension of these more primordial breeding populations, a cluster of kinship circles created by endogamy (where mate selection is confined to specific groups) and territoriality (physical proximity of its members and relative isolation from nonmembers). An ethny represents a reproductive strategy for maximizing fitness beyond the narrower confines of kinship, because by forming an ethny—even a very large one of millions of people—individuals create bonds with those who can help preserve their fitness, whether by actually sharing genes or, more typically, by reciprocal acts of altruism with fellow ethnys. An ethny is, therefore, a manifestation of more basic "urges" to help "those like oneself." Although ethnys become genetically diluted as their numbers increase and become subject to social and cultural definitions, the very tendency to form and sustain ethnys is the result of natural selection, which produced biological tendencies for people who share genetic material to help each other.

Thus, sociobiology provides an evolutionary explanation—a highly controversial one, we might add—for why members of an ethnic group band together and maintain distinctiveness. While this perspective has not gained a wide following among sociologists, sociobiology has taken center stage in the field of biology; as a result, we need to be aware of theories emanating from this quarter.

Human Ecology Theories

Also drawing inspiration from biology are ecological theories stressing the forces of competition, selection, and "speciation" of distinctive ethnic groupings. Robert Park's assimilation theory was couched in a larger ecological framework for analyzing urban areas (Park, 1916; Park and Burgess, 1924). This framework emphasized that living patterns in urban areas are produced by competition for scarce resources—land, housing, and jobs.

Human groups exist in a kind of Darwinian struggle for survival, each trying to find a viable social niche. Thus, as populations migrate to urban areas, they accelerate the level of competition for resources with those already present and, Park believed, set in motion the processes of accommodation and assimilation.

More recent ecological theories stress that competition for resources often escalates the level of conflict between ethnic subpopulations, forcing subordinate ethnic groups into segregated housing niches and a narrow range of economic positions. Once members of an ethnic group find such niches, their boundaries and distinctiveness are preserved, thereby making them easier targets of discrimination. Susan Olzak (1986, 1992) is one of several scholars working in human ecology tradition. Her theory holds that violence between ethnic subpopulations, especially attacks by members of the dominant group on subordinate groupings, occurs when members of subordinate ethnic subpopulations move into the occupational and housing niches of superordinate groups. Acts of violence against these mobile subordinates increase as members of the dominant subpopulations feel threatened. For example, Olzak (1992) has documented Anglo-Saxon Protestant attacks on nineteenth- and twentieth-century European immigrants in two scenarios: (1) when the number of immigrants expanded and (2) when economic recessions occurred. She concludes that under these conditions European immigrants were seen as a threat to the housing and occupational niches occupied by Anglo-Saxon Protestants (Roediger, 1991). These two conditions could provide reasons for the dramatic intensification of white violence against African Americans as they began to leave the rural South in the early decades of this century and to emigrate to northern cities as a low-wage labor force in tight labor markets, although it should be emphasized that African Americans and white Americans had come into conflict as early as the 1830s (Roediger, 1991). As greater numbers of African-origin people migrated north, European immigrants who had recently secured a foothold in American society felt threatened and, as a result, attacked blacks and developed intense prejudices, some of which persist to this day.

These ecological theories emphasize the relative size of ethnic subpopulations, their patterns of migration, their movement into various social niches, and their competition with other ethnic groups in markets for housing and jobs. Out of such competition come conflicts, often violent, that maintain prejudices and boundaries between antagonistic ethnic subpopulations. Thus, competition does not always lead to easy assimilation, as Park (1950) hoped, but to partitions and pluralism, punctuated by tension and conflict.

Power and Stratification Theories

Stratification theories emphasize how the process of discrimination produces overrepresentation of members of ethnic subpopulations in various social classes. All of these theories place considerable emphasis on the mobilization of power in order to control where ethnic groups are placed in the class system. Yet, each stresses a somewhat different aspect of how power is used to create systems of ethnic stratification.

Caste Theories

In the early 1940s, W. Lloyd Warner and colleagues described black–white relations as constituting *a caste system* in which African Americans were confined to lower socioeconomic positions, denied access to power, prevented from intermarriage, and segregated in their own living space (Warner, 1941; Warner and Srole, 1945). African Americans thus constituted a distinctive caste that white Americans maintained for their own privileges.

Oliver C. Cox (1948) added a Marxist twist to this argument, emphasizing that the capitalist class of owners and managers of industry has been crucial to the castelike subordination of African Americans. The importation of slaves was a business enterprise in which European capitalists bought and sold cheap labor—slaves—to capitalistic plantations in the South. Once capitalists set this pattern of using Africans as a source of cheap labor and higher profits, it needed to be legitimated by highly prejudiced beliefs and stereotypes based on the biological characteristics of the "black race." Thus, exploitive practices are tied to the actions and interests of economic elites who mobilize power and ideologies in order to have a ready, desperate, and low-cost labor pool available for exploitation. From these early caste theories, the emphasis on power and stratification has taken a number of directions. Let us examine some representative theories.

Colonialism Theories

Colonialism theories draw inspiration from the analysis of the dynamics of European colonialism in the past. *External colonialism* is the process by which one nation controls the political and economic activities of another, less developed and less powerful society. Robert Blauner (1969:396) has identified four components of what he termed the *colonization complex:* (1) forced entry into a territory and its population, (2) alteration or destruction of the indigenous culture and patterns of social organization, (3) domination of the indigenous population by representatives of the invading society, and (4) justification of such activities with highly prejudicial, racist beliefs and stereotypes.

This basic theory has also been used to study *internal colonialism* (Blauner, 1969, 1972), where the dynamics of the colonization complex are seen to operate *within* a society. From the internal colonization perspective, much of the history of ethnic relations in America has involved the establishment of successive internal colonies of people who are not white and who are dominated by descendants of the original Anglo-Saxon Protestant colonists. For example, African Americans constitute a colony within white America because institutionalized discrimination maintains white control over the economic, educational, and political opportunities of many African Americans. This situation, it is argued, is little different from that in South Africa, where until recently a white minority, who were the descendants of early Dutch and German colonists, exerted control over the black population.

The motivations behind internal colonialism in the United States were twofold: (1) the need for cheap labor to increase profit and (2) the desire to take and control land, first from the Native Americans and later from the Mexicans. As Robert Blauner (1969) notes, the desire for inexpensive labor led to the creation of slavery; the desire to control the agricultural base and land of Mexicans in the Southwest was the reason white Americans pushed Mexicans into a low-wage labor pool. Similarly, the attempted genocide of Native Americans was a way for Europeans to take their land, forcing those who survived to live on reservations—a very visible type of internal colony.

In order to create internal colonies, government must actively participate. It must provide the coercive force needed to control those who are "colonized," while legitimating patterns of domination with laws. Thus, by virtue of their control of the state, the descendants of early European white immigrants have been able to create and sustain internal colonies for long periods of time.

Split-Labor Market Theories

Split-labor market theories are much like ecological theories in their emphasis on competition between ethnic groups for resources, but they bring the mobilization and use of power to the forefront. Indeed, split-labor market theories make up for what is often considered a deficiency in ecological theories: the lack of sufficient attention to power and how the dominant class in society uses power to foster ethnic antagonism for its own benefit. *Split-labor market theories* emphasize that markets for labor become partitioned, with members of certain ethnic groups being confined to some jobs in the labor market and not allowed to work in other, typically higher-paying jobs. The pressure to split the labor market comes from those in the more powerful ethnic populations who fear that they might lose their advantage if the labor market were to be opened up to other groups who would be willing to work for less and who would increase the supply of labor relative to the market's demand, thereby driving wages down as more workers compete for jobs.

Edna Bonacich (1972) has developed the most important split-labor market theory. This theory has been applied to black–white relations in America (Bonacich, 1976) and to ethnic populations in other societies. The basic argument is that capitalists, or those who own and manage large businesses, have an interest in high profits. One way to raise or maintain profits is to keep labor costs low, so capitalists try to import cheap labor in order to undercut higher-wage labor. Thus, for example, low-wage African American workers were imported from the South by northern industrialists as "strike breakers" in the 1920s and 1930s in order to undermine the efforts of white workers to unionize and to develop a power base for securing higher wages and better working conditions (Bonacich, 1976). And, just as ecological theory would predict, acts of violence against African Americans increased dramatically in the 1920s.

Threatened workers sometimes react not only violently to efforts at undermining their wages but also politically and economically. At times they enlist government to exclude an ethnic group, but this is almost always impossible when powerful capitalists have an interest in supporting and sponsoring an influx of low-wage workers. A fall-back strategy is for threatened workers to create formal and informal ways of "splitting the labor market" such that a subordinate minority is excluded from the more privileged positions in this market. As a result, members of the subordinate ethnic group often find themselves forced to compete with each other for a narrow range of less privileged and less secure positions. For example, as we will see in later chapters, for over a century after the Civil War African Americans were excluded from most skilled craft unions and included in only some positions in industrial unions, creating a split in the labor market between its white and black sectors.

Thus, competition involves more than two antagonistic ethnic groups; it also involves third parties who wield power and who wish to maximize profits by stimulating competition between ethnic groups in labor markets. Such actions fuel both competition and threat, leading to discrimination ranging from acts of violence to institutionalization of a split-labor market.

Split-Class Theories

Class theories emphasize economic exploitation of the lower classes by those in the higher classes. Added to this dynamic, however, is the recognition that each class includes segments or sectors that are isolated and hence subject to discriminatory practices. Theories of this sort, such as one developed by Mario Barrera (1979), generally begin with a Marxian view of the class system composed of (1) capitalists who control the investment of capital and who thereby regulate production and the purchase of labor; (2) managers who do the administrative work for capitalists and who, thereby, have control of workers; (3) petit bourgeoisie who own small businesses and buy labor; and (4) members of the working class who constitute the majority of workers and who sell their labor for salaries and wages. Aside from the conflicts of interest among these classes, Barrera argues, there are splits *within* each class along ethnic lines. Members of some ethnic subpopulations are subordinate within a class and are often relegated to the less desirable, lower-paying, and less secure jobs within this class. Moreover, these members can become a reserve labor force within a class, especially the large working class, where they constitute a pool of excess labor that can be hired when needed for low wages and thrown back into the pool when not needed.

For example, within the working classes, subordinate ethnic minorities were until recently almost always excluded from the most desirable jobs—unionized crafts positions (carpenters, plumbers, electricians, sheet metal workers, welders, machine workers, and the like)—and dramatically overrepresented in low-skill, low-pay, and low-job-security positions (day laborers, seasonal workers, and domestics). This is still the case, though somewhat less so, for African, Latino, and Native Americans. In Europe, Jews were historically confined to a few positions (trade, finance); even today in the United States, Jews are overrepresented in certain middle-class occupations and businesses (retail sales in certain spheres such as clothing, as well as accounting, finance, college teaching, and medicine), but they tend to be underrepresented in other spheres. Or, many Asian groups—Koreans, Vietnamese, and Chinese, for example—are confined to small retail and service businesses and underrepresented in other middle-class occupations and professions. Thus, there are splits in social classes, just as there are in labor markets. Indeed, splits in labor markets may extend beyond lower-paying jobs and operate in other, more affluent and privileged spheres.

Middleman Minority Theories

One process that creates splits in the middle class is described by *middleman minority theories.* Not all ethnic groups occupy lower castes and classes, nor are all confined to internal colonies. In fact, some are overrepresented in the petit bourgeoisie, or small businesses that often rely on family labor and ethnic networks (for credit, customers, and other needed aspects of doing business). They are *middlemen* along several potential dimensions: (1) They have middle, or moderate, levels of resources; (2) they serve as distribution links between producers of goods and those who buy them; and (3) in Marxist terms (Bonacich, 1973), they are the "go-betweens" (as small retail store owners) between members of elite classes and subordinate classes.

The various explanations for the formation of middleman minorities are basically the same (Blalock, 1967; Bonacich, 1973; and Turner and Bonacich, 1980): Certain minorities bring to a host society entrepreneurial skills and perhaps some capital. Ironically, these very attributes pose a threat to dominant groups, and so, these minorities are excluded from many middle-class positions and allowed to operate only those businesses that serve their own ethnic group, other oppressed ethnics, and, occasionally, more elite ethnic groups. Once these "middlemen" become lodged in these middle niches, movement to economic niches controlled by dominant groups is threatening and, hence, likely to engender discrimination, which keeps its ethnic victims confined. The clients of middleman minorities, especially those in the lower social classes, also tend to exhibit hostility toward the petit bourgeoisie, who are viewed as mercenary and exploitive. For example, tensions have emerged between African American residents and Korean business owners in ghetto areas. As demonstrated by the attacks on these businesses during the rioting in Los Angeles in the early 1990s, this hostility can translate into violence. At other times, boycotts against a middleman minority—as in the case of certain Korean stores in New York—are initiated as a way to vent hostility against perceptions of maltreatment. Such hostilities from potential competitors and clients force the members of a middleman minority to withdraw into an ethnic enclave and to be perceived as "clannish," thereby perpetuating hostility toward them.

We have now presented in very general terms the range of theories on ethnic relations. There are many variations of the theories discussed above, but the basic types of theoretical approaches have been summarized. As is evident, each theory stresses some processes, while ignoring others. Some appear to apply to a single ethnic group in America, whereas others seem more general and generic. How, then, can this theoretical diversity be pulled together in an analysis of ethnicity in America? Our answer to this question is to create an even more general theory that can incorporate the strong points of existing theories, while simplifying the explanation of ethnic relations. Good theory should not be complicated; rather, it should be simple and parsimonious.

A UNIFIED THEORY OF ETHNIC RELATIONS

Let us begin by emphasizing the central force in ethnic relations: *discrimination* against a subordinate subpopulation. The greater the level of discrimination and the more it is institutionalized across many social arenas, then the more likely is a subpopulation to develop and retain a distinctive ethnic identity. Thus, if forms of discrimination, such as violence, exclusion, selective inclusion, and segregation, are practiced against a subpopulation, its members will become a clearly identifiable ethnic group. Conversely, the less the discrimination practiced against an identifiable subpopulation, the less distinctive will be its ethnicity and the more likely it is that it will assimilate.

Of course, at times elements of ethnicity are retained without the threat of discrimination. For example, many white ethnic groups—Irish Catholics, Poles, Italians, and others in America—have tried to maintain elements of their ethnicity, such as holidays, festivals, religion, and community organizations. These ethnic elements are not immediately apparent, however; they do not define and distinguish these subpopulations in a highly visible way. Moreover, all these ethnic groups were at one time victims of discrimination; and so the effort to retain ethnicity is a holdover effect of past discrimination, in which members of the subpopulation selectively retain certain symbols and rituals of the past. Other ethnic groups, such as the Basque in America, have retained a considerable number of their ethnic traditions without ever having experienced high levels of overt discrimination. This maintenance of ethnicity has been accomplished by retaining Basque communities, patterns of intragroup marriage, important rituals and festivals, and language. Even here, though, assimilation is slowly occurring because there is relatively little outside discrimination to force Basques to retreat into their ethnic traditions. Thus, ethnicity can be retained, to an extent and for a while, without discrimination; ultimately, however, the intensity of discrimination determines whether a subpopulation remains distinctively ethnic in culture, behavior, and organization or becomes assimilated into the societal mainstream.

Another force involved in creating and maintaining ethnicity is the degree of *identifiability* of members of a subpopulation. To be targets of discrimination, members of a subpopulation need to be visible and readily identified. And so, the more distinctive members of a subpopulation are, the more likely are they to become targets of discrimination.

There are several bases for distinctiveness. One is biological, and so, the more members of a subpopulation can be singled out in terms of biological features, such as skin color and eye shape, the more readily they can become targets of discrimination. It should come as no surprise, then, that the two ethnic groups most discriminated against in American society have been African Americans and Native Americans; after all, they can be identified biologically. Asians and Latinos have had a similar experience. Identifiability is also cultural—language, religious beliefs, normative practices, and other symbol systems. For example, if an American subpopulation uses a language other than English, has distinctive religious practices that deviate from Judeo-Christian traditions, and reveals norms that sanction behaviors and demeanors that are at odds with the American mainstream, they become distinctive and identifiable. As a consequence, they are likely targets of discrimination. Behavioral and organizational characteristics also create identifiability. When members of an ethnic population have a noticeable interpersonal demeanor (such as speech styles, body language, or dress) and when they have organizational structures, (such as deviant kinship patterns, church practices, and business arrangements), they can become targets of discrimination.

Discrimination and identifiability are mutually reinforcing. If people can be identified and singled out for discrimination, then such acts of discrimination and their institutionalization force their victims to "remain with their own kind" where they interact, intermarry, and maintain their distinctive cultural, organizational, and behavioral patterns. Sometimes this maintenance of ethnic patterns is a defensive reaction, and other times it is merely the only option for segregated and excluded peoples. Most typically, however, it is a mixture of the two. Once a subpopulation is forced to maintain its identity as a result of discrimination, ironically it becomes an easier target for further discrimination. This is particularly likely to be the case if rates of marriage within the ethnic group maintain biological distinctiveness, but other bases of distinctiveness—cultural, behavioral, and organizational—are also important. As biological, cultural, behavioral, and organizational features of a subpopulation become intertwined and intercorrelated, then the members of a subpopulation become ever more visible targets of discrimination. This cycle of identifiability, discrimination, maintenance of identifiability, and further discrimination is often difficult to break—as has certainly been the case for African Americans, Native Americans, most Latinos, and some Asians (Aguirre and Baker, 1993). In contrast, for ethnic groups who are not biologically distinguishable because of skin color or facial features, it has been easier to break the cycle and to filter into the mainstream, as has been the case for members of most white European ethnic groups.

Identifiability and discrimination affect the levels and types of valued resources available to an ethnic subpopulation, such as income, power, and prestige. Other resources are also important, such as human capital (skills and education) as well as financial capital (savings) that ethnics bring with them when they come to America. But ultimately discrimination determines what resources members of a population can have and how resources can be used. Even for those immigrants who bring human and financial resources with them, discrimination shapes how and where their imported resources can be used, and as a consequence, it will affect the kinds and levels of resources that can be accumulated. For existing ethnic groups in the lower socioeconomic stratum and for those immigrants who do not bring human or financial capital with them, discrimination keeps them from acquiring resources. Whether channeling the further acquisition of resources among those with some capital or denying them to those without capital, discrimination works to maintain identifiability indirectly because the levels and types of resources that members of a population possess influence their behavioral, cultural, and organizational characteristics. When a population has little money, low levels of education (and hence prestige in a credentialed society like the United States), and few channels of acquiring power, it develops distinctive characteristics which, in turn, make its members easier targets for further discrimination. For example, African Americans, Native Americans, and most Latinos have become even more visible as targets of discrimination because of their low *shares of valued resources.* Or when a population uses its financial resources to make more money but is excluded from positions of power and prestige, it also becomes distinctive, often arousing hostility over its wealth. As a result, it becomes a target of discrimination. For instance, most Asian middleman minorities have experienced this phenomenon, as have Jews over centuries of persecution in Europe and somewhat more muted discrimination in the United States.

Figure 2.1 is a diagram of the relationships among *discrimination, identifiability,* and *resource levels.* If a population can be easily identified, it is likely to be a target of discrimination; if there is discrimination, this population develops a typical share of resources, which in turn increases its identifiability. We have added to this cycle another feature: *degree of ethnic stratification.* If a pattern of resource shares becomes discernible, then it usually creates distinctive pockets of ethnicity within the strata of society. For example, if African Americans are consistently overrepresented in the lower social strata, this situation increases their identifiability as somehow "not measuring up" to societal standards, and, as a result, it provides a further basis for discrimination which, in turn, perpetuates their meager shares of resources and their location in the stratification system.

As discrimination denies people access to resources, it limits their capacity to fight back or to move away from their situation. If a subpopulation

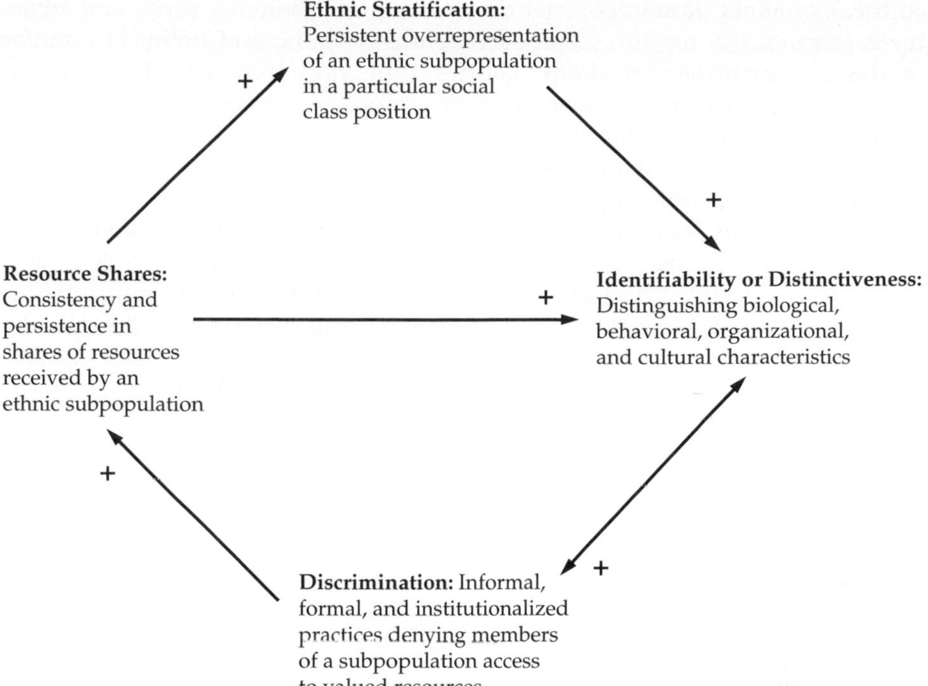

FIGURE 2.1. Cycles of discrimination, identifiability, resource shares, and stratification.

does not have access to channels of power, how can it fight discrimination? If it does not have access to a good education, which leads to job opportunities and prestige, how does it become upwardly mobile? If it does not have money, how does it improve? Thus, resource shares also determine how people respond to discrimination; if their options are limited, they are more likely to accept their plight and, as a consequence, remain identifiable targets of further discrimination.

Figure 2.1 illustrates the reinforcing dynamics in the cycle of discrimination, identifiability, resource shares, and stratification—as denoted by the positive signs on the arrows. Each one increases the values of the other in the direction specified by the arrows. If these were the only processes involved in the cycles, they would be difficult to break. But other forces are involved, some of which work to intensify these cycles, a few to mitigate their effects.

Why do people discriminate? Is identifiability the only reason? Ethnic identifiability alone is not enough to generate the high levels of discrimination that perpetuate the cycles portrayed in Figure 2.1. At least one additional force is needed: *a sense of threat.* If a subordinate ethnic group is perceived as threatening the political power, the economic well-being, the cultural symbols (language, customs, values, and beliefs), the social structures (community organization, social clubs, rituals, and holidays), and/or the basic institutions (economy, politics, family, church, school, and medicine) of a dominant ethnic group, this perception will translate into hostility, fueling the fires of discrimination. For example, slavery may have persisted long after it was economically viable because there was great fear about the social, economic, and political consequences of a large mass of freed slaves. This fear mobilized considerable hostility toward black people in the decades before and after the Civil War, resulting in violent acts (hangings, shootings) and efforts to reinstitutionalize in law and practice the oppression of African Americans (Turner and Singleton, 1978; Singleton and Turner, 1975; and Turner, Singleton, and Musick, 1984). A more recent example is the large influx of Latinos, especially Mexicans, into the United States, which has aroused fears about its effects on the economy, the existing balance of power, and schools. This fear has resulted in hostility and discriminatory practices. Recent Asian immigrants—Koreans and Vietnamese, for instance—are sometimes seen as a threat to small-business owners because many of them possess both human and financial capital and are willing to work long hours with pooled family labor. They are, in essence, more successful than some white ethnic groups in many entrepreneurial niches, thereby arousing hostility. Moreover, their success in these niches limits opportunities for other ethnic groups—African Americans and Latinos, for example—who may wish to start small businesses as a way to rise from their particular place in the system of ethnic stratification. The result is hostility and discrimination against these middleman minorities. Thus, the greater the sense of threat experienced by superordinate ethnic groups (and, at times, subordinate ones as well) over the influx or existence of another ethnic subpopulation, the greater is their hostility toward this subordinate population and the more likely are they to engage in discriminatory acts and to institutionalize these acts.

What forces create a sense of threat? Is distinctiveness enough? Our sense is that two additional features of an ethnic subpopulation operate to generate hostility. One is the *size* of an ethnic population. A large number of immigrants or a large subordinate ethnic group poses a threat because they might (1) work for less money than the dominant ethnic groups (out of desperation for job opportunities), (2) upset the balance of political power if they become enfranchised, and (3) change existing cultural and organizational patterns if they influence the mainstream. Thus, African Americans and Latinos pose a threat to the dominant Anglo-Saxon population because of their large numbers; and as a result, they are discriminated against in order to preserve what white ethnic groups see as "the American way of life." When an ethnic group is large, intense discrimination, fueled by a sense of threat, will usually force them to the bottom of the stratification system because there are too many people to be channeled into a narrow range of middleman minority niches and because they cannot be allowed to "dilute" the dominant culture and its institutions. Of course, when ethnic groups are denied access to resources and pushed into a lower socioeconomic group, they maintain their ethnicity, which increases the identifiability that poses a threat—often more imagined than real. But more is involved: Large numbers of oppressed ethnic subpopulations sometimes become hostile, which causes the dominant ethnic groups to experience an escalated sense of threat. Intense discrimination against a large ethnic population only exacerbates the level of threat that prompted the discrimination; hence the cycle of threat, discrimination, hostile reaction to discrimination, escalated threat, and renewed discrimination is perpetuated.

Another force that creates a sense of threat is the *entrepreneurial resources*—occupational skills, education, money, and organizational abilities—that an ethnic population possesses. Usually, ethnic groups with entrepreneurial resources are small; hence, through discrimination, it is possible to channel them into a narrow range of middleman minority niches or a limited number of professions. The ability of these ethnic groups to outperform segments of the dominant population in economic enterprises is threatening and arouses hostility, which results in efforts to confine them to niches and positions that reduce head-to-head competition with the members of the dominant population and, perhaps, places them in competition with other subordinate minorities. Under these conditions, the resentment of the victims of discrimination is reduced because they can enjoy economic success in at least some activities. For example, because many Asian immigrants in America possess entrepreneurial resources, they have been shunted into middleman minority niches or selected professions. Yet, over time, it is difficult to maintain this kind of confinement because these ethnic groups, and their successive generations of offspring, possess skills, capital, and education that make them valuable in the mainstream; and if they can acquire at least the veneer of the cultural mainstream, they can often penetrate mainstream institutions. And because their numbers are relatively small, coupled with increased rates of intermarriage with members of the dominant ethnic subpopulation, their penetration is less threatening and arouses less hostility than would be the case with larger ethnic populations.

Thus, the level of threat posed by superordinate ethnic groups is increased not only by their distinctiveness but also by their size and entrepreneurial resources. Large numbers of ethnic groups threaten to "overrun" the mainstream, and the possession of entrepreneurial resources among ethnic groups threatens entrenched small businesses and professions.

How is this sense of threat and hostility sustained over time? The answer resides in another central aspect of ethnic relations: *negative beliefs and stereotypes.* Here is where prejudice becomes a significant force in ethnic relations. When dominant ethnic groups feel threatened, they develop prejudices and portray those who threaten them in a negative light. If the sense of threat is severe, these negative portrayals are codified into a series of beliefs and stereotypes about the perceived undesirable characteristics and qualities of a subordinate ethnic population. Ironically, such portrayals tend to heighten the potential "menace" of the ethnic group, thereby escalating the sense of threat, which, in turn, leads to more negative portrayals. For example, the initial justification for not freeing slaves in America was that they were "childlike" and hence incapable of "managing for themselves" (Turner and Singleton, 1978). But as the abolitionist movement gained momentum, and as the sense of threat experienced by some white Americans increased correspondingly, these portrayals became ever more vicious, shifting to a view of black males as sexually aggressive and as lusting after white women whom they were prepared to rape if ever set free. Such portrayals escalated the sense of threat in the minds of white southerners, resulting in ever more aggressive discrimination against African Americans. According to Jordan (1968:151) the perception that "Negro men lusted after white women" intensified white prejudice.

Codified beliefs and stereotypes not only escalate the sense of threat, which then ratchets up the level of discrimination, but also legitimate discrimination: If an ethnic group has undesirable qualities, it is only appropriate that they be segregated and excluded from the mainstream. And as discrimination sets in motion the cycles outlined in Figure 2.1, it appears to justify itself because the victims of discrimination tend to maintain those biological, behavioral, cultural, and organizational features that are portrayed in a negative light by stereotypes. As a consequence, the failure of ethnic groups to "change" (ignoring the obvious fact that discrimination prevents change) escalates the sense of threat and organizes the negative beliefs and stereotypes into a codified dogma. For example, Jews in Europe were denied access to many positions and forced into a narrow range of retail, finance, and professional niches; as they operated successfully in these niches and did not change their ethnic characteristics, the stereotypes about them—clannish, anti-Christian, financially ruthless, and so on—became ever more codified, thereby justifying more hostility, discrimination, and prejudice.

In Figure 2.2 we have expanded the model of discrimination presented in Figure 2.1 to include those specific variables that will guide our analyses of ethnicity in America. First we need to know the *resource shares* of an ethnic group as a rough measure of the effects of discrimination. On this basis, we can ask if the ethnic population under examination is firmly lodged in a *system of ethnic stratification.* For if an ethnic subpopulation as a whole is overrepresented in poverty or low-income positions, we can be sure that discrimination has been at work. Or, if it is confined to a narrow range of business and professional niches, we can also be certain that discrimination does exist or has existed. Next, we can review the history of *discrimination* against this ethnic group, paying particular attention to its institutionalization in the economic, governmental, and educational structures. We should also understand how and why an ethnic group remains *distinctive* or *identifiable* and, as such, an easy target for discrimination. We must then delve into questions about the *sense of threat* engendered by an identifiable ethnic population and how this sense of threat is related to its size and entrepreneurial resources. Then, we can turn to the *negative beliefs* and

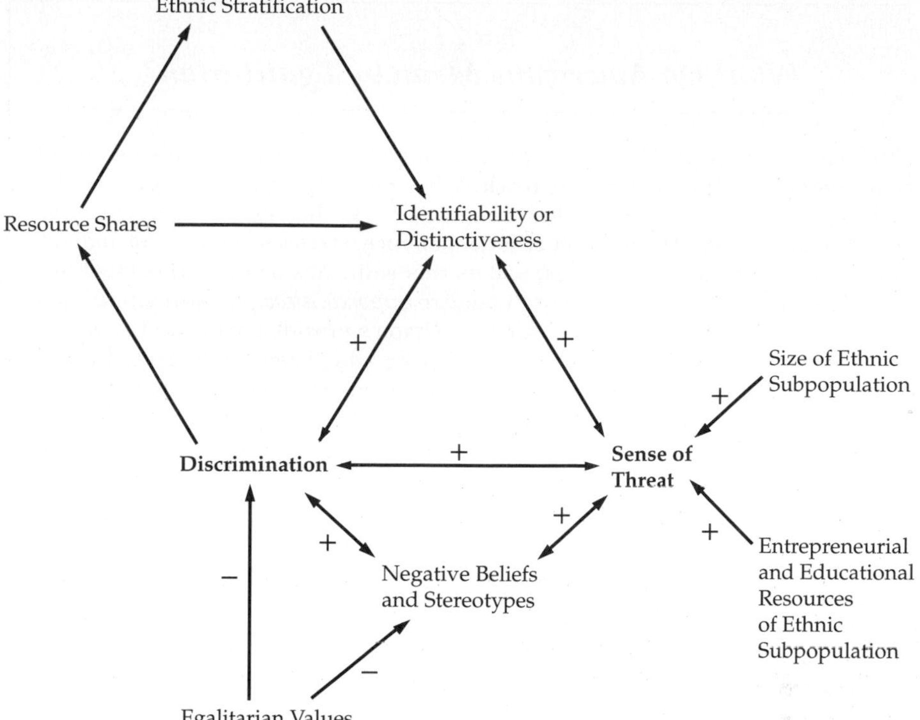

FIGURE 2.2. A general model of ethnic relations.

stereotypes to see how they have legitimized discrimination, while escalating the sense of threat. Finally, we need to examine the impact of *egalitarian values* imposing challenges to prejudicial beliefs and stereotypes about an ethnic group and to patterns of institutionalized discrimination that have denied this group access to resources. In this context, we can assess political and social movements that have arisen in recent years or that are likely to emerge in the future.

How can these self-reinforcing processes be broken? Rebellion and revolt, political mobilization, formation of a social movement, and other acts may force dominant ethnic groups to make concessions. Also, the existence of egalitarian values, as portrayed in the lower right portions of Figure 2.2, may stimulate change. The negative arrows pointing to prejudicial and negative beliefs as well as to discrimination indicate that such values stand in contradiction to prejudice and discrimination. Of course, in societies without such values, the cycles portrayed in Figure 2.2 are allowed to operate, up to the point of revolt and conflict. But in the United States, where values of equality and freedom are pervasive, they legitimate opposition movements to discriminatory practices—for example, the abolitionist movement that denounced slavery and the civil rights movement that culminated in a

Box 2.1

What Do Americans Mean by Egalitarian?

Affirmative action policies have, over the last two decades, generated so much controversy that it is reasonable to ask: Why the controversy? The answer ultimately resides in two approaches for realizing egalitarian values. The first, clearly stated in the Declaration of Independence, stresses equality for individuals rather than social categories; and as this value has become translated into social policies, the goal has been to equalize *opportunities for individuals.* The second approach, initiated under Richard Nixon's presidency in the 1970s, emphasizes equality for groups; and as this policy has been implemented under more recent affirmative action programs, the focus has been on *equality of results.*

As Seymour Martin Lipset (1993: 209) has argued, these policies represent a clash of two basic American values: egalitarianism versus individualism. *Individualism* stresses that people get ahead through their own efforts and hard work; and when combined with *egalitarianism,* the result is a commitment to providing compensatory help to those individuals whose circumstances keep them from realizing their full potential for hard work and success. But, when equality is stressed over individualism, the commitment is to assuring that certain categories of people—minorities and women, for example—achieve proportionate representation and results when compared to those who have been more advantaged. In this latter commitment, emphasis is on giving preferences to certain categories of individuals in order to compensate for past discrimination.

Public opinion polls in the United States have been consistent and overwhelming in their endorsement of individualistic egalitarianism. The American public is opposed to group-preference approaches; and even among minorities, who could be helped by these approaches, a clear majority is opposed to them as well. Yet, Americans are strongly in support of programs that will help individuals, *as individuals* rather than as a social category, overcome the disadvantages that come with present and past discrimination. It should not be surprising, then, that affirmative action—when seen as group preferences—should be

series of federal laws in the 1960s formally outlawing discrimination. Without the existence of such egalitarian values in the dominant culture, oppressed ethnic groups must accept discrimination, migrate to a more favorable environment, or incur the risks of rebellion. Historically, acceptance and migration have been the most common responses of subordinate ethnic groups; protest by a subordinate minority is usually crushed, unless the population is large and the dominant groups weak, or unless the ethnic group has allies within or outside the society. Only recently in world history have egalitarian values become a powerful force; patterns of discrimination and ethnic stratification have been a prominent feature of human societies for millennia. Since egalitarian values are hardly universal in the world so hotly debated, and that Americans have come to disagree with virtually all policies based upon a group-preference interpretation of egalitarianism. Whether this feeling on the part of the American public is good, bad, right, or wrong in some ultimate moral sense is less relevant than the fact that Americans view group preferences as unfair. In contrast, they do not feel that compensatory efforts—special programs in education and job training, for example—are unfair; indeed, Americans see these kinds of efforts as necessary to overcome present, as well as the legacy of the past, discrimination.

Another basic American value is *humanitarianism*—that is, those who have suffered through no fault of their own should be helped. In the minds of most Americans this value is mixed with individualism and egalitarianism to produce a clear desire for programs to help individuals realize more opportunities, regardless of their social category. Those who are poor and who have been victims of discrimination need compensatory help *as individuals* to realize their potential. This is as far as Americans appear to be willing to go in their humanitarianism; relatively small percentages of Americans believe that categories of individuals should be given preferential treatment. Indeed, programs which are perceived to give preferential treatment to social categories—whether this perception is accurate or not is another matter—are seen as undesirable. Hence, efforts on the part of policy makers to overcome the effects of present and past discrimination will need to be careful in constructing these programs; if they are not, programs will encounter negative evaluation by the conditional humanitarianism of most Americans: equality of opportunity is okay; equality of outcome through group preferences is not okay.

Yet, it can be asked: Without group preferences, can the cumulative effects of discrimination over hundreds of years really be overcome? Can any compensatory educational program, for example, overcome the effects of being raised in a graffiti- and bullet-marked public housing project infested by gangs and drug dealers? Or, can women ever overcome discrimination by anything but group preferences in assuring their access to job categories dominated by men? In reality, the answer to these questions is probably no, but Americans think otherwise; and hence, programs to realize egalitarian values in the face of past and present discrimination will always be limited by what the public perceives as fair and unfair.

today, ethnic stratification and tensions will remain part of human society in the future. This is assuredly the case when one considers that the United States, which subscribes to powerful egalitarian values, has yet to break the cycles portrayed in Figure 2.2.

The definitions in Chapter 1, coupled with the theoretical explanation offered in this chapter, provide us with a means for examining ethnic relations in America. More specifically, the model depicted in Figure 2.2 can be viewed as a springboard for discussion about each ethnic subpopulation to be examined in the chapters to follow.

When noticeable differences of an ethnic subpopulation are perceived to pose a threat, they lead to discrimination. Large ethnic populations or smaller ones with entrepreneurial skills are most likely to generate a sense of threat among dominant ethnics. This sense of threat leads people to construct negative beliefs and stereotypes about ethnics; and these beliefs are used to legitimate discrimination.

Discrimination, itself, also encourages beliefs that can make such discrimination seem legitimate; and once codified, these beliefs encourage further discrimination. The effects of additional discrimination are to limit resource shares of ethnic groups, maintain their identity and vulnerability to discrimination, and to force them into habitual locations in the stratification system; as these effects occur, a renewed cycle of threat, prejudice, and discrimination is unleashed against ethnic groups who "refuse to change" (again, ignoring the obvious reasons for why it is difficult to change).

The forces delineated in the theoretical model portrayed in Figure 2.2 will become the chapter headings and sections in subsequent discussions. They will provide a framework for systematically reviewing the past, present, and future of the most prominent ethnic subpopulations in America. And, they will do more. Because these headings are derived from a theoretical model, they contribute to an explanation of *why* an ethnic subpopulation and members of the dominant Anglo-Saxon Protestant culture have formed a particular pattern of tension-provoking relations. By examining how the forces portrayed in Figure 2.2 have operated and interacted for a particular ethnic population, we will be able to explain what has occurred in the past, what is going on today, and what will likely happen in the future.

SUMMARY

Theories attempt to explain why a phenomenon exists and how it operates. Theories explaining ethnicity are diverse, each capturing an important dynamic but none incorporating all the key forces in ethnic relations. Assimilation theories emphasize the process by which members of an ethnic population become part of the mainstream of a society, but they do not adequately account for the persistence of ethnic differences and the conflicts these differences generate. Theories of ethnic pluralism arose in reaction to the "melting pot" basis of assimilation theories, arguing that the maintenance of ethnicity is often a way of coping with discrimination. More recent biological theories propose the possibility of human genetic tendencies to identify with and support members of their distinctive ethnic heritage. These biological theories are as controversial as earlier and often ethnocentric, if not racist, theories. Ecological theories emphasize that competition for scarce resources is a key force in creating and sustaining ethnic relations and that patterns of domination and subjugation among ethnic groups reflect this competition over valued resources such as jobs, incomes, and housing.

All stratification theories argue that ethnic groups are overrepresented in particular social strata because of the unequal distribution of power.

Caste theories stress that many minority groups have been historically pushed to the bottom of the class system with rigid barriers preventing mobility out of this position. Colonialism theories emphasize that minority populations often become exploited "colonies" within a society—much like their international counterparts, where one nation subjugates the members of another and extracts their resources without a proportionate return. Split-labor market theories draw attention to the fact that patterns of discrimination are often created and sustained through the partitioning of labor markets so that dominant subpopulations can continue to enjoy their privilege while denying subordinate ethnic groups access to jobs and income. Split-class theories argue that divisions and partitions *within* social classes exist, with the least powerful typically confined to a lower class in order to maintain the privilege of the dominant sector within a class. Middleman minority theories use elements from split-labor market and split-class theories to explain how small pockets within ethnic subpopulations, mostly in a narrow range of business and entrepreneurial positions, emerge and succeed in the socioeconomic mainstream.

Finally, this chapter has sought to take the main tenets of each theory and synthesize them into a general model of ethnic discrimination in America. This model stresses several interrelated factors: ethnic identifiability, the threat that an ethnic population poses, the prejudicial stereotypes that are articulated, the resources possessed by an ethnic population, the size of an ethnic population, and the position of a subpopulation in the stratification system.

POINTS OF DEBATE

Each of the theories summarized in this chapter suggests points of debate, some of which are enumerated below.

1. Is assimilation the desired outcome of ethnic relations? Today, many argue that America must be a "pluralistic society," but this raises the question: How much pluralism is possible? Historically, no society has endured without a cultural core that absorbs elements of diverse ethnic populations while remaining intact. When "ethnic pluralism" translates into competing cultural cores, history has shown that societal disintegration follows. When "ethnic pluralism" refers to a limited range of traditions such as religious beliefs and rituals, distinctive ceremonies and holidays honoring a cultural heritage and important figures in this heritage, and even maintenance of a secondary language, the disintegrative potential of ethnicity is reduced. Can the cultural core, which is examined in Chapter 3, absorb important components of diverse ethnic populations? Must ethnic groups assimilate, and, if so, to what degree? What are the consequences for society if assimilation does not occur? To what degree are members of the dominant Anglo-Saxon cultural core

willing to accommodate change?

2. Stratification theories emphasize that discrimination forces some ethnic groups into either lower-class positions or a narrow range of middleman positions. Inequality is one of the most volatile forces in human organization; when inequality takes on an ethnic dimension, it is doubly volatile. Because the socioeconomic position of many ethnic groups in America is the result of discrimination, it is reasonable to ask: How can the remaining patterns of discrimination be eliminated, or at least reduced? What can be done to compensate descendants of those who have experienced the most discrimination and those who live with the legacy of such discrimination? To the "second American dilemma," discussed in the points of debate section in Chapter 1, we now add a caveat: People who have been subjugated for a long time become angry and strike back. Americans need to consider how they are to avoid the dangers of ethnic violence as a form of retaliation by those in lower socioeconomic positions.
3. Ethnic stratification is sustained by mutually reinforcing cycles (see Figures 2.1 and 2.2); how can these cycles be broken? The identifiability cycle, especially when based upon physical features, can be broken by intermarriage. How willing are the members of both subordinate and dominant ethnic groups to accept this type of assimilation? When members of the dominant culture, as well as other subordinate ethnic groups, feel threatened, discrimination and prejudice emerge. How is this cycle to be broken, especially as competition for resources (as emphasized by ecological theories) intensifies? Are there enough jobs, houses, or educational credentials to go around? Are those who have these resources willing to see others acquire them if it costs them some of their own privilege? How much, if anything, are people willing to give up in the name of ethnic peace and egalitarianism? What are the consequences if privileged Americans are not willing to give up anything?

CHAPTER 3

The Anglo-Saxon Core and Ethnic Antagonism

Relations between ethnic groups almost always involve elements of domination and subordination: One ethnic subpopulation is able to impose its culture and institutional arrangements on another. In the United States, this process of cultural and institutional domination is complex because of the immigration of so many diverse ethnic groups, but one fact is clear: Anglo-Saxon culture and institutions often dictate and define what other ethnic populations must become (Gordon, 1964). Each ethnic minority in America has been expected to adapt to this Anglo-Saxon core; and each has experienced discrimination by those who have sought to maintain the cultural symbols and institutional structure of this core. Thus, before exploring the lives of the most prominent ethnic minorities in the United States, let us explore the history of those dominant sociocultural traditions that have been imposed upon other ethnics.

EARLY COLONIZATION OF AMERICA

The Anglo-Saxons

The term "Anglo-Saxon" is a bit of a misnomer; it derives from northern Germanic tribes—the Saxons and Angles—that invaded England in the fifth and sixth centuries, displacing other tribes whose lives had already been disrupted by the invasions of the Celts from continental Europe and later the Romans. Other invaders followed, such as the Normans from France; and as a result, a considerable amount of mingling among continental and English cultures ensued. Thus, the English settlers who came to America were, themselves, a product of a long history of conquest and blending of ethnic subpopulations. For not only were Scots and Welsh (the remnants of the old Celts) part of the early "English" settlements, but in some areas significant numbers of Germans (as many as one-third in Pennsylvania) and Scandinavians were to follow, blending together with these "English Americans" to form the cultural core of America.

The term "Anglo-Saxon" (or one of its variants, "WASP"–White Anglo-Saxon Protestant) denotes a northern European cultural and institutional complex of ethnic traditions fused with, and dominated by, the English who were the first to settle North America in large numbers and to begin the process of colonization. We use the terms "Anglo-Saxon" and "WASP," therefore, to denote an ethnic complex consisting of northern European ethnic stock with light, "white" skin; Protestant religious beliefs; Protestant-inspired values based on individualism, hard work, savings, and secular material success; and English cultural traditions (language, laws, and beliefs) and institutional structures (politics, economics, and education).

The Early Colonists

Although the early colonizers were predominantly English, there were significant numbers of Welsh and Scots. At first, the Welsh maintained their own communities, and even language traditions, but by the late 1600s, they were assimilated into the English core. Scots constituted a much larger population, coming from both the Highlands and Lowlands as well as from Ireland (where many Scots had earlier migrated). Like the Welsh, they were almost fully assimilated into English culture by the end of the seventeenth century. A few Irish also lived in the early settlement communities, but the flood of Irish immigrants was to come much later.

Germans constituted the largest of the non–British Isle segment of early colonists, with almost all coming from the Protestant north. Later German immigrants were non–Protestant Catholics and Jews, but the early Germans were close to the English in terms of culture and institutional practices. Thus, it was not difficult for these Germans to change in ways compatible with English culture, although some distinctive German traditions remained in isolated communities. Other northern Europeans, such as Scandinavians, were not as prominent as Germans; their peak period of immigration was not to come until the late nineteenth century. Continental Europeans, such as the Dutch and French (who were settling in larger numbers in Canada), also immigrated, but again, they did not come to the early colonies en masse.

Thus, by the close of the eighteenth century in the aftermath of the Revolutionary War and in the early phases of the emergence of the United States as a nation, the American Historical Association (1932) estimates that 60.1 percent of the free, nonslave population was English, 14.0 percent Scotch and Scotch-Irish, 8.6 percent German, 3.6 percent Irish, 3.1 percent Dutch, 3.0 percent French or Swedish, and 7.6 percent other ethnic nationalities. The English dominated numerically for the first two centuries, especially if one includes other ethnic groups from the British Isles. This dominant group established the cultural and institutional agenda of the United States.

THE CULTURAL AND INSTITUTIONAL LEGACY OF EARLY COLONIZATION

The Core Culture

Language

Perhaps the single most important cultural legacy of the early settlers was the English language. Language was to become a litmus test for subsequent immigrants' right to be "American," for the early settlers demanded that English be spoken and that other immigrant populations adopt this language or suffer the consequences. Indeed, there was great agonizing over the "mongrelization" of the white, Anglo-Saxon culture by immigrants who spoke other languages. These concerns exist today, as is clearly evident in the "English-as-the-official-language" campaigns in Congress and some states.

Basic Values

Many of the core values of America come from English Protestantism, as Max Weber [1905–1906 (1930)] emphasized in his famous analysis. As Weber stressed, the British brought with them to the Americas *ascetic Protestantism,* as personified in Puritanism, which emphasized salvation, hard work, abstinence from temptation, and religiosity. Weber's portrayal of asceticism—discipline, hard work, efficient use of time, rationality, accumulation and profit without moral temptation—can all be seen in the core values of America. These values, in turn, have been used as a yardstick to see if ethnic immigrants "measure up." Those ethnic groups who have not been deemed hardworking, efficient, and disciplined have become targets of prejudicial beliefs and discriminatory practices.

Legal Tenets

The basic tenets of American law owe much to British traditions, as modified by the colonists' adoption of ideas from the eighteenth-century French philosophies. Law is to rule; people are to be equal before the law; laws are to be enacted by representatives of the people; and concentrations of power are to be limited or held in check by law. Despite the blending of French and British philosophical and legal traditions, much of the actual substance of early law in the colonies was English in origin. For example, the specific rights of property holders and obligations established by contracts were considered as important in the actual wording of substantive laws as the broader philosophical and constitutional concerns about equality, freedom, and justice. This disjuncture between general constitutional principles, on the one hand, and state and local laws protecting property rights, on the other, enabled patterns of legally sanctioned discrimination to persist until the latter decades of this century.

The dominant systems of symbols in America—language, values, and laws—derive from the early English settlers. These core cultural components have, of course, been intermingled with those of other cultures and altered in accordance with changing circumstances, but more noticeable is the continuity of these symbols and their capacity to define how members of ethnic groups must speak, think, and behave.

The Core Institutional Structures

Economic Institutions

The early American settlers came primarily for economic reasons. Colonial settlement was geared to the extraction of raw materials for English commerce and the creation of new markets for English goods. Other reasons for settlement—to escape religious persecution, to reduce the population, to arrest the Spanish and French advance in the hemisphere, and to search for a quicker passage to India—were secondary to the desire of the English Crown and commercial interests to develop America in ways that increased England's prosperity. The chartering of companies and granting of territory were the initial vehicles for transporting commercial capitalism to the colonies. Here, emphasis was placed on private property, contracts, and markets. The drive to take land, develop farms, kill or displace Native Americans, and import slaves was fueled by the effort to create markets that sent raw materials across the Atlantic and brought back finished goods from commercial and emerging industrial interests in England.

The Revolution freed this market-oriented economy from the chartered companies of the English Crown and created what eventually was to be a dynamic form of capitalism that relied upon disadvantaged and inexpensive ethnic labor. The enslavement of Africans was the first manifestation of this use of ethnic populations to extract profits; the mass killing of Native Americans was ultimately for the economic gains that came with their land and resources; the conquest of Mexican Americans in the Southwest marked a similar appropriation of land and subordination of an ethnic group for economic gain; finally, the large-scale importation of white ethnic groups from other parts of continental Europe and Asians from the East was used to sustain further expansion of industrial development. Thus, the legacy of early British commercial capitalism evolved into a system that depended upon subordinated ethnic labor—a situation that persists to the present day.

Political Institutions

As with legal tenets, the structure of government in the United States reflects the blending of seventeenth-century British political traditions (Hunnington, 1966) and eighteenth-century French social philosophy. The early colonists' concepts of decentered nationhood, representative government, decentralized power, and rule by law were greatly supplemented in the post-Revolutionary era by French thinking on equality, justice, individual rights, representative democracy, and checks and balances among legislative, judicial, and administrative branches of government. The result was a constitutional democracy that expounded high principles about justice, equality, and freedom but which also gave much political autonomy to local communities and the states.

In actual practice, this decentralized system allowed for considerable disjuncture between lofty constitutional principles—freedom, equality, and justice—and the actual operation of government. Both local and state laws perpetuating slavery, justifying land appropriation from Native Americans and Mexican Americans, and encouraging discrimination against ethnic groups employed as inexpensive laborers existed alongside egalitarian constitutional tenets. Moreover, these highly discriminatory laws and political practices were often sanctioned by all branches of the federal government in the name of territorial expansion, industrial and commercial development, private property rights, and, most importantly, *states' rights.* This same system existed within a democracy that attacked discrimination on the political and legal battlefields. The result was that ethnic groups and their allies from the dominant core gradually overcame the most blatant and formal patterns of discrimination by making appeals to constitutional principles, by taking power at the local level, and by forcing legislative changes in the laws at all levels of government.

Educational Institutions

Before the Revolution, schooling was private and available only to affluent, mostly Anglo-Saxon, citizens. Education was based largely on the tenets of English Protestantism, the core values that Protestantism spawned, the culture of western and northern Europe, and the views of commerce and politics held by the early English settlers. This early private system did not reach a large proportion of the population, but it became the model for the public schools, which later proliferated as an explicit and acknowledged means to "Americanize" newer and non-Protestant immigrants in the latter part of the eighteenth century and throughout the nineteenth and twentieth centuries. What typified these early schools and many public schools thereafter was an Anglo-Saxon Eurocentric curriculum. And, even as a system of private Catholic schools, along with other religious institutions, began to emerge, the substance of the secular curriculum in these schools contained the core values and beliefs of the early northern European settlers. Only recently has this curriculum begun to accommodate the realities of non-European immigration and of the legacy of slavery and Native American genocide. In many instances, however, this new material is viewed as a supplement to the core white, Anglo-Saxon, middle-class thrust of the school culture and curriculum. These new materials are designed as supplements to efforts at Americanizing those who were unsuccessfully assimilated, such as those Native Americans and African Americans who remain at the fringes of society, those who have resisted full assimilation like Mexicans and other Latino individuals, and those new immigrants, such as recent Asians, who must learn western and American ways.

Religious Institutions

The English brought with them Anglican and Congregational Protestantism, although these religions were not dominant by the Revolutionary era. The religious tone of the society was decidedly Protestant, however, with other religions, particularly Catholicism and Judaism, viewed most suspiciously. In fact, Will Herberg (1960) has argued that Catholicism, Judaism, and non-British Protestantism all accommodated themselves in terms of the language used in their services, the organization of their religious schools, and the format of their rituals. As increasing numbers of non-English Protestants and non-Protestants immigrated to America in the post-Revolutionary era, tolerance for religious pluralism became evident; yet this was a pluralism among unequal partners, for English religious traditions dictated how each religion was to be tolerated. To this day, hostility exists toward those religions that do not conform to the style and format of Protestantism.

ANGLO-SAXON HEGEMONY AND THE DYNAMICS OF ETHNICITY

The Domination of the Anglo-Saxon Core

We can conclude, then, that the core cultural and institutional structures of the United States have been disproportionately influenced by the early English settlers. As founders of America, the English did not have to compete with rival cultural symbols and institutions from another equally developed population. For, although Native Americans helped many of the early settlers survive the early winters, their institutional structures were unlikely to survive those of peoples from a much more technologically developed society. Unless the first settlers wanted to return to hunting and gathering or simple horticulture, Native American institutions could not out-compete those brought by an economically and militarily more developed population. Native Americans and their institutional structures were destroyed and displaced, as was their culture.

Once Anglo-Saxon culture and institutional structures were in place, Anglo-Saxons could set the terms of competition among ethnic groups—the nature of the playing field, the rules of the game, and the players who would be allowed in the game. In so doing, they could force other cultures and institutional systems to adapt and adopt Anglo-Saxon ways. A conquering ethnic group, which had conquered and displaced the founding native stock, can usually establish itself before other ethnic migrants arrive and, as a consequence, will almost always be able to dominate.

Today, with two hundred years of immigration to complement the ancestors of African slaves, Latinos, and Native Americans, the descendants of Anglo-Saxons still hold a disproportionate number of elite positions (see Feagin, 1989:75–78, for a brief review). Not only are core cultural and basic institutional structures Anglo-Saxon but the elite members of this group are overrepresented by the descendants of those who came before the Revolution. Because these elite members have the power to influence beliefs and policy, Anglo-Saxons can disproportionately determine the cultural climate and institutional policies of American society today. We are not concluding that there is a concerted conspiracy to do so; rather, the elite Anglo-Saxons and their many assimilated allies from other ethnic groups, especially later European immigrants, simply view certain symbols and arrangements as more desirable, workable, and fair. Indeed, they are likely to believe that these symbols and arrangements offer the best chance for the disadvantaged to do better in American society.

The dominance of white ethnic groups, especially those in the Anglo-Saxon core as well as others who have adopted this core culture, is reflected in their economic well-being. White ethnic groups have lower rates of poverty and higher levels of wealth than Native Americans, African Americans, and Latinos (Farley, 1990:238; U.S. Bureau of the Census, 1991a, b, and c). Some Asians match or exceed non-Latino white Americans in income and wealth (see Chapter 7), but this fact does not detract from the basic point: White ethnic groups from the original core and later white immigrants who suffered enormously *until* they were absorbed into the core do well compared to those who were brought as slaves (African Americans), those who were killed by European diseases or instruments of violence (Native Americans), and those who were displaced by conquest in the Southwest (Mexican Americans). Latinos and Asians have also suffered, but not to the same degree as those whose human and material resources were taken away or used to build the society.

The Anglo-Saxon Core and the Dynamics of Discrimination

The imposition of the Anglo-Saxon core has not always been benign in the past, nor is it today. The dominance of the Anglo-Saxon core has led to patterns of ethnic antagonism along the lines discussed in Chapter 2. As each new ethnic group arrived, it posed a threat to this core: These ethnic groups tended to be non-Protestant, sometimes non-Christian; they were willing to work for less; they were sufficiently numerous to tip local balances of political power; they placed new burdens on schools and housing; and they brought different languages, values, beliefs, and other symbol systems. This threat led to negative and prejudicial stereotyping of these newly arrived ethnic groups based on their inability to conform to the Anglo-Saxon core; these prejudicial beliefs legitimized discrimination in jobs, housing, education, and politics. Such discrimination was relatively easy to practice because recently arrived ethnic groups are identifiable in terms of culture (language, beliefs, traditions, values), behavior, imported institutions (religion, family), and, for many, physical appearance (skin color, facial configurations). Those who could adapt to Anglo-Saxon culture by changing their

White supremacist groups, like the Ku Klux Klan, strive to preserve U.S. society from nonwhite persons.

cultural or behavioral norms experienced less discrimination, especially if they were white. Groups who remained identifiable, were small in number, and possessed entrepreneurial skills tended to find middleman minority niches, even in the face of intense discrimination. Groups who were identifiable, large in number, and without skills or other resources tended to occupy lower socioeconomic positions.

Each wave of immigration, coupled with the "emancipation" of African Americans and the conquest of Native Americans and Mexicans, set in motion these discriminatory dynamics. In the early years of settlement, in the seventeenth and eighteenth centuries, Africans were enslaved and Native Americans conquered; however, with the "freedom" and emergence of each new population, the Anglo-Saxon core had to adjust to the threat against their predominance.

Germans and Scandinavians began to migrate to America in the late eighteenth century and continued throughout the nineteenth century, as did many English. Their presence posed less of a threat to the Anglo-Saxon core than other ethnic populations, however, because of their Protestant and northern European heritage. But for other ethnic groups, the dynamics of discrimination were accelerated by new threats.

Abolitionist pressures to free slaves heightened the sense of threat in

Box 3.1

The Anglo-Saxon Core and Demographic Change

In 1996, the U.S. Census Bureau estimated that Latinos and Asians will account for more than half of the growth in the American population over the next fifty years. The total population of the United States in 1996 was 262.8 million persons, and it will increase to 393.9 million people by the year 2050. Population growth in America is quite modest, about 1 percent per year; and the Census Bureau expects even this modest rate to drop to levels below those ever recorded since the census was initiated in 1790. Yet, even as the overall birth rate drops, there are differences in the respective rate among ethnics; and coupled with immigration, the ethnic composition of the society will change, and dramatically so over the next fifty years. Indeed, in California, which is now 30 percent Latino and which may have a Latino majority within the next forty years, can be seen reflected the future of America.

The official forecast for the nation as a whole for the year 2050 is as follows (with current percentages in parentheses): non-Hispanic whites, 52.8 percent (currently, 73.6%); Latinos, 24.5 percent (10.2%); African Americans or blacks, 13.6 percent (12%); Asian and Pacific Islanders, 8.2 percent (3.3%); and Native Americans, 0.9 percent (0.7%). Thus, non-Hispanic whites will constitute a bare majority in fifty years, placing a great burden on the Anglo-Saxon core to accommodate a certain degree of "Latinoization." California will, of course, experience even greater pressures to become more culturally Latino. Moreover, as the Asian count increases, some accommodation will have to occur here, although the Asian minority in America today is broken down into many distinct cultures and, hence, will not exert the same influence as the more unified Latino cultural complex. The African American population will not grow very much as a proportion of the total, although continued pressure to incorporate the distinctive culture that emerged out of slavery and centuries of oppression will, no doubt, persist. Native Americans will perhaps have the least influence because of their small numbers, although what remains of the many cultures that once existed will continue to be preserved.

But, one thing is very clear: America will still be dominated by the sociocultural complex of northern Europe, but it may have to change significantly over the next fifty years. Change is always difficult, and typically very threatening to those who are used to having their cultural ways dominate. Just how much change will ensue is difficult to estimate, but America in the year 2050 will be a very different place. The Anglo-Saxon core will still dominate and set many of the standards that others must meet, but these standards will have changed to accommodate the demographic realities of the next half century.

the South, and also in the North. As the country expanded westward, nations of Native Americans were successively conquered in the Indian Wars of the 1800s and shunted to various reservations. They were viewed as a constant threat by the white settlers who had taken their land and destroyed their culture. Irish Catholics, the first of the non-Protestant Europeans, came between the 1830s and 1860s. Their large numbers unsettled the Anglo-Saxon core in America's key cities. The Chinese—the first Asian ethnic population—came in the 1850s to 1870s as railroad workers. Their nonwestern ways posed a threat to the western extensions of the Anglo-Saxon core. The Mexicans of the Southwest were colonized and thrown off their land beginning in the 1850s. Those who remained in the United States were relegated to low-wage jobs—a situation that was exacerbated by the Mexican migration into the Southwest throughout the twentieth century. In the 1880s through the first decades of the twentieth century, Italians, Jews from eastern Europe, and Poles entered in large numbers. The Japanese and Filipinos also straddled the century mark, coming as agricultural workers, often via Hawaii, to the West Coast and bearing with them the "threat" of Asian and South Asian culture.

African Americans began to migrate to the Northeast and Midwest in the early decades of the twentieth century, competing with the white ethnic groups for employment. Puerto Ricans came to the Northeast in large numbers, from the 1940s to the present, standing with pride in their Latin heritage. Cubans came to south Florida in the 1960s and 1970s. Their presence evoked less fear because of their anti-communist views and desire to return to Cuba; but their large number and Latin culture pinch at Anglo sensibilities. And in the 1960s to the present, new Asian groupings—Koreans, Vietnamese, Taiwanese, Chinese, Filipinos—have migrated to the United States. Each wave of immigration and migration has posed a threat to the integrity of the Anglo-Saxon core.

Although the culture and institution building of each wave of immigrants have broadened the culture and structure of American society beyond the original Anglo-Saxon core, this broadening has always involved the assimilation of immigrant cultures to the Anglo-Saxon core. Even with accommodation, however, the more visible dynamic has been ethnic antagonism—born and sustained by threat, prejudice, and discrimination—between the new and the older cultural core.

SUMMARY

Ethnic relations in America have been profoundly influenced by the cultural systems and institutional structures of the first colonizers. This is almost always the case when a more powerful population invades the territory of a less powerful population and, then, seeks to settle there. Throughout world history, this process has occurred again and again, but the "new world" added a different twist. The settlement and expansion of the conquering population required the accommodation of new waves of immigrants. Some immigrants were imported as slaves, but most came voluntarily from Europe and Asia. As Native Americans were virtually eliminated and isolated on reservations, and Mexicans were conquered and deposed,

America became, literally, a land of opportunity for immigrants and migrants. The rapid industrialization of the East and Midwest, along with the expansion of agriculture and ranching in the West, created new opportunities, which stimulated a massive wave of immigration. Among the Europeans, those from the north were the first to come, followed by central and southern Europeans. Most of these Europeans initially settled in the East and emerging Midwest; later, they moved farther west. In addition to these white immigrants, Asian immigrants began to settle on the West Coast; some came before most northern and southern Europeans, but most came at about the same time as these Europeans.

These early immigrants, as well as those who arrived in the latter part of the twentieth century, have had to confront the Anglo-Saxon core, itself an amalgam of cultural and institutional systems of the British Isles, coupled with significant infusions from German, Dutch, Scandinavian, and French cultural traditions. This core consisted of such cultural elements as the English language, English values and beliefs, and English legal tenets, along with mostly northern European institutional structures in economy, government, education, and religion. This core represented the environment that other ethnic groups would have to adapt to, adopt, or live with the consequences. For white ethnic groups, assimilation was easier because of their European heritage and, most important, their skin color; for Asians, physical identifiability and nonwestern culture posed greater problems; for freed slaves, skin color coupled with extreme prejudice and discrimination made it very difficult to adapt to, much less adopt, all the elements of the core; for more recent immigrants—particularly Asians and Latinos—adjustment has not been easy because of the threats that these immigrants pose not only to many members of the Anglo-Saxon core but also to those earlier immigrants who have yet to fully adapt to this core.

Each wave of immigration, as well as each internal wave of migration of former slaves and natives, has activated the dynamics of discrimination discussed in Chapter 2 and modeled in Figures 2.1 and 2.2. Each ethnic group has altered the Anglo-Saxon core, but only to a point; the persistence of ethnic tension indicates that not all ethnic groups can, or want to, assimilate.

POINTS OF DEBATE

Some of the most hotly contested issues in America today revolve around the conflict between subordinate ethnic groups and members of the dominant Anglo-Saxon core. Often as a reaction to discrimination, but also as a matter of preference, ethnic minority groups have sought to cultivate and maintain their distinctive cultural features and patterns of social organization, even if this means that they conflict with the Anglo-Saxon core. The resulting tension and conflict engenders many questions, some of which follow:

1. How flexible can the Anglo-Saxon core be in accommodating the key elements of other cultures and remain the core? Many argue that Amer-

ica must become pluralistic, but to what degree and at what expense? If a society has no clear cultural or institutional core, is such a society viable?

2. Has the existence of blatant and established discrimination in America forced ethnic groups to discard assimilation as an option? If so, has the United States passed the critical point where accommodation is less likely than ethnic conflict? If this is so, what is to be done? What is the future of the United States if ethnic subpopulations polarize around distinctive cores?
3. Has the Anglo-Saxon core been inflexible, as is often charged by the victims of discrimination? There are clear signs that a considerable amount of change has occurred, as reflected in the massive contributions of all ethnic groups to the culture and structure of American society. Even those populations that have experienced severe discrimination have assimilated some elements of their culture, albeit only those elements peripheral to the core values, beliefs, and institutional arrangements that organize the society. Can the Anglo-Saxon core absorb more? Are ethnic groups willing to give up more of their cultural and institutional core in order to decrease the polarization between cores? If the answer is no to both questions, what is America's future?

CHAPTER 4

African Americans

Imported as slaves, treated as property to be bought and sold, denied citizenship rights, and considered less than human for much of American history, most African Americans have not been able to enjoy the benefits that come with living in the United States. The legacy of two hundred years of slavery, thirty years of post–Civil War oppression, and another century of systematic discrimination in housing, employment, education, and virtually every social sphere persists. Even as many of the old forms of discrimination have been dismantled since the mid-1960s, discrimination remains a central part of the African American experience (Jaynes and Williams, 1989; Farley and Allen, 1987; and Schafer, 1993).

The effects of three hundred and fifty years of oppression are not suddenly undone, for the weight of the past stands as a barrier in the present (Pinkney, 1984). How does one overcome, for example, the effects of residing in inner-city slums and public housing projects, growing up in single-parent households, living in a social climate where most young men have lost hope of finding employment and women are welfare-dependent, attending crowded and often dangerous schools, and walking down crime-ridden streets (Caputo, 1993; Bullard, 1991)? These conditions did not suddenly emerge; rather, they are the product of past discrimination, and now they operate as a new kind of discriminatory barrier. White Americans often fail to recognize this fact. Indeed, African Americans are frequently condemned for not overcoming these barriers, as if centuries of massive oppression could be quickly eradicated by individual initiative and drive (Farley, 1987; Hughes and Madden, 1991; and Blauner 1989). And so, even now, when institutionalized discrimination has been greatly reduced, the damage of the past remains, and few in the United States are seriously addressing this damage. Moreover, even as formal discrimination has decreased, subtle patterns of informal discrimination persist. As a result, today many African Americans are still denied equal access to the valued resources of society.

RESOURCE SHARES OF AFRICAN AMERICANS

The Impoverishment of African Americans

One very good indicator of how well, or badly, a subpopulation is doing in the United States is the rate of poverty. According to the U.S. Bureau of the Census (1995), approximately 13.5 percent of the population is defined as "poor," where in essence people's incomes do not meet government-established standards for adequate food, housing, clothing, and other necessary resources. These standards have varied over the last fifty years, as have the income levels necessary to meet them, but they have remained constant in the last decade.

African Americans are disproportionately poor, as Table 4.1 documents. As of 1994, close to 33 percent of African Americans were living in poverty; and this figure might be higher if the government's outmoded method for calculating poverty more accurately reflected the actual costs for many necessities of living (see Turner, 1992, for a review). The figures in Table 4.1 are, in one sense, encouraging: The poverty rate for African Americans is below that of the 1960s because of the War on Poverty programs, coupled with important civil rights legislation. But these statistics must be qualified by several considerations. First, the poverty rate is still very high; at least ten million African Americans are poor. Second, because of changes in the definition of poverty in the mid-1960s, only the data for 1970 and 1990 are comparable; if this comparison is made, poverty rates for African Americans in the current decade are the same as they were over twenty years ago. Third, while the poverty rate for African Americans declined after 1900, it is on the rise again, indicating that the commitment to eradicate poverty and discrimination in the 1960s was not renewed in the 1980s and 1990s.

The Income of African Americans

In absolute terms, the income of African Americans has increased, even taking inflation into consideration. But, relative to whites, blacks have not

TABLE 4.1. Percentage of Black and White Americans Living in Poverty

Year	Black	White
1994	33.1	12.2
1990	30.7	10.0
1980	31.0	9.0
1970	33.5	9.9
1960	55.1	18.1

Source: U.S. Bureau of the Census, 1979, 1983d, 1989, 1991c, and 1995.

made any real gains, except for a brief period after the programs of the 1960s were implemented. Thus, blacks have not been able to close the gap in income, which means that they have not increased their share of the resource pie (Rolison, 1993; Drinan, 1991; and Geshwender and Carroll-Seguin, 1990).

Table 4.2 shows the ratio between black and white median family income from 1950 to 1994. With the exception of 1970, the ratio of black to white income has remained relatively the same since 1950. The 1980s saw a drop in the ratio to the levels of the 1950s and 1960s. The decrease after 1970 is the result of (1) cutbacks in government job programs for the poor in general and African Americans living in the inner city in particular, (2) dramatic decreases in the number of relatively unskilled jobs in the economy, and, most importantly, (3) the rapid rise in female-headed single-parent families in the black population over the last two decades, at a time when white families increasingly became dual-income families (Jackson, 1995).

The income ratios in Table 4.2 do not reflect an important consideration: the increase in the African American middle class. Today, nearly one in seven black families earns over $50,000, compared to one in seventeen in 1967. Since the ratio of black to white income includes the incomes of this higher-income black middle class, poor blacks are much worse off relative to whites. Thus, the figures in Table 4.2 represent the average incomes of both African Americans who escaped poverty and those who did not; and since the figures extend to the 1950s, when there were very few middle-class blacks, these statistics show that more African Americans are poor now than in the past. Moreover, among these poor, a significant amount of income is derived from welfare and other government programs and, hence, does not signal participation in the job market, the occupational system, and the mainstream of American society. This lack of participation results in a pattern of marginalization among many in the African American community—a pattern that is difficult to change.

TABLE 4.2. Black Family Median Income As a Percentage of White Median Income

Year	Ratio of Black and White Income
1994	0.55
1990	0.59
1980	0.56
1970	0.64
1960	0.55
1950	0.54

Source: U.S. Bureau of the Census, 1979, 1983d, 1989, 1991c, and 1995.

The Occupation Distribution of African Americans

There have been dramatic changes in the distribution of jobs among African Americans. In 1960, only 13 percent of blacks could be labeled "white-collar workers," whereas in 1990, 50 percent held white-collar jobs (see Table 8.1 on page 204). Yet this apparent improvement is somewhat misleading, for several reasons. First, this 50 percent still lags behind the 58 percent white-collar niche held by whites. Second, African Americans are underrepresented in the higher-paying white-collar occupations and overrepresented at the lower-paying end of the stratum (Swinton, 1989). Third, the increase in white-collar employment among African Americans is only partially the result of a decrease in discrimination; much of the change is due to a shift in the occupational structure away from manual labor to low-paying clerical work. Fourth, as Farley and Allen (1987) discovered, the only group of blacks who have parity with their white counterparts are college-educated women; yet they must confront the glass ceiling that operates to keep women in lower-paying clerical jobs. Fifth, the increasing number of blacks in white-collar jobs is not paralleled by a similar increase of African Americans in professional and managerial positions. Sixth, blacks are overrepresented in menial and low-paying service jobs, and their participation in salaried blue-collar jobs has declined since the 1970s (reflecting changes in the economy, but reducing their opportunities for those entry-level jobs that have been the springboard for other ethnic groups).

For many African Americans, occupational life has improved, but the picture is not quite as rosy as it appears on the surface (Gabriel, Williams, and Schmitz, 1990). This fact becomes evident when we compare the unemployment rates of blacks and whites as shown in Table 4.3. In 1994, over 11 percent of African Americans were unemployed, compared to 5.3 percent of whites—a ratio that would be much greater if all those blacks who have given up the search for work were included. As the data in the table indicate, the gap between black and white rates of unemployment has been increasing; since the 1970s, the ratio of black to white unemployment has

TABLE 4.3. Unemployment Rates for Black Workers Compared to White Workers

Year	Percentage of Black Unemployed	Percentage of White Unemployed	Ratio of Black to White Unemployment
1994	11.5	5.3	2.2
1990	11.3	4.7	2.4
1980	13.2	6.3	2.1
1970	8.2	4.5	1.8
1960	10.2	4.9	2.1
1950	9.0	4.9	1.8

Source: U.S. Bureau of the Census, 1991c, 1993, and 1995.

risen from a little over 2 to 1 to almost 2½ to 1. These differences, it bears repeating, all would be much greater if those who stopped searching for work had been included.

Part of the explanation for the higher unemployment rate for African Americans is the greater percentage of black workers in service jobs, where employment is less secure, and in blue-collar jobs which, over the last forty years, have been decreasing. Some unemployment can be attributed to discrimination: More black workers are laid off than white workers (Lewis, 1989).

Unemployment denies people access to resources such as money and dignity. The unemployed often turn to the welfare system, which further erodes their dignity and which, in light of Congress's effort to "reform" welfare in 1996, will force many onto the streets. Moreover, unemployment makes it difficult, if not impossible, to build a stable life around home, family, and hope for the future (Eggers and Massey, 1992; Caputo, 1993; and Schneider and Phelan, 1990).

Educational Attainment of African Americans

Today, access to good jobs, income, and other resources depends upon a person's educational credentials. African American attendance in schools has, of course, been a hotly contested issue—from the early efforts at desegregation in the 1950s and 1960s to the controversy over forced busing in the 1970s and 1980s (Boozer et al., 1992). This situation alone signals the institutional inequities that have prevented blacks from attaining educational credentials equivalent to white Americans. Despite the desegregation controversy, which still rages on today, African Americans have made significant gains over the last decades in securing credentials that have increased their access to valued resources. As Table 4.4 shows, the gap between blacks and whites with high school diplomas has been closing over the last

TABLE 4.4. Educational Attainment Levels of Blacks and Whites*

	High School†		*College*‡	
Year	Blacks, %	Whites, %	Blacks, %	Whites, %
1994	73	82	13	23
1990	66	79	11	22
1980	51	69	8	17
1970	31	55	4	11
1960	20	43	3	8

*Persons 25 years old and over.
†Four years or more of high school.
‡Four years or more of college.
Source: U.S. Bureau of the Census, 1995.

thirty years. Moreover, for most of this period, the percentage of African Americans who have completed four years of college increased, but so did the percentage of whites, thereby sustaining the wide gap between blacks and whites.

Housing of African Americans

Housing is a valued resource. Where one lives determines access to other resources—jobs, good schools, clean air, peace and quiet, lack of crime, and so on (Bullard, 1993; Whetstone, 1993). African Americans have endured a tremendous amount of discrimination in housing, and, as a consequence, they are disproportionately confined to the inner cities (Jaynes and Williams, 1989; Wildausky, 1990; and Farley, 1995). Furthermore, they are segregated more than any other large ethnic population in the United States. Table 4.5 shows the residential segregation index for blacks in representative metropolitan areas: A low number indicates mild levels of segregation, whereas a high score represents high levels (a score of 100 would signal complete segregation of blacks). Among the sixteen metropolitan areas with the largest black population, however, the index score rises considerably to about 80 (Jaynes and Williams, 1989:27). As the black population increases in a metropolitan area, the level of segregation increases dramatically. Yet, as the most recent analysis of segregation between blacks and whites indicates, the peak period of segregation may now have passed (Farley and Frey, 1994), although Table 4.5 reveals that considerable segregation persists. Table 4.6 underscores the fact that the degree of segregation is very high in the most segregated metropolitan areas. Even in the least segregated metropolitan areas, the index scores are still rather high. However, the recent reductions in white–black segregation can be accounted for by increases in the Latino population. Census data classify Latinos as white, and this ethnic group has nearly the same levels of poverty as blacks (McKinney and Schnare, 1989), and hence, these poor Latinos have become integrated with blacks in urban poverty.

TABLE 4.5. Trends in Residential Segregation of African Americans

Year	Degree of Segregation, %
1990	58*
1980	53
1970	59
1960	56

*Estimate based on preliminary data from 1990 census. In addition, an examination of tract data from the 1980 and 1990 U.S. census shows that the black population continues to be the most segregated group in U.S. society (Harrison and Weinberg, 1992).
Source: McKinney and Schnare, 1989; U.S. Department of Housing and Urban Development, 1991.

TABLE 4.6. Segregation Indexes for Most and Least Segregated Metropolitan Areas, 1990

Most Segregated		Least Segregated	
Gary, Ind.	91	Charlottesville, Va.	45
Detroit, Mich.	89	Danville, Va.	45
Chicago, Ill.	87	Killeen, Texas	45
Cleveland, Ohio	86	San José, Calif.	45
Buffalo, N.Y.	84	Tucson, Ariz.	45
Flint, Mich.	84	Honolulu, Hawaii	44
Milwaukee,Wisc.	84	Anaheim, Calif.	43
Saginaw, Mich.	84	Cheyenne, Wyo.	43
Newark, N.J.	83	Ft. Walton Beach, Fla.	43
Philadelphia, Penn.	82	Clarksville, Tenn.	42
St. Louis, Mo.	81	Lawrence, Kan.	41
Ft. Myers, Fla.	81	Fayetteville, N.C.	41
Sarasota, Fla.	80	Anchorage, Ala.	38
Indianapolis, Ind.	80	Lawton, Okla.	37
Cincinnati, Ohio	80	Jacksonville, Fla.	31
Average	84	Average	42

Source: Farley and Frey, 1994:33.

Segregation of African Americans means that this minority is concentrated in inner cities and in city public housing. The result is that African Americans have (1) reduced access to jobs (because many companies have moved to the suburbs), (2) reduced capacity to go to good schools (because many inner-city schools are underfunded, overcrowded, and plagued with problems ranging from drugs and crime to high dropout rates), and (3) reduced ability to live and grow up outside the sphere of rampant crime, drug use, and gang activity (Calmore, 1993).

Life Span of African Americans

In 1993, the U.S. Department of Health and Human Services issued a report that black men and women were living longer—sixty-six years for men, and approaching seventy-five years for women (U.S. Department of Health and Human Services, 1993). Yet, the large gap between the life span of whites and blacks persists with white males living nearly seven years longer than black men and white women living nearly five years longer than black women. On average, then, blacks die nearly six years before whites (Jaynes and Williams, 1989:41, 395). Life is, indeed, a valuable resource, and, statistically, African Americans have less of it than white Americans.

Aside from life span, another indicator of general health and access to the medical system is the infant mortality rate, which, in general, is very high in America compared to other industrialized nations. While both white and black infant mortality rates have declined over the last fifty years, the black rate remains over twice that for whites (Jaynes and Williams, 1989; National Center for Health Statistics, 1991). Low birth weight is the cause of most early fatalities, indicating that premature babies and undernourished babies are a major contributor to the high infant mortality rate for African Americans; this fact, in turn, reflects the poverty, malnourishment, young age, single-parent status of mothers and inadequate neonatal care for black families (Reed, 1990).

In subsequent years of childhood—from ages 1 to 4, and from ages 5 to 14—large differences exist between the mortality rates for blacks and white Americans. In the 1 to 4 age range, black children have mortality rates just under twice those for white children, whereas in the 5 to 14 age range, the difference declines considerably. Thus, if an African American child survives the early years, his or her chances for survival increase until adolescence; then, black male homicide rates jump dramatically—to over ten times those for whites—and thereby increase the mortality rate for African Americans (Jaynes and Williams, 1989:416–417). If a black child survives adolescence and early adulthood, more typical health risks—heart disease, cancer, and stroke—become the major cause of death, occurring 30 to 40 percent more often among blacks than whites (Jaynes and Williams, 1989:418). It is clear, then, that death is a more immediate, present, and likely danger for blacks at most stages of life than it is for whites.

Thus, African Americans do not have the same level of access to money, jobs, education, housing, and health care as white Americans and, as we will see, other ethnic groups (Wallace, 1990). Our goal is to understand how and why this inequity exists. In seeking an explanation, we will use our discussion in Chapter 2; and in fact, the reader may want to review Figures 2.1 and 2.2 before proceeding. As the model in Figure 2.2 predicts, the explanation for the plight of African Americans resides in easy identifiability as targets of discrimination, large numbers and lack of entrepreneurial skills, negative stereotyping and prejudice by members of the dominant society, and victimization through both institutionalized and informal discrimination.

THE DYNAMICS OF DISCRIMINATION AGAINST AFRICAN AMERICANS

Identifiability of African Americans

Being black poses a problem in a white world: You stand out, and dramatically so. Black and white are perceived as opposite colors; a black person cannot easily "blend" into a predominantly white America. Skin color is, in the biological sense, a minor genetic trait; but in the sociological sense it is anything but minor. Identifiability makes people easy targets of discrimination. Most members of white ethnic groups look like the dominant population, and most Latinos are not physically identifiable as members of an ethnic group. Black people cannot shed their color, but commingling has occurred since the Africans were pressed into slavery, resulting in generations of individuals with various degrees of dark skin pigmentation. Interethnic marriages have increased somewhat in recent decades, further influencing the color balance of the American population. Yet, skin color, no matter what the permutation, continues to identify some as targets of discrimination.

Sociocultural traits also contribute to discrimination. Poverty and unemployment statistics for African Americans reflect their disproportionate representation in the lower classes; demeanor, speech, and dress further distinguish many members of the African American community. These characteristics are reinforced by black culture, which has evolved in reaction to slavery and the discrimination that blacks have endured since "emancipation."

Even when socioeconomic standing and/or culture are not obvious, skin color alone remains as a basis of discrimination. For example, Joe Feagin (1991) conducted in-depth interviews with black middle-class members and found that they experienced discrimination in public places, such as restaurants, stores, swimming pools, and parking areas. Thus, to be denied service, told to go, or to suffer epithets are still very common for blacks in America. The prejudice and discrimination that middle-class African Americans live with cannot be attributed to class or culture, but simply to skin color.

Negative Beliefs about African Americans

More than any other ethnic population in the United States, and perhaps in the world, African Americans have been the victims of negative beliefs and stereotypes. Negative beliefs have also reinforced the identifiability of blacks, making them unique in a negative way. Such stereotypes have then been used to legitimize discrimination in a society whose core values are based on liberty, freedom, and equality (Staples, 1975; Andrews, 1994).

In the early period of slavery, from 1650 to 1820, whites viewed Africans as "uncivilized heathens," "bestial," "sexually aggressive," and as suffering the "curse of God" who made them black (Jordan, 1968; Turner and Singleton, 1978). Although there is some debate as to whether all white southerners held such hard views (Roediger, 1991:24), these beliefs changed somewhat when abolitionists in the North challenged them. Slavery became a "positive good," protecting Africans from their "savage impulses" and responding to their "childlike dependency." Yet, even in the abolitionist North, stereotypes portrayed Africans as ignorant, lazy, and immoral (Fredrickson, 1971:51). During this period the "black Sambo" stereotype evolved (Boskin, 1986), which portrayed black people as childlike, helpless, shuffling, and fumbling (but with potentially aggressive tendencies).

After the Civil War, when the short-lived but significant gains of radical Reconstruction were undone, African Americans were portrayed as inferior because they had not been able to take advantage of the *equal opportunities* offered by Reconstruction. Even in enlightened circles, blacks were often portrayed as not having progressed as far as whites on the evolutionary scale; so, without segregation as well as supervision and control, African Americans would revert to their more primitive state. In the South, this state was perceived to be one of laziness, criminality, and lustfulness (especially for white women, a belief which conveniently overlooked some slaveholders' lust for black women); in the North, this state was one of childlike docility and kindness that needed to be channeled (by whites). Whether vicious or benign, treatment of African Americans was based on the belief that black people are biologically inferior and must be segregated (Fredrickson, 1971).

Between the world wars, from 1914 to 1941, evolutionary theory and results on intelligence tests were interpreted to confirm as "scientific fact" the inferiority of blacks, although social scientists began to attack this position and to argue that the differences between black people and white people (as well as all "races") were the result of environmental rather than biological differences. Yet, the prevailing belief continued to advocate segregation as necessary and desirable in order to prevent "black inferiority" from diminishing the white biological stock.

The post–World War II period saw a dramatic shift in beliefs about African Americans. A consensus slowly emerged in more progressive circles that segregation was harmful, that blacks were not innately inferior, that the appearance of inferiority reflected cultural deprivation stemming from undesirable environments, and that improvements in schooling, job opportunities, and neighborhoods were the key to making life better for African Americans. Such progressive beliefs began to shape broad public perceptions (though not universally), and perhaps more significantly, they began to affect federal governmental policies, at least to a degree. Yet, many still believed that integration was unnecessary and undesirable. During this period of domination by liberal beliefs, a domination which culminated in the 1960s, a more subtle form of negative stereotyping occurred: Even if their "inferiority" were totally environmental, African Americans were still seen as inferior.

Over the last two decades, beliefs have continued to change (Schuman, Steeh, and Bobo, 1985); yet there is little consensus. Some people think that liberal policies have gone too far: Affirmative action, or measures designed to rectify past patterns of discrimination, is often seen to discriminate against white people; busing destroys neighborhood schools; and integration forces people to live near those whom they would rather avoid. Others believe that liberal policies have encouraged African Americans to depend on government for welfare, jobs, and education, thereby preventing many blacks from improving their lives. Many others, fearing the emergence of an urban underclass of angry, unemployed youth, have called for more government spending on programs to provide opportunities for African Americans.

Some have urged the government and the private sector to provide real rather than illusory opportunities. Others feel that individuals and communities must develop their own resources to break the cycle of poverty and government dependency. This last outlook has gained some currency over the last few years and has been used to cut back federal aid programs for the poor in general and African Americans in particular. Some believe that "minorities are getting too much" at the expense of whites (Kluegel and Bobo, 1993). The passage of Proposition 209 (California Civil Rights Initiative) by the majority of California voters in the 1996 November election was fueled by the belief that "minorities had received more than their share" at the expense of white persons. And, in response to these sentiments, the welfare reform of 1996 will assure that the poor will get less, and for a shorter period of time.

The history of beliefs about African Americans is based on one tenet: Blacks are not equal to whites. At one time, African Americans were believed to be biologically inferior; now many believe they are culturally inferior. No matter how benign and progressive the beliefs, they are based on the premise that black people are different.

In many respects, white Americans' attitudes toward African Americans have changed (Jaynes and Williams, 1989:116–128; Marger, 1991:26): Ninety percent now think that black and white children should go to the same schools (up from 63 percent in 1963); 75 percent would not object to inviting an African American to dinner (up from 50 percent in 1963); 75 percent do not think it is right to keep blacks out of white neighborhoods (up from 45 percent in 1963); 72 percent do not believe that there should be laws against intermarriage between blacks and whites (up from only 37 percent in 1963). Yet, the intensity of feeling among some whites regarding school busing, black welfare mothers, and affirmative action signals strong negative sentiments toward African Americans (Kluegel and Bobo, 1993). African Americans are well aware of these feelings and must live with the uncertainty of not knowing when or where negative responses to them might erupt. Although black culture has penetrated mainstream white culture to a significant degree, subtle and complex negative beliefs persist, making blacks vulnerable to informal discrimination (Gomes and Williams, 1990). These beliefs discourage efforts to deal with the legacy of past discrimination, as it has been legitimated by a long history of negative stereotyping.

Institutionalized Discrimination against African Americans

Legal Discrimination

Dominant beliefs usually become codified into laws; in turn, these laws sanction certain types of behavior. So it was with beliefs about blacks in America, against whom it was once legal to discriminate. Moreover, undermining and, often, defying the law are informal discriminatory practices that are not codified but that are deemed appropriate in a climate in which the law makes discrimination acceptable.

Legal Discrimination under Slavery and in Its Aftermath. It is difficult to determine whether the first Africans in America were slaves or indentured servants; the historical record is not clear on this point (Jordan, 1962). By the 1650s, however, there is evidence that some colonies had laws distinguishing between white and black servants, with black servants and their children consigned to servitude for life. By the early eighteenth century, the broad legal framework of slavery in the South had become clearly codified (Stampp, 1956; Starobin, 1970:7):

1. Blacks were to be slaves for life.
2. Slaves were *both* property and persons; owners held title to blacks as property and had some responsibilities to blacks as persons.
3. Children would inherit their mother's status as a slave.
4. Christian baptism did not automatically lead to freedom.
5. Marriages between blacks and whites were prohibited.
6. Blacks could not acquire or inherit property.
7. Blacks could not engage in litigation or enter into civil contracts; they could not testify against whites in court, nor could they sit on juries.

Such codes reaffirmed beliefs about the "bestiality" of slaves and legitimized slavery by making it acceptable for white Americans to buy slave labor. In the North, the laws were considerably more benign, but few questioned the biological inferiority of blacks or the existence of economic, educational, and political discrimination (Litwack, 1961:30–38; Fredrickson, 1971:1–43, 1981, 1988). With the admission of border and southern states to the Union in the early 1800s, a considerable amount of debate in Congress ensued over the legal rights of African-origin people. The coexistence of free blacks in the North and slaves in southern and border states made it difficult to define the constitutional rights of slaves in the growing Union. The issue was effectively avoided in 1821 when Missouri was admitted to the Union, for Congress enacted a loosely worded law that allowed the states to legislate as they pleased, with the proviso that no citizens "shall be excluded from the enjoyment of any of the privileges and immunities to which such citizen is entitled under the Constitution of the United States." Thereafter, until the Civil War, northern laws were increasingly relaxed, while southern legislatures passed ever more restrictive laws.

Abolitionist pleas for at least "humane treatment" of the "inferior race" were beginning to have a small impact on public opinion, and those states with few black residents began to accord them broader citizenship rights. However, these formal laws contradicted informal *Jim Crow practices* of the North, which, despite the lofty tenets of formal laws, excluded most African Americans from access to jobs, education, and housing (Woodward, 1966).

It appears likely that the abolitionist ideology was used retroactively to justify a massive northern invasion of the South for economic and political

Box 4.1

The Execution of Black Slaves

The following table provides some descriptive statistics for black slave executions in the United States between 1641 and 1865. Most black slave executions occurred in deep South states. While black slaves were more likely to be executed for theft in deep South states, black slaves were just as likely to be executed for murder and rape regardless of geographical region. In general, black slaves were most often executed for murder followed by participation in a slave revolt, rape, theft, arson, and poisoning. The most common form of execution was hanging, and most executed black slaves were males.

Selected Characteristics of Black Slave Executions in the United States, 1641–1865

	*Deep South States**		*Border States†*		*Northern States‡*		*Total*	
	N	%	N	%	N	%	N	%
Criminal offense								
Murder	566	78	105	15	52	7	723	100
Rape	110	77	22	15	11	8	143	100
Theft	115	92	7	6	3	2	125	100
Slave revolt	207	84	8	3	31	13	246	100
Arson	45	67	7	10	15	23	67	100
Poisoning	51	88	2	3	5	9	58	100
Method of execution								
Hanging	1,351	85	158	10	87	5	1,596	100
Breaking on the wheel	31	47	3	5	32	48	66	100
Gibbeted	20	95	0	0	1	5	21	
Gender								
Male	1,179	83	136	10	106	7	1,421	100
Female	119	79	19	13	13	8	1,551	100

*Alabama, Arkansas, Florida, Georgia, Louisiana, Mississippi, North Carolina, South Carolina, Texas, and Virginia.
†Kentucky, Maryland, Tennessee, and West Virginia.
‡Illinois, Massachusetts, Missouri, New Jersey, New York, and Pennsylvania.

Source: Aguirre and Baker, 1996.

reasons. Nevertheless, the war abolished forever the institution of slavery, and, hence the economic base of the South. In 1866, this was formerly ratified in the Thirteenth Amendment.

In reaction, southern states began to enact *black codes* restricting the rights of freed slaves. These codes were enforced through violence, which, for the remainder of the century, was to become the key to maintaining black subordination to whites. The details of these codes varied, but several restrictions were common to all of them. Blacks could not (1) vote, (2) serve on juries, (3) testify against whites, (4) carry arms, and (5) enter certain occupations (depending upon the state). The codes also stated that black vagrants could be consigned to forced labor. Thus, after the Civil War, the free South was unified in its attempts to impose new legal restrictions upon African Americans.

In reaction to these codes, the violence used to enforce them, and perceptions that President Andrew Johnson was being too conciliatory toward the South, radical Republicans in Congress began to assume control of Reconstruction. The radicals in Congress mounted a two-front legal attack on discrimination in the South by advocating (1) the division of the South into military districts and the enforcement of new constitutional conventions on each southern state and (2) the passage of the Fourteenth and Fifteenth Amendments, which were ratified by northern and reconstituted southern states in 1868 and 1870, respectively. The Fourteenth Amendment was an extension of an earlier civil rights act (vetoed by Johnson, and then overridden by Congress) that was designed to overrule the emerging *black codes.* The Fifteenth Amendment extended suffrage to African Americans. Reforms in the South were soon followed by the Civil Rights Act of 1875, which outlawed northern Jim Crow practices. In this way, Congress forced the South and, to a lesser extent, the North to accept black participation in mainstream American life.

Had radical Reconstruction continued over several generations, institutional discrimination in America would have been markedly reduced. However, by 1880, the radical Republicans had lost control of Congress and the presidency. Almost immediately, new exclusionary laws were passed at local and state levels. These laws were, in essence, a codification of informal practices of segregation and exclusion, reinforced by the ever-present threat of white violence (Williamson, 1984:229). In turn, the Supreme Court began to legitimize the reemergence of Jim Crow practices in the 1890s. First, the Court declared unconstitutional the Civil Rights Act of 1875, thus denying African Americans access to public conveyances and amusement facilities used by white Americans. Then, in 1896, the Court ruled in *Plessy v. Ferguson* that segregated facilities for blacks and whites were not in violation of the Thirteenth and Fourteenth Amendments to the Constitution, since, as the Court declared: “If one race be inferior to the other socially, the Constitution cannot put them on the same plane” (Pinkney, 1969:28).

Codifying exclusionary and segregationist practices in the highest laws of the land firmly established the culture and structure of discrimination in America, in both institutional and informal practice (Cella, 1982; Horiwitz and Karst, 1969). It was with this national legal legacy that blacks entered the twentieth century (Steele, 1990). During this period, African Americans became increasingly urban. In the North, however, a myriad of discrimina-

Box 4.2

A Century after Plessy v. Ferguson

On June 7, 1892, Homer Plessy became part of an incident that would shape the entire twentieth century in America. Plessy was self-described as one-eighth "colored," and on this day he refused to move out of the "whites only" railroad car on the East Louisiana Railroad traveling between New Orleans and Covington. Plessy was seen to violate a two-year-old state law in Louisiana that required "separate but equal" facilities for blacks and whites. Plessy's refusal was staged to test the state law, but the Louisiana decision went against him.

The issue was important because throughout the South, except for South and North Carolina as well as Virginia, segregation laws had been rapidly emerging for intrastate travel on the railroads which, at this time, was the major means of long-distance travel. In the 1890s, it was not inevitable that black–white segregation would occur; it was, instead, entirely possible that these emerging state laws could be struck down and the process of integration—however slow and difficult—could have proceeded. The case went to the Supreme Court, and the history of black–white relations in America was forever changed in 1890. Justice Henry Billings Brown—a man who had grown up in the North—wrote for the majority opinion and argued that facilities need not be identical to be equal, and if blacks see their segregation as inferior, "it is not by reason of anything found in the act, but solely because the colored race chooses to put that construction on it." Thus, if blacks saw their segregation as a signal of inferiority, it was in their minds, not in the legal mandate. Writing a strong dissent was Justice John Marshall Harlan, a Kentuckian who had even been a Confederate officer, who predicted just what happened: the *Plessy v. Ferguson* decision would become the legal mantle for creating segregated facilities in all spheres, not just public transport.

It was not until the early 1950s that the *Plessy v. Ferguson* decision was overturned, but by then much of the damage had been done. White America had begun to move: up the occupational ladder, into the suburbs, into better schools, into colleges and universities, and into post–World War II prosperity. Blacks had been shut out during these critical decades between the *Plessy* decision and the *Brown v. the School Board* decision in 1954 which declared segregated schools to be inherently unequal.

Source: Adapted from a syndicated column by Edwin M. Yoder, Jr., and from C. Vann Woodward's *The Strange Case of Jim Crow,* 1996.

tory laws prevented black integration into white institutions and black participation in the world of white American affluence. Many did not consider such laws illegal or immoral; they were legitimized by the highest court in the land and reflected the post–Civil War belief that blacks had been given a chance and had demonstrated their inferiority. These court decisions were subsequently reversed, but informal discrimination in housing, jobs, education, and other spheres persists to this day. Such formal legal barriers and the informal climate of discrimination they created make up the struggle for equality by African Americans in the twentieth century.

Legal Discrimination in the Twentieth Century. Through the first half of the twentieth century, state and local codes discriminated against blacks in many vital areas of life. In education, African Americans in the South attended segregated and inferior schools, a circumstance supported by state and local codes and enforced with threats of and actual violence from the white community. In housing, Federal Housing Authority (FHA) codes prevented integration of housing subsidized by the FHA, which confirmed and reaffirmed restrictive covenants in trust deeds (that certain ethnic groups could not own property in an area) and discriminatory lending practices of bankers. In the job market, most craft unions and many industrial unions established rules that either restricted or forbade black membership or created separate black auxiliary (and less powerful and effective) unions; in both cases, these practices prevented African Americans from moving beyond a narrow range of lower-paying jobs. In politics, especially in the South, state and local governments enacted voting laws that were differentially enforced for blacks and whites, a practice that kept African Americans disenfranchised. For example, in the 1890s, Alabama, Georgia, Louisiana, Mississippi, North Carolina, South Carolina, and Virginia all enforced literacy tests for blacks but not for whites (Bell, 1973). Since two-thirds of the black population in these states was illiterate at that time, the vast majority of African Americans were disenfranchised. In contrast, illiterate whites could have the literacy requirement waived if they owned property or if they revealed a "good character" or could understand English. Across all sectors of society, then, African Americans confronted laws and rules that excluded them.

From this blatant legal discrimination—which reinforced and encouraged informal discrimination in housing, schools, jobs, and politics—the civil rights movement was born. For two decades, in the 1950s and 1960s, blacks and sympathetic whites organized to eliminate the legal basis of discrimination. They employed a broad array of tactics—lawsuits culminating in Supreme Court decisions, mass protests, boycotts, sit-ins, and lobbying in Congress. The first big legal victory was the 1954 Supreme Court decision in *Brown v. Board of Education of Topeka, Kansas,* which declared segregated schooling inherently inferior and, hence, discriminatory (Kluger, 1975). By the 1960s, public opinion outside the South had become sympathetic to the black struggle. The result was the enactment of a series of significant laws—the Voting Rights Act of 1965 and the civil rights acts of 1964 and 1968. Congress passed these laws to eliminate legal and informal discrimination in employment, unions, housing, voting booths, and schools.

These laws were not enacted until one hundred years after the Civil War. Although they have helped African Americans enormously in the latter half of this century, these relatively recent laws cannot reverse the damage done by a long history of legal discrimination. Indeed, it was during the one hundred years since the Civil War that the United States was transformed into an affluent, industrial society; yet many African Americans were not allowed to be beneficiaries of this national success.

Undoing the legacy of legal discrimination is a formidable challenge to American society in the waning years of this century. Unfortunately, the 1980s and early 1990s have not evidenced a strong commitment to meeting the challenge. In fact, there have even been efforts to weaken some laws; for example, the Reagan and Bush administrations sought to soften the Voting Rights Act by limiting funding for its enforcement by the Justice Department, and by supporting a civil rights law that virtually eliminated the Voting Rights Act. Moreover, attempts to reinterpret other laws in the courts, especially with respect to the affirmative action policies stemming from the Civil Rights Act, and to enforce laws selectively, particularly with respect to job and housing discrimination, have been made by Congress and the presidents of the 1980s and 1990s. Most important is the virtual absence of political will to create laws to help African Americans overcome the cumulative effects of legal exclusion from the American mainstream. This lack of political will exists because the majority of Americans believe that today the inequities African Americans experience are the result of their lack of motivation and individual effort (Kluegel and Smith, 1986; Kluegel and Bobo, 1993). When a voting majority does not see the present problem, it is difficult to redress past discrimination. It is not surprising, then, that many African Americans continue to meet obstacles in their efforts to participate fully in the institutional structure—economy, education, politics, and housing—of the society.

Nowhere is the lack of knowledge about the cumulative effects of discrimination more evident than in the area of "affirmative action." The civil rights laws of the 1960s, as interpreted by Executive Order 11246, required organizations doing business with, or receiving funds from, the government to increase minority representation in those organizations (Jaynes and Williams, 1989:316). In practice, these government mandates applied primarily to businesses receiving (directly or indirectly) government contracts, and to education, especially higher education. As affirmative action policies were more rigorously enforced in the 1970s and early 1980s, they became increasingly unpopular. Charges (both legal and informal) of "reverse discrimination" could be heard from some white employees and students. Moreover, one effect of affirmative action was the creation of informal quotas favoring members of minority groups and, to a lesser extent, women in male-dominated occupations and in the sphere of education; this public perception that quotas do indeed exist is then used to validate the charge that some whites are the victims of discrimination. This charge has led many people to believe that affirmative action no longer is about equality of opportunities but of results, or group preferences. Yet, without affirmative action, or a similar policy, how are the effects of past discrimination to be overcome? Without some degree of preference afforded African Americans affected by past discrimination, many will have difficulty achieving equality with white Americans in school and in the workplace.

In recent decades, the courts have issued somewhat contradictory decisions (Marger, 1991:528; Jaynes and Williams, 1989), perhaps reflecting the public's ambivalence over affirmative action. In some cases, such as *Weber v. Kaiser Aluminum* in 1979, the Supreme Court ruled that employers could use "race" as a criterion for hiring and could employ quotas. A year earlier, however, in *Bakke v. The Regents of the University of California,* the Supreme Court ruled in favor of Bakke, a white male who had been denied entrance into medical school because of quotas for minority students. During the Reagan and Bush administrations, the Supreme Court, which had been generally supportive of affirmative action, began to shift as new appointees to the Court began to influence decisions. Recent decisions not only have weakened the impact of affirmative action but have also made it more difficult for members of minority groups to prove in court that they have been victims of discrimination. As the Court's composition shifts again in the 1990s, it is difficult to predict the fate of affirmative action programs, but it is unlikely that any new laws will be enacted to bolster affirmative action programs in light of the general public's hostility to such programs (Takaki, 1987:223–232; Kluegel and Bobo, 1993). Indeed in 1996, the first major decision since *Bakke v. The Regents of the University of California* went against the University of Texas (*Hopwood v. Texas*) which had sought to use "race" as a criterion for special admission policies; and in a highly controversial decision in 1996, the Board of Regents of the University of California eliminated race and ethnicity as criteria for special admission to the university, a decision that will be challenged in the courts but that, like the *Hopwood* ruling, will work against affirmative action as it was practiced in the 1970s and 1980s.

Economic Discrimination

Slavery and Its Aftermath. Prior to the Civil War, the economic organization of the South became heavily dependent upon a large slave population. While the historical record does not mark precisely when slavery was first institutionalized, it is clear that by 1670 most black people in America, adults and children, had been forced into lifelong servitude. Slavery became rapidly institutionalized because of the agricultural economy emerging in the South. In contrast to the North, which was beginning to industrialize and urbanize by the time of the American Revolution, the South remained heavily agricultural, relying on the export of cotton, tobacco, hemp, rice, wheat, and sugar. While different states tended to specialize in only some of these crops, they all had one feature in common: the reliance upon an inexpensive and relatively large labor pool to cultivate large tracts of land. It is not clear whether slavery was the most efficient form of agricultural organization (see Fogel and Engerman, 1974; Genovese, 1965; and Williamson, 1984:12–14), but the shortage of labor and the abundance of land in the southern colonies placed a high value on involuntary labor. As a result, slaves were used to initiate the plantation system, and once initiated, the system was operated to "keep in line" a large and potentially volatile population. The initial importation and enslavement of blacks in the seventeenth century was facilitated by the early settlers' cultural beliefs about the "bestial" nature and less-than-human status of Africans (Jordan, 1968). Such negative beliefs facilitated the accelerated pace of enslavement, a process that violated the core values of American society.

The distribution of slaves in the South reflected the economic priorities and power relations within that part of the country (Stampp, 1956; Starobin, 1970:5). By 1860 there were about four million slaves in the South. Over 50 percent were owned by only 12 percent, who held the large tracts of fertile land that formed the basis of the southern economy. Slavery emerged and persisted largely because a small group of politically powerful landowners required cheap labor and made slavery acceptable in the agricultural sector of the economy, and then, to a very limited extent, in mining, iron production, textile manufacturing, and small industry (Lewis, 1979, 1989; Lander, 1969). Thus, by the dawn of the Civil War, most agriculture in the southern economy and a few industrial and craft sectors (Newton and Lewis, 1978) relied upon slave labor. The institutionalization of slavery in the southern economy, plus the fear of retaliatory violence by slaves, partially accounts for the resistance of this "peculiar institution" to change (Stampp, 1956).

The South countered abolitionist attacks on slavery by further codifying beliefs based on the "Sambo" stereotype (Turner and Singleton, 1978; Boskin, 1986). Although most abolitionists did not hold the Sambo stereotype, even the most radical abolitionist believed in the intellectual inferiority of blacks (Fredrickson, 1971). Differences in the northern and southern belief systems no doubt reflected the respective economic dependency of the northern and southern economies on slave labor. Because few blacks lived in the North, its economy remained unaffected by abolition or the colonization of the black population. In the South, however, the loss of slave labor threatened widespread disruption of the southern economy and lifestyle.

Only a war between the states could break the culturally legitimized institution of slavery in the South. During the brief period of radical Reconstruction, large numbers of blacks gained access to many skilled trades and began to assume ownership of farms. But as noted earlier, Congress in 1877 changed its legislative mind toward ethnic relations. For thirty years thereafter African Americans were systematically excluded from skilled nonfarm occupations and thrust into tenant farming or low-wage labor for white landowners or into menial labor and domestic work in both rural and urban areas. Such a dramatic reversal of the economic policies of radical Reconstruction was legitimized by the limited conception of "equality" of the then-dominant laissez-faire ideology (economic and individual activity should go unregulated) and by the Social Darwinism ("survival of the fittest") of the late nineteenth century.

By the turn of the century, 90 percent of all African Americans remained in the South, with 75 percent living under oppressive conditions in rural areas. For a number of reasons, the quality of life for African Americans, especially those in rural areas, worsened dramatically during the early years of this century (Hamilton, 1964): (1) The high birthrates of rural families began to exceed their ability to secure sufficient income in the depressed economy of the South; (2) the nature of agriculture changed dramatically with mechanization and the consequent displacement of black labor; (3) the cotton industry, on which many blacks depended for survival, began to move to the Southwest and, then, was devastated by the boll weevil; and (4) many whites used violence—beatings, burnings, and lynchings—to maintain black subordination (Williamson, 1984:180–223; Rable, 1984; Tolnay and Beck, 1992; and Aguirre and Baker, 1991). These and other "push factors" led blacks to migrate from the South into the urban

White violence against African Americans has historically been a means of control and domination. Here, into the 20th century, two blacks were hanged without trial or due process for supposed crimes against whites.

areas of the North. By 1914, these "push factors" were combined with "pull factors" from northern cities: The onset of World War I had cut off European migration while rapidly expanding the very industrial production that had for decades drawn European migrants to American cities. Suddenly, there were economic opportunities for African Americans in northern cities, with the result that between 1914 and 1920, nearly one million blacks migrated to urban areas in the industrial North. This migration was to be the first of a series of large-scale shifts in the black population; by 1960 over three-fourths of that population resided in cities, with only one-half remaining in the South. Patterns of economic discrimination became urban as opposed to rural, and national in contrast to regional.

Many of the early migrants to northern cities initially found jobs during the peak of wartime production, but they also encountered white discrimination and violence (Bonacich, 1976). African Americans tended to live in segregated tenements that early European migrants had abandoned because of their dilapidated and unsafe condition; when blacks ventured into white neighborhoods and into certain occupations, acts or threats of violence frequently occurred. For example, twenty-five "race riots" broke out between June and October of 1919 (Turner, Singleton, and Musick, 1984). This violence was intensified as black laborers were used as strikebreakers in corporate America's effort to stifle the union movement. Whites attacked blacks, then black workers retaliated, bringing a counterattack by whites. The resulting violence forced police to quell such riots. The hostility toward blacks, based on the threat of job displacement, persists today in many urban areas of the Northeast and Midwest.

With the end of wartime production and the onset of the great depression of the 1930s, the economic situation of African Americans worsened once again. Unemployment and hunger increased, and even welfare allocations were differentially distributed among blacks and whites (Pinkney, 1969:33–34). The New Deal ushered in some changes, but the capacity of nascent civil rights groups to generate change was limited. Wage and job discrimination and exclusion from unions continued until well after World War II.

World War II, like World War I, caused a massive black migration to urban areas in both the North and South. As African Americans became concentrated in key wartime industries in urban areas, they began to exert political pressure, forcing President Roosevelt to ban discrimination in wartime industries and pressuring the Congress of Industrial Organizations (CIO) to allow some black workers into the unions' ranks (although most unions, especially craft unions, used informal means to keep black workers out, or in low-paying positions).

Patterns of Present-Day Discrimination. The effects of slavery and established patterns of discrimination remain today, as Tables 4.1 to 4.4 document. Black workers are overrepresented in farm and menial service jobs; they are underrepresented in professional and managerial occupations; they are twice as likely to be unemployed; they earn slightly over one-half the wages of white workers; and they are three times as likely to be poor. This legacy of slavery costs all Americans a great deal in terms of (1) lost productivity among the large pool of potential black workers; (2) lost consumption of gainfully employed African Americans, which could, in turn, encourage production for all workers; (3) lost tax revenues from African Americans who lack a steady job; and (4) lost federal, state, and local revenues allocated to social welfare programs in order to maintain black households.

The legacy of economic discrimination has been compounded by other conditions over the last two decades:

1. The decrease in skilled and semiskilled blue-collar jobs in the economy at a time when most employment barriers have been eliminated
2. The movement of employment opportunities to the suburbs, making employment difficult for inner-city blacks to secure because of past housing discrimination (see the section on this topic, discussed later in this chapter)
3. The decline in industrial union power and membership at a time when they have become fully open to blacks
4. The increase in low-paying service jobs relative to the higher-paying and skilled blue-collar jobs that historically allowed many white immigrant ethnic groups to assimilate and become upwardly mobile
5. The influx of new immigrants who compete with black workers and small-business owners for jobs
6. The national fiscal crisis, which has reduced the amount of money available for social programs in general, and poverty programs in particular
7. The resurgence of conservative beliefs that government cannot and should not try to solve the economic problems of African Americans (Indeed, government is now seen as part of the problem in that it supports welfare dependency.)

Thus, the economic plight of today's African Americans is difficult to address, even though many of the legal barriers to discrimination have been removed. Yet, even though legal and institutional discrimination has receded, more subtle patterns of informal discrimination persist.

Many African Americans today continue to pay a penalty for their skin color when seeking jobs—assuming that they live in an area where they have access to jobs. For example, in 1991, the Urban Institute in Washington, D.C., sent teams of black and white men as job seekers to over four hundred interviews for jobs advertised in the newspapers of Washington and Chicago. The workers were matched with identical qualifications. The results showed that 15 percent of the white applicants received job offers compared to 5 percent of the African Americans. During the job selection process, white men advanced to the next round of interviews 20 percent of the time, whereas black men did so only 7 percent of the time. White men reported rude or otherwise unfavorable treatment during the job-seeking process 27 percent of the time, while the corresponding figure for black men was 50 percent. Thus, despite Americans' beliefs that affirmative action guarantees African Americans favorable treatment, this study indicates that African Americans still experience discrimination.

Once employed, African Americans often are not promoted because of informal discriminatory practices, especially in white-collar corporate jobs. In another pioneering study on women and minorities in nine of the Fortune 500 corporations, the U.S. Department of Labor (1991) found a "glass ceiling" blocking these groups from access to "corporate pipelines" leading to managerial and executive positions. African Americans, in particular, experience this subtle, almost invisible barrier in a variety of ways. First, blacks and other minority groups are more likely than whites to be placed in human resources and public relations positions, which, unlike sales and production jobs, are off the "fast track" to management. Second, blacks are more likely than whites to be excluded from networks, mentor programs, and policy-making committees; as a result, they do not acquire the contacts, information, and experience necessary for movement up the corporate ladder. Third, hiring at the executive level is typically conducted outside the human resources and personnel departments, without concern about affirmative action and without systematic efforts by corporate executives or their "head hunter" search firms to create a diverse pool of applicants. Instead, informal networks and discussions usually influence hiring at the higher levels of a corporation, the kind of contact from which African Americans are routinely excluded.

African Americans often encounter another pattern of informal, and perhaps at times inadvertent, discrimination when attempting to set up a business. For many white Americans, owning and running a business has been one path to affluence. For African Americans, however, this path is strewn with obstacles. African American–owned businesses tend to be economically marginal, labor-intensive proprietorships that must withstand heavy competition from entrepreneurial immigrants vying for the same clientele. Also, it is more difficult for black Americans to secure credit than it is for white Americans since lending agencies use criteria that favor those with "white credentials" (such as higher education, current collateral, and high credit ratings) and those who intend to service white shopping center clientele. However, while all small businesses are high-risk ventures, there is no evidence that black businesses in ghetto neighborhoods are any more risky than white ventures in white neighborhoods. For example, in the 1960s the Small Business Administration began extending loans in terms of criteria other than credit history and collateral. In 1964, for example, 98 of 219 special loans went to African Americans; and only 8 of the 219 loans became delinquent and none were liquidated (Turner and Singleton, 1978). For a while the Minority Business Development Agency helped expand minority-owned businesses, but in the 1980s its resources and programs were cut back. Such cutbacks are a form of discrimination, especially when it is recognized that African Americans do not receive Small Business Adminis-

Box 4.3

African Americans Still Face Job Discrimination

A recent study by the Urban Institute in Washington shows that African American job applicants with the same qualifications as white applicants face discrimination in hiring at the rate of about three times as often as whites.

That's an alarming finding, but there's also another problem minority job seekers face: Most minorities live in the city while jobs are in the rapidly expanding suburbs. Even if job discrimination were ended, many minorities wouldn't be able to get jobs because of the lack of transportation to the suburbs.

"The continued movement of jobs away from the city, where many African Americans live, to suburban areas divests our community of desperately needed jobs and business opportunities," James W. Compton, president of the Chicago Urban League, writes in *NorthStar News & Analysis,* a national African American news magazine. But even the most forward looking companies with aggressive minority hiring programs are stymied by the lack of mass transportation to link inner city neighborhoods with outlying areas.

Gary Orfield, professor of political science and education at the University of Chicago, observes that "the fundamental mismatch between burgeoning suburban jobs and concentrated inner city poverty is a root problem for the poor blacks in the city."

"Nationwide, there is a strong concentration of good, entry-level jobs that pay decently, but they're located on the outer edges of the whitest part of suburbia." Minority women are doing "barely" better than minority men as they often are able to get clerical jobs downtown, Orfield said.

Major corporations nationwide have been moving to the suburbs since World War II. "I think racism is an important factor," Orfield said. "People be-

tration loans proportionate to their numbers in society. Almost thirty years later, the Federal Reserve Board of Boston issued a report showing that blacks were 60 percent more likely than whites to be rejected for bank loans (Smith, 1992). Thus, the public's perceptions of "preferences" for blacks are inaccurate.

Part of the informal process of discrimination is the criteria defining a good worker—criteria that are biased against African Americans in favor of white Americans. For instance, employers look at formal education credentials, which white Americans are more likely to have, for jobs that do not require them. Or, to take another example, only white speech styles and personal demeanor associated with middle-class subculture (which, in reality, are seldom related to actual job performance) are preferred in certain jobs (Jaynes and Williams, 1989:321). Invidious discrimination is thus built into the hiring practices of many of America's businesses—a discrimination that perpetuates the disadvantaged position of African Americans.

lieve blacks have inferior educations, that black neighborhoods are dangerous and that blacks are more likely to join unions. Also, where managers want to live is a leading determinant of where factories are located."

But there also are strong business reasons to relocate. "Business facilities in the city are suffering from functional blight and can't take advantage of modern methods of manufacturing or merchandising," said Bill Miller, professor of geography at Carthage College in Kenosha, Wisconsin. "Employers need a lot of space for new buildings and parking."

Miller notes that "even in the most depressed city neighborhoods, land values often are higher than those of far suburban cornfields. Often, to get new industry, the suburb will offer tax credits. The suburbs also have other amenities, from the quality of the school system to the number of golf courses."

Ideally, the geographer says, mass transit that is efficient and reasonably inexpensive should be built linking city and suburbs. "The mass transit systems, such as they are, are pitiful, built to accommodate a city that no longer exists," he says. "Every other developed nation in the world puts the U.S. to shame with respect to mass transit. But budgets are being cut instead of increased."

The effect on employment is "depressing," Miller says. "Every time workers who live in the city and are qualified for a job cannot get to and from the workplace everyone loses: the workers, who feel worthless because they don't have a job and who would pay taxes if employed, and taxpayers, who may have to pay for welfare."

Lack of transportation, the geographer says, is "just one part of the many problems of the inner city, but it adds to the emergence of a permanent underclass."

Source: Chicago Tribune, 1992.

Political Discrimination

Without political power, it is difficult to diminish discrimination in a society. Until recent decades, African Americans have been almost completely disenfranchised, with little or no political power. Even today, blacks' participation in the political arena is not proportionate to their numbers because of the long-established pattern of exclusion. Several historical facts explain the level of political participation in the black community today:

1. Prior to the Civil War, blacks held the right to vote or hold office in only five states (all northern with very small black populations).
2. In the nineteenth century, blacks voted and held office in significant numbers only during the brief period of radical Reconstruction following the Civil War.
3. In the 1870s, congressional commitment to Reconstruction waned. When the presidential election of 1876 became deadlocked in the Elec-

toral College and was thrown into Congress, Republicans abandoned the principles of Reconstruction in order to "buy" southern votes. The result was that blacks were systematically excluded from the polls, with virtually complete disenfranchisement in the South by 1895 (Kousser, 1974; Williamson, 1984:224–284).

4. Through a variety of tactics—from poll taxes through "literacy tests" to threats of violence—blacks living in the South remained politically excluded from the 1890s until well into the 1960s (Daniel, 1973). Urban blacks who lived in the North and South had somewhat more voting power, but a broad array of tactics kept many African Americans disenfranchised and diminished the power of those who participated in local and national elections.

Thus, the relative lack of black political power is largely a result of the long history of intended and deliberate political exclusion, especially in the South. The patterns of political discrimination have continued well into this century with strategies such as the poll tax, the "literacy test," and the "Constitution test," which were differentially enforced for African Americans and poor whites. When these measures were declared illegal, administrative obstruction—long lines, much paperwork, elaborate documentation of residence, and so forth—effectively prevented most African Americans from registering to vote. Underlying these obstructions was the frequently implemented threat of white violence visited on the homes of those blacks who sought to register to vote or who actually voted.

It was not until the mid-1960s that many of these exclusionary tactics were declared unconstitutional. With the Voting Rights Act of 1965, political participation among blacks increased. However, the removal of these roadblocks and a growing political consciousness among African Americans caused discriminatory political strategies to shift from denying the vote to diluting the impact of black voting power by gerrymandering congressional districts in order to "break up" the ghetto as a voting bloc and spread its votes among two or more districts where whites outnumbered the now-divided African American vote.

In the decades following the civil rights movement and the Voting Rights Act of 1965, African Americans have made significant political gains, especially at the state and local levels (Jaynes and Williams, 1989:208–209; Welch, 1990). Although black voter participation still lags behind that of whites, the elimination of most barriers to black electoral participation has led to significant changes. For example, approximately three hundred mayors are African American; most of the largest cities in the United States are governed by black mayors. Many city, county, and state legislators, municipal judges, constables, and sheriffs, and some standing and select committee chairs in Congress are black. Yet, even with this kind of political representation, African Americans still constitute considerably less than 2 percent of all elected offices and officials in the United States (Joint Center for Political Studies, 1990; National Roster of Black Elected Officials, 1989). Moreover, at the national level, where important

Crime, violence, drug use, and other pathologies often typify African American neighborhoods. Increasingly, African Americans seek to "take back" their communities by demanding that drug pushers and users be arrested and prosecuted.

policy decisions affecting blacks will be made, African Americans are not proportionately represented: only 5 percent of Congress members are black; there are no black senators; and there are very few African Americans in top-level positions in the executive branch of government (Pohlmann, 1990; White, 1985).

Even in areas where African Americans have made real gains—political influence and control of large cities—they have come at a time when political and economic power has shifted to the suburbs and, because of the fiscal problems of most large cities, to state and federal government. Black political control of the large cities really means that black officials must deal with the financial, educational, and social problems that were created by past discrimination and that caused many whites to move to the suburbs. "Control" over cities marked by poverty, gangs, deteriorating schools, high levels of crime, deficit budgets, slums, empty industrial buildings, and expensive social services is not likely to improve the political power base situation of African Americans. City politics does not greatly influence national politics, which is where most important political decisions affecting the welfare of African Americans are ultimately made.

African Americans are almost always elected in locations where they are the majority—with only a few exceptions. Significant numbers of white Americans tend not to vote for black candidates, and so African Americans usually have power only where there is an overwhelming black constituency. Thus, while significant gains in political power are evident, African Americans remain underrepresented in the political system, a system that often fails to address their problems and needs.

Educational Discrimination

Educational Discrimination before and Immediately after the Civil War. By the dawn of the Civil War, all southern states had enacted compulsory ignorance laws for slaves. These laws, which some slaveholders chose to violate, prohibited whites from teaching slaves to read, write, and calculate. Moreover, clandestine schools for slaves operated everywhere in the South; and many freed slaves received education in segregated public facilities (Turner, Singleton, and Musick, 1984). In some states, such as North Carolina, literacy among blacks reached as high as 43 percent, but in the deep South literacy was probably no more than 10 percent.

In the North, educational opportunities were much better for African Americans in the decades before the Civil War. Religious groups, some municipalities, and a number of philanthropists created educational opportunities for blacks. Yet, these opportunities were not universally available. At the higher-education level, the first black university—Lincoln University in Pennsylvania—opened its doors to a few students. In 1833, Oberlin College became the first *mainstream* college to admit African Americans in significant numbers.

After the Civil War, the establishment of free public schools in both the North and South was initiated (Cash, 1941:3–102). Yet, much of the education of African Americans occurred in private schools sponsored by religious societies and philanthropists. By the 1870s, state legislatures had mandated free public education for all citizens, and by 1880, one-third of all black children were registered in school (Weinberg, 1977:45–54). But during the 1880s, the tide turned against black education. Public funding at the local level slowed considerably, although African Americans were required to pay taxes for all schools, both white and black. In some southern states, government spending on African American schools became voluntary. Between 1870 and 1905, the sixteen southern states in which 90 percent of all southern African Americans lived spent one-fourth as much on black schools as they spent on white schools. Most of these black schools were vocational, providing literacy and teaching the rudiments of a trade.

By the dawn of the twentieth century, literacy among African Americans had increased to as much as 40 percent (Turner, Singleton, and Musick, 1984), but still, a system of dual education was firmly in place. This system of separate and decidedly unequal schools became more pronounced as blacks began to move to urban centers in the North and South.

Educational Discrimination in the Twentieth Century. In the urban areas of the North and South, school attendance and literacy increased, but in a segregated school system. In this system, the South spent two to three times as much on white students as on black students, assuring that the latter would receive an inferior education (Bullock, 1967). Moreover, despite gains in literacy within this unequal system, illiteracy among African Americans was six times that among whites, and as late as 1969, it was still four times that of whites. It was not until 1975 that black enrollment in schools reached parity with white enrollment (Turner, Singleton, and Musick, 1984:123). But the quality of education for African Americans was consistently inferior for the simple reason that schools were segregated. Between 1920 and 1940, the pattern of segregated schools spread throughout the United States. In the South, state legislators, local political figures, school boards, and courts all worked to create a separate educational system; in the North, housing discrimination and threats of white violence produced residential segregation, which led to separate school systems.

As this dual system was established, blacks and their white supporters began to raise questions (Kluger, 1975). In the late 1940s and early 1950s, the National Association for the Advancement of Colored People (NAACP) and The Urban League began to push not only for African American voting rights but also for equality in education. This effort culminated in the NAACP's successful appeal in 1954 before the Supreme Court stating that separate schools are unequal and, therefore, are in contradiction to the Fourteenth Amendment to the Constitution *(Brown v. Board of Education of Topeka).* In rendering this landmark decision, however, the Supreme Court did not set a timetable for its implementation. Hence, local school boards dragged their feet, citing complexities and the need for additional time. Indeed, local officials routinely ignored court orders for desegregation. During the 1960s, however, black and white activism increased and led to the passage of the Civil Rights Act of 1964, which strengthened the federal government's hand in forcing the states to comply with desegregation orders; and hence, under the threat of withholding federal funds and military coercion, the states increased school integration, especially in the South.

A series of court decisions in the 1970s reinforced the push for school integration. In 1971 *(Swann v. Charlotte-MecKlenburg Board of Education),* the Supreme Court ruled that busing was an appropriate tool for achieving integration; in 1973 *(Keyes v. Denver School District No. 1),* the Court ruled that evidence of government actions to maintain segregation, such as site selection for schools or manipulation of attendance zones, was sufficient to require desegregation using busing and other means. Yet, in another series of decisions in the 1970s, the Court rejected the regionalization strategy, which would require suburban districts to be part of the desegregation effort in large cities. This latter set of decisions, coupled with white protests and violence over busing, have made the desegregation of the inner city a difficult process. And so, in the 1990s, half of all black students attended schools in which minority groups were overrepresented (Feagin, 1989:244).

In the period between 1920 and 1960, most black students in the South attended black colleges. In the 1950s, however, forced desegregation of state universities in the South began; today, there is little evidence of discrimination in admissions to public universities in either the South or North. At private colleges and universities, the picture is more complicated. A combination of sincere efforts to comply with affirmative action and fear of losing federal funds has led most private colleges and universities, especially those heavily involved in government-funded research, to recruit and assist members of minority groups, especially African Americans. For some institutions less dependent on federal monies, both explicit and covert discrimination in admittance procedures continues. Yet, current efforts by colleges and universities to recruit and assist African Americans have not succeeded in stemming the decrease in African American enrollment, particularly among males (Jaynes and Williams, 1989:340–341).

African Americans have endured a long history of exclusion from the education system; even today they are overrepresented in poor, minority-filled schools. While the data are inconclusive, some findings show that blacks who attend integrated schools are more likely to graduate, attend college, and live in integrated neighborhoods (Feagin, 1989:242). Thus, to the degree that African Americans continue to cluster in the inner city, they are more likely to attend segregated schools and less likely to attend college. In addition, housing segregation remains an important cause of discrimination in education.

Housing Discrimination

One's place of residence determines access to other valued resources—jobs, schools, public facilities, health care, and social services. When African Americans experience discrimination in housing, they become isolated from the mainstream and are, in effect, excluded from other social arenas, even if there is no intent to discriminate in these arenas. For example, housing discrimination has confined many African Americans to inner cities at a time when jobs have moved to the suburbs and transportation systems to the suburbs have decayed. In fact, housing discrimination works against African Americans not only in their efforts to find work but also in their capacity to gain access to decent schools, public facilities, and services.

The first black migrants to northern cities were forced—not only by their meager resources but also by threats of white violence and discriminatory landlord policies—into the decaying cores of the cities. While the wartime industries of World War I provided many jobs, and while the geographical concentration of cities allowed easy access from the ghetto to work, a *pattern* of African American residential isolation in urban areas had been initiated. This pattern was often formalized in communities by restrictive covenants that forbade integrated neighborhoods. During the great depression of the 1930s, when economic opportunities vanished in the North and elsewhere, black migration to the cities waned. During this period the federal government enacted highly discriminatory legislation that forged the current profile of urban America.

The most significant piece of legislation was the federal act creating the Federal Housing Authority and the FHA mortgage loan guarantee program, which subsidized home mortgages for whites. In the post–World War II period, the FHA and the related Veterans Administration (VA) mortgage guarantee programs stimulated the rapid flight of white Americans from the cities to the suburbs. African Americans were prevented from joining this flight because of discriminatory administrative rules of law that stated that neighborhoods of "mixed races" could not be subsidized by the government. From 1950 to 1962, the year when President Kennedy finally issued an executive order to the contrary, the practice of providing FHA and VA loan guarantees primarily to white neighborhoods continued. Even after 1962, FHA policy was "ineffectively integrationist."

Industry and commerce began to follow the white population to the suburbs; and eventually, as assembly-line production with its need for large tracts of land came to dominate sectors of the economy, industry began to pull residents out of the cities. As industry and workers moved out of the city, commerce and service industries followed. Some African Americans were able to commute to these jobs, but as mass transit services began to deteriorate in the post–World War II period, commuting became difficult. At the same time, as the tax base that financed city schools diminished, schools with heavy concentrations of black students languished for lack of financial resources. Furthermore, large suburban communities began to exert enormous political power in metropolitan and statewide government. Thus, urban–suburban segregation, largely created by FHA law, has profoundly limited African Americans' access to jobs, quality schools, and political power.

To cope with the consequences of this segregation, other federal laws have been enacted, but they have not eliminated slum conditions, and, more importantly, some have exacerbated patterns of segregation. One of the key legislative acts of the New Deal initiated public housing, which, by 1937, had acquired the social purpose of eliminating substandard housing. Unfortunately, changes in the law in the late 1930s turned administration of the public housing projects over to the cities, resulting in housing projects that were built in existing slum areas, which, in turn, perpetuated black confinement to the inner city. Urban renewal in the decades since the 1950s was another major attempt to revitalize slum areas and to restore the decaying downtown commercial areas in order to attract middle-class suburbanites back to the city. The result of the program was the destruction of slum housing, which forced the poor into public housing projects where few wished to live. Model cities programs, introduced in the 1950s through the 1960s, have not done much better because they do not attack the basic problem—urban–suburban segregation.

A crucial Supreme Court decision made even more difficult the breakdown of urban–suburban inequities. In 1973 the Court ruled that suburban communities do have zoning control over patterns of land use in their communities. This ruling allowed local suburban governments to alter the zoning of land tracts to keep public housing and federally subsidized homeownership programs for African Americans out of the suburbs.

Important civil rights legislation of the 1960s has been ineffective in counteracting discrimination because (1) it has often gone unenforced because the civil rights division of the Justice Department is understaffed, underfinanced, and, in the 1980s, unsympathetic and (2) it has placed the burden of litigation on the *individual* against whom discrimination has occurred—a personally and financially arduous process.

More importantly, this legislation does not address the fundamental need for a *mass* migration of African Americans to the suburbs (or, a mass white migration to the cities). Of course, any such policy would encounter resistance in local communities, which, under the 1973 Supreme Court ruling, can "zone out" government-sponsored housing for African Americans. One of the ironies of housing laws is that from the mid-1930s until the mid-1960s, whites were given mortgage subsidies by the FHA and VA to move into the suburbs en masse, whereas current laws prevent a similar mass exodus of blacks. Moreover, current Supreme Court rulings prevent the implementation of massive federal programs to integrate the suburbs. Thus, suburban integration must happen slowly, on an individual-by-individual basis. These laws reinforce the discriminatory belief that the absence of African Americans from the suburbs is a result of their failure to avail themselves of "equal" educational and economic opportunities that would allow them to buy a house there.

Throughout the period of suburbanization of whites and confinement of blacks to the cities informal practices of *redlining* have persisted whereby residents of integrated neighborhoods or residents of less affluent neighborhoods with large numbers of African Americans have difficulty securing home mortgages. These practices are now so well documented that special enforcement of antiredlining laws now occurs; but because of the subtlety of the practice, it is often difficult to catch and prosecute the offenders. And even if one could assume that all redlining could be stopped, much of the damage has already been done: African Americans have been denied home ownership because banks would not lend them the money, while equivalently positioned whites have received mortgages and have been able to enjoy the benefits of home ownership (Minerbrook, 1993; Huskisson, 1988; U.S. Commission on Civil Rights, 1996).

STRATIFICATION OF AFRICAN AMERICANS

Affluent and Poor African Americans: The Widening Gap

As a result of legal, economic, political, educational, and housing discrimination, a majority of black Americans has been pushed to the bottom rungs of the stratification system. They tend to have few resources, as we documented at the outset of this chapter, and even fewer prospects for the future. Some African Americans have "made it" out of poverty and the lower socioeconomic stratum. Indeed, the percentage of black families that earn more than the national median family income—around thirty-five thousand dollars per year—has increased dramatically over the last decade, to nearly 25 percent. Also, the number of black families earning over fifty thousand dollars per year has increased significantly—perhaps as much as 40 percent. At the same time, poverty rates for African Americans have remained very high—around 30 percent of all African Americans and around 50 percent of households headed by black women (U.S. Bureau of the Census, 1991c: 16–17). African Americans are divided by social class, and although many middle-class African Americans still encounter discrimination in public places, in jobs, in housing, and in education, they no longer live in poverty.

Many of those outside the middle class live in slums or, even worse, public housing projects in the inner city; they live in crime-ridden and dangerous neighborhoods; they send their children to inferior schools; they work—if they can find work—for low wages in jobs with little security, few benefits, and an uncertain future; they seek help from the welfare system, which erodes their self-respect and which, with new "reforms," will be even less helpful; and if they are women, they are often raising their children alone. Indeed, a majority of black children are now raised by single parents, most of whom are women living in poverty. Thus, the situation for poor blacks has been made worse by the disruption to the family structure.

The African American Underclass: Myth or Reality?

Many white Americans are concerned—indeed, even fearful—of perceived trends in the urban minority population, especially urban African Americans: more babies born out of wedlock; more unmarried women on welfare; more violent crime; more drug use and related crime; more school dropouts and illiteracy; and more unemployed males. Some believe that these social and economic ills are concentrated in "the American underclass" which is presumed to be mostly black (Auletta, 1982). Currently, debate rages in the media, public, and academia over just what this underclass is, who belongs to it, how big it is, and how fast it is growing (Zinn, 1989; Fainstein, 1993). Definitions vary, but a reasonable one is the convergence of "a number of social ills including poverty, joblessness, crime, welfare dependency, fatherless families, and low levels of education or work related skills" (Ricketts and Sawhill, 1988:316). Some sociologists are convinced that the black underclass represents a major problem in America (Wilson, 1987).

Documentation of this underclass among African Americans reveals, however, a somewhat different picture (Jencks, 1991:28–102): The proportion of black single mothers collecting welfare has declined since 1974; violent crime rates among blacks have declined; black dropout rates from schools have declined in the 1980s; the gap in secondary school graduation rates has closed; and the percentage of 17-year-olds with basic reading skills steadily rose in the 1980s. However, some problems have grown

Box 4.4

Reparations to African Americans

Should reparations to African Americans be supported by the U.S. government in order to compensate for the injustices they suffered—that is, removal from their native lands and their enslavement in the United States? The Civil Liberties Act of 1988 provided reparations to people of Japanese ancestry to compensate for their internment during World War II. Every Japanese person who was interned at a camp was awarded twenty thousand dollars and a formal apology from the U.S. government. Could similar legislation be enacted for African Americans?

According to Verdun (1993), there are five periods of political activism that promoted reparations to African Americans. The first period was "inspired by the tension between the Union and the Confederacy and the attendant desire to restructure the South in order to enhance the Union's military advantage" (p. 600). The U.S. Congress in 1861 enacted legislation that gave President Lincoln the power to seize property used by the Confederacy and to free slaves engaged in arms or labor against the United States. The confiscated land would be distributed to the freed slaves. President Lincoln believed that "emancipated slaves should have land as an economic base upon which to establish themselves" (p. 602).

The second period took place at the turn of the twentieth century and was "motivated by the response of African Americans to the poverty and racism that prevailed in the South" (p. 602). During this time period, African Americans were fleeing oppressive conditions in the South by migrating north, or to Africa, and by demanding land and political power. The efforts to get Congress to enact legislation that would provide economic relief to African Americans were initiated by "Walter R. Vaughan, a white businessman from Selma, Alabama, who also started the first ex-slave pension and bounty organization," and "Mrs. Callie D. House and Reverend Isaiah H. Dickerson, who . . . established the National Ex-Slave and Mutual Relief Bountys Pension Association in 1894 . . ." (pp. 602–603).

worse: joblessness for males has risen, and the number of babies born out of wedlock has increased to over 65 percent among African Americans, resulting in an increase in single mothers. These data, then, do not support the existence of an African American underclass. The minority of African Americans who do meet the criteria of membership in an underclass receive much publicity, and the much larger African American population is further stigmatized by their activities.

Threats and Hostility toward African Americans

White hostility toward African Americans, and the resulting discrimination, have been fueled by a sense of threat. During slavery, many working-

The third period occurred during World War II and focused on Mississippi Senator Theodore Bilbo's efforts to "propose a bill creating a Bureau of Colonization and providing for the migration and colonization of negroes to newly acquired territories" (p. 603).

The fourth period covered the civil rights movement of the 1960s and the early 1970s. A significant event during this period was the promotion of the Black Manifesto in 1969 that targeted white Christian churches and Jewish synagogues. The Black Manifesto demanded 500 million dollars from the churches and synagogues but made no demands of the federal government. According to the manifesto, the money would be divided as follows: 200 million dollars to purchase land for cooperative farms; 80 million dollars to establish black publishing companies and television networks; 170 million dollars to establish a black college in the South, a research center, and a skills training center; 30 million dollars to establish a welfare rights organization and a labor defense fund; 20 million dollars to establish a trade association that would facilitate trade between the United States and Africa.

The fifth period is identified as the post–Civil Liberties Act era beginning in 1989. U.S. Representative John Conyers introduced a bill (Congress Bill H.R. 1684) in 1989 that would "create a commission to study the institution of slavery, subsequent de jure and de facto racial and economic discrimination against African Americans, and the impact of these forces on living African Americans" (p. 606). In 1991, Massachusetts State Senator William Owens introduced a bill (Owens Bill S. B. 298) that provided for "payment of reparations for slavery, the slave trade, and invidious discrimination against the people of African descent born or residing in the Commonwealth of Massachusetts" (p. 606).

Thus, there have been efforts over the past one hundred and thirty years to award reparations to African Americans. However, none of these efforts has had any results. Why? According to Verdun, "Opponents of reparations to African Americans are so overwhelmingly entrenched in the rightness of their position that they conceptualize the cry for reparations as frivolous, meritless, and divisive" (p. 607).

class whites, encouraged by slaveholders, feared the release of large numbers of blacks into the labor market and society in general (thereby destroying the "southern way of life"). When northern industries used African Americans as strikebreakers in the first decades of this century, white workers feared the loss of their jobs. Today, many white Americans fear "black violence" (fostered by the riots of the 1960s and 1990s, the gang activities of the 1980s and 1990s, high crime rates, and the perception of a growing "underclass"). Moreover, specific fears about the "costs" of welfare as well as the "taking" of jobs through affirmative action have added to white fears.

These fears have translated into negative stereotypes of African Americans as prone to crime and violence, as morally and sexually promiscuous,

Box 4.5

Why Do Black Immigrants Do Better Than U.S.–Born Blacks?

The *London Economist* posed the above question, as unpopular as it might be. But the facts speak for themselves: Blacks who immigrate to America do better economically than those who were born and raised in the United States. Some of the explanation for the difference comes from the fact that recent African-origin immigrants are among the most highly educated members of American society, and hence, they have the credentials and resources to be successful in the job market or in establishing a business. Yet, Caribbean-origin blacks also do better than native-born African Americans; and these individuals come from a very poor part of the world. Thus, why should they do better? The answer to this question reveals something of what has occurred to African Americans as a result of past and present discrimination.

Black immigrants are, first of all, more likely to be married than native African Americans. Black immigrants' households bring in more money because more people in the family are working, even for wages that are somewhat lower than working African Americans. Two-thirds of Caribbean families are headed by a couple, whereas the same percentage of African American families are headed by a single parent. Black immigrants also appear to bring more entrepreneurial motivations and skills, and hence, they are more likely to start a business, especially since they have pools of rotating credit that they can draw upon. Even Haitians in Miami, a rather poor group, are more likely than African Americans to start a business because of their access to capital in rotating credit clubs and systems in which immigrants pool their capital and loan this capital out to targeted entrepreneurs who then pay the pool back. As the pool keeps being replenished, it is loaned out again and again to targeted businesses, typically those just getting started.

Mary Waters of Harvard, who has studied this situation, notes that the advantages of first-generation immigrants appear to dissipate for subsequent generations. Among West Indian students, for example, the third generation was experiencing downward mobility, indicating that the immigrant drive was being undermined by forces in American society. Those who cling to the immigrant culture do better, but ironically, those who assimilate into the broader American culture begin to do poorly—just the opposite of what occurred to white ethnics.

This downward mobility is a good marker of the barriers that blacks confront in the world around them. As long as immigrants are seen as "different" or as "good blacks," they do better. Once they become American blacks, they must endure the same discrimination and prejudicial beliefs as the descendants of American slaves.

as unwilling to work, and as draining the white taxpayers through welfare dependency. In turn, these stereotypes have been used to justify informal discrimination, to dismantle or underfund programs to help the urban poor, to be negligent in enforcing laws or policies prohibiting discriminatory practices against black workers, and, most importantly, to hesitate in mounting a serious effort at job creation for African Americans. The result is that African Americans' share of valued resources has not increased appreciably over the last two decades, even as formal discrimination has been greatly mitigated. This fact is used to further the negative belief that African Americans have "not taken advantage of their equal opportunities." For example, most media portrayals of black youth revolve around gangs and criminal activity in an attempt to symbolize their purported unwillingness to "take advantage of opportunity" in U.S. society (Lyman, 1990; Reed, 1993; and Gomes and Williams, 1990).

RESPONDING TO DISCRIMINATION

Protest during Slavery

During slavery, African Americans were severely limited in what they could do to protest their situation. White violence and the plantation system, coupled with easy physical identification of black-skinned individuals, were extremely effective in maintaining oppressive social control. Music represented one form of protest; *Negro spirituals* depicted the troubles and dissatisfaction of African slaves. Sabotage, such as the burning of barns and destruction of farm tools, was another form of protest. Slaves also practiced quiet resistance, by faking illness and working slowly. Suicide and infanticide (to keep children from being enslaved) were other forms of protest. Running away was perhaps the most effective protest, although being caught meant severe punishment. The *Underground Railroad* to the North for freed slaves, created by northern abolitionists and humanitarians, made this form of protest somewhat successful. Open, and frequently violent, revolt was not uncommon throughout the slave era; Nat Turner's revolt in 1831 was the most famous because sixty whites were killed.

Protest after Slavery

The problem for freed slaves was to build institutions that could, in turn, become resources in their fight for greater equality. After the fall of radical Reconstruction, this became extremely difficult because of the imposition of Jim Crow laws and white violence. Yet, institutions were being built. The church became perhaps the most important and effective institution because it was difficult for whites to deny African Americans the right to worship; indeed, white Americans tended to see the church as pacifying the

Box 4.6

Whites Myths about Blacks

WHITE MYTH: BLACKS LACK MOTIVATION.

According to a 1990 NORC poll, whites (62 percent) tend to believe that blacks are lazier than whites, and whites (78 percent) tend to believe that blacks prefer welfare to being self-supporting.

Fact: During most of the twentieth century blacks were more likely to work than whites. There was a larger proportion of black men than white men in the workforce from 1890 until after World War II, and the proportion of black women in the workforce outpaced the proportion of white women until the mid-1990s. Up until 1970 black males, 20 to 24 years old, had higher labor force participation than their white counterparts. Presently, the labor force participation of black and white women is almost identical, while black men are slightly less likely (69 percent) to be in the labor force than white men (74 percent). However, blacks are disproportionately represented on the welfare rolls. Numerous surveys have shown that blacks are on welfare as a result of social and structural factors, such as segregation and discrimination, rather than personal choice.

WHITE MYTH: BLACKS ARE VIOLENCE-PRONE.

The 1990 NORC poll found that almost half of the white respondents believed that blacks are more violence-prone than whites.

Fact: Black persons, especially young black males, commit a disproportionate share of crime—blacks account for about 45 percent of all arrests for violent crime. The disparity between black and white arrest rates partly results from the fact that blacks are more likely than whites to *ask* police to arrest juveniles. While the majority of victims of black crime are black, it is whites who are more likely to feel unsafe than blacks.

WHITE MYTH: BLACKS NO LONGER FACE JOB AND HOUSING DISCRIMINATION.

Seventy-five percent of the respondents in a 1990 Gallup poll believed that blacks have the same chance as whites to get a job for which they were quali-

African American community. In reality, church leaders were the most effective protest organizers in the twentieth century.

Education represented another institution that was slowly built. Historically, gaining access to public schools had been difficult; yet black attendance, even in segregated schools, increased dramatically from the end of the Civil War until today. In the 1990s, black high school graduation rates are on a par with those of whites, although new problems in dropout rates have emerged in the late 1990s. A system of private *Negro colleges* emerged in the late 1800s as a means to circumvent the exclusion of African Americans from private and state colleges in the South. Over time, a public

fied. In addition, 53 percent of the respondents also believed that blacks were given "too much consideration" in job hiring. A 1992 survey conducted by the Federal National Mortgage Association reported that whites believe that blacks have the same chance as whites of getting affordable housing.

Fact: The Department of Housing and Urban Development (HUD) has conducted numerous tests of housing discrimination. In general, the HUD tests have shown that in slightly more than 50 percent of the time, real estate agents discriminate against black applicants, tend to steer black applicants to minority neighborhoods, and avoid providing mortgage assistance to black applicants. The Federal Reserve Board has also found that black applicants are twice as likely to be rejected for a mortgage than white applicants with the same socioeconomic background.

Regarding the workplace, the Urban Institute conducted, in 1991, a study of white and black male college students who applied for entry-level jobs in Chicago and Washington. The study found that discrimination is an active selective dimension in the hiring process and that white applicants are more likely than black applicants with the same qualifications to advance further in the hiring process.

WHITE MYTH: BLACKS BLAME EVERYONE
BUT THEMSELVES FOR THEIR PROBLEMS.

A 1991 NORC poll found that the majority (57 percent) of white persons believe that blacks have worse jobs, income, and housing than whites because they aren't motivated to better themselves.

Fact: A 1992 Gallup poll of 511 blacks found that while 25 percent believe that the only way to improve their condition was to pressure government to address their needs, 67 percent believe that blacks should try harder to solve their own community's problems, and to better themselves and their families.

Source: U.S. News & World Report (Nov. 9, 1992), pp. 41, 43–44.

African American college network was created. Today, the challenge in higher education is to increase enrollment of black students in formerly exclusionary universities and, simultaneously, to sustain the black colleges, which were once the main source of higher education for African Americans in the South.

African Americans had begun to vote in large numbers during Reconstruction, but political organization was difficult in the post-Reconstruction South because of intense efforts to disenfranchise blacks (Williamson, 1984:224–258; McAdam, 1982:65–67, 1988). Indeed, only with the massive migration out of the South from 1910 to 1930 did African Americans gain

Box 4.7

Black Churches on Fire

Reverend David Upton was awakened by a ringing telephone at 4 a.m. on January 8, 1996. The voice on the other end of the telephone line simply said, "The church is on fire." The reverend walked through a half-foot of snow to watch his two-story brick church building burn. "I thought of all the memories—the services, the weddings, the children baptized," Upton said. "Our child-care center was on track to open in a month. Everything was just going up in smoke." When the fire settled down to a smolder, Upton noticed that someone had painted "Die Nigger Die!" and "White Is Right!" on the church's back door.

The Center for Democratic Renewal, which monitors white supremacist groups and hate crimes from the Martin Luther King Jr. Center in Atlanta, has found that forty-five Southern black congregation churches were attacked between January 1990 and February 1996. While no arrests have been made in thirty-three of forty-five attacks, all the people arrested for the other twelve attacks were white males aged 15 to 45. All of those arrested have expressed links with white supremacist groups. President Clinton asked Attorney General Janet Reno to provide assistance with the arrest and conviction of persons setting black churches on fire. Reno brought together in February 1996 a working group of one hundred agents from the Bureau of Alcohol, Tobacco, and Firearms (ATF), and the Justice Department's civil rights division. Reno's efforts ran into trouble, however, when it was found that two of the ATF agents had participated in "Good Ol' Boy Roundups"—white supremacist gatherings in Tennessee.

One of the few strong institutional systems organizing contemporary

political clout, albeit only in their new northern location; and even there, white violence and other tactics kept black voters from gaining political access. In 1940 in the South, no more than 10 percent of the eligible black voters were registered in any state; in most southern states the registration was under 5 percent, and for four states it was under 1 percent (McAdam, 1982:79). Yet, the existence of the NAACP and its frontal attack on Jim Crow during the 1930s led to a series of favorable Supreme Court decisions that reenfranchised African Americans in enough numbers to form an important voting block. During and after World War II, the black migration continued to the North and West, where the climate of political oppression was less severe. The stage was then set for the political mobilization of the 1960s (for a review of the NAACP and the career of Thurgood Marshall, see Rowan, 1993).

Violence was a common occurrence in the post-Reconstruction era, right up through the interwar years. Until the 1940s, most violence by African Americans was in reaction to the violence initiated by whites, but from the 1940s on, and particularly in the 1960s, black rioting emerged as an effective form of protest, calling attention to problems and, at the same time,

African Americans is religion, and especially the black churches that emerged in the South and spread throughout the United States. During the civil rights movement of the 1950s and 1960s, black churches were frequently burned, as retaliation against the black ministers and their white compatriots who were at the forefront of the movement. In 1996, President Clinton responded to what appeared to be a rash of black church burnings in the South—a situation that was reminiscent of the 1950s and 1960s. Between 1995 and 1996, there were seventy-three burnings of black churches, a figure that received considerable media attention.

More careful examination of the records revealed an interesting fact: Churches—both black and white—are among the favorite targets of arsonists because they are often empty and unguarded and because many are in somewhat remote and isolated rural areas. Moreover, many of those that are burned are constructed of wood or wood framing. Thus, during the period in which black church burnings increased, so did the arson rates for white-dominated churches. Yet, even taking into account these considerations, the various investigations into the burnings revealed that at least one-quarter of the black church burnings were "racially motivated." It is not likely that the burnings of white churches were similarly motivated, and so while the media and the president may have overstated the issue somewhat, there is ample reason to be concerned. If twenty of the seventy-three burnings in the year between 1995 and 1996 were clearly done because of anger toward African Americans, this figure represents a form of discrimination that white Americans do not have to face. True, they face crazy arsonists, but not arsonists who hate them because of the color of their skin.

Source: Associated Press, May 5, 1996.

prodding fearful white Americans into limited responses to alleviate these problems.

The Last Fifty Years

Beginning in the 1940s and escalating during the 1950s and 1960s, black protest against continued subjugation took an array of forms: The NAACP continued to press its case in the courts, winning such important decisions as *Brown v. Board of Education of Topeka;* individual protests, such as Rosa Parks's refusal to go to the back of the bus, became the rallying cry for boycotts and other forms of collective protest; organized, nonviolent demonstrations, largely orchestrated by religious leaders such as Martin Luther King, Jr., became an extremely effective tool in calling attention to and mobilizing broader sentiments against the continued segregation of public facilities (from lunch counters to schools); voter registration drives, especially after the Voting Rights Act of 1965, dramatically increased the voting power of African Americans; urban violence in the form of riots escalated in the 1960s, calling attention to and forcing a response from government;

Nonviolent protest proved to be the most effective tool in securing for African Americans their civil rights. Here Martin Luther King, Jr., leads a civil rights march.

militant black political organizations and parties, such as the Black Panther party, the Student Nonviolent Coordinating Committee (which became violent), and the Black Muslims all began to advocate that acts of white violence and oppression should be met with equal force (for a history of the Black Panther party, see Hilliard and Cole, 1993).

These protests created a climate in the 1960s for the passage of a series of civil rights laws, which, in turn, facilitated more protest, more voter registration, more legal redress of grievances, more individual actions against acts of discrimination, more awareness among the general public about the plight of African Americans, and, for a time, more militancy in "black power" parties and organizations. For the first and only time since radical Reconstruction, the federal government, under Lyndon Johnson's Great Society initiative, seriously addressed the problems of the poor in general and African Americans in particular with a broad array of programs. During this period African Americans made significant gains in income and educational attainment, in assistance in housing and medical care, and in job training. Many of these gains have been undone over the last two decades; others have remained static. Today, even in the wake of the Los Angeles riots of 1992—the most costly in history—violent protest is less effective in the 1990s than in the 1960s. More effective is the growing voting power that has come with increased voter registration among African Americans.

Box 4.8

African American Women in the Civil Rights Movement

The most famous leaders of the civil rights movement are men, with Dr. Martin Luther King, Jr., being the most famous of all. But women were also leaders, playing key roles in initiating protests, mapping out strategies, and mobilizing necessary resources. Below are some of the most prominent and important black women in the civil rights movement:

Rosa Parks: Known for her December 1, 1955, refusal to surrender her seat to a white passenger in a crowded Montgomery, Alabama, bus, she was the spark for the Montgomery bus boycott.

Ella Baker: She was an officer of the National Association for the Advancement of Colored People, a founder of the Southern Christian Leadership Conference, and a supporter of the Student Nonviolent Coordinating Committee.

Daisy Bates: With the support of the NAACP, she played a major role in the integration of the Little Rock, Arkansas, public schools. Single-handedly she spearheaded a grassroots community campaign to enroll black children in all-white public schools.

Mary Burks: As founder and first president of the Women's Political Council (WPC) of Montgomery, Alabama, she led the WPC in the Montgomery bus boycott of 1955–1956.

Constance Motley: Serving as an associate counsel for the NAACP Legal Defense Fund over a period of twenty years, she prepared legal briefs for *Brown v. Board of Education* (1954).

Autherine Foster: She was the first black student at the University of Alabama (1956).

Diane Nash: While a student at Fisk University, she was a key figure in the sit-in movement of the 1960s to remove segregation from restaurants, lunch counters, and theaters in Nashville, Tennessee.

Juanita Mitchell: In April 1942, she directed a citizen's march of two thousand people on Maryland's capitol in Annapolis that resulted in the appointment of the Governor's Interracial Commission, the appointment of black police officers, and an investigation into charges of police brutality in the black community.

Margaret Wilson: In 1975, she became the first black woman to serve as chair of the board of directors for the NAACP.

Source: Bernice M. Barnett. 1993. "Invisible Southern Black Women Leaders in the Civil Rights Movement: The Triple Constraints of Gender, Race, and Class." *Gender & Society* 7(2):162–182. Jessie C. Smith (ed.). 1992. *Notable Black American Women.* Detroit, MI: Gale Research. Darlene C. Hine (ed.). 1993. *Black Women in America: An Historical Encyclopedia.* Brooklyn, NY: Carlson Publishing.

The long history of protest has been, at best, only partially effective in combating discrimination. Protest has brought improvement in the economic, political, and social positions of African Americans, but the continued existence of poverty, segregation, and subtly institutionalized discrimination emphasizes that the descendants of the slaves must live under conditions that no other minority group in American history has had to endure. These conditions will, in the future, be the driving force behind further protests—from the violence of alienated gang members, through the retreat and separatist sentiments of some groups and organizations, to the legal assault on the more subtle forms of discrimination.

SUMMARY

African Americans were brought to the United States as slaves and were denied access to the most basic resources, even after slavery ended. Blacks have thus experienced higher rates of poverty, lower incomes, more segregation in housing, higher rates of unemployment, less access to higher education, and shorter life spans than virtually all other groups of Americans. Discrimination is relatively easy to practice against African Americans because their black skin makes them easy to identify. Historically, African Americans have had to endure some of the most vicious negative beliefs, which have been used to justify discrimination in jobs, housing, education, and all institutional spheres in American society. These beliefs and patterns of discrimination have been fueled by the white perception of a "black threat." These forces have combined to institutionalize discrimination against black Americans.

In the legal arena, free and enslaved blacks were initially denied all rights of citizenship. In the period after slavery up to the 1960s, African Americans have had to overcome a combination of laws, court decisions, and enforcement practices that sought to deny them access to the resources enjoyed by white Americans. In the economic sphere, black workers have been denied access to all categories of jobs, although in recent decades many African Americans have made dramatic progress in securing good jobs. As slaves, blacks were simply excluded from the political process. Their manumission followed by the rapid collapse of radical Reconstruction introduced Jim Crow practices that kept blacks from registering to vote. The civil rights movement begun in the late 1950s opened the door for large numbers of African Americans to participate in the American political process. In the educational arena, black slaves were deliberately kept illiterate; after slavery their exclusion from the educational system was maintained as long as possible, especially in the South. Separate schools for blacks and whites, as well as black colleges, represented the fall-back position during most of this century; and only over the last few decades has a significant amount of school integration occurred, although such integration is still hampered by white resistance and the segregation of blacks from white neighborhoods.

In housing, African Americans are the most segregated minority in America, save for those Native Americans confined to reservations. Such segregation was created by white violence against blacks who ventured into white neighborhoods, by lending policies of banks, and by governmental housing programs.

This system of institutionalized discrimination has confined African Americans to the lowest strata of the class system in America, although in recent decades a significant proportion of the black population has been able to overcome discrimination and move into the middle classes. This movement has only highlighted the fate of those who have not been mobile.

POINTS OF DEBATE

African Americans are the only minority in America that was imported against their will as slaves. This situation existed until 1865, ending with the Civil War. However, except for the brief period of radical Reconstruction, new forms of vicious discrimination ensued. For most of the twentieth century, blacks were systematically denied access to jobs, housing, politics, and education, while being subjected to white violence and negative stereotypes. The legacy of these forces haunts America today, posing what we termed the "second American dilemma": How is this legacy to be undone? In answering this question, some hotly debated issues emerge.

1. Does white America owe black America compensation for past acts of discrimination? If so, how much? Most Americans are now against forced busing to integrate schools. Many are antiwelfare, believing that welfare mothers have babies in order to increase their allotments; some are against higher taxes to support any social action programs. Some white Americans want to build more prisons to house those they fear. Many are more willing than in the past to live in integrated neighborhoods but worry (needlessly) about loss of property values. At the same time they complain about reverse discrimination when confronted with affirmative action programs that may limit their employment future. In light of these beliefs and attitudes, it will be difficult to address the legacy of the past, even if white America is sympathetic in the abstract. But are white Americans willing to live with the consequences of these attitudes? This poses another point of debate.
2. The legacy of discrimination against black Americans is manifest in two directions: One is the hard work and effort by many to overcome discrimination, the other is the entrapment of millions of African Americans in the pathologies of decaying urban areas. These pathologies revolve around drug use, violent crime, gang activity, high dropout rates from schools, very high rates of out-of-wedlock births, and an increasing

number of single-parent households. Can America allow this to continue and not experience the consequences of these pathologies? Are Americans willing to allow them to fester, thereby putting a harder and potentially more volatile edge on black–white relations in America?

3. Yet, even in the wake of the most expensive riot in American history, Americans remain remarkably insensitive to the depth of the problems. Indeed, they continue to visualize the plight of African Americans in very individualistic terms, as a character flaw of blacks and not the structure of society. Can white Americans continue to blame the victims of discrimination, and not their ancestors, if not themselves? Anglo-Saxons tend to assume that they are a rational people who pragmatically assess costs and benefits. If blacks are not wise enough to realize the consequences of crime, drug use, out-of-wedlock babies, and unstable families, then they must accept the costs. But the costs will not be only on the victims; they spill over into the society in the form of the enormous costs associated with building more prisons, with health care brought about by violence and despair, with alienated youth in gangs and drug distribution, with the loss of productive activity and the corresponding welfare burden, and with violence affecting the schools and so many mainstream aspects of American society. Thus, can Americans continue to hold such a narrow view of human behavior without addressing the more deep-seated forces behind these problematic issues?

CHAPTER 5

Native Americans

Leif Ericson and Christopher Columbus were comparative newcomers to the Americas. Long before their "discoveries," people began to cross the land bridge connecting Alaska with the Asian continent, perhaps as long ago as forty thousand years. They came in search of food, hunting wild game and gathering indigenous plant life, and they settled the entire face of North, Central, and South America. As they settled in distinctive niches, they evolved diverse cultures. And some, such as those among the Maya, Incas, and Aztecs, developed cultures and organizational structures as sophisticated as those in other parts of the world. In what was to become the United States, however, the several hundred societies and perhaps as many as three hundred language groups of the native people were comparatively simple, making them highly vulnerable to conquest by white Europeans. Some were hunters and gatherers, others focused on fishing, a few on herding, and some on horticulture. All constituted viable societies, but upon contact with Europeans, they were to be wholly or partially destroyed. The history of Native Americans[1] after European contact is thus one of conquest and domination.

ON THE VERGE OF EXTINCTION

We can only estimate how large the Native American population was prior to its contact with the Europeans. In 1860, Emmanuel Domenech (1860) es-

[1]*A note on terminology:* Our use of the term "Native American" is intentional. First, we use it to emphasize the presence of the population prior to the arrival of European explorers. Implicit is the observation that Native Americans were not "discovered." Second, the term "Native American" encompasses a number of indigenous nations. Jaimes (1992:113) has noted, "American Indian Peoples whose territory lies within the borders of the United States hold compelling legal and moral rights to be treated as fully sovereign nations."

timated that the precontact population was between 16 and 17 million. One of the limitations of early estimates, however, is that they represent subjective impressions and extrapolations based on early contacts with villages and settlements (Snipp, 1989:6). The first generally accepted scientific estimate of the sixteenth-century Native American population was produced by James Mooney (1928), who estimated the North American aboriginal population to be about 1.2 million persons at the time of European contact. A more recent estimate puts the precontact population between 2 and 5 million (Snipp, 1989), although some still argue that the number was in fact much larger.

Figure 5.1 illustrates the decrease in the Native American population between 1600 and 1850, from around 2.5 million (a conservative estimate) to only around 200,000 (Spinden, 1928). This decline can be viewed only as genocide, or the virtual elimination of a population. Lack of immunity to European diseases, or what some have called "ecological warfare"; displacement from lands and consequent starvation; widespread killing in "war"; and cold-blooded murder account for this sudden drop (Merrell, 1984;

FIGURE 5.1. The Native American population from 1850 through 1990.

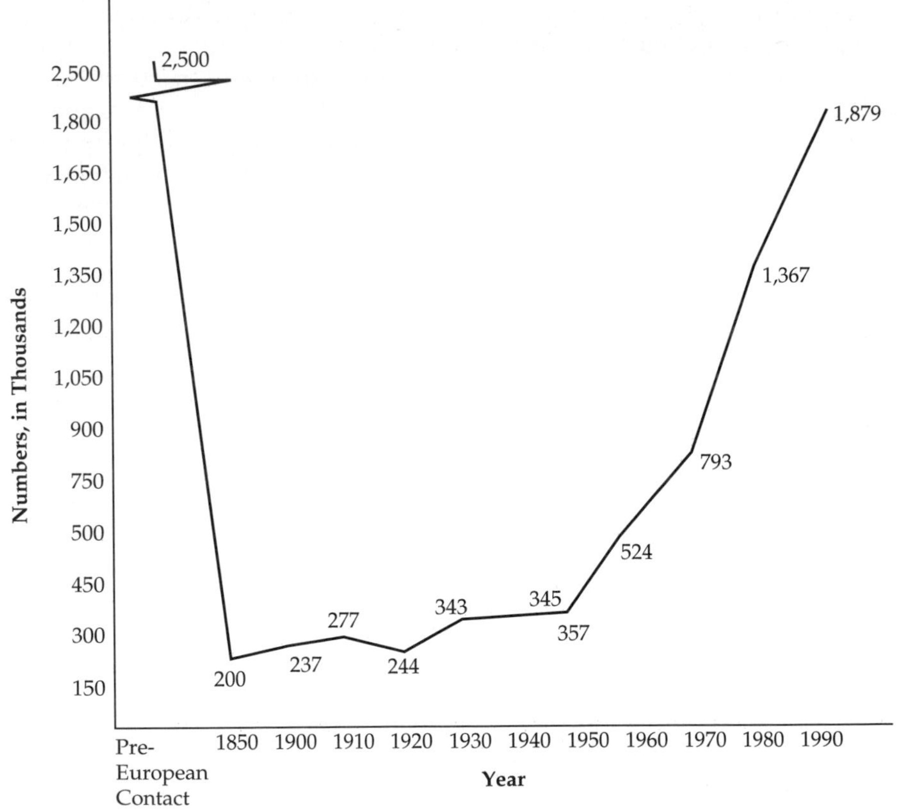

Crosby, 1976). Thus, if we needed an indicator of discrimination against Native Americans, a tenfold drop in the size of the population is as good as any. But this figure does not tell the whole story, for even as the population has replenished itself over the last one hundred and fifty years, it has done so amid the residue of those conditions that led to attempted genocide.

In this century, with the exception of the 1920s, the Native American population has grown for each census period. Part of the decrease in population during the 1920s has been attributed to an influenza epidemic. By 1930, however, the population was again growing, and by 1950, this growth began to accelerate, a trend that Snipp (1989) suggests constituted a Native American "baby boom" equivalent to the postwar boom among white Europeans. The result was that between 1950 and 1990, the Native American population grew by 426 percent. (Table 5.1 shows the numerical increase between 1980 and 1990 of the top twenty Indian tribes in the United States.) This increase was due to the fact that public policy toward Native Americans began to change in 1950, and attitudes shifted from fear and hate to sympathy and guilt. Improved health care resulted in lowered infant mortality rates and increased life expectancy for adults.

Another factor in this growth is the increased willingness of Native

TABLE 5.1. Top Twenty Indian Tribes by Population Increase between 1980 and 1990

Tribe	Increase between 1980 and 1990	Percent Change between 1980 and 1990
Cherokee	458,868	59
Navajo	66,665	42
Sioux	28,713	37
Chippewa	32,386	44
Choctaw	36,011	72
Pueblo	12,778	30
Apache	17,469	49
Iroquois	14,339	38
Lumbee	22,257	78
Creek	17,594	62
Blackfoot	16,028	73
Chickasaw	11,205	109
Thono O'Odham	3,579	27
Potawatomi	7,004	72
Seminole	5,201	50
Pima	3,352	29
Tlingit	4,908	52
Alaskan Athabaskans	4,062	40
Cheyenne	1,891	19
Comanche	2,400	27

Source: U.S. Bureau of the Census, 1994b.

Americans to be identified as such, resulting in the increased capability of government agencies, such as the U.S. Bureau of the Census, to identify them. The "self-pride" movements among disadvantaged ethnic groups in the 1960s, for example, increased the ethnic awareness of Native Americans; it became a matter of pride to identify oneself as an "Indian" because the term no longer carried such negative connotations and stereotypes. Indeed, some researchers have suggested that the increase in the Native American population between 1960 and 1980 is not solely the product of health programs (Passel, 1976; Passel and Berman, 1986; and Clifton, 1989) but, rather, a marker of increased ethnic pride as more and more people were willing to proclaim themselves as "American Indian" on U.S. census forms. However, increased ethnic pride may result in a high "overcount" of the American Indian population (see Box 5.2). According to Passel (1993), while 54 percent of the growth in the American Indian population between 1960 and 1990 can be attributed to demographic factors, 46 percent of the growth can be attributed to nondemographic factors. One of the most salient nondemographic factors is enhanced self-identification as an American Indian. Thus, there may be as many persons that perceive themselves as American Indians as there are "real" American Indians.

Though Native Americans live throughout the United States, almost half of the population resides in the West, primarily in the southwestern states of California (19 percent), Arizona (16 percent), and New Mexico (11 percent) (Paisano, 1992). Outside of the Southwest, the largest concentrations of Native Americans are found in Oklahoma (20 percent) and North Carolina (6 percent). And, contrary to popular belief, the majority of Native Americans do not reside on or near a reservation (Table 5.2).

TABLE 5.2. Geographical Distribution of Native Americans, 1980 and 1990

	1980		*1990*	
Location	Number	Percent	Number	Percent
Region				
Northeast	79,038	6	125,148	6
North Central	248,413	17	337,899	17
South	372,825	26	562,731	29
West	722,769	51	933,456	48
Residence areas				
Reservation	355,761	25	411,000	22
Near reservation	213,457	15	281,000	15

Source: U.S. Bureau of the Census, 1983b, 1992b; and Edna Paisano, Selected Social and Economic Characteristics for the American Indian, Eskimo, and Aleut Population for Selected Areas, 1990. Presented at the Meeting for the Census Advisory Committees on the American Indian, and Alaska Native, Asian and Pacific Islanders, Black and Hispanic Populations for the 1990 Census.

RESOURCE SHARES OF NATIVE AMERICANS

Compared with other ethnic populations in the United States, Native Americans have been severely constrained in their interaction with mainstream society. This isolation is the result of the numerous treaties between the U.S. government and the Native American tribes, which marginalized and subordinated them, thereby limiting their opportunities to secure valued resources (Deloria, 1976).

Income of Native Americans

The average income of Native Americans is lower than that of white Americans. Overall, Native American median income was 59 percent of that for white Americans in 1970, 66 percent in 1980, and 65 percent in 1990 (Snipp, 1989; Paisano, 1992). Thus, despite the gains made in the 1970s, Native Americans have not closed the income gap over the last decade. These income differences between white Americans and Native Americans reflect different patterns of occupational distribution.

Occupational Distribution of Native Americans

Native Americans are underrepresented in white-collar occupations and overrepresented in service occupations. For example, in 1990 almost 42 percent of Native Americans were employed in white-collar occupations (managerial and professional; technical, sales, and administrative support) compared with 61 percent of white Americans. In contrast, 39 percent of Native Americans are employed in blue-collar occupations (service; operators, fabricators, and laborers) compared with 24 percent of white Americans (Table 5.3).

Occupational distributions for Native Americans are also based on their patterns of residence. In general, Native Americans living on the reservation are more likely to be employed in blue-collar occupations, whereas off-reservation Native Americans are more likely to be employed in white-collar occupations. Moreover, according to Snipp (1989:239), "About 32 percent of Indian men and 37 percent of Indian women living on or near a reservation are employed by federal and local government authorities, compared with 16 percent of men and 17 percent of women residing in nonreservation areas." Many of the government-created jobs for Native Americans living on reservations have been low-paying ones, particularly during the 1970s. Although federal programs have been instrumental in providing an array of public works jobs in trades and construction, like all such "make-work" it is subject to political more than economic forces and does not, therefore, lead to steady employment patterns. The larger percentage of Native Americans living on reservations in service occupations (contrasted with those living off the reservation) may not, according to Snipp (1989:241), "constitute a

TABLE 5.3. Occupational Distribution among White Americans and Native Americans, 1980 and 1990

	White American Population, %		*Native American Population, %*	
Occupation	1980	1990	1980	1990
Managerial and professional	23.7	28.3	15.1	14.4
Technical, sales, and administrative support	33.4	32.9	23.9	27.4
Service	12.3	10.2	21.0	17.7
Farming, forestry, and fishing	2.6	2.4	5.0	3.8
Precision production, craft, and repair	11.9	12.0	12.9	15.0
Operators, fabricators, and laborers	16.2	14.2	22.3	21.7

Source: U.S. Bureau of the Census, 1985; 1990 census-detailed EEO occupations file.

major source of employment for the American Indian labor force. . . . It is most likely that many traditional occupations for American Indians, such as traditional crafts (especially those purchased mainly by other Indians), provide a livelihood insufficient for survival and consequently may be practiced as an avocation and not as a principal source of income."

Educational Attainment of Native Americans

On average, the levels of education attained by Native Americans are below those attained by white Americans, although outcomes (e.g., completed years of schooling) at the high school and college levels have increased for the Native American population over the last few decades (see Table 5.4). However, Native Americans still account for less than 1 percent of the undergraduate and graduate and professional degrees awarded in the United States (see Table 5.5).

The gains in education for Native Americans at the high school level may have been affected by the politics of education in the 1970s. During that time, both federal and state governments sought to improve high school graduation and college attendance rates of minority groups in general. Programs such as Upward Bound, for example, sought to increase the presence of minority high school graduates on college campuses; and while these education initiatives dramatically increased the high school graduation rates for Native Americans, a comparable increase in college completion did not materialize. Despite the fact that college graduation rates more than dou-

TABLE 5.4. Educational Levels Attained by White Americans and Native Americans, 1970, 1980, and 1990*

	Less Than Five Years of School			*Four Years or More of High School*			*Four Years or More of College*		
	1970	1980	1990	1970	1980	1990	1970	1980	1990
White Americans	4.5	3.2	2.4	54.5	69.6	79.6	11.3	17.4	22.2
Native Americans	7.7	8.4	6.6	22.0	55.5	63.5	3.8	7.7	9.3

*Persons 25 years old and older.

Source: U.S. Bureau of the Census, 1973a, 1985; 1990 Census of Population and Housing Summary, Tape File 3C.

TABLE 5.5. The Postsecondary Progress of Native Americans, 1981 through 1992

	1981		*1990*		*1992*	
Population	Undergraduate Degrees, %*	Graduate/ Professional Degrees, %†	Undergraduate Degrees, %	Graduate/ Professional Degrees, %	Undergraduate Degrees, %	Graduate/ Professional Degrees, %
White	87	89	85	88	84	86
Black	7	6	7	5	7	6
Latino	3	2	4	3	4	3
Asian	2	2	3	3	4	4
Native American	‡	‡	‡	‡	‡	‡

*Includes associate's and bachelor's degrees.
†Includes master's, doctor's, and first professional degrees.
‡ < 1 percent.

Source: U.S. Bureau of the Census, 1995.

bled for Native Americans between 1970 and 1990, the gap in college completion between the whites and Native Americans closed very little.

Life Span of Native Americans

Ignoring for the moment the genocidal practices of the past, Native Americans currently do not live on average as long as whites. Life expectancy, for example, for Native Americans in 1990 was 71 years compared to 74 years for whites (National Center for Health Statistics, 1991). Access to health care helps account for this difference, particularly the limited availability of prenatal care for Native Americans which increases the chances of babies being born with low birth weight that, in turn, results in infant mortality.

In general, Native Americans have higher death rates during their life course than white Americans. In contrast to whites, Native Americans are twice as likely to be victims of accidents (motor vehicle accidents, drownings, and unintentional injuries such as household fire), more likely to be victims of homicide, twice as likely to commit suicide, and almost three times as likely to die from heart disease (U.S. Department of Health and Human Services, 1993). Thus, life is a resource that is less available to Native Americans than to whites and other ethnic groups.

Housing of Native Americans

Native Americans tend to have lower-quality housing than whites. They are less likely to live in owner-occupied housing, more likely to live in a mobile home, more likely to live in a smaller (that is, number of rooms) home, and more likely to have extra persons per room in each household (U.S. Bureau of the Census, 1973b, 1983a, 1993). Also, the quality of domestic life for many Native Americans is very different from that of most white Americans. For example, fewer Native American households have complete bathrooms, and fewer have access to public water, public sewers, complete kitchens, and telephones. In 1990, 5 percent of the Native American population lived in housing units that lacked complete plumbing facilities, compared to 1 percent of the U.S. population. In addition, Native Americans tend to live in households that lack complete kitchen facilities (5 percent), depend on well water (17 percent), and are not connected to a public sewer system (67 percent). Comparable figures for the U.S. population are 1 percent, 14 percent, and 76 percent, respectively.

Aside from the quality of life in most Native American dwellings is the issue of where these dwellings are located. Some 25 percent of the native population lives on government-regulated reservations, separated and isolated from the general population, and another 15 percent live near the reservation. Thus, around 40 percent of the Native American population is dramatically segregated, not just by neighborhood but by territory. This situation, the legacy of past discrimination, forces a significant percentage of Native Americans to be dependent on economic opportunities on and around

The housing of Native American individuals and families is often substandard.

the reservation, which, typically, is isolated from mainstream society (U.S. Commission on Civil Rights, 1975). Most Native Americans view this isolation in a positive light, as a way to recapture their quickly vanishing culture (Ambler, 1990). On the negative side, however, this segregation has increased dependency on the federal government, which in the past has not demonstrated great sympathy for maintaining Native American cultures.

Poverty of Native Americans

It should not be surprising that the majority of a population that suffered virtual genocide, that remains partially isolated on reservations, that tends to have lower incomes than others, that is disproportionately underrepresented in white-collar jobs and the professions, that tends to die earlier than other ethnic groups, and that has a lower average level of education would be living in poverty. In the 1970s, the U.S. government officially acknowledged that Native Americans were the most impoverished group in the United States and that this population lived in conditions rivaling those found in the Third World (U.S. Department of Health, Education and Welfare, 1976). For example, at that time, 14 percent of Native Americans lived in crowded housing, 67 percent lived in houses without running water, 48 percent lived in houses without toilets, and 32 percent had no means of transportation. Thirty-three percent of Native American families were living below the poverty line compared to 8.6 percent of white families. Ten years later, 24 percent of Native American families were living below the poverty line compared to 7 percent of white families (Aguirre, 1990), and by 1990, conditions had worsened, with almost 36 percent of Native American families living below the poverty line (see Table 5.6).

THE DYNAMICS OF DISCRIMINATION AGAINST NATIVE AMERICANS

Identifiability of Native Americans

Movie stereotypes aside, it is not so easy to identify Native Americans physically, for such characteristics as high cheekbones, reddish complexion, black hair, almond-shaped eyes, and very little male facial hair are not universal among Native Americans, and any of these characteristics can be found among other populations (Snipp, 1989:26). In contrast to these popular notions of who "Indians" are, more explicit biological definitions seek to highlight the five genetic features unique to Native Americans: earwax texture, organic compounds in urine, blood types and Rh factor, fingerprint patterns, and the ability to taste the test chemical phenylthiocar bamide (Snipp, 1989). Although trivial in any genetic sense, some of these characteristics, especially those related to "blood quantum," were to become the bases for constructing a social definition of who is "Indian." The need to define an Indian based on "blood quantum" became important at the turn of the nineteenth century when the U.S. government took an active role in determining land rights for Indians and non-Indians in the western United States (Meyer, 1991; Harmon, 1990; and Smitts, 1991).

In the late nineteenth century, the U.S. government made a systematic attempt to identify Native Americans. Jaimes (1992) suggests that this effort stemmed more from an interest in limiting treaty obligations than in

TABLE 5.6. White American and Native American Families Living Below Poverty Levels, 1970 through 1990

	Population, %	
Year	White American	Native American
1970	8.6	33.2
1980	7.0	23.7
1990	9.8	36.1

Source: U.S. Bureau of the Census, 1973a, 1985; 1990 Census of Population and Housing Summary, Tape 3C.

Box 5.1

What's in a Team Name?

The use of an ethnic label as a mascot is perhaps one of the most degrading things that can happen to a population. It is a sign of disrespect and low regard. If one doubts this conclusion, let us rename some prominent teams: The Washington Negroes, the Florida State Jews, the Cleveland Italians, or the Atlanta Wasps. Or, let's construct some new names that reflect the ethnicity of an area: The Los Angeles Dodgers can become Los Angeles Mexicans; the San Francisco 49ers can become the San Francisco Chinamen; the Anaheim Angels can become the Anaheim Viets; the Chicago Bears can become the Chicago Pollacks; the New York Giants can become the New York Spics.

In the United States, no ethnic group other than Native Americans is used as a mascot. Yet, when efforts are made to change the name of a sports team on the basis of this inappropriate usage, there is often resistance. Some teams, such as the Stanford Cardinals (formerly the Indians), have changed their names, but most have not.

promoting collective identity among native peoples. The vehicle for doing so was a "blood quantum" measure, or the degree of "Indian blood" an individual possessed. The Dawes Act of 1887, also known as the General Allotment Act, empowered the government to "test" blood levels to identify someone as an "Indian" and thereby entitled to government treatment under treaty obligations. If this degree was below certain levels, then treaty obligations could be ignored.

To this day the "percentage of Indian blood" is an important bureaucratic marker for who is entitled to government assistance and who qualifies for special programs, such as affirmative action. For example, in 1986 the Department of Health and Human Services proposed that one-fourth blood quantum was a requirement for receiving medical services at Indian Health Service clinics (Snipp, 1989). In adopting this approach—which no other ethnic population must submit to—the government presumes that blood makes "Indians" a distinct race with certain behavioral propensities (Bieder, 1980). More materially, the earlier Dawes Act used "blood" to determine who was eligible for land or, more important, who was not entitled to land because of insufficient "Indian blood." As a consequence, between 1887 and 1934, the land base to which Native Americans were entitled was reduced from 138 million acres to 48 million acres (House Committee on Indian Affairs, 1934). For those Native Americans who did qualify to receive land, most found that the allocated land was arid or semiarid, almost useless for agriculture. In contrast, the most attractive and fertile native-occupied land was reserved for nonnative populations (Deloria and Lytle, 1983).

Box 5.2

Ethnic Pride and Native Americans

When white patrons at Romo's restaurant in Holbrook, Arizona, learn that their host is half Navajo and half Hopi, they frequently exclaim, "I'm part Cherokee!" The host smiles and secretly rolls his eyes. More bahanas *(whites) are jumping on the Indian bandwagon.*

The increased interest in declaiming one's ethnic identity as "Native American" has resulted in rapid increases among Native Americans in large metropolitan areas and in the expansion of Native American industries.

POPULATION GROWTH

- American Indians increased their numbers by 101 percent between 1980 and 1990 (46,200 persons in 1990) in the New York–Northern New Jersey–Long Island area.
- The American Indian population increased by 82 percent between 1980 and 1990 (45,700 persons in 1990) in Oklahoma City and by 66 percent in Phoenix (38,000 persons in 1990).
- In general, the 38 percent increase between 1980 and 1990 in the number of persons that identified themselves as Native American exceeded the growth rate of blacks (6 percent) and whites (13 percent), but not Latinos (53 percent) or Asians (108 percent).

NATIVE AMERICAN INDUSTRIES

- Native American special trade contractors, a total of 2,268 firms, had 97 million dollars in receipts.
- Native American–owned food stores had receipts of 54 million dollars, and Native American–owned automotive dealers and service stations had receipts of 65 million dollars.
- The business ownership rate for Native American–owned firms is 12.1 Native American–owned firms per 1,000 Native Americans in the South, 10.3 in the West, 9.6 in the Northeast, and 7.4 in the Midwest.

Source: Fost, 1991.

Negative Beliefs about Native Americans

Despite their visibility in U.S. popular culture, Native Americans did not occupy a meaningful place in the sociohistorical fabric of U.S. society (Churchill, 1993). In the past, Native Americans often were either "noble savages" or "savage redmen" in movies and on television. Native Americans were stigmatized as pastoral relics in an industrial society: the cigar store

Indian and the Indian face engraved on the nickel. Moreover, Native Americans often are portrayed as partially mute in popular culture. In American literature, "the Indian" tends to be a passive witness to others' actions. For example, Queequeg in *Moby Dick,* Tonto in *The Lone Ranger,* and Chief Broom in Ken Kesey's *One Flew Over the Cuckoo's Nest* do not speak. The same may be rightly said of most other Native American characters inhabiting the pages of Euroamerican fiction (Durham, 1992:428). And even the depiction of Native Americans as silent has resulted in a set of negative beliefs (Osborne, 1989; Jones, 1988; and Churchill, 1992).

Savage Redmen

The portrayal of the Native American as a ruthless killer of white settlers in movies and television can be traced to the early stages of European contact (Stedman, 1982). As Europeans moved westward, they discovered that they would have to either remove the Native Americans from their lands or learn to share the land. Rather than attempt to live alongside the natives, European settlers decided to take the land. When the natives resisted, European settlers produced the ruthless savage stereotype (Brown, 1970; Shively, 1992). The death of European settlers was seen as a savage act imposed upon innocent people. Such stereotypes became common in the media of the time, which tended to sensationalize and caricature, and promoted a tidal wave of anti–Native American sentiment (O'Connor, 1980).

"Fat Cat" Capitalists

Land has always been a pivotal feature in conflicts between Native and white Americans. One of the more recent negative beliefs is that Native Americans have become "fat cats" from the minerals and resources on their land—a belief that is empirically wrong in light of their poverty rates (Anderson, 1992). At issue is the potential wealth in Indian lands—oil, natural gas, uranium, or other resources. Churchill and LaDuke (1992:241) note that "approximately one-third of all western U.S. low-sulphur coal, 20 percent of known U.S. reserves of oil and natural gas, and over one-half of all U.S. uranium deposits lie under the reservations."

The stereotype of Native Americans as "fat cats" is negative in that it implies that Native Americans are undeserving of these resources. Similar to the early stereotype of Native Americans as "unwanted land occupants," the negative portrayal of Native Americans as "fat cats" reinforces their perceived threat to white society and its control of resources. This stereotype has facilitated the federal government's transfer of mineral-rich Native American lands to U.S. control (LaDuke, 1981) and has limited the amount of opposition by white society in the appropriation of these mineral-rich lands. For example, the bulk of the ore-bearing portion of the copper belt found on the Papago reservation during the 1920s was removed from the Papago domain by the U.S. Congress.

Negative stereotypes not only emerged out of conflict with Native Americans, but became an active force in legitimizing virtual genocide, in

Box 5.3

Who Were the Real "Savages"?

Historical analyses dispute the stereotype of the wagon train of white settlers being attacked by hordes of "screaming Indians" (Hurtado and Iverson, 1994). Between 1840 and 1860, when the Plains migrations occurred, some 250,000 white settlers crossed the Great Plains on their way farther west. During this period 362 white Americans and 426 Native Americans died in all the recorded battles. Cooperation was much more common between migrants and natives. For example, regarding Indian and white relations on the California frontier, Hurtado (1982:245) has noted that "instead of resisting the whites, restricting settlement, and impeding development, California's Indians worked obediently in the whites' fields and homes in return for food and shelter."

The real savagery came from federal troops and federal agents who sought to pacify the Native Americans, killing them arbitrarily and making their lands available to the white settlers. While the Native Americans certainly defended themselves, most of the massacres were of Native Americans who were shot or sent to reservations. In the early 1800s, Governor William Henry Harrison of Indiana expressed concern that "a great many of the Inhabitants of the Fronteers [*sic*] consider the murdering of the Indians in the highest degree meritorius" (quoted in Edmunds, 1983:262). As Figure 5.1 demonstrates, the vast majority of Native Americans were killed by 1850.

encouraging land grabs, and in establishing patterns of institutionalized discrimination. For in a society that values equality of opportunity, blatant discrimination had to be justified if it was to be institutionalized.

Institutionalized Discrimination against Native Americans

Legal Discrimination

The early European explorers and settlers described the Native American as innocent, ingenuous, friendly, and naked. In a sense, the Native American was seen as childish—one of the early stereotypes about them (Jarvenpa, 1985). As more European settlers arrived, English concepts of property—land transfer, titles, deeds—were inserted into the relations between the settlers and the natives (Delgado and Stefancic, 1992). It is not surprising to find, then, that much of discrimination against Native Americans was tied very closely to the legalistic legitimation of land grabs by European settlers. The bulk of this discrimination is found in legal documents, especially treaties, that defined the nature of Native Americans' presence and residence on their own land.

The taking of Native American land by whites was also legitimized by the principle of *Manifest Destiny,* in which "European Americans believed that through divine ordination and the natural superiority of the white race, they had a right (and indeed an obligation) to seize and occupy all of North America. . . . During the nineteenth and twentieth centuries, the philosophy of Manifest Destiny was accompanied by several pieces of legislation that accomplished under . . . law that which would not have been legally justifiable through military force" (Morris, 1992:67). Some of the central pieces of legislation that defined the U.S. government's relationship with Native Americans include the following (Churchill and Morris, 1992).

- *The Indian Removal Act (1830).* Andrew Jackson used this act to force the mass relocation of the Creek, Cherokee, Choctaw, Seminole, and other Indian nations during the 1830s. The intent was to open up the territory east of the Mississippi for settlement by white Americans and their African slaves.
- *The Major Crimes Act (1885).* This act allowed the United States to extend its jurisdiction into Native American territories. Since the sovereignty of Native American territories was defined by treaty, this act nullified the treaty's purpose, which had permitted Native Americans to exercise their own jurisdiction within their own territories.
- *The General Allotment Act (1887).* Also known as the "Dawes Act," this act was designed to break up the collective ownership of Indian lands by requiring Indians to identify themselves by means of a "blood quantum" code. Under the act, "full-blood Indians" received the deeds to land parcels over which the U.S. government exercised control for twenty-five years, and "mixed-blood Indians" received "patents in fee simple"—basically land rental agreements—and were forced to accept U.S. citizenship. As a result of the act's implementation, the United States acquired over 100 million acres of Native American land between 1887 and 1934.
- *The Indian Citizenship Act (1924).* This act confers U.S. citizenship on all Native Americans born within the territorial limits of the United States. The act's purpose was to curtail the demand for indigenous identity among Native Americans. To protest, the Hopi and Onondaga refuse to acknowledge the act by issuing their own tribal passports.
- *The Indian Claims Commission Act (1946).* There is some speculation that this act originated, in part, as a response to the role the United States played at the Nuremberg trials. The act was designed to provide legal recourse to those Native Americans who felt that their land was unjustly taken away from them. The act established the Claims Commission, which was responsible for hearing cases brought forward by Native Americans. The commission, however, was not empowered to return land to any Native American; rather, it was required to assign a monetary value to the land in question—"at the time it was taken." As a result, awards given out by the commission tended to be very small. In general, the act gave the United States the tool with which to legitimize its claim to Native American lands.
- *The Relocation Act (1956).* This act created job training centers in urban

areas for Native Americans. The purpose of the act was to force Native Americans off the reservation by offering job training opportunities only in urban areas. Native Americans participating in the job training programs were required to sign formal agreements that they would not return to their reservations.

- *The Alaska Native Claims Settlement Act (1971).* The act removed the sovereign status of the Indian nations in Alaska by incorporating them into the United States. Approximately 44 million acres of Native American lands were turned into U.S. assets. The importance of this act is that the incorporation of Native American lands included the oil beneath and the timber on top.

Treaties were the first step in the colonization of Native Americans. Most of the legal concepts—such as land deeds and land tenure—were foreign to natives, but they accepted treaties as a "good-faith" attempt at coexistence with the whites. Native Americans perceived treaties as a recognition of their sovereignty as Indian nations and assumed that they were on an equal legal footing with the United States. The second step in the colonization of native Americans was congressional legislation, such as the acts reviewed above, which became a tool for displacing Native Americans from their lands (Mcdonnel, 1991; Parker, 1989). Congress's efforts to alter the original treaties with Native American nations were motivated by the white settlers' demands for yet more land. Without their land, Native Americans lost their sovereign status and became a fully colonized population.

All these manipulations of the law increasingly undermined the promises of the 1787 Northwest Ordinance:

> The utmost faith shall always be observed towards the Indians; their land and property shall never be taken from them without their consent; and in their property . . . they shall never be invaded or disturbed . . . ; but laws founded in justice and humanity shall from time to time be made, for preventing wrongs being done to them, and for preserving peace and friendship with them.

Such laws, as it turns out, were used as a tool for doing great wrong.

Political Discrimination

Native Americans were historically caught in an awkward position: The treaties defined each native nation as a "foreign" government, though heavily regulated by the U.S. Congress. Hence, the members of these "Indian nations" could vote and exercise their political rights within their "tribe" and "tribal council," but until 1924 with passage of the Indian Citizenship Act, they could not vote outside their reservation. Even after 1924, when Native Americans could vote, discriminatory practices—literacy tests, poll taxes, informal discrimination, gerrymandering of districts—were used to discourage voting. Thus, Native Americans were excluded from full political participation and from assuming local, state, and national political offices. Coupled with regulation by the Bureau of Indian Affairs (BIA), whose key administrators have traditionally been whites, Native Americans were limited in their ability to determine their fate on the reservations where they could vote. John Collier, for example, Commissioner of Indian Affairs from 1933 to 1945, accused the Bureau of Indian Affairs of despotism rooted in rules and regulations that sought to dispossess Indians from their lands and increase the Indians' impoverishment (Kelly, 1975; Kunitz, 1971).

In recent years, Native Americans have gained more political power. They have increased their numbers at the voting booths and, consequently, in political office—particularly at local levels. Also, the BIA has become less restrictive and more sensitive to the needs and interests of its clients. Yet, the legacy of past discrimination remains today, and its consequences for the Native Americans need to be discussed.

The Political Consequences of Being Conquered "Nations." As we have noted, treaties were utilized to subdue and then dislocate Native Americans from their land—thereby opening up the land to white settlers. By dislocating them from their lands, the federal government removed the basis—land—on which Native Americans could demand political sovereignty (Deloria, 1969; Brown, 1970); with a reduced territorial land base over which they could exercise political power, Native Americans lost power

Box 5.4

What's in a Gravesite?

Obviously, dead bodies are in a gravesite. Only Native Americans, as a conquered people, have had to endure the desecration of their gravesites and the religious-cultural significance of these sites. Let us propose an alternative scenario: A crew of Native American archaeologists arrives at a cemetery in which members of an ethnic group are buried. They lay a grid over the site, and with careful picking, dusting, sorting, and recording, they then empty the gravesite of its bones. These are then carted back to a reservation, where they are stored in large drawers, labeled and numbered, and used for research by Native American scholars who want to know about a particular ethnic group. Perhaps some of the bones are reassembled and put on display; maybe some are dressed up in native costumes and put on display in a reservation museum.

Few non–Native Americans would tolerate such treatment of their ancestors. And yet, many Americans cannot understand why Native Americans are upset at the desecration of their ancestral burial grounds.

In an attempt to prevent further removal of artifacts from Indian burial grounds, the U.S. Congress approved the Native American Graves Protection and Repatriation Act of 1990 (Coughlin, 1994). Two important provisions in the act are (1) museums are required to notify tribal groups of remains for which the tribes may have a claim or cultural link and (2) goods excavated on federal or tribal land belong to the Indian tribal group that claims the goods.

vis-à-vis white Americans. According to Deloria (1992) the concepts embedded in the treaty agreements between Native Americans and the federal government were rooted in the idea of the European ministate. European states would utilize diplomatic relationships, such as treaties, to coexist with other populations within a territory. However, such relationships enabled the stronger, more powerful participant to dominate the weaker, less powerful participant. As a result, the door was open to take land from or to colonize the land of the weaker participant, and as colonization proceeded, less care and concern in negotiations with Native Americans was necessary.

Native Americans entered treaty agreements with the belief that they would be accorded equal political status with the United States and did not perceive treaty agreements as the basis by which an expanding nation, the United States, would usurp their lands. According to Deloria (1992:269), it was Native Americans' misperception of treaty agreements that resulted in their being regarded as "suspect" in the political infrastructure of U.S. society:

> Formal diplomatic relations were established with the various indigenous peoples and international political status was accorded them. The difficulty, however, was one of perception. European mini-states had family relationships with the rulers of larger nations, they were contiguous to the powerful countries of Europe, and they represented long-standing historical traditions going back to the time of original settlement when the barbaric tribes had divided the Roman Empire. Indians could not claim this history and since they were of a different "race," and had different religions, languages, and cultures altogether, their political rights, even when phrased in European terms, were always considered to be intellectually suspect.

Treaties were a blatant expression of political discrimination by the United States against Native Americans. To enhance the political colonization of Native Americans established by treaty, the federal government utilized legislation such as the Major Crimes Act (1885), General Allotment Act (1887), Indian Citizenship Act (1924), and Indian Reorganization Act (1934) to extend its jurisdiction over Native American lands (Williams, 1990). This legislation gave the federal government absolute control over land tenure and the political governance of "Indian nations." Indeed, the federal government increased the role of nonnatives in tribal decision making, and according to Robbins (1992:90), this colonial administration of natives often operates under the guise and illusion of self-determination by tribal councils:

> The current reality is that American Indian governance within the United States has been converted into something very different from that which traditionally prevailed, or anything remotely resembling the exercise of national self-determination. Through the unilateral assertion of U.S. "plenary power" over Indian affairs, a doctrine forcefully articulated in the 1885 *United States v. Kagama* case, the status of indigenous national governments has been subordinated to that of the federal government. . . . Under legislation such as Public Law 280, which emerged during the

> 1950s, the status of Indian nations has been in many cases again unilaterally lowered by the United States, this time to a level below that of the states, placing the indigenous governments affected by the change in approximately the same postures as counties. . . . In sum, it is accurate to observe, as has been noted elsewhere, that American Indian nations within the geography presently claimed by the United States exist in a condition of "internal colonization."

Political Control by the BIA. The BIA was originally housed in the War Department (the precursor to the current Department of Defense), a clear signal that the bureau was designed to control a conquered people. Later, the BIA was moved to the Department of the Interior, but a bureaucratic pattern had already been set. Because Native Americans were a conquered enemy, tight regulation of their internal political affairs could be justified. Only federal prison inmates, and perhaps the Confederacy in the brief period of radical Reconstruction after the Civil War, have experienced this degree of external control by government. Some kind of protective agency like the BIA was perhaps necessary when it was established in 1825, the period when genocide was at its peak. But the consequence of bureaucratic regulation has been much like that of contemporary welfare programs: It created dependency; it undermined Native American culture; it denied its clients self-respect; and it most significantly undermined the capacity for self-governance. Even today, as greater efforts are being made at encouraging self-governance, the colonized status of Native Americans on their reservations thwarts such efforts. In turn, the lack of self-governance and the dependence on the federal government is used to justify continued government intrusion, thereby perpetuating the colonized and dependent status of many Native Americans.

Much of the problem resides in the structure of the BIA itself. As a highly centralized bureaucracy with its central offices located in Washington, D.C., the bureau is too removed from its clients. From this central office, the bureau fans out into area administrative offices, then to around sixty field installations, such as boarding schools and irrigation projects, and finally into several hundred minor installations. Until recently (and even today but less so than in the past) too much authority has resided in Washington and the area offices, which are staffed primarily by nonnatives. The result is that those closest to the problems of Native Americans in the field installations have the least authority and must constantly seek higher approval by nonnative administrators.

In addition to this source of inefficiency and insensitivity to the needs and problems of its clients, the BIA bureaucracy must cope with myriad tribal rules, archaic legislative acts, recent legislation, and judicial precedents when seeking to make important decisions. For example, there are close to 400 treaties, well over 5,000 legislative statutes, hundreds upon hundreds of Interior Department and solicitor rulings, over 600 opinions submitted by the attorney general, around 100 tribal constitutions, almost that many tribal charters, and vast numbers of BIA administrative procedures. With this complex load, decisions are made slowly and given unnecessarily detailed review. Administrators become ritualists who lose sight of the goal of the BIA—to assist Native Americans—and, instead, often view the interests of the BIA and its clients as opposed. The conflict between Native Americans and the BIA is most evident in the area of economic discrimination. The BIA–administered treaties, bureaucracy, and efforts to thwart Native American self-determination have inhibited economic development on the reservations.

Economic Discrimination

One reason European explorers ventured to the New World was to find lands they could exploit. These European explorers assumed that by conquering as many "foreign" lands as possible, the economic power of their country would increase. The settlers that came to what is now the United States also saw land as necessary for establishing their own economic base in their new surroundings. The treaties between the federal government and the Native American nations were a crucial step in colonizing the natives; these treaties, and later acts of Congress, displaced natives from their lands, making these lands accessible to white settlers. As a result, Native Americans became economically colonized—their lands were not under their control to use as an economic tool. For example, Jaimes (1992:127) notes that the manner in which the federal government robbed Native Americans of their economic power could be highly devious:

> In constricting the acknowledged size of Indian populations, the government could technically meet its obligations to receive "first rights" to water usage for Indians while simultaneously siphoning off artificial "surpluses" to non-Indian agricultural, ranching, municipal, and industrial use in the arid west. The same principle pertains to the assignment of fishing quotas in the Pacific Northwest, a matter directly related to the development of a lucrative non-Indian fishing industry there.

The loss of their lands or resources undercut Native Americans' economic infrastructure; they were unable to derive a livelihood from stock raising, herding, and agriculture. For example, in 1940, 58 percent of the Navajo reservation derived a livelihood from raising sheep and farming, but by 1958 the number had dropped to below 10 percent. Speaking for the Native Americans, Winona LaDuke (as quoted in Jaimes, 1992:128–129) states that the denial of livelihood has produced poverty and hopelessness:

> [We] have the lowest per capita income of any population group in the U.S. We have the highest rate of unemployment and the lowest level of educational attainment. We have the highest rates of malnutrition, plague disease, death by exposure and infant mortality. On the other hand, we have the shortest life-span. Now, I think this says it all. Indian wealth is going somewhere, and that somewhere is definitely not to Indians. I don't know your definition of colonialism, but this certainly fits into mine.

Unemployment and dependency on welfare are the results of economic discrimination (Tinker and Bush, 1991; Ainsworth, 1989). According to

Morris (1992:70), what makes the economic condition of Native Americans unique is the amount of political and economic control as well as manipulation exercised by the BIA. The BIA often creates employment opportunities for Native Americans that keep them tied to governments. According to a report prepared by the U.S. Commission on Civil Rights in 1976, on the Navajo reservation, for example, 35 percent of the working-age population was employed year-round, leaving 65 percent of the working-age population unemployed; of the 35 percent, the majority (over 60 percent) was employed in government programs. The unemployed population is likely to depend on federal subsidies (e.g., welfare) for their livelihood, and federal programs employing only a small proportion of Navajo people assure the dependence of a larger proportion on the welfare system. Churchill and LaDuke (1992) argue that this pattern of maintaining Native Americans at a subsistence level has continued through the 1980s and into the 1990s. Indeed, the budgetary cutbacks in social services during the Reagan and Bush administrations threatened even the base subsistence of Native Americans.

One effort to increase the resources available to Native Americans, and in turn to increase their degree of independence, has been to seek agreements with corporations to extract resources from reservation lands in exchange for rents and profit shares. Although the BIA has lead the way in this effort, the economic condition of Native Americans (largely created by past BIA actions) places them in a poor bargaining position. Moreover, the corporations often gain a low-wage labor force and a nonregulated work environment, especially with respect to safety and health codes for workers.

The economic dependence of Native Americans on federal employment programs and social services increases their colonized status in the United States, even when negotiating with private corporations. Native Americans experience economic discrimination that prevents them from utilizing their central asset—land—to become economically self-sufficient. As a consequence, they remain economically dependent on government on the one side and potential victims of predatory practices of economic enterprises on the other.

Educational Discrimination

Education was a key element in efforts to colonize Native Americans. In general, formal education was designed to facilitate submission; it is not surprising, therefore, that the "education" of the Native American population began very early after the arrival of the Europeans. For example, as early as 1611, French Jesuit missionaries established schools along the St. Lawrence River to educate Indians in the French manner (Mulvey, 1936). During the early 1600s, Spanish Jesuits in California developed a system of mission schools that focused on teaching Indians in Spanish as required by the Spanish government (Bishop, 1917). These early educational efforts emphasized "conversion" of the native to European culture and language, with the result that Native American languages and cultures were suppressed. Noriega (1992:373–374) has noted:

> In effect, the system by which Native Americans are purportedly "educated" by Euroamerica has from the onset been little more than a means by which to supplant indigenous cultures. This has had, or at least has been intended to have, the predictable effect of demolishing the internal cohesion of native societies, thereby destroying the ability of these societies to resist conquest and colonization.

The Educational Model. The educational model imposed on Native Americans by Europeans was rooted in the boarding school. Children were required to attend schools away from their homes, where they were rarely permitted to visit their families. The Bureau of Indian Affairs promoted the boarding schools as the best vehicle for assimilating Indian youths into American society (Trennert, 1982). As a result, Indian youths were often removed from their homes at the age of 6 and were not returned to their homes until the schooling was completed around the age of 18. When "educated" Native American children returned home, they had often lost much of their own culture and their place in this culture. As Noriega (1992:381) notes, "Altogether, the whole procedure conforms to one of the criteria—the forced transfer of children from a targeted racial, ethnic, national, or religious group to be reared and absorbed by a physically dominating group—specified as a Crime Against Humanity under the United Nations 1948 Convention on Punishment and Prevention of the Crime of Genocide."

Native American families attempted to prevent the dislocation of their children by hiding them from education authorities. Lummins (1968) documents efforts by the Hopi to prevent Mormon missionaries from sending their children to the Intermountain School in Utah. After Hopi parents refused to hand their children over to the Mormon missionaries, federal troops were called in to round up the children. The Hopi greeted the troops by showering them with rocks. The troops subdued the Hopi, rounded up the majority of their children, and sent them to a boarding school in Utah. One result of the Mormon missionaries' involvement in Indian education was the fracturing of the Hopi into two factions—*Mormon Hopi* and *traditional Hopi* (Titiev, 1944; Thompson and Joseph, 1944).

Higher Education. While boarding schools were designed to dislocate native youths from their tribes and families, higher education focused on two concerns: (1) vocational training rather than advanced academic studies and (2) the mainstreaming of Native Americans into white society (Wright and Tierney, 1991). Despite the efforts of Dartmouth and Harvard to educate select Native American students, tribal resistance to higher education was widespread. Historically, Native American tribes have regarded the higher education of their youths as a last step in their isolation from the tribe. For example, the Six Nations' response to an invitation from the College of William and Mary in 1744 to send their sons to the college was (as quoted in Wright and Tierney, 1991:13) the following:

> We love our children too well to send them so great a Way, and the Indians are not inclined to give their Children learning. We allow it to be good, and we thank you for your Invitation; but our customs differing from yours, you will be so good as to excuse us.

The Indian Reorganization Act of 1934 was the U.S. government's first step in shaping higher education policy for Native Americans. Until then, religious missionaries and charities had initiated efforts in this area. The Indian Reorganization Act of 1934 attempted to increase Indian participation in higher education by establishing loan and scholarship programs, but students remained reluctant to pursue a higher education because they regarded college as a hostile and alienating environment.

It was not until the 1970s that Native Americans were able to address the issue of tribal colleges. The Indian Self-Determination and Education Assistance Act of 1975 and the Tribally Controlled Community College Assistance Act of 1978 were instrumental in shifting control of higher education from the federal government to the tribes. Native Americans could now develop a higher education system that was neither paternalistic nor assimilationist in its goals. As a result, there are now twenty-four tribally controlled colleges in eleven western and midwestern states (Wright and Tierney, 1991). Together, these institutions service about ten thousand students and enroll about four thousand five hundred students on a full-time basis. However, these colleges are dependent on the U.S. federal government for their financial existence. It may be that higher education for Native Americans may not survive as long as it is dependent on a government that has a history of ignoring the cultural and social rights of the tribes. As Wright and Tierney (1991:17) have observed:

> Because Indian students most often live in economically poor communities, tuition is low and local tax dollars do not offer much assistance. Congress has authorized up to $6,000 per student, but, in reality, the amount released to the colleges decreased throughout the Reagan era so that by 1989 the amount generated for each student was only $1,900. . . . One would think that if the government was serious about increasing opportunities for Indian youth, then colleges would be provided the funds necessary to aid those youth.

The history of formal education for Native Americans has been marked by deprivation of their cultural, linguistic, and social identity. Boarding schools were developed with a paternalistic goal—to civilize the "savages" by having them trade in their moccasins for shoes, their language for English, and their cultural beliefs for traditional western religion (Bartelt, 1992). Overall, higher education has not created the same opportunities for self-fulfillment and advancement available to white Americans or other minority groups.

STRATIFICATION OF NATIVE AMERICANS

By almost any indicator—median income, years of schooling, job classification, housing, medical care, life expectancy—Native Americans are at or near the bottom of the resource-distribution system. Their socioeconomic position is perpetuated by the reservation system: Native Americans are isolated from the broader society in the government's effort to maintain bureaucratic control and in their own attempt to preserve what is left of their indigenous cultures. Coupled with the fact that much of their land (which could serve as an economic base for mobility within and between Native American and non–Native American class systems) has been lost, the prospect for economic development on reservations is uncertain. Those nations located on land rich in natural resources have some hope if they can secure capital and avoid nonexploitive relations with both the government and the private sector.

The impoverishment of the Native American population emerged and persisted because of the dynamic processes outlined in Chapter 2 (see especially Figure 2.2). Native Americans were readily identifiable because of their cultural and organizational distinctiveness, and they have historically posed threats to white Americans, many of whom saw them as potentially inhibiting the growth and expansion of society (Russell, 1994). As a result, a range of negative beliefs—from "the savage" to "the fat cat"—has legitimized discriminatory practices: attempted genocide under the guise of war, continued acts of violence and murder, isolation on reservations, land grabbing, denial of voting rights, removal from traditional lands to new and unfamiliar reservations, efforts to force Native Americans to conform to European culture, stealing of mineral and resource rights, and rigid bureaucratic control by agencies of the federal government. All these forces sustained the identifiability of Native Americans while denying them resources. The result was the creation of not only a colonized population but also an ethnic caste.

To break this cycle of discrimination, individual Native Americans face difficult choices: to stay on impoverished reservations and try to preserve what is left of their culture or to enter a Eurocentric society that is not prepared to facilitate their upward mobility. In either case, the majority of Native Americans will remain isolated in either the lower socioeconomic stratum of mainstream society or the impoverished reservation system.

RESPONDING TO DISCRIMINATION

War As a Nonviable Response

The initial response of Native Americans to the European invasion of their homelands appears, on balance, to have been one of cooperation and accommodation, punctuated by acts of violence. As it became evident to Native Americans that their territories were to be occupied and that they were to be displaced, more conflict occurred. Given their numerical and technological disadvantage, however, war was not a viable response for the Native Americans. Indeed, war led to near extinction. By 1871, the remaining Native Americans and their nations had been conquered, moved to reservations, and made wards of the federal government.

Retreatism As Another Nonviable Response

One response of colonized populations is to mount retreatist social movements in the belief that supernatural powers will intervene and return the people to some idealized era. Among Native Americans such *millenarian movements* occurred frequently in the latter part of the nineteenth century and remain in some form to this day.

The most famous millenarian movement occurred in the 1870s among the Great Plains natives in *Ghost Dance groups* who were responding to a vision that Native Americans would return on a train in great numbers just as the earth swallowed up all white people. When this did not occur, the movement died down, but a decade later, a new Ghost Dance vision stimulated another movement. Although these movements did not persist, they initiated some cooperation among tribes, an initiative that would have increasing significance.

As the Ghost Dance movement receded, *peyotism* spread through the Great Plains. A mild hallucinogen, peyote gave religious ceremonies a new power because of the experiences induced. This movement sought to develop an intertribal religion, mixing some elements of Christianity and Mormonism that had been forced upon them with holdovers from their own religions. This movement was assailed, especially because drugs were involved; nonetheless, under the constitutional protection of religious freedom, it became organized as the Native American Church in 1918 and affiliated with Christian groups (Price, 1978). Over the decades, Native American criticism of Christianity has mounted, but membership continues to increase. The Native American Church was the first successful effort at *pan-Indianism,* the unification of Native American nations for explicitly political purposes (Stewart, 1987).

Pan-Indianism

In a sense, the Ghost Dance groups represented pan-Indianism; the peyote sacrament evolved into the Native American Church, which has taken on explicitly political goals. The Iroquois Confederation represented an earlier version of pan-Indianism but was confined to the Iroquois, as were a number of similar confederations dating back to the time of the first contact with Europeans.

It was only after decades of BIA domination that Native Americans began to unite in significant numbers (Snipp, 1986). The National Congress of American Indians (NCAI) was the first truly nationwide organization to represent Native Americans and to engage in active lobbying in Washington (much as the NAACP and Urban League have done for African Americans). This organization has had numerous successes in overcoming restrictive laws and abusive bureaucratic practices by the BIA. Perhaps its greatest accomplishment was to establish the Indians Claims Commission, which has been active and successful in returning land to Native Americans and in remunerating Native Americans for past abuses.

The American Indian Movement (AIM) represents a more radical movement to organize Native American nations to pursue political goals, a movement dominated by Plains tribes. The founders, Clyde Bellecourt and Dennis Banks, began by using both confrontational tactics—such as patrols to monitor the police—and more subtle strategies such as alcohol rehabilitation and school reform. The AIM is best known for its confrontations with the federal government and the BIA. *Fish-ins* to protest government interference with traditional Native American fishing areas, seizing Alcatraz Island in the San Francisco Bay in 1969, and the Wounded Knee confrontation brought considerable media notoriety to the AIM and, perhaps even more importantly, sensitized many white Americans to the plight of the descendants of the first Americans (Eagle, 1992).

Under President Nixon in the 1970s, some progress was made in addressing Native American grievances. But the intensity of confrontation has not diminished; indeed, it has intensified because of the accurate perception that the progress of the 1970s has waned in the 1990s and that the government relies on conservative tribal leaders' judgments in making policies. Moreover, infighting among factions of Native American militants has escalated the violence, as has the perception that a civil rights movement much like that among African Americans could be more successful (Schaefer, 1990:196). Yet, the influence of the AIM appears to be waning, and a new point of conflict has emerged: control and development of the resources on and under Native American land.

The Economic Battle

In 1975, the Council of Energy Resource Tribes (CERT) was formed, with the goal of forming an OPEC-like cartel to coordinate the development of, and perhaps manipulate the market for, the resources on reservation land. Vast reserves of oil and other key resources are located on Native American lands. Yet, the effort to develop and control these resources has not been highly successful. A few notable exceptions can be found, but CERT has threatened many people and mobilized large mineral and energy companies in ways that may be counterproductive to Native American economic advancement, although the long-term efforts of CERT may prove otherwise.

Other economic development programs are based on the special status of reservation lands as sovereign nations—albeit easily invaded and highly

Sioux Indians briefly occupied Alcatraz Island in 1969, planting a flag asserting their rights given them in 1868 (to claim "unoccupied government land"). U.S. Marshals were quick to deny them this right.

regulated nations. The use of reservations for gambling has increased over the last decade; the shift from bingo and card parlors to much more sophisticated gaming resorts has been financed and managed by hotel and gambling interests from nonreservation locations, such as Las Vegas and Atlantic City. These new kinds of enterprises provide employment and cash flow for tribes, but they rarely lead to independence from outside economic interests, who take the lion's share of profits and who maintain management control of the hotels and casinos. Moreover, gambling invites further government regulation in an effort to avoid the infiltration of organized crime and other illegal activities.

Thus, through organized protest, punctuated by sporadic violence, Native Americans have significantly reduced the government's abusive practices. Yet a basic dilemma remains: Much of Native American culture is gone, and yet assimilation into the Eurocentric mainstream is difficult and, for many, undesirable. If economic development, self-governance, and increased prosperity are to be achieved on the reservation, then new cultural traditions, new sources of start-up capital, and new relations with government and industry will have to be created. Pan-Indian organization, effective lobbying, and strategic protests offer the best hope for the future.

SUMMARY

Long before Europeans discovered the Americas, earlier immigrants from Asia had settled and established viable societies. These societies were, however, comparatively simple; though they had existed for thousands of years, they were no match for the Europeans who by 1850 had virtually eliminated the native populations of the Americas. The conquest of "American Indians" and their subsequent confinement to reservations has left a legacy of discrimination rivaled only by the treatment of African Americans, who were imported as slaves. In terms of income, access to jobs, educational attainment, rates of poverty, standards of housing, and life span, the original Americans rank at the bottom on almost all shares of valued resources in the society.

This situation has been sustained by the identifiability of Native Americans and the embellishment of "distinctiveness" by the government's emphasis on "blood" and other biological features (rather minor ones). Such identifiability has been accompanied by highly unfavorable stereotypes of Native Americans as savages, cigar store Indians, fodder for killing by "noble" cowboys, reservation drunks, fat cat capitalists, and many other vicious stereotypes. Only recently have these stereotypes been mitigated by more favorable portrayals of Native Americans, and yet, they still must endure the disrespect of being used as athletic team mascots and victims of archaeological assaults—facts which indicate that the more recent media images are only superficial improvements. Identifiability of Native Americans was encouraged by a system of government categories and policies. This system, along with negative stereotyping, has legitimized discrimination in treaty agreements that have been routinely violated by Anglos, in policies and practices by the Bureau of Indian Affairs, in political discrimination in voting, in the interpretation of citizenship rights of the first Americans, in the loss of ownership of much of their lands and the economic potential of these lands, in job discrimination, and in educational discrimination from inferior schools on and off the reservation. By any indicator of well-being, Native Americans are worse off than any other ethnic population in America because of discrimination.

Native Americans have fought this discrimination, first by unsuccessful wars, then by retreatism in the face of their conquest, and now by active movements to foster a pan-Indian culture. The call of pan-Indianism engages Native Americans in political and legal protest and, most importantly, develops administrators who can, perhaps, enhance the potential wealth of the remaining native lands.

POINTS OF DEBATE

Many Americans see the conquest of the native population as an outcome of war, fought fair and square. Yet no other population conquered by the Anglo-Saxon core has had to endure the discrimination experienced by Native Americans. Indeed, in this century, efforts have been made to help rebuild the conquered nations around the world and to establish friendly and mutually beneficial relations with their inhabitants. Such has not been the case for American Indians who were displaced from their land, confined to reservations, regulated by government, and cheated at almost every turn by both government and large-scale economic enterprises. The legacy of this treatment of America's true natives now raises important points of debate.

1. Should the lands, or at least portions of them, that were taken in violation of treaties be given back to the Native Americans, or should they be compensated for the loss of their most valuable asset? Most white Americans are against any such effort; but in a society that values the principle of justice within the rule of law and order, should not past violations of the law be redressed in some way?
2. Should Native Americans be encouraged to enter the mainstream of the society or stay somewhat isolated on the reservations, preserving what is left of their cultures? To do the former would require enormous expenditures in creating new educational and job opportunities, whereas the latter, without subsidizing the economic development of the reservations, would perpetuate the current situation. How can either policy mitigate white Americans' resistance to public expenditures for welfare or their increasing fear of the development of Native American lands? Even more recent use of lands for gambling, which whites and other ethnics use and enjoy, generates protest from adjacent communities who fear a change in their lifestyle. Is such protest legitimate in light of the lifestyle adjustments forced on the first Americans over the last two centuries?
3. Is it time to dismantle the Bureau of Indian Affairs and allow Native Americans to go their own way? Or is the bureau necessary to protect Native Americans from predatory practices and to facilitate economic development? Or, is some other form of government assistance needed, a form not so rooted in past patterns of exploitation?

CHAPTER 6

Latinos

As the dominant Anglo-Saxon ethnic stock maintained the enslavement of African Americans and continued the conquest of the Native Americans, a new point of ethnic conflict emerged in the middle of the last century. This conflict was perhaps inevitable in light of the fact that Anglo-Saxon America was surrounded on its southern and western borders by Spanish-speaking populations. The Spanish had exerted their influence on the southern portions of the northern hemisphere, Central and South America, as well as the island populations off the shores of Florida and the Deep South. Inevitably the two cultures would clash—a clash that revolves around the uneasy relations between the Anglo-Saxon core and various white ethnic groups from other European societies, on one side, and Latinos, on the other.

The term "Latino" does not denote a unified ethnic population (Jones-Correa and Leal, 1996; Portes and MacLeod, 1996). While the Latino population in the United States consists of three major groups—Mexicans, Puerto Ricans, and Cubans—it also incorporates immigrants from Central and South America who have arrived in noticeable numbers during the past two decades (Munoz, 1989; Jaffe and Boswell, 1980). Mexican Americans make up 64 percent of all Latinos; Puerto Ricans and Cubans together constitute 16 percent (U.S. Bureau of the Census, 1994). The remaining Latino population is made up of persons from diverse societies in Central and South America that immigrated to the United States, primarily in response to political upheavals (Portes, 1990; Rodriguez, 1987). Persons from Central America, however, do not constitute a clearly defined and noticeable ethnic subpopulation in the same way as do persons from Mexico, Puerto Rico, and Cuba. This chapter, thus, concentrates on these latter three subpopulations, which constitute about 85 percent of all Latinos in the United States.

RESOURCE SHARES OF LATINOS

Poverty Levels of Latinos

As can be seen in Table 6.1, the poverty rate for Mexican Americans and Puerto Ricans is more than twice that of non-Latinos, while the poverty rate for Cuban Americans is slightly higher than the rate for non-Latinos. Most Mexican American (46 percent) and Puerto Rican families (60 percent) living below the poverty level are headed by females; and a noticeable number of Mexican American (37 percent) and Puerto Rican (48 percent) families in poverty are headed by a non-high school graduate. By contrast, 24 percent of non-Latino white families are headed by women, and 16 percent of poor non-Latino white families are headed by a non-high school graduate (U.S. Bureau of the Census, 1994).

Income of Latinos

The median income of all Latino families is below that of non-Latino families (see Table 6.2). Mexican American families currently earn about 61 percent, Puerto Rican families about 57 percent, and Cuban American families about 87 percent of the median income for non-Latinos. The income gap between Cuban American and non-Latino families is smaller than for either Mexican Americans or Puerto Ricans. Interestingly, Mexican American families earned 70 percent and Puerto Rican families earned 66 percent of the Cuban American median family income in 1994. Table 6.3 shows that the earnings of both Latino males and females are below those of non-Latinos. While Latino income decreased as a proportion of non-Latino income between 1983 and 1993, the decrease is much more noticeable for Latinas.

Occupational Distribution of Latinos

Table 6.4 shows that relatively more persons in the non-Latino population (29 percent) and in the Cuban American population (22 percent) work in

TABLE 6.1. Poverty Rates for Latinos

	Population Living in Poverty, %			
Year	Non-Latino	Mexican American	Puerto Rican	Cuban American
1994	13.5	31.8	38.7	19.9
1990	9.2	27.7	30.4	12.5
1980	6.3	21.4	33.4	11.2
1970	7.8	26.8	28.2	13.1

Source: U.S. Bureau of the Census, 1973a, 1983a, 1991b; March 1994 CPS.

Box 6.1

The Latino Marketplace

The Latino marketplace is booming! While some sectors of the U.S. marketplace may be shrinking, the growth of Latino-owned businesses is expanding in the United States. Between 1987 and 1992 the number of Latino-owned businesses increased 76 percent, from 489,973 in 1987 to 862,605 in 1992. During the same period, U.S. firms increased 26 percent, from 13.7 to 17.3 million. Receipts for Latino-owned businesses increased by 134 percent between 1987 and 1992, from $32.8 to $76.8 billion. In contrast, receipts for all U.S. firms increased 67 percent during the same time period, from $2 to $3.3 trillion.

In 1995, Latino purchasing power stood at about $220 billion. One can observe from the statistics below that Los Angeles had the largest number of Latino-owned businesses and the highest index of Latino purchasing power. However, Miami accounted for a larger share of the 1995 revenue for Latino-based businesses.

Top Five Latino Markets

	Total	Los Angeles	San Antonio	Chicago	New York	Miami
1995 Latino population	28,410,000	5,781,949	694,909	1,016,079	4,288,857	1,284,612
1995 Latino purchasing power	$220.30 b*	$48.47 b	$8.15 b	$8.37 b	$28.67 b	$13.22 b
1995 Latino TV media expenditures	$517.1 m†	$109.17 m	$11.75 m	$21.50 m	$45.28 m	$56.00 m
1995 Latino radio media expenditures	$321.2 m	$74.17 m	$15.06 m	$17.50 m	$32.25 m	$50.66 m
1995 Latino print media expenditures	$142.5 m	$55.12 m	$4.37 m	$11.71 m	$22.45 m	$22.75 m
1995 Latino-owned businesses	1,211,144	159,275	28,242	25,073	55,126	107,212
1995 Revenue of Latino-owned businesses	$127.95 b	$14.02 b	$3.01 b	$3.64 b	$6.63 b	$20.85 b

* In billions of dollars.

† In millions of dollars.

Source: www.hispanstar.com.

TABLE 6.2. Latino Income as a Percentage of Non-Latino Income

Year	Mexican American, %	Puerto Rican, %	Cuban American, %
1994	61	57	87
1990	63	57	89
1980	67	64	80
1970	69	70	83

Source: U.S. Bureau of the Census, 1973a, 1983a, 1983b, 1991b; March 1994 CPS.

managerial and professional occupations, whereas 11 percent of Mexican Americans and 19 percent of Puerto Ricans have these jobs. A noticeable number of Mexican American workers (33 percent) are farmers and laborers; 19 percent of Puerto Ricans hold such positions; and 20 percent of Cuban Americans have these jobs—a figure that approaches the 24 percent for all non-Latinos. This occupational distribution offers some insight into the reasons for differences in median earnings among the three Latino groups. The concentration of Cuban American persons in managerial, professional, technical, and sales occupations versus the percentage of Mexican Americans and Puerto Ricans in service, production, and laborer occupations accounts for the disparity in earnings among Latino populations. Managerial, professional, and technical occupations are associated with higher pay, more job security, and better fringe benefits than are service, production, and labor occupations.

Educational Attainment of Latinos

Table 6.5 shows that the levels of education attained by Latinos are below those attained by all non-Latinos, a fact that places Latinos at an enormous disadvantage in a credential-oriented society. The education levels attained by Mexican Americans and Puerto Ricans are lower than those attained by

TABLE 6.3. Latino Income Differentials Relative to Non-Latino Income

		Latinos	
Year	Total Latino Population*	Males†	Females‡
1993	0.62	0.63	0.77
1988	0.64	0.61	0.80
1983	0.67	0.67	0.91

*Latino income as a proportion of non-Latino income.
†Latino male income as a proportion of non-Latino *male* income.
‡Latino female income as a proportion of non-Latino *female* income.
Source: U.S. Bureau of the Census, 1994.

TABLE 6.4. Occupational Distribution among the Latino Population, 1994 through 1970*

	Non-Latino, %				*Mexican American, %*				*Puerto Rican, %*				*Cuban American, %*			
Occupation	1994	1990	1980	1970	1994	1990	1980	1970	1994	1990	1980	1970	1994	1990	1980	1970
Professionals, managers	28.9	27.3	26.4	25.4	10.9	11.3	14.2	10.2	18.5	17.1	16.6	15.6	21.7	24.0	22.6	23.4
Clerical workers, salespeople, craftspeople	31.2	33.2	39.7	40.2	22.7	25.3	36.9	30.4	31.5	31.4	45.3	47.8	33.1	33.9	45.3	45.2
Operatives, service workers	23.9	23.8	27.2	28.5	33.9	31.7	37.7	42.2	31.1	31.8	32.2	30.3	25.4	25.8	25.7	24.3
Farmers, laborers	15.8	15.7	6.7	5.9	32.5	31.7	11.2	17.2	18.9	19.7	5.9	6.3	19.8	16.3	6.4	7.1

*Persons 16 years and older.

Source: U.S. Bureau of the Census, 1973a, 1983a, 1983b, 1991b; March 1994 CPS.

TABLE 6.5. Levels of Education Attained by Latinos and Non-Latinos*

	High School, %†				*College, %*‡			
Year	Non-Latino	Mexican American	Puerto Rican	Cuban American	Non-Latino	Mexican American	Puerto Rican	Cuban American
1994	83.4	46.7	59.4	64.1	23.4	6.3	9.8	16.2
1990	79.6	44.1	55.5	63.5	22.2	5.4	9.7	20.2
1980	69.6	38.1	45.9	34.6	17.4	4.9	5.6	12.2
1970	62.6	33.3	43.8	33.4	14.1	4.3	3.4	12.6

*Persons 25 years old and older with high school and college degrees.

†Four years or more of high school.

‡Four years or more of college.

Source: U.S. Bureau of the Census, 1973a, 1983a, 1983b, 1991b; March 1994 CPS.

Cuban Americans; most notably, the majority of Mexican Americans have not completed four years of high school. On the college level, the number of Mexican American students who have completed four years is less than the number of Puerto Rican college graduates and slightly less than one-third the number of Cuban American college graduates. In general, between 1970 and 1994, Cuban Americans and Puerto Ricans made larger educational gains than Mexican Americans, although all three Latino populations lag significantly behind non-Latinos.

Life Span of Latinos

Life expectancy statistics show discrepancies between the Latino and non-Latino populations. In 1988, only 58 percent of Mexican American mothers, 63 percent of Puerto Rican mothers, and 83 percent of Cuban American mothers, compared with 80 percent of white non-Latino mothers, received prenatal care (National Center for Health Statistics, 1991). Puerto Rican mothers are more likely (9.4 percent) to give birth to infants with low birth weight than Mexican American (5.6 percent), Cuban American (6.0 percent), or white non-Latino mothers (5.3 percent). Cuban Americans have the lowest mortality rate (7.3 percent) compared to Mexican Americans (8.7 percent), Puerto Ricans (12.5 percent), and the white non-Latino population (8.8 percent).

Death rates for the Latino population are little studied because death certificates identify "race" rather than ethnicity (Becerra et al., 1991). Still, an analysis of Latino death rates by the National Center for Health Statistics (1991) found that: (1) The leading cause of death for both Latino and white American children 1 to 14 years of age was unintentional injury (for example, fires, drowning, motor vehicle injury); however, approximately 20 percent of Latino children aged 1 to 14 were the victims of homicide, compared to 5 percent of white children. (2) The leading cause of death for Latino and white young adults aged 15 to 24 was unintentional injury, but homicide accounted for 25 percent of Latino deaths, compared to 4 percent of deaths among white Americans. In contrast, suicide accounted for 12 percent of deaths among young white adults, and 4 percent among Latinos in this age category. (3) In Latino and white cohorts aged 25 to 44, heart disease was the leading cause of death. The AIDS virus was the second leading cause of death for Latinos and the fifth leading cause of death for the white population. (4) The leading cause of death among both the Latino and white populations 45 years of age and older was heart disease.

What are the reasons for the discrepancies in life expectancy between these two populations? One reason is limited access to health care. The higher incidence of low birth weight among newborn Latino children reflects two aspects of the health care delivery system: the limited availability of affordable health care in general and prenatal care in particular (Ginzberg, 1991) and the lack of affordable health care coverage for the Latino population (Treviño et al., 1991). These limitations prevent most

Latina mothers from obtaining neonatal services until the eighth or ninth month of pregnancy, when they can then utilize health care services available through social welfare programs. Less neonatal care translates into greater risks for infants.

Another reason for shorter life expectancy is violence (Martinez, 1996). The large proportion of deaths due to homicide among Latinos in the 1 to 14 and 14 to 25 age ranges reflects the risk of living in areas with high crime rates and the presence of gang violence. For example, Latino youth are four times more likely than white youth to be the victims of gang violence (U.S. Department of Justice, 1991b and c). Latino youth are also more likely than white youth to feel unsafe or threatened while attending school (U.S. Department of Justice, 1995).

Housing of Latinos

Housing segregation limits opportunities by confining an ethnic group to areas where jobs, education, health care, and security are less available (Santiago and Wilder, 1991). Thus, minority ethnics not living among the dominant groups in a society will have reduced access to resources (Palm, 1985; Lopez, 1986). In their study of the Latino population in the United States, Bean and Tienda (1987) recorded the following patterns of residential segregation: (1) Puerto Ricans living in the New York City area are highly segregated residentially. This segregation pattern is based largely on racism. Since some Puerto Ricans are of African heritage, they are more likely to be relegated close to African American neighborhoods, which tend to be isolated from white American neighborhoods. (2) Mexican Americans in the Los Angeles area experience less residential segregation than Puerto Ricans in New York City. Since Mexican Americans constitute 22 percent of the Los Angeles area's population (and Latinos, in general, an even greater percentage), their large numbers increase the probability of contact in residential areas. (3) Compared with Puerto Ricans and Mexican Americans, Cuban Americans in the Miami area experience the lowest level of residential segregation and the highest rate of contact with the white population. Bean and Tienda (1987:177) concluded that the consequences of Latino segregation

> are uncertain, but probably depend on the extent to which it is voluntary or involuntary. In this regard, Puerto Ricans are clearly at greatest risk of being denied equal access to spatially determined resources like education, health, security, and employment.

In sum, then, Latinos have less access to valued resources—income, education, health care, and housing—than white Americans, although degrees of access to these resources vary among the three Latino groups (Aponte, 1991). Cuban Americans clearly have more access than either Puerto Ricans or Mexican Americans; and Mexican Americans have the least access of the three groups, despite the fact that they are less residentially segre-

Box 6.2

Latino Children at Risk

According to the National Coalition of Hispanic Health and Human Services Organization (COSSMHD), Latino children are the second largest group of children in the United States after non-Latino white children. The majority (90 percent) of the increase in the number of Latino children is the result of fertility and legal immigration. However, as the number of Latino children has increased, so has their risk of becoming victims in U.S. society. For example:

- 33 percent of Latino children are uninsured compared to only 12 percent of white children.
- 39 percent of Latino children live in poverty compared to only 16 percent of white children.
- The rate of Down's syndrome per 100,000 births is 12 percent for Latino children compared to only 8 percent for white children.

Growing population

Number of children by racial, ethnic group, in millions:

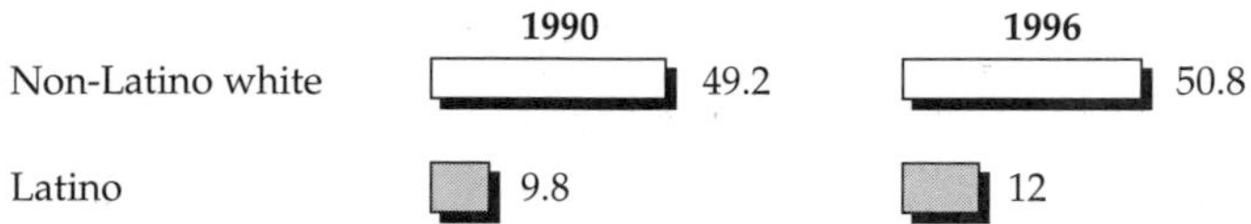

	More are uninsured . . . Percent of school-aged children without health insurance, by ethnicity:	**. . . and poor** Poverty rate for children:	**More are dropouts** Dropout rate for twelfth graders:
Latino	30%	39%	18%
White	13%	16%	9%

Most nonimmigrant
U.S. 1990 Latino population by immigrant status:

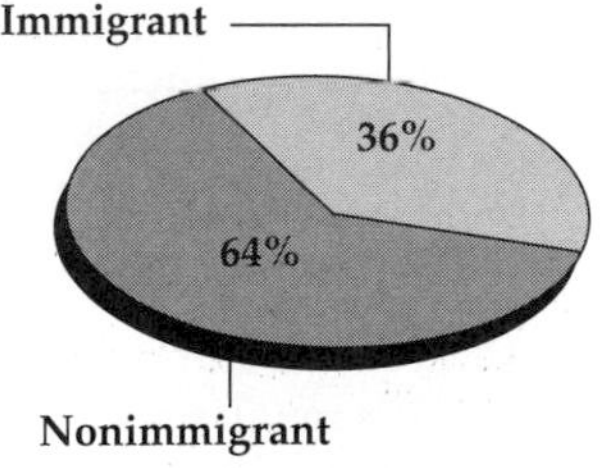

Fewer in Head Start
Percent of children enrolled:

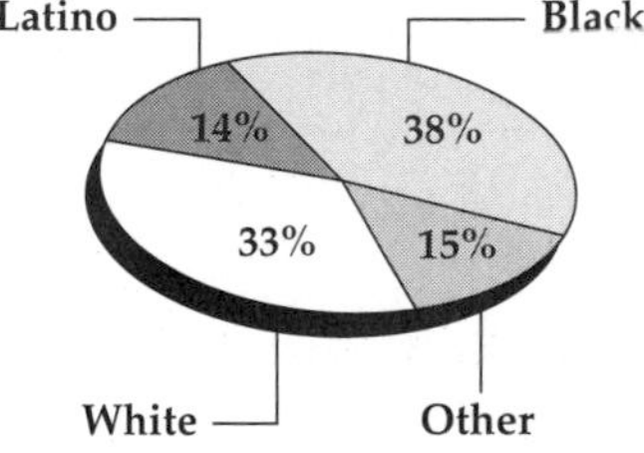

Source: National Coalition of Hispanic Health and Human Services Organizations, 1996.

gated than Puerto Ricans. Let us now examine in more detail each of these three populations, in order to understand the specific forces that have determined their respective resource shares.

MEXICAN AMERICANS

Identifiability of Chicanos

Language and culture have set those of Mexican origin apart from mainstream society. The proximity of Mexico to the United States, coupled with frequent contact across the 2,000-mile border, has preserved the Spanish language as a prominent feature of social intercourse between the two cultures (Aguirre, 1980, 1984, 1988). Unlike many European immigrants who cut their ties with their homelands, Mexican Americans, or Chicanos, have had less incentive to abandon their native culture (Langley, 1988). Indeed, early Mexican American settlers regarded the Southwest as *their* homeland until the Anglo-Saxons invaded and made it part of the United States.

Box 6.3

The Identifiability of Latinos

In his book *Latinos: A Biography of the People* (1992), Earl Shorris examines the Latino experience in the United States by asking Latinos and Latinas to discuss issues of ethnic identification and survival in the United States. Regarding ethnic identification, Shorris documents the manner in which Latinos perceive themselves and other Latinos. For example:

> Raymond del Portillo, who headed up San Francisco's initial effort at bilingual education, is the son of a Cuban father and a Mexican mother. . . . From his unique viewpoint del Portillo offers these observations about the cultural extremes of the three nationalities. "Cubans," he said, "are aggressive, assertive, and sometimes appallingly arrogant. There is a steadfastness and loyalty among Mexican Americans, but their docility is sometimes disappointing. And the feistiness of the Puerto Rican is understandable. They're tough, very tough, either because of life on the island or prejudice in New York, they're tough, but not bitter." (p. 63)

Leobardo Estrada, a demographer at UCLA whose work takes him to every Latino community in the country, says that a visitor must prove himself in different fashion for each group. For the Cubans, the litmus test is language: One must not only speak Spanish, but speak the language well, with a vocabulary of synonyms and the ability to use arcane verb forms. Puerto Ricans judge a person by his or her familiarity with the island; one must know not only the cities but the towns and villages as well. To establish oneself with Mexican Americans, it is necessary only to be a professor, so great is the reverence for education in the Mejicano and Mexican American culture (p. 63).

The maintenance of language and other features of Mexican culture have served to segregate Mexican Americans, perpetuating incentives to marry within the Latino population and to sustain traditional behavioral and social patterns (such as birth rates and family structure). Many Mexican Americans speak Spanish or speak English with an accent, have slightly darker skin than most Americans of European descent, and are overrepresented in certain occupations (see Table 6.4). Taken together, these differences create a relatively high degree of identifiability which, historically and currently, is the basis for discrimination. To understand the dynamics of this discrimination, as well as the sense of threat and prejudicial beliefs that sustain such discrimination, we need to review briefly the history of the Mexican American population. This overview tells the story of a population of conquered people (similar to Native Americans), imported menial labor (similar to African Americans, but without the extremes of slavery), and generally unwanted and illegal immigrants.

The History of Mexican Americans: Conquest, Displacement, and Exploitation

Early History: The Conquest

By 1602, a handful of Spaniards had explored most of the southwest borderlands—from Galveston to San Diego, from Sonora to Santa Fe, and from the west coast of Mexico to Monterey. In time, the Spanish settlements in the Southwest came to consist of a fairly rooted colony in New Mexico, an easily held and fairly prosperous chain of missions in coastal California, and a number of imperiled settlements in Texas and Arizona. By 1790, the population of the Southwest, estimated at 23,000, was almost entirely Spanish-speaking (American Council of Learned Societies, 1932).

The presence of a large Spanish-speaking population in the Southwest facilitated, to a degree, the adjustment of the incoming Anglo-Saxons because they could adopt much of what was useful. For example, Spanish and Native American words were incorporated into the English vocabulary, and styles of architecture found in the Southwest—the one-story ranch house and buildings with tiled roofs, adobe walls, patios, and verandas—were adopted (Hernandez-Chavez et al., 1975).

Between the Battle of San Jacinto in 1836 and the Gadsen Purchase of 1853, the United States came to acquire most of the Southwest. A significant event in Mexican American history was the Treaty of Guadalupe Hidalgo in 1848, which concluded the war between the United States and Mexico (Estrada et al., 1988; Hietala, 1985). This treaty guaranteed to all Mexicans living in the "new" American territory a number of basic rights: full American citizenship, retention of Spanish as a recognized and legitimate language, political liberty, and ownership of property. The treaty was rarely enforced, however, which opened the door to social and political exploitation.

Despite the guarantees of the Treaty of Guadalupe Hidalgo, the Anglo-Saxons assumed the right to impose the English language on all the inhabitants of the Southwest (Villareal, 1988). Laws were written in English, leaving Spanish speakers ignorant of the law, especially laws protecting their property; Spanish was not used in the courts; and school instruction in Spanish was forbidden. As a result, Mexicans were at a disadvantage in protecting their property, in seeking redress through the courts, and in acquiring an equal education. Mexicans living in the Southwest soon became the objects of prejudice (Pitt, 1966).

For Mexican Americans, the period leading into the early nineteenth century involved loss of land, social status, culture, and language. This group became a minority in the United States by being conquered (Acuña, 1981), and as the Anglo-Saxon population settled in the Southwest, and as control of the Southwest borderlands passed into their hands, Mexican Americans became an ever more subordinate ethnic minority.

After 1848, when the Anglo-Saxon population opened the Southwest for expansion, major economic transformations ensued. The loss of social, political, and economic status relegated Mexican Americans to a source of cheap labor. Hence, the major thrust of Anglo-Saxon economic development of the Southwest was in labor-intensive industries—agriculture, mining, and railroads (Barrera, 1979). As this development increased, more people from south of the border immigrated to U.S. territory. For example, between 1890 and 1900 the Mexican-origin population in the Southwest grew from about seventy-five thousand to over half a million (McWilliams, 1968).

The arrival of large numbers of Mexican immigrants threatened the precarious socioeconomic status of those already living in the Southwest. Since the majority of immigrants from Mexico were illiterate and poor, they were willing to accept the lowest wages; as a consequence, the white American population tended to regard all Mexicans, including ancestors of the original land holders in the Southwest, as "cheap labor." Indigenous Mexican Americans were perceived by the Anglo core as no different from poor Mexican immigrants—a perception that pushed virtually those of Mexican extraction to the bottom rungs of the stratification system (Murguia, 1975).

Mexican Americans in the First Half of the Twentieth Century

Immigration of Mexicans into the Southwest was closely linked to the economy. On the U.S. side of the border, as labor-intensive industry expanded, the demand for cheap labor served as a "pull" factor for Mexican immigrants. On the Mexican side of the border, the revolution of 1910 to 1917 operated as a "push" factor for Mexicans seeking refuge and employment. The push out of Mexico was reinforced by the fact that employers in the United States were looking for a source of inexpensive labor to compensate for the shortage of American workers created by World War I. Soon, Mexicans became a subordinate labor force: paid less than white American laborers for the same work, concentrated in the low-paying occupations, and often indebted to their employers for food and shelter.

As the southwestern economy fluctuated, employers often had too many workers and not enough work. Ironically, the need for cheap labor to run the labor-intensive industries of the Southwest also created the need to eliminate the presence of surplus labor during economic downturns. For example, between 1870 and 1930 immigration policy was relatively unrestricted for Mexican immigrants, who were allowed to enter the United States on an open-door policy to fill the need for labor. But the great depression of 1929 changed immigration policy dramatically. As white Americans lost jobs and homes, anti-Mexican feelings emerged; and as whites increasingly competed with those of Mexican origin for low-wage jobs and welfare benefits, white resentment toward "Mexicans" grew. The result was a repatriation movement for Mexicans, a movement that included both indigenous Mexican Americans and those who had more recently immigrated. Between 1929 and 1935 over a half million Mexicans were repatriated (Hoffman, 1974; Humphrey, 1941; and Chavira, 1977).

While immigration initiatives such as Operation Wetback were deterrents to illegal immigration, they were not effective in stemming the demand for inexpensive labor. An interesting feature of immigration reform in the 1980s was its focus on employers; rather than continue to fixate on the number of Mexicans crossing the border, the U.S. Congress placed the

Box 6.4

Chicano Farmworkers and Pesticides

Chicano farmworkers who pick and harvest America's agricultural crops face tremendous risks from the pesticides sprayed on the crops. In particular, since children make up a large share of the farmworker pool, the risks of cancer and/or learning disability that might result from exposure to pesticides for them are of national concern (Taylor, 1973; Benavides, 1981; and Mores, 1993). In an attempt to discuss the health danger of pesticide exposure to farmworkers, the House of Representatives Select Committee on Aging (1992) held a series of hearings. Maria Gomez spoke before the Select Committee on Aging (1992:10–11) regarding her experience as a farmworker:

> My name is Maria Gomez. I live in Pharr, Texas. I have been a worker in the field for twenty years.
>
> First of all, I would like to talk about pesticides in work. Little by little they have been killing us because there is no regulation for these pesticides. Back in 1985, they were already using planes to spray the fields, and I was in my home asleep when one of these planes flew over my home and sprayed, and the spray came into my house.
>
> The doctors are not trained as to what reaction the pesticide has on the body and what other complications you could have with the medication. The medication that was given to me produced high blood pressure. This was also complicated by the fact that I was picking cantaloupe melon in the field; it is in the heat of the day and the sun also caused some of these side-effects.

burden on employers (Bean, Vernez, and Keeley, 1989; Bean et al., 1990). For example, in 1986 Congress implemented the Immigration Reform and Control Act (IRCA) to prohibit employers from hiring illegal immigrants and to establish a monitoring system for employer compliance. Yet, a study to examine the progress of the IRCA found that the enforcement of employer sanctions is weak, that few criminal and civil fines have been assessed against employers, and that a low degree of cooperation between employers and the Immigration and Naturalization Service prevails (Fix and Hill, 1990).

Negative Beliefs about Chicanos

As the process of subordinating the indigenous Mexican population in the Southwest began, Mexicans were portrayed in highly negative and stereotyped terms (Reisler, 1996). Many slaveholders, and former slaveholders, who had settled in the Southwest in the second half of the nineteenth century, portrayed Mexicans as an inferior "race," biologically tainted by Indian blood. The early perception of Mexicans as "greasers" (presumably, because some once greased wagon wheels) and as cowardly originated after the defeats of the Mexican Army in the 1880s (Meyer, 1978; Ortego, 1973; and Keller, 1985). Those who insisted that Mexicans constituted a distinctive "race" thus based their negative stereotypes on biological and, hence, on what was viewed as unalterable traits. As a result, during the first decades of the twentieth century, fear was expressed in Congress and in diatribes by white nativists that the "white race" would be "mongrelized" because of excessive contact with Mexicans, who many regarded as lazy, shiftless, lawless, and potentially violent (Stoddard, 1973; Almaguer, 1994).

These stereotypes persist in the second half of this century (Duran and Bernard, 1973). Males of Mexican origin have been portrayed as "banditos" (fat, lazy, thieving, and immoral) or as overly "macho" and violent street criminals. Mexican American women have been viewed as young seductresses or as passive mothers of violent gang youth and wives of lazy husbands (Simmons, 1973; Mazon, 1984; and Paredes, 1977). Consequently, "Mexican-looking" people, Spanish-speaking people, or individuals who speak English with a Spanish accent must endure prejudice about their character, honesty, work ethic, and reliability (Martinez, 1969). These beliefs have justified past discrimination; now they legitimize current treatment of Mexican Americans. Negative beliefs about Mexican-origin persons in the United States are reinforced by the depiction of Mexicans as deviants—especially as criminals or drug dealers—in the mass media (Keller, 1985; Robinson, 1963). The focus by the television and newspaper media, for example, on Mexican Americans and Mexicans carrying the Mexican flag in protests against Proposition 187 in California fueled nativist sentiments in the Anglo population, sentiments that supported the discrimination of Mexican Americans (Aguirre, 1995a).

The Dynamics of Discrimination against Mexican Americans

Economic Discrimination

Despite the anti-Mexican sentiment of the 1930s and the resulting repatriation movement, the United States sought assistance from Mexico during the 1940s to fill labor shortages in agriculture created by World War II. In 1942 the United States and Mexico established a labor contract system known as the "Bracero Program." Participating Mexican workers were granted temporary visas and labeled *braceros* (hired hands). The Bracero Program operated from 1942 to 1964. During its existence about five million Mexican workers entered the U.S. labor force as legal seasonal workers (Garcia, 1980).

The U.S. Congress used the Bracero Program as a way of reducing the number of illegal immigrants from Mexico. By extending the Bracero Program beyond World War II, Congress sought to provide some relief for the struggling U.S. Border Patrol, which had been relatively ineffective in its control of illegal immigration. In 1954, for example, Congress allowed the Border Patrol to launch *Operation Wetback,* which targeted Mexican immigrants who did not have papers identifying them as braceros. Congress gave the Border Patrol blanket authority to stop and search any "Mexican-looking" person. Between 1954 and 1959, the patrol returned 3.8 million people to Mexico (Grebler, Moore, and Guzman, 1970). Operation Wetback reinforced the perception among Mexican Americans that their presence in the United States would always be marginal and tenuous.

Mexican Americans in the Second Half of the Twentieth Century

Comparatively speaking, Mexican immigration between 1970 and 1990 was overshadowed by immigration from Central and South American countries. In contrast, most of the growth of the Mexican American population between 1970 and 1990 was the result of high birthrates of those already living in the United States (McCarthy and Valdez, 1986).

The identification of Mexican Americans as a colonized people has perpetuated discriminatory economic practices. One source of discrimination was built into the wage structure of the Southwest. The availability of Mexican workers created a depressed labor market, providing only limited menial jobs with very few economic rewards and benefits (Romo, 1989).

Economic discrimination against Mexican Americans has been aggravated by a number of circumstances. First, until the 1960s, many labor unions actively discriminated against Mexican Americans (Grebler, Moore, and Guzman, 1970). As a consequence, Mexican American workers were prevented from moving to higher-wage and skill positions which, in turn, could serve as the springboard for further mobility by subsequent generations—much as union jobs had done for white European immigrants. Today, although institutionalized discrimination has declined, the economy has shifted away from industrial work, thereby reducing the number of bet-

A Chicano pride rally in Sacramento, California, focuses attention on the need to eliminate negative stereotypes about Chicanos.

ter-paying jobs and forcing many Mexican Americans onto the welfare rolls or into service, agriculture, and light-industrial jobs with low wages, little security, and no benefits. Second, the existence of a large unemployed Mexican American labor pool, either just across the border or in urban areas, has depressed wages and kept workers from demanding new benefits—lest they be fired and replaced by more eager and pliant workers. Third, the undocumented citizenship status of many Mexicans has driven down wages because undocumented aliens will rarely protest wages and working conditions—unless they wish to run the risk of being deported.

The imposition of the English language on Mexican Americans not only contradicted the intent of the Treaty of Guadalupe Hidalgo but also caused a form of economic discrimination (Falcon and Campbell, 1991): Because laws were changed from Spanish to English and court proceedings were conducted only in English, land grants written in Spanish were deemed worthless, and Mexican Americans were forced to rent their own land (Aguirre, 1982). In the Southwest, where land ownership became a measure of power, Mexican Americans soon became second-class citizens, displaced from their land and forced into the low-wage labor market.

Chicanos, however, did not always accept economic domination passively. "Social banditry" emerged, a phenomenon that reinforced prejudicial beliefs. For example, Las Gorras Blancas (the White Caps) was a group of Mexican American social bandits around 1887 who protested their loss of land by cutting down fences and burning property acquired by white ranchers—especially those who had obtained land through manipulation of the English-speaking court system (Barrera, 1985). Las Gorras Blancas received widespread support in the Chicano community, but this support was not strong enough to sustain a major challenge to the erosion of Mexican American land rights. Today, protest has diminished in the wave of undocumented workers and illegal aliens. Indeed, all protest invites harsh response in a political climate that is highly receptive to mass deportation of Mexicans who have recently come to the United States.

Some Mexican American protests against economic discrimination have been remarkably effective, however. In the 1960s, Cesar Chavez unionized the farmworkers. Through the effective use of media, personal charisma, and well-organized boycotts and strikes, Chavez and his colleagues greatly improved the working conditions and wages of agricultural workers. To this day, United Farm Workers of America operates effectively to improve wages and working conditions—most recently extending its lines of battle to include the dangers of chemical pesticides to both workers and consumers. Yet, the limited success of the Mexican American farmworkers has not been matched by Mexican Americans living in cities. Urban Chicanos remain vulnerable to an oversupply of undocumented labor and the actions of law enforcement agencies.

Legal Discrimination

The use of English by the Anglo core as the language of the courts, despite guarantees to the contrary in the Treaty of Guadalupe Hidalgo, has been a crucial step in depriving Chicanos of justice. For example, in an analysis of Mexican American prisoners who had been executed between 1890 and 1986, Aguirre and Baker (1989) note that Mexican American prisoners given capital sentences had lower rates of appeal than either white American or African American prisoners because either they did not understand the legal rights communicated to them in English or they were unable to communicate in English with the court. The inadequate defense of Mexican American prisoners increases their number in the prison population, thus reinforcing prejudicial beliefs that they are criminally prone, or natural "hardcore criminals."

Perhaps more significantly, because many Mexican Americans are subjected constantly to questions about their citizenship, they have been abused by those enforcement agencies—first the Texas Rangers and later the Immigration and Naturalization Service (INS), Border Patrol, and state highway police—designed to detect, capture, and deport "Mexicans." Special law enforcement agencies charged with the task of targeting a particular ethnic subpopulation are often a license for discriminatory abuse.

The strain between the Mexican American population and the mainstream legal system was established early with the creation of the Texas Rangers. According to Grebler, Moore, and Guzman (1970), the Texas Rangers were created in 1835 as a symbol of white American control over the social progress of the Mexican American. Though their primary purpose was to protect the Texas Republic from the Mexicans, the Texas Rangers spread their law enforcement presence throughout the Southwest. The rangers were given wide latitude in their treatment of Mexicans and Mexican Americans; and, as a consequence, beatings, lynchings, firing squads, and dismemberment were common (McWilliams, 1968). In fact, the general view of many Chicanos and Mexicans is that "every Texas Ranger has some Mexican blood. He has it on his boots" (Murguia, 1975).

Similar to the Texas Rangers, the U.S. Border Patrol was created in 1924 to protect the United States from Mexican infiltration. Congress gave the patrol the authority to apprehend those suspected of illegal entry into the United States and to search persons and property within 25 miles of the U.S.–Mexico border (Grebler, Moore, and Guzman, 1970). The primary target of the Border Patrol became the "wetbacks"—Mexicans who crossed over to the United States by swimming across the Rio Grande River. The patrol became ever more oppressive in its efforts to apprehend illegal aliens, cruising the streets in Mexican American neighborhoods and stopping any "Mexican-looking" person who acted in a suspicious manner (McWilliams, 1968). Through its actions the Border Patrol communicated to the Mexican American community their tenuous place in American society.

Two major efforts of the Border Patrol had a significant impact on the Mexican American population. First, the Border Patrol deployed enforcement procedures during the great depression of the 1930s to deport Mexicans who were identified as burdens to U.S. society. Second, as noted earlier, they initiated Operation Wetback in 1954 to combat the "wetback invasion" of illegal aliens, allowing as many as 3.8 million Mexicans to be deported without due legal process (Grebler, Moore, and Guzman, 1970). These two efforts by the Border Patrol resulted in the deportation of longtime Mexican American residents of the United States, Mexican American parents and their children born in the United States, along with immigrant Mexicans. These massive efforts served to brand the remaining Chicanos wrongfully as second-class citizens.

Studies of police tactics in small communities have shown that Mexican

Americans are victims of prejudiced attitudes, indiscriminate searches and detentions, and high arrest-conviction rates (Aguirre and Baker, 1994; Morales, 1972, 1973; and Welch et al., 1984). The 1970 report of the U.S. Commission on Civil Rights, *Mexican Americans and the Administration of Justice in the Southwest,* identified several discriminatory police actions: use of excessive force, verbal abuse, discriminatory treatment of juveniles arising from the nonnotification of parents, and random stops and searches. A decade later, the papers presented at the National Latino Conference on Law Enforcement and Criminal Justice documented similar patterns of police abuse in the Chicano community (U.S. Department of Justice, 1980). This same pattern of abuse persists in the 1990s.

Fears about the enforcement of laws regarding citizenship status were demonstrated dramatically in the response to the amnesty provision of the 1986 Immigration and Reform Act (IRCA). This provision allowed many undocumented immigrants to apply for legal residence. While over 1.7 million undocumented aliens did apply, this figure was far below the estimated 3 million who were eligible for amnesty. At the same time that amnesty was offered, new restrictions on immigration were imposed, including penalties (not strictly enforced thus far) on employers who give jobs to undocumented workers and screening of welfare applicants for migration and citizenship status. The effectiveness of the IRCA now seems questionable; undocumented Mexicans continue to enter the Southwest, and documented workers and legal citizens are subject to abuse by law enforcement agencies targeting "Mexican-looking" people.

Educational Discrimination

When the Mexican American population was employed primarily as agricultural workers in the early 1900s, virtually no formal education was offered to children; and it was well into the 1930s before the lack of schools for Mexican American children was considered a problem. As schools were built, segregation prevailed as a result of housing segregation, local ordinances, and gerrymandering of school and district lines. Even as integration increased in the 1970s and 1980s, Mexican American teachers, administrators, and counselors were dramatically underrepresented in school systems.

This virtual absence of Mexican American school personnel, coupled with powerful local pressure exerted by white Americans, created an Anglo-Saxon American school culture, even in predominantly Mexican American neighborhoods and districts. Mexican American children were thus placed in a school system that was alien to their culture. Although children in European ethnic groups often have the same experience in school, they do not have to endure the legacy of discrimination that echoes in the curriculum and practice of the U.S. public school system. Chicano children sometimes experience ambivalence at home because of their parents' close ties to their Mexican homeland and custom. They are torn between two cultures—the Mexican culture of their family and the American culture of the school and broader society. Moreover, because the school system has always been designed to "Americanize" immigrants, students living in the two cultures—that of the Mexican homeland across the border and that of their new or temporary place of residence—have often become alienated in schools. Because many Mexican American schoolchildren resisted heavy-handed efforts at Americanization, they were placed in segregated schools, under constant pressure to become "American" (Grebler, Moore, and Guzman, 1970; Sanchez, 1951; Rubel, 1966; and San Miguel, 1987). For example, Mexican American children who spoke Spanish in school were often the victims of corporal punishment from teachers (for example, spanking with a paddle); Mexican American children were ridiculed by teachers if they brought burritos or tacos to school for their lunch. In the end, "good" American citizens were those Mexican American children who rejected their ethnic identity and culture.

In the only other major study conducted on the education of Mexican Americans in the Southwest, the U.S. Commission on Civil Rights (1972) found that teachers tended to ridicule Mexican American students who spoke English with an accent, exclude them from classroom discussion, refrain from asking them questions during classroom lessons, and punish them corporally for speaking Spanish in the classroom or on the school playground. The commission (1972:48) concluded its report by stating:

> The basic finding of the Commission's study is that school systems of the southwest have not recognized the rich culture and tradition of the Mexican American students and have not adopted policies and programs which would enable the students to participate fully in the benefits of the educational process.

Contributing to the sense of alienation in the school was the belief that Mexican American children needed only a rudimentary education before they dropped out and entered the low-wage labor pool. This belief, in turn, became a self-fulfilling prophecy: Schools imposing mainstream American culture on Mexican American children, with little sensitivity to or appreciation of their place in two active cultures, caused children to become unhappy in school, which led them to drop out.

The Elementary and Secondary Education Act passed by Congress in 1968 allocated some funds for bilingual education. The hope was that, if Spanish-speaking children could be sensitively introduced to English and the dominant Anglo-Saxon-European culture, their education would prove more effective, thereby reducing dropout rates. Yet very little bilingual education actually ensued in the early 1970s, and only with a 1974 Supreme Court decision *(Lau v. Nichols)* prohibiting schools from ignoring the language difficulties of national-origin minority groups did bilingual education increase. Currently, bilingualism in schools is not universal (Aguirre, 1995b; Macias, 1993). More recent political movements for "English only" as the official language of all Americans, culminating in the passing of formal laws in several states, have slowed the progress of bilingual education (Adams and Brink, 1990; Califa, 1989; Juarez, 1995). For example, in November 1986, voters in California approved Proposition 63 declaring English as the official language of the state. The importance of Proposition 63 is that it was approved by the voters in a state with a sizable population of non-English speakers. Other states that have approved English-only amendments and that have large numbers of non-English speakers in the state's population are Arizona, Colorado, and Florida. Moreover, the effectiveness of bilingual education in helping Mexican American children is the subject of intense debate (Padilla and Benavides, 1992; Imhoff, 1990).

As a result of these discriminatory factors, many Mexican American children leave school early. Today fewer than 50 percent graduate from high school (Aguirre and Martinez, 1993). Without an education in a society that values it, the economic prospects of Mexican American youth are indeed dim (Aguirre and Martinez, 1984).

Political Discrimination

With the signing of the Treaty of Guadalupe Hidalgo in 1848, Mexicans living in the Southwest became citizens of the United States. However, the disregard for the rights granted to Mexicans in the treaty placed the latter in a relatively powerless position. At times, Mexicans responded to their colonization—for example, the mobilization of Las Gorras Blancas, mentioned earlier—but the majority of the Mexican population did not develop a cohesive political identity with which to challenge the Anglo population. By the 1920s, however, Mexican Americans were awakening to the reality that they would be politically powerless as long as the mainstream white population perceived them as foreigners. Thus, first attempts to create a political identity focused on integration into mainstream American society (Garcia and de la Garza, 1977). For example, in 1921 in San Antonio, middle-class Mexican Americans formed the *Orden Hijos de America* as a signal to the white population that they were interested in participating in U.S. society—even at the expense of accepting negative stereotypes for their behavior. In 1929, the *League of United Latin American Citizens (LULAC)* was founded in Corpus Christi, Texas, by Mexican Americans who chose to refer to themselves as "Latins" in order to reinforce their loyalty, in the eyes of white Americans, to the United States (Marquez, 1993).

Later, Mexican American veterans returning from World War II encouraged increased political activity in their communities. These war veterans saw that they were returning to a country in which they were regarded as second-class citizens. Two of the most significant political organizations arising out of the efforts of these war veterans during the 1940s and 1950s were the *G.I. Forum* and the *Community Service Organization* (Hero, 1992). The G.I. Forum advocated the rights of Mexican American war veterans, sought representation in Congress, encouraged voter registration, and focused attention on the segregation of schoolchildren. The Community Service Organization was formed in Los Angeles as a community-based organization to encourage Mexican American participation in local, state, and national elections.

Despite these efforts to increase political participation, Mexican Americans remained politically underrepresented in the 1960s. Yet, this was a period of awakening in the Mexican American community, as political events stimulated political awareness. For example, the "Viva Kennedy" movement in the 1960s presidential campaign, the land rights movement led by Reyes Tijerina to reclaim land in northern New Mexico, the farmworkers' movement led by Cesar Chavez, the rise of La Raza Unida as a political party in Texas were all manifestations of a newfound political awareness.

The post-1970s signaled a period of political decline among Chicanos, although various radical political parties, such as the La Raza Unida in Texas, formed to wage local political campaigns. As Hero (1992) has noted, most of the political organizations formed before 1970 became involved in moderate political activities—voter registration, legal challenges to redistricting, and lobbying efforts at the local and state levels. As a result, political efforts within the Chicano population have shifted to the development of traditional political techniques with which to forge a unified social, economic, and political identity.

In the 1990s, Mexican Americans are politically underrepresented at all levels of political life: at the local level (mayors, city council members, school board members, county supervisors, sheriffs), at the state level (state legislators, court judges and justices, and governors), and at the national level (congressional representatives, senators, federal judges, and high-level executive appointees) (Hero, 1990). During the 1980s and early 1990s, the Republican White House had little incentive to initiate efforts to redress this imbalance of power because Mexican Americans traditionally vote overwhelmingly for the Democratic party. Some progress is now being made at the local and state levels in those cities and districts where Mexican Americans outnumber non-Latinos, but even here progress is slow. For example, Los Angeles, which is now close to 50 percent Latino, elected its first Chicano representative, Gloria Molina, to the Los Angeles Board of Supervisors in 1991. Without political power proportionate to their numbers or their needs, Mexican Americans have found it difficult to address other forms of discrimination (Garcia, 1996).

Stratification of the Mexican-Origin Population

As a consequence of the long history of economic, legal, educational, and political discrimination against individuals of Mexican origin, Chicanos are disproportionately overrepresented in lower socioeconomic positions in American society. As a population, they tend to be more successful than African Americans and Native Americans, but they remain disproportionately locked into agricultural labor, urban barrios with high crime and little hope, and jobs that have few benefits and no future.

The negative beliefs about Mexican Americans—prone to criminality, lazy, un-American, uneducable, overly macho or seductive, welfare burdens, gang-oriented and violent—have legitimized discrimination and aroused fears among non-Latinos. Like all institutionalized patterns of discrimination, those against Mexican Americans are an outcome of perceptions that this population is a threat. At one time Europeans saw Mexicans as a military enemy. More recently, those of Mexican origin have posed a series of threats: as a low-wage labor pool that could potentially undercut higher-wage labor, as a political threat to European American ways of speaking and thinking; as a threat to social order arising from criminality and gang activity, and, most recently, as a numerical threat in the Southwest, where they are rapidly becoming a numerical majority. In turn, as the number of Mexican Americans has increased, new threats have emerged and old ones have been intensified. For example, fears about the schools' being overrun, about loss of white control of local politics, about burdens on the welfare and health care systems, about lost jobs for non-Latinos, and about the loss of white mainstream cultural hegemony have all escalated. These fears fuel discrimination, even in an age when antidiscrimination laws are well established. This discrimination can be subtle—housing discrimination, low educational expectations, biased hiring practices—or it can be blatant—English-only political movements and attacks on bilingualism. The result is a population stuck in the lower stratum of American society.

PUERTO RICANS

The forces that created the minority population of Puerto Ricans stand in marked contrast to those that forged the Mexican American community. Puerto Ricans became U.S. citizens in 1898, when the United States annexed Puerto Rico, and the Jones Act of 1917 allowed Puerto Ricans free access to the U.S. mainland, long before the island became a commonwealth in 1952. By the 1940s, the U.S. census indicated that 70,000 Puerto Ricans had settled on the mainland, but during the 1950s, almost 20 percent of the island's population migrated to the United States (Fitzpatrick, 1987). By 1970, over 800,000 Puerto Ricans were living on the U.S. mainland, 57 percent of whom were island-born. In 1993, the Puerto Rican population on the U.S. mainland was estimated at 2.4 million (U.S. Bureau of the Census, 1994).

Both "push" and "pull" factors have affected the Puerto Rican migration. First, the island's size, 35 miles wide by 100 miles long, has generated problems of overpopulation; many island residents view the United States as a place to improve their living standard—especially the opportunity for adequate housing and employment (Maldonado-Denis, 1972). Second, conferring full U.S. citizenship rights on island residents meant that Puerto Ricans could enter the United States without having to confront restrictive immigration legislation, such as quotas and harassment by enforcement agencies like the Border Patrol and the INS. Third, lowered costs for air travel between San Juan and New York City have encouraged movement to and from Puerto Rico.

Identifiability of Puerto Ricans

As with other Latinos, Puerto Ricans are identifiable by their language, although they are far more likely to be bilingual than Mexican Americans. Puerto Ricans are also frequently visible in terms of their skin color, categorized by some as "black" if they are particularly dark or as Latino if they have a lighter skin tone. In fact, because the island of Puerto Rico has been a U.S. colony since the late 1800s, the cultural differences between Puerto Ricans and white Europeans are less critical than are perceived biological differences—a situation that is the reverse for Mexican Americans. Because some perceive Puerto Ricans as members of a distinct "race," discrimination can become intense.

Negative Beliefs about Puerto Ricans

Like Mexican Americans, Puerto Ricans are at times considered lazy, submissive, and immoral, with propensities for crime and gang violence (Wagenheim, 1973; Lopez, 1973; Díaz-Cotto, 1996). Because poor Puerto Ricans are concentrated in a few cities, and mostly in the New York City area, they are viewed as a drain on the welfare system and social services. Much like African Americans, they are stigmatized on the basis of their welfare dependency, large families, and lack of stable employment. These beliefs create a sense of threat among some in the white population and legitimize the resulting patterns of discrimination.

The Dynamics of Discrimination against Puerto Ricans

Economic Discrimination

As is the case with Mexican migrants, the timing of Puerto Rican migration to the United States has been related to cycles in the U.S. economy. During the 1950s job recruiters would go to the island of Puerto Rico to recruit workers for the increasing number of sweatshops in the garment industry (Morales, 1986). The targets of these recruiting efforts were farmworkers in the sugar cane industry; the inability of Puerto Rico to offer these farmworkers urban jobs caused many to migrate to the United States in hopes of increasing their economic well-being (Ayala, 1996). Despite increased industrialization in Puerto Rico during the 1960s, people continued to leave the island because the Puerto Rican economy failed to absorb the growing population of unemployed farmworkers (Maldonado, 1976; U.S. Commission on Civil Rights, 1976).

Increasing unemployment and factory closings in the United States during the 1970s did not stem the tide of migration from Puerto Rico. At the same time, however, a pattern of return migration from the United States emerged, despite an unemployment rate of 20 percent in Puerto Rico (Morales, 1986). As Bean and Tienda (1986:25) summarize:

> The persistent inability of many island migrants to secure steady employment on the mainland, coupled with the displacement of Puerto Rican

> workers from declining textile and garment industries in the northeast during the decade of the 1970s, set in motion a return migration process whose scale and duration cannot be predicted.

Puerto Ricans have experienced job discrimination in much the same form as both Mexican Americans and African Americans. Those who lack fluency in English have not performed well on occupational screening tests, even for menial manual jobs. Those with darker skin color have often been excluded from skilled trade and craft unions, which, in the 1990s, remain predominantly white. Specifically in New York City, Puerto Ricans have been negatively affected by structural changes in the city's economy away from the kinds of blue-collar jobs that provided an economic and social springboard for white ethnic groups. Similarly, Puerto Ricans who have moved to other northeastern cities have experienced the same shift in occupational structure, resulting in limited job opportunities. Unlike Mexican Americans who are widely dispersed across urban and rural areas of the Southwest, and similar to urban African Americans, Puerto Ricans are concentrated in cities with a declining industrial and union base, forcing them to take temporary and low-wage jobs. Moreover, informal discrimination operates, much as it does for urban African Americans, to block Puerto Ricans from higher-wage occupations and to keep them in a large, oversupplied labor pool sustained by the welfare system. Coupled with housing discrimination almost equal to that experienced by African Americans (indeed, African American and Puerto Rican neighborhoods are often contiguous or overlapping), access to jobs far from their neighborhoods, caused by inadequate public transportation routes, is limited (Mendoza Report, 1978).

Poverty rates for Puerto Ricans exceed those for Mexican Americans; many return to Puerto Rico, even though job prospects are dim there. This mobility creates the same problem for Puerto Ricans as it does for Mexican migrants: Movement back and forth disrupts family life, reduces the chances for building a stable employment history, and inhibits full integration into mainstream American culture, all of which further limit economic opportunities for Puerto Ricans.

Legal Discrimination

The problems Puerto Ricans face with respect to the U.S. criminal justice system are due to the fact that "the police are often seen as oppressors who do not speak the language, do not understand the culture, and lack empathy and sensitivity when acting in what otherwise would be a minor or routine situation" (Carro, 1980:369). In 1965, Chicago's Puerto Rican community rioted for three days to protest against police brutality (Cruz, 1995). The Puerto Rican community felt that they had been the victims of police brutality since their arrival in Chicago in the 1950s (Padilla, 1987). A detailed study (Sissons, 1979) of how U.S. criminal justice organizations treat Puerto Ricans found the following: Puerto Ricans are victims of language discrimination in the courts; Puerto Ricans are persecuted for some activities that are legal in Puerto Rico, such as playing the numbers and cockfighting; Puerto Ricans are more likely to be institutionalized than placed on probation; and, compared with white Americans, Puerto Ricans receive longer sentences for the same criminal acts.

Educational Discrimination

The concentration of Puerto Ricans in low-wage occupations, coupled with rampant housing discrimination, has limited their ability to move both within and out of urban environments, especially New York City. Consequently, many Puerto Rican children attend schools in which they are the majority; this de facto segregation limits educational opportunity (Fitzpatrick, 1987).

The concentration of a large portion of the Puerto Rican population in low-wage seasonal jobs, along with movement to and from the island of Puerto Rico, creates waves of unemployment, thereby increasing the chances that Puerto Rican youth will drop out of school in order to help the family by obtaining a job in the low-wage seasonal sector. As a consequence, only about 60 percent of Puerto Ricans have completed high school and less than 10 percent have completed college.

Within the schools, language skills are an issue for many Puerto Rican children. Relatively few teachers and administrators are Latino, and so the culture of the school system is unfamiliar. Spanish speakers often are labeled as "learning disabled" due to their limited English-speaking skills and understanding of Euro-American cultural traditions. Language barriers, movement to and from the island, and the need to help support the family in temporary jobs all contribute to a high dropout rate among Puerto Rican youth, and to marginal career opportunities for many.

Political Discrimination

Puerto Ricans are underrepresented in local, state, and national politics. Even in New York City, where it could be expected that their numbers would translate into political power, Puerto Ricans are not prominent in city government, the judicial system, state legislatures, or Congress (Falcon, 1984, 1988). Part of the problem is that only about 20 percent of registered Puerto Ricans vote, a pattern that reflects deeper problems.

One reason for political disempowerment, as Hero (1992:40) notes, is that "Puerto Ricans often do not see themselves as permanent residents on the U.S. mainland—that is, they feel that they will someday return to the island—they do not develop deep political attachments on the mainland." As a consequence, they do not mobilize effective and stable bases of power, despite their large numbers in key cities. A second source of apparent political apathy is that big-city political machines traditionally have paid little attention to the Puerto Rican population. These machines tended to be dominated by white Americans of European origin who saw little need to respond to a sojourning ethnic group. Moreover, Puerto Ricans traditionally have been more politically radical and left-wing than politicians in entrenched city machines found acceptable; these politicians typically do not feel the need to respond to extremist political voices. Consequently, as networks of power were being constructed in large cities during the 1930s and 1940s, Puerto Ricans were excluded, and the legacy of this exclusion persists today, even as many political machines are being dismantled (Hardy-Fanta, 1993). Without an established network of patronage appointments and informal ties, it is difficult for Puerto Ricans to exert power proportionate to their numbers. Without political power, it is almost impossible to attack other forms of discrimination in housing, schools, the workplace, and the courts.

Puerto Ricans have reacted to their relative powerlessness, on both the island and the mainland. A nationalist movement on the island seeks separation from the United States, but the majority want statehood or the current status quo. While the platforms of the Republican and Democratic parties advocate statehood for Puerto Rico, the fact that it has not been achieved says a great deal about the reluctance of Congress to incorporate formally a Spanish-speaking population into the Union. On the mainland, a number of community service organizations have sought to organize legal services, family counseling, voter registration, political debate, and women's consciousness within the Puerto Rican community. Efforts have also been made to increase attendance in the city school systems (Fitzpatrick, 1987).

In contrast to these quiet organizational efforts, some strategies have been more aggressive. Perhaps fueled by President Johnson's effort in the 1960s to reduce poverty, political militancy grew among Puerto Ricans. One manifestation of this militancy was the emergence of the Young Lords, who used community services such as providing hot lunches and patrolling schools for drug dealers to focus attention on the plight of the Puerto Ricans in New York City (Baver, 1984; National Puerto Rican Coalition, 1985). The Young Lords also became involved in nationalist politics that advocated the severing of ties with the island of Puerto Rico.

Despite some of the strides Puerto Ricans have made, they remain politically isolated, even in areas where their numbers are great. Without political power, the ability to overcome social and economic stratification is limited.

Stratification of Puerto Ricans

Discriminatory practices against Puerto Ricans are legitimized by highly prejudicial beliefs. These practices and beliefs are ultimately fueled by a sense of threat among non-Latinos in the cities where Puerto Ricans are concentrated. Some white Americans fear that Puerto Ricans will "dilute" white European culture, that they will have to pay for increased social services to Puerto Ricans who are unemployed and have too many babies, that they will lose their jobs to Puerto Ricans who will work for less, that they will have to share local political power, that they will lose control over the

Eurocentric curriculum in schools, and that they will become the victims of gang violence and crime.

Aside from the barriers created by prejudice, Puerto Ricans must battle an economic system that fails to accommodate them. They cannot easily move into middleman minority niches; their numbers are too large in key cities and their entrepreneurial skills are lacking. Without a firm foothold in the economy, the educational system, or the political arena, most Puerto Ricans living in the United States have slid to the lower stratum of American society, although a sizable minority has been mobile to the middle and upper-middle classes.

CUBAN AMERICANS

Fewer than 50,000 Cubans lived in the United States before Fidel Castro overthrew the regime of Fulgencio Batista in 1959 (Perez, 1980). This coup led to an exodus of Cubans seeking political asylum during the 1960s. By 1970, over a half million Cubans resided in the United States (Massey, 1983); and by the end of the 1970s, Cuban American communities were firmly established in south Florida. Although the Cuban population grew to slightly over one million persons by 1993, it is the smallest segment of the Latino population relative to the Mexican American and Puerto Rican segments. Its relatively small size and concentration in Florida, especially Miami, has created a Cuban American ethnic enclave with an economic base in small business (Wilson and Portes, 1980).

Several factors differentiate the arrival of Cubans in the United States from that of Mexicans and Puerto Ricans. First, the Cubans came to the United States as political refugees of communism; hence, they were perceived as desirable in light of the politics of the cold war. Their arrival stimulated the U.S. Congress to enact legislation creating a resettlement program for Cubans that provided job training, employment assistance, small-business loans, mortgage assistance for home purchases, educational services (such as bilingual instruction), and reimbursement for school districts educating Cuban children (Rogg, 1974).

Second, the majority of early Cuban refugees were from the upper and middle classes, with professional and technical training as well as entrepreneurial skills and resources; these attributes could shield them from menial work and low-status occupations. Although many Cuban refugees did have to accept low-paying jobs on their arrival, the legislation approved by Congress allowed them to retrain so that they could pursue business and professional options. This opportunity enabled many refugees to transpose their occupations and professions in Cuba to the United States.

The opportunity for Cuban Americans to gain upward mobility has had visible results: Cuban-owned enterprises in Miami increased from 919 in 1967 to more than 8,000 in 1980; close to one-third of all businesses in

The entrepreneurial skills of Cuban refugees in Miami are quite visible among the shops and restaurants that focus on Cuban culture.

Miami are Cuban-owned; 75 percent of the workforce in construction is Cuban, and 40 percent of the industry is Cuban-owned; Cubans control 20 percent of the banks in Miami, accounting for 16 out of 62 bank presidents and 250 vice presidents (Wilson and Portes, 1980; Bach, 1980). In 1988, five of the ten largest Latino businesses were located in Dade County, Florida (Shorris, 1992).

In 1980, Fidel Castro emptied Cuban prisons and mental hospitals, declaring that "all" who wished to leave Cuba could do so. Thus began the *Mariel boatlifts,* from the Cuban port of Mariel to south Florida. An entirely different population of Cubans entered the United States, a predominantly darker skinned, poorer, and often unemployable population. The composition of the Cuban population in the United States thus began to shift. Many of these more recent refugees created problems for the U.S. government and the Cuban community in south Florida in the areas of employment, crime, housing, and welfare services (Boswell, 1985).

Negative Beliefs about Cuban Americans

Cubans were not faced with the same level of language, cultural, or social discrimination encountered by Mexican Americans in the Southwest or Puerto Ricans in the cities of the Northeast. For example, the appropriation of funds by Congress to create bilingual multicultural public instruction in Dade County, Florida, guaranteed that Spanish-speaking Cuban children could maintain their Spanish-language skills while acquiring English-language facility (Pedraza-Bailey and Sullivan, 1979). As a result, Cuban children were not perceived as foreigners in public instruction, as Mexican Americans were in the Southwest.

Cubans were also welcome in the United States because they were anti-Castro and anticommunist. Whereas Mexican Americans and Puerto Ricans were treated as territorial minority groups, Cubans were regarded as refugees waiting for the removal of Castro from power. Although many Americans did not initially expect Cubans to remain in the United States, as the Cubans assimilated into American society, they were perceived as industrious, intelligent, and law-abiding (Bryce-Laporte, 1982).

The Mariel boatlift in 1980 altered many Americans' perceptions of Cubans. Hostility toward Cubans has increased, and, coupled with the growing recognition that most Cubans are here to stay, hostility toward them has escalated (Portes and Rumbaut, 1990). Moreover, African Americans in south Florida have begun to discriminate against Cubans in reaction to their own increasingly subordinate economic status. Many African Americans living in this region are now competing with low-wage labor from Cuba. As the welfare and social services burden of the Mariel boatlifts has reduced benefits for African Americans, the latter's intolerance has increased, culminating in a series of riots in Liberty City and Overtown, Florida.

The Mariel experience may have triggered latent white and manifest African American resentment toward Cubans. As Miami has expanded its image as a bilingual–bicultural community, resentment from the non-Latino community has increased. In November 1980 voters in Dade County approved an English-only ordinance that reversed a policy of official bilingualism established by the Board of County Commissioners in 1973 with the official support of Congress. An analysis of the voting patterns showed that non-Latino white citizens voted overwhelmingly for the English-only ordinance because they wanted to limit the increasing Latinization of south Florida. Positive perceptions of Cubans as anticommunist refugees have shifted to a more negative belief based on their language as well as their Latino cultural roots, their more recent criminality and violence, and their success in "Latinoizing" south Florida.

The Dynamics of Discrimination against Cuban Americans

Economic Discrimination

The arrival of Cubans as political refugees triggered a response from the federal government that insulated them from many of the economic obstacles faced by Mexican Americans and Puerto Ricans. To the government, the comparatively small numbers of Cubans meant that social and educational programs could focus on mainstreaming Cuban refugees into the U.S. economy. As a result, the Cuban American population has been overrepresented in white-collar professions and businesses, while being underrepresented in agricultural and blue-collar occupations (Boswell, 1985).

The entrepreneurial skills of many Cuban refugees allowed for the creation of an ethnic enclave—"Little Havana" in Florida—that facilitated the economic transition of newly arrived Cuban refugees (Wilson and Portes, 1980). The emergence of Cuban-owned firms, especially in Dade County, Florida, provided employment opportunities for other Cuban refugees. These opportunities made it possible to stratify Cuban refugees as employers or low-wage earners, with the result that Cuban-owned firms reproduced in microcosm the stratification evident in pre-Castro Cuba. Indeed, as in the pre-Castro era, Cubans in lower-paying jobs have been subject to the exploitive economic practices of entrepreneurial Cuban business owners.

The arrival of the *Marielitos* in the United States in 1980 added a new stratum to the socioeconomic structure of the Cuban American population. The majority of the Marielitos were single, black, adult males with a criminal background. The arrival of the Marielitos in Dade County was so dramatic that the county's unemployment rate jumped from 5 percent to 13 percent (Boswell, 1985). The unwelcome reception given to the Marielitos by the American public was reinforced by the Cuban American community in Miami as well. Like other dark-skinned minority groups in the United States, the Marielitos were exploited as a cheap-labor pool that could be hired and fired at will.

Legal Discrimination

The comparatively high socioeconomic status of the early Cuban migrants, the relative recency of their arrival in the United States, and their image as anti-Castro, anticommunist political refugees have limited their involvement with the U.S. legal system. The majority of the Cuban American population resides in an economic and social niche that insulates them from unnecessary contact with law enforcement agencies. There are, however, two exceptions to this situation, both centering on the Marielitos.

First, the 1980 Mariel boatlifts created a logistical problem: Where were an estimated 125,000 Cuban refugees to be housed? The Carter administration responded by using Eglin Air Force Base as a processing center for the Marielitos (Boswell, 1985). The majority of the Marielitos regarded their move to Eglin as an attempt by the president to institutionalize them, a reminder of their status as prisoners in Cuba. As a result, soon after their arrival in Eglin, the Marielitos rioted and federal troops were called in. The Marielitos were the first segment of the Cuban American population to come in conflict with U.S. law enforcement agents in much the same way as the unwanted Mexican immigrants.

Second, the arrival of the Marielitos in Miami brought unexpected social problems to the Cuban community. A large number of the Marielitos had been Cuban prisoners because they were drug addicts (Page, 1980). Not surprisingly, their arrival increased the incidence of drug use in Miami's Cuban population. Since the majority of the Marielitos were black, the African American community in Miami perceived them as a threat to the positive relationship it had forged with law enforcement agencies; if crime-prone and drug-using Marielitos were mistaken for African Americans, the latter would suffer at the hands of law enforcement agencies. As a result, African Americans pushed for a distinction between Marielitos and themselves in treatment by the law—a pressure that only increased discrimination against newly arrived Marielitos.

Educational Discrimination

In contrast to the prejudice and discrimination experienced by Mexican Americans and Puerto Ricans in the educational system, Cubans were offered educational programs as a vehicle for assimilation into U.S. society. Hence, the education of Cubans in the United States has not been associated with the production and perpetuation of inequality. Indeed, the average level of education attained by the Cuban American population is higher than that of the non-Latino white population (Bean and Tienda, 1987).

The recent "English as the official language" movement has been particularly strong in south Florida, and it has changed the receptiveness of schools to bilingual and special programs for Cubans at the very time that the most needy members of this population—the Marielitos—have entered the educational system (Castro, Haun, and Roca, 1990; Dyste, 1990). Consequently, more recent, poor, and black Latino immigrants will be more likely to experience the same types of educational discrimination as other Latino migrants.

Political Discrimination

The initial waves of Cuban refugees to the United States were members of the professional, entrepreneurial, and/or upper classes in Cuba, who, like most people in affluent social strata, were politically conservative. Their self-perception as "exiles" and their commitment to preserving the class distinctions eliminated by Fidel Castro caused a majority to align themselves with the conservative politics of the Republican party (Torres, 1988). According to Hero (1992), the Reagan administration was instrumental in promoting conservative politics in the Cuban American population. For example, the Cuban community lobbied for the creation of Radio Jose Marti and for aid to the Nicaraguan contras. The Cuban community has also exhibited its ability to serve as a voting block for Republican party candidates to the Florida state legislature. Moreover, in local community politics, Cubans have been highly successful in securing seats on city councils and school boards. Such success, however, has caused political backlash from African Americans, who overwhelmingly vote against Cuban candidates, and, increasingly, from white Americans who are also threatened by Cuban political success.

With the fall of communism as a cold war threat, and with the social and economic problems associated with more recent Cuban immigrants, the success of Cuban Americans in politics may begin to level off. Also, African and white Americans may feel threatened by Cuban politicians as national politics moves away from its forty-year obsession with containing communism. Thus, despite the success of Cubans in the political arena, political discrimination against them may well increase over the next decade.

Stratification of Cuban Americans

If there is a success story among the Latino population it is Cuban Americans. Their entry into this country was a positive one. The U.S. government created social, educational, and occupational programs that allowed them to transfer their social and economic positions in Cuba to the United States. They lead other Latinos in educational, economic, and occupational attainment. In some cases, the Cuban American population has outpaced the non-Latino white population. Despite the recency of their arrival in the United States, most Cuban Americans enjoy a privileged position in U.S. society relative to other Latinos (Nelson and Tienda, 1985; Rodriguez, 1992). Stratification is more evident *within* the Cuban community, however. Recent immigrants are more likely to be black, less skilled, poor, unemployable, drug-addicted, and criminal; like their counterparts within the African American community, they may eventually constitute a volatile subpopulation. Those who are willing and able to work may be exploited by their employers, as is the case with many other Latinos and African Americans. Thus, while Cubans as an aggregate are highly successful, considerable inequality and stratification within the Cuban population exist (Perez, 1986).

As African Americans and white Americans feel more threatened by the Cuban American presence, discrimination against, and stratification of, Cubans are likely to increase. The English-only movement in Dade County, Florida, is perhaps a harbinger of a new, more intense wave of institutionalized discrimination.

SUMMARY

With the Spanish conquest of Mexico, Central and South America, and parts of the Caribbean islands, Spanish-speaking populations surrounded the English-speaking Anglo-Saxon core in the United States. Inevitably they were to come into conflict, with the Anglo-Saxon core winning all of the important confrontations. The consolidation of formerly Spanish territories as part of the United States (or at least as part of its sphere of influence), coupled with subsequent patterns of immigration and settlement from formerly Spanish-controlled areas, has created a highly dynamic and fluid situation in which the Latino population will soon be America's largest minority. Most of this large Latino minority will be of Mexican origin, with significant numbers of Puerto Ricans, Cubans, and both Central and South Americans.

The largest group in the Latino population, Mexican Americans, lags behind Puerto Ricans and Cuban Americans in educational attainment, income, and occupational status. Chicanos are thus at the bottom of the Latino population, whereas Cubans are at the top and Puerto Ricans somewhere in between. Rank in resource distribution and stratification is the result of intense and institutionalized discrimination against those of Mexican origin, somewhat less severe discrimination against those from the island of Puerto Rico, and more favorable treatment of those early anti-Castro Cuban refugees, with growing discrimination against those who have immigrated recently.

Among Mexican Americans, the retention of the Spanish language, as well as other cultural traits, sustains their identifiability, making them easy targets of discrimination since the Mexican-American War. Continued immigration, both legal and illegal, from Mexico has maintained this identifiability, which has been codified into negative stereotypes ranging from portrayals of males as "banditos" and, later, as macho and violent street criminals to images of young women as seductresses and of mature women as overbreeding, passive mothers of street gang members, and the accepting wives of lazy husbands or macho men. These beliefs help to sustain discrimination in jobs and wages in both rural and urban settings in every facet of life. They legitimate maltreatment by the legal system since the early betrayals of the Treaty of Guadalupe Hidalgo by Anglos. The educational system fails to recognize the special learning problems of Spanish-speaking youths who are members of a culture that has not fully abandoned its original home or accepted its new home. In politics a wide variety of tactics, from gerrymandering to intimidation by the Immigration and Naturalization Service and the Border Patrol, have kept Mexican Americans disenfranchised relative to their numbers in the population. Such patterns of discrimination are sustained by widespread fears among non-Latinos about the rapidly growing size of the Spanish-speaking population and what this will mean for Anglo culture and institutions.

Among Puerto Ricans, who became U.S. citizens through the annexation of Puerto Rico and the Jones Act, which gave them free access to the mainland, discrimination has taken a somewhat different pattern than among the Mexican-origin population. Puerto Ricans are visible not only because of their language and culture but also because a significant portion of the population bears the dark skin of their African origins. For both segments of the Puerto Rican population, negative stereotypes of them as lazy, sneaky, clannish, crime-prone, violent, and welfare-dependent have been used to justify discrimination in jobs, in treatment by law enforcement, and in schools. At least 40 percent of the over-25 age groups have not completed high school. In politics they are underrepresented even in those areas with very high numbers and concentrations of Puerto Ricans. In housing they are victimized by high segregation. Because Puerto Ricans continue to be concentrated in the urban Northeast, they are perceived as a threat to non-Latino whites in this region of the country, thereby guaranteeing continued patterns of discrimination.

Among Cuban Americans, who have been treated as desirable anticommunist refugees of the Castro regime in Cuba rather than as undesirable immigrants, discrimination has been much less intense. Since the early waves of Cubans were upper and middle class with technical, professional, and business skills, they were not subjected to the same intense stereotypes as other Latinos. However, the more recent waves of poor and often criminal Cubans, many of whom are black, to the mainland have escalated the level of discrimination. Coupled with the recognition by many, especially those in south Florida, that Cubans are here to stay, negative stereotyping much like that experienced by Puerto Ricans is beginning to accelerate, foretelling of future discrimination.

Until the last decade, Cubans were able to prosper economically, often with the help of programs sponsored by the federal government. Their success and refugee status shielded them from entanglement in the legal or law enforcement system, to become politically successful and powerful in south Florida. Educationally they achieve at a rate higher than non-Latino whites. But as poorer Cubans have entered the country, they have brought many of the problems of the poor—from crime to drug abuse—and this shift will change the perception of Cubans in the future.

Increasingly, all Latinos are seen as a threat because their numbers are increasing relative to the European-American stock. This threat has reinvigorated old prejudicial beliefs against Latinos and legitimated new patterns of discrimination in schools, in the activities of law enforcement agencies, in politics, and in the job markets for low-skilled workers. Mexican-origin people suffer the most discrimination and prejudice because they are the largest, fastest-growing, and, hence, the most threatening of the Latino ethnic groups. But recent Cuban refugees still suffer a great deal of discrimination and prejudice within and outside the Cuban community; and unskilled Puerto Ricans have a difficult struggle in the financially burdened cities of the Northeast. In the near future, then, Latinos will come to rival African Americans for the dilemma they pose to the Anglo-Saxon core in a free and democratic society that values equality of opportunity.

POINTS OF DEBATE

As the size of the Latino population grows and as white ethnic Americans approach being a bare majority of the total population, the sense of threat among non-Latino Americans will increase, potentially setting into motion new and intense forms of discrimination. Yet, the very size of the Latino population by the midpoint of the twenty-first century will not only pose a threat to non-Latinos but serve the Latino population as a resource for economic and political power against the discrimination that ensues from the threat. In any case, the next fifty years will pose a number of volatile points of debate.

1. Can English be maintained as the ascendant language, or are parts of the country to become bilingual? Non-Latino Americans intensely feel that all immigrants must learn English, but because Latino immigrants remain close to their country of origin, Spanish remains the language of everyday use among large numbers of Latinos. Should this use of language and other non-Anglo cultural traits be suppressed? Or are Americans going to have to change their views about bilingualism in America? In either case, debate and action will be intense.
2. Because the Latino population will be so large and a clear majority of the population in the Southwest, the patterns of assimilation evident for other minority populations may not occur. Latinos may be able to carve out a social niche within the Anglo-Saxon core, maintaining their own economic, cultural, educational, and religious institutions. The intensity of feeling in the Southwest about language will thus be magnified many times over, as Anglos seek to stop this potential subsociety in America. What will happen? Violence? Mass exodus of non-Latinos? Adjustment and accommodation of non-Latinos to a dual culture and society? Or will this confrontation of lifestyle and culture be avoided? There is no clear answer to these questions, indicating that ferment and debate will be intense—as is already evident.
3. Americans do not feel that they "owe" Latinos compensation for past acts of discrimination in the same way that they owe African and Native Americans. This lack of "collective guilt," coupled with rising fears about the Latinoization of American culture, will pose a real problem for non-Latino Americans who resent with ever greater intensity the invasion of their territory, institutions, and cultural patterns. How is this resentment to be mitigated? Can it be reduced? Or are non-Latino Americans and Latinos on a collision course? And what will be the outcome of this collision as it intensifies from the political posturing of today to the dramatically escalated rhetoric and potential political empowerment of tomorrow?

CHAPTER 7

Asian Americans

Praised for their industriousness, heralded for their educational attainments, and lauded for their economic success, Asian Americans are often viewed as the "model minority." Indeed, most Americans believe that the success of Asian Americans stems from a combination of industriousness and avoidance of discrimination (McQueen, 1991). But the history of Asian immigration tells a very different story, and the persistence of negative stereotypes and acts of discrimination reflect past patterns that persist today, though in more subtle and muted form (Takaki, 1989; Matthaei and Amott, 1990).

The first Asians to arrive in the United States in significant numbers were the Chinese, who initially worked in the gold mines of California in the 1850s and, later, in building the transcontinental railroad. By the early twentieth century, the Chinese were joined by increasing numbers of Japanese, Filipinos, Koreans, and Asian Indians. By the 1920s, this immigration decreased dramatically in reaction to a series of highly restrictive immigration laws enacted by the U.S. Congress and targeted at immigrants from Asian countries. Later, in the period after World War II, these laws were liberalized, opening the door to a new wave of Asian immigration (Hing, 1993).

Asians made up 1.5 percent of the U.S. population in 1980 and 2.9 percent in 1994, indicating that their numbers have increased by 108 percent over the last fourteen years (U.S. Bureau of the Census, 1995). Over 40 percent of the Asian American population is comprised of Chinese and Filipinos, followed respectively by Japanese, Asian Indians, and Koreans (U.S. Commission on Civil Rights, 1992). The increase in the Asian population in the United States is mirrored in the numbers of Asians living on their home continent: Sixty percent of the world's population lives in Asia (Suzuki, 1989).

People tend to lump Asians together because of their physical appearance, but each subpopulation has a distinct language, culture, and organizational pattern. Indeed, much of the subtle discrimination against Asians comes from the failure to recognize and appreciate their differences. Yet, for our purposes it is useful to consider Asian Americans together in order to describe what they all have in common—the experience of being victims of negative stereotyping, prejudice, and discriminatory practices directed at Asians living in America.

RESOURCE SHARES OF ASIAN AMERICANS

Impoverishment of Asian Americans

Table 7.1 summarizes poverty statistics for both the white American and Asian American populations. From 1970 to 1980, poverty rates for both populations were roughly similar; but in 1990 and 1994, they increased for Asians. Between 1980 and 1990 the poverty rate for white Americans increased by 6 percent, whereas the Asian American poverty rate rose by 57 percent, primarily because the more recent Asian immigrants—Vietnamese, Cambodians, Laotians, and Pacific Islanders—tend to be indigent. Between 1990 and 1994 the poverty rate increased by 22 percent for white Americans and 9 percent for Asian Americans. The increase in the poverty rate for Asian Americans (70 percent) between 1980 and 1994 was more than twice that for white Americans (30 percent). These figures undermine the image of Asian Americans as the model minority, immune to social inequalities and the problems associated with poverty (U.S. Commission on Civil Rights, 1992a).

Income of Asian Americans

Table 7.2 shows that the median income of Asian Americans is higher than that for white Americans. However, the net gain in income between 1980 and 1994 was the same for both white Americans and Asian Americans. One must interpret the data in Table 7.2 in light of the figures in Table 7.2, which report an increase in the Asian American poverty rate relative to that for white Americans. These two sets of figures also reveal that the

TABLE 7.1. Poverty Rates among White Americans and Asian Americans

Year	White Americans, %	Asian Americans, %
1970	10.9	11.5
1980	9.4	9.0
1990	10.0	14.1
1994	12.2	15.3

Source: U.S. Commission on Civil Rights, 1988, 1992; U.S. Bureau of the Census, 1992a; March 1994 CPS.

TABLE 7.2. Median Household Income and Number of Workers per Household for White Americans and Asian Americans, 1980, 1990, and 1994

	White Americans			*Asian Americans*		
	1980	1990	1994	1980	1990	1994
Median household income	$20,835	$36,915	$40,884	$22,713	$42,245	$44,456
Number of workers in each household, %						
0	12.3	13.9	14.5	7.8	10.4	16.3
1	32.9	26.5	26.8	29.2	26.5	31.8
2 or more	54.9	59.7	58.7	63.0	63.1	51.9

Source: U.S. Bureau of the Census, 1992a; U.S. Commission on Civil Rights, 1992; March 1994 CPS.

Asian American population can be characterized as divided between those growing richer and those who remain poor (U.S. Bureau of the Census, 1992a; U.S. Commission on Civil Rights, 1992).

Three main factors contribute to the higher incomes of Asian Americans (Cabezas, Shinagawa, and Kawaguchi, 1990). First, in a larger proportion of Asian American families, both spouses work. Second, because Asian American children tend to live with their parents for a longer period than do white American children, they become contributors to the household income. Third, Asian families are larger on average, thus more wage earners live in each household (Suzuki, 1989; U.S. Commission on Civil Rights, 1980, 1988). Consequently, the income figures for Asian American families do not reflect the fact that it takes more Asian American wage earners per household to attain the income level of the average white American household.

Occupational Distribution of Asian Americans

Statistically, it is undeniable that Asian Americans are successful in the employment area. According to the figures in Table 7.3, Asian Americans outnumber white Americans in several desirable occupations. For example, the proportion of Asian Americans in executive, managerial, and administrative occupations increased by 9.5 percent between 1980 and 1994, compared to an increase of only 5.1 percent for white Americans; 66 percent of the Asian American population was employed in executive, managerial, administrative, technical, sales, and administrative support occupations in 1994 compared to 60 percent of the white population.

The occupational success of the Asian American population, especially compared to other minority groups such as African Americans and Latinos, needs to be qualified, however. Hurk and Kim (1989) argue that the occupational accomplishments of Asian Americans create a "false con-

TABLE 7.3. Occupational Categories for White Americans and Asian Americans* Age 16 and Over, 1980 and 1990

	White Americans, %			*Asian Americans, %*		
Occupational Category	1980	1990	1994	1980	1990	1994
Managerial and professional specialty	24.3	27.4	29.4	24.8	31.9	34.2
Technical, sales, and administrative support	31.3	33.2	30.3	30.3	33.8	31.5
Service	11.5	12.5	12.7	15.9	15.2	15.1
Farming, forestry, fishing	2.9	2.6	2.9	1.9	0.7	1.2
Precision production, craft, and repair	13.4	11.0	11.1	9.9	7.7	6.9
Operators, fabricators, laborers	16.6	13.3	13.6	17.3	10.8	11.1

*Includes Japanese, Chinese, Koreans, and Filipinos.
Source: U.S. Commission on Civil Rights, 1986; U.S. Bureau of the Census, 1992a, 1992b; March 1994 CPS.

sciousness" among Asian Americans that disguises their patterns of underemployment. That is, Asian Americans accept, to a degree, the stereotype that they are successful in light of their visibility in high-status occupations (doctors, engineers, scientists, entrepreneurs, etc.). As a result, they develop a false consciousness in believing that Asian Americans are more successful than they are unsuccessful (Gee, 1993). Yet, despite their representation in high-status occupations, most Asian Americans hold jobs in the *lower levels* of these professions (Osako, 1984; Duleep and Sanders, 1992; Sue, Zane, and Sue, 1985; and Cabezas et al., 1989). For example, the placement of Asian Americans at lower levels in their professions has resulted in a noticeable pattern according to Ronald Takaki (1966:43):

> This very image can produce a reinforcing pattern: Asian-American professionals often find they "top out," reaching a promotional ceiling early in their careers.

For example, in a study of Asian workers in management positions in local, state, and federal government agencies in the San Francisco area, Amado Cabezas found that most of the Asian American workers were at the bottom of the managerial tier, indicating that Asian Americans had lower salaries than their white counterparts (U.S. Commission on Civil Rights, 1979). Similarly, in a study of managers in U.S. corporations, it was found that "Asian descent" had a negative effect on becoming a manager (Chiu, 1994:1089):

> The probability that an Asian man will become a manager is seven to eleven percentage points lower than for a white man. The study was adjusted for English-proficiency and was limited to American-born Asian Americans, so that language proficiency and cultural barriers could not account for these findings.

Thus, because of a "glass or bamboo ceiling," many Asian Americans have not fully benefited from their mobility into the professional and management ranks (Equal Employment Opportunity Commission, 1985). The notion of a *glass or bamboo ceiling* refers to the perception held by Asian Americans that, due to negative stereotypes of them, they are limited, despite being qualified, for advancement in professional occupations. Some of these negative stereotypes are rooted in the perceptions that Asian Americans are unaggressive, have poor and/or limited communication skills in English, and are too technical to be effective managers (Nguyen, 1993). As Chiu (1994:1090) has noted: "Asian Americans continue to be denied employment opportunities simply because they speak English with a foreign accent."

The overall occupational success of the Asian American population has reinforced the image of that population as the model minority, an image that belies their difficulty in integrating fully in the professional world, especially its upper echelons (Thomas, 1995; Kang, 1996). Acceptance of the image by both Asian Americans and white Americans also creates the illusion that the Asian American population is not subject to social problems and does not need help from either the state or federal government (Hu, 1989; Lee, 1993). As Crystal (1989:405) has noted:

> In reality, the "model minority" myth has obscured many serious problems in the Asian community and has been used to justify omitting Asian Americans from federal funding and some special minority programs. Moreover, the Asian-American success story has been turned into a weapon against other minorities by persons who deny the existence of racism in America.

Educational Attainment of Asian Americans

The Asian American population is regarded as the most educated group in U.S. society (Grove and Wu, 1991). A review of the data in Table 7.4 shows that Asians do indeed have higher graduation rates from high school and college than whites. Between 1980 and 1990, however, a 10.2 percent increase in the number of white high school graduates brought both groups closer to parity. However, the increase in the number of Asian American high school graduates between 1980 and 1990 was only 47 percent of the increase in the white population, indicating possible problems in the area of education for Asian Americans.

In 1994, 41.2 percent of Asian Americans had completed four years of college or more, compared to 23.1 percent of white Americans, a figure that

TABLE 7.4. Educational Outcomes for White Americans and Asian Americans, Age 25 and Older, 1980 and 1994

	High School Graduates, %			*Completed 4 or More Years of College, %*		
	1980	1990	1994	1980	1990	1994
White Americans	68.9	79.1	82.0	17.3	24.8	23.1
Asian Americans	75.1	80.6	84.8	33.4	44.3	41.2

Source: U.S. Bureau of the Census, 1983a, 1983b, 1983c, 1992a; March 1994 CPS.

accounts for their occupational success. The college completion figures in Table 7.4 often are utilized to argue that there are no barriers to higher education for Asian American students. In particular, these numbers do not reflect the existence of restrictive admission policies against Asian American college applicants. Asian American student activists argue that although college applications submitted by Asian American students increased by over 70 percent between 1980 and 1990, the number of Asian American students accepted decreased by almost 80 percent (U.S. Commission on Civil Rights, 1992).

At Harvard, Brown, Princeton, Yale, Stanford, and the University of California, a pattern of lower admission rates for Asian American applicants was discovered, even though those applicants had academic qualifications equal to those of white applicants (Bunzel and Au, 1987; Nakanishi, 1988; and Takagi, 1990). Interestingly, some college admission officers have contended that restrictive admission policies for Asian American applicants are important "because Asian American college admits would overshadow white college admits" (Takagi, 1990). This pattern of underadmitting qualified Asians has been justified as a way of overcoming "reverse discrimination" that would hurt qualified white applicants; in fact, it is a form of direct discrimination against Asian Americans, for whom "quotas" *limiting* (not increasing) their numbers apparently exist (Kang, 1996).

Housing of Asian Americans

The existence of "Koreatowns," "Little Tokyos," "Chinatowns," "Little Saigons," and "Little Manilas" indicates patterns of residential segregation among Asian American populations. Many Asian Americans have chosen to settle in large metropolitan areas in order to enhance their social, cultural, and economic development in U.S. society (Wong, 1976; Lyman, 1986; and Cabezas, Shinagawa, and Kawaguchi, 1986–1987); and as a consequence, their concentration in these areas produces a high degree of residential segregation.

Using a *segregation index* based on the percentage of the population

Box 7.1

Earnings and Education: A Dilemma for the Model Minority

One of the indicators used to gauge the success of a population is "returns of education." The table below shows that across all categories of educational attainment the median earnings of the Asian American population are lower than the median earnings of equivalently educated white Americans. The discrepancy is more apparent for the category "4 or more years of college." While the proportion of the Asian American population in this category is 65 percent greater than the proportion of the white population, the median earnings of the latter are 105 percent greater than the median earnings of the former. For Asian Americans, then, the returns of education are not comparable to those for white Americans.

	Less Than High School		*4 Years of High School*		*1–3 Years of College*		*4 or More Years of College*	
	White Americans	Asian Americans	White Americans	Asian Americans	White Americans	Asian Americans	White Americans	Asian Americans
Median earnings*	17,054	14,876	22,053	19,288	26,737	24,211	36,134	34,469

*1990 year-round, full-time workers 25 years and older.
Source: U.S. Bureau of the Census, 1992a.

that would need to move into white neighborhoods to achieve complete desegregation, the U.S. Commission on Civil Rights (1992) listed the results for five groups in the Asian Americans: Japanese (42 percent), Chinese (52 percent), Filipino (55 percent), Korean (55 percent), and Vietnamese (69 percent). Based on the segregation index for each group, then, Japanese Americans are the least segregated and Vietnamese Americans are the most segregated. Researchers have suggested that the segregation index also reflects the groups' country of origin and length of residence in the United States (Langberg and Farley, 1985; Montero, 1981). Japanese Americans have a lower segregation index because they tend to be American-born and have resided longer in the United States. In contrast, Vietnamese Americans have a higher segregation index because the majority are foreign-born and have resided in the United States for a shorter period of time. Although the segregation index is useful, the separation of Asian and white Americans cannot be fully explained in terms of self-selection, nativity, and length of residence. Discrimination is also involved, as we will see shortly.

Life Span of Asian Americans

There are negligible differences between Asians and whites on factors associated with life and death. According to the National Center for Health Statistics (1991), Asian Americans have a lower death rate due to accidents and homicides than white Americans. For example, in 1990 the death rate per 100,000 population by accidents was 22 for Asians and 40 for whites, while the rate per 100,000 population for homicide was 29 for Asians and 49 for whites.

Box 7.2

A Note on Pacific Islanders

In 1990, Pacific Islanders made up about 5 percent of the Asian population in the United States (Barringer et al., 1993) or about 365,000 persons. While the Pacific Islander population increased by 46 percent between 1980 and 1990, their proportion of the Asian–Pacific Islander population actually decreased because other Asian populations experienced even greater numerical increases—especially, Southeast Asian populations. The Pacific Islander population is divided into three groups based on region of origin: Polynesians (85 percent of the total), Micronesians (14 percent), and Melanesians (1 percent). Hawaiians are the largest segment in the Polynesian population followed by Samoans and Tongans. Guamanians are the largest segment in the Micronesian population, and Fijians are the largest segment in the Melanesian population.

An examination of Table 7.5 shows that the majority (66 percent) of Hawaiians in the United States live in the state of Hawaii. In contrast, the majority of Samoans (51 percent), Guamanians (51 percent), and Fijians (82 percent) live in the state of California. Comparatively speaking, a larger proportion of the Pacific Islander population residing in the United States is found in the state of California—a not unexpected finding given California's proximity to countries in the Pacific Rim.

In general, the Pacific Islander population is relatively youthful compared to the median age of the U.S. population, 21 years of age versus 30 years of age. Educational outcomes for the Pacific Islander population show that the population is enrolled at comparable levels in secondary schools (26 percent) and college (17 percent) with the U.S. population as a whole (at 25 percent and 20 percent, respectively). Since most Pacific Islanders enter the U.S. labor market as immigrants, they tend to be clustered in blue-collar occupations; and because of this fact, Pacific Islanders are underrepresented in managerial and professional occupations. Poverty in the Pacific Islander population varies by group. Tongans (22 percent), Samoans (30 percent), and Micronesians (38 percent) have a higher rate of poverty than the total U.S. population (with 13.5 percent being poor). Hawaiians (16 percent) and Guamanians (14 percent) have a slightly lower rate of poverty than other Pacific Islanders, but still a rate that is higher than the national average.

TABLE 7.5 Pacific Islanders in Selected States by Group, 1990

Group	Size of Various Pacific Islander Populations in 1990	*Percentages of Pacific Islanders Living in Key States*				
		Hawaii	California	Washington	Texas	Utah
Hawaiian	211,014	66	16	3	1	1
Samoan	62,964	24	51	7	2	3
Guamanian	49,345	4	51	8	5	*
Tongan	17,606	18	45	3	4	22
Fijian	7,036	4	82	4	1	1
Palauan	1,439	25	28	8	5	*

* Less than 1 percent.
Source: U.S. Commission on Civil Rights, 1992.

THE DYNAMICS OF DISCRIMINATION AGAINST ASIAN AMERICANS

Like other ethnic subpopulations in the United States, Asian Americans are victims of inaccurate perceptions by others of society (Thornton and Taylor, 1988; Stephan and Stephan, 1989; and Sodowsky et al., 1991). Stewart Kwoh, director of the Asian American Legal Center, has observed:

> Asian Americans have been viewed as non-citizens. . . . Historically, we (Asians) have all been considered immigrants, temporary visitors, or foreigners. Even though we are not immigrants, Asian Americans, when they move out of Asian neighborhoods, are seen as new immigrants (U.S. Commission on Civil Rights, 1986:31–32).

As the number of Asian immigrants to the United States increases in the next decades, so will the perception that all Asians are recent arrivals to the United States. The perception that all Asian Americans are foreigners increases their visibility in U.S. society and reinforces negative beliefs and stereotypes that are used to legitimize discrimination.

Identifiability of Asian Americans

In the United States, Asians are unique in their physical appearance. Their skin and hair color, as well as facial characteristics (especially the epicanthic fold), make Asian Americans very noticeable in American society. This identifiability, coupled with the misconception that Asian Americans are recent immigrants, has resulted in an anti-Asian climate in the United States. For example, according to the U.S. Commission on Civil Rights (1992), anti-Asian slogans, signs, and slurs are widespread:

- In California, the word "JAP" was spray-painted on the door of a Japanese American state legislator.
- In Houston, Texas, public health officials harassed Chinese and Viet-

namese restaurant owners for not adopting "American" standards of cleanliness.

- A car constructed as a caricature of a Japanese face dropping a bomb on Detroit was displayed at an automobile exhibit in Flint, Michigan.
- Bumper stickers have appeared on cars in Los Angeles with the following messages: "Toyota-Datsun-Honda and Pearl Harbor," and "Unemployment Made in Japan."

Anti-Asian sentiment in the United States has targeted Asian Americans as scapegoats for many of the social ills facing the U.S. economy.

Negative Beliefs about Asian Americans

Stereotypes of Asian Americans have shifted from those stereotypes characterizing them as sneaky, obsequious, or inscrutable to the stereotype of the model minority (Chun, 1980; Hurk and Kim, 1989). According to this stereotype, all Asian Americans are hardworking, intelligent, and successful. Although this stereotype appears to be positive, it can also have negative implications. The most important of these is the perception that Asian Americans do not experience the same social and economic problems of other populations. Consequently, homelessness, poverty, unemployment, crime, and other problems of the Asian American population are often ignored (Crystal, 1989).

Another negative belief about Asian Americans is that many are recent immigrants (Hosokawa, 1982). For example, Asians are commonly asked, "Where did you learn English?" Diane C. Yu, a member of the California Commission on Racial, Ethnic, Religious, and Minority Violence, has noted that when acquaintances ask her where she was born, they are reluctant to accept "the United States" as a response; they are appeased when she mentions that her parents came from China (U.S. Commission on Civil Rights, 1986).

Portrayals in movies and television have also created persistent stereotypes (Delgado and Stefancic, 1992; Wong, 1978). Early on, Asians were portrayed in movies as cunning and savage. As anti-Asian sentiment grew, especially after the bombing of Pearl Harbor, they were depicted as tricky and devious (Wong, 1978). During World War II, most movies promoted anti-Japanese sentiment by depicting Japanese as master criminals (ironically, the role of master criminal was usually played by a white actor in makeup). These stereotypes built upon those created in 1919 by William Randolph Hearst who began an anti-Asian film serial that promoted the image of Asians as the "yellow peril."

In the public mind, Asian Americans often are regarded as "foreigners" because their status in U.S. society is often associated with foreign policy between Asia and the United States (Takaki, 1993; Schrieke, 1936). As relations between Asia and America fluctuate, so does public sentiment in the United States toward Asian Americans. For example, when the Japanese automaking industry increased its share in the United States, in certain segments of the population living in certain locations sentiment became anti-Asian. In some cases, anti-Asian sentiment has produced violent and tragic results. For example, the 1982 killing of Vincent Chin, a Chinese American, in Detroit was the result of his killers' resentment of Japanese automobile exports to the United States. As Asian automobile plants have been established in the United States, much of this intensity had receded, but the potential for a new wave of anti-Asian sentiment remains, as industries export jobs to lower-priced labor in Asian countries.

Even as excessively negative beliefs have moved some to violence against Asian Americans, a series of more subtle and invidious beliefs has emerged (Sodowsky, Lai, and Plake, 1991). For example, the model minority becomes the "yellow peril" when Asian Americans are accused of taking jobs from white Americans, African Americans, and Latinos (Chang, 1993). Also, tensions between Japan and the United States have created various waves of "Japan bashing." Another negative belief stems from "Buy American" campaigns, which contain subtle anti-Asian messages, despite the fact that America's two biggest trading partners are European.

Finally, Asians' occupational niche as a middleman minority group that sells to non-Asians has created the same kinds of negative beliefs that emerge against all middleman minority groups—that they are clannish, secretive, dishonest, and devious. The Chinese were labeled with these negative epithets early on, but in recent decades these beliefs have been revived with a new intensity as Asian Americans have established small businesses in the neighborhoods of other disadvantaged minority groups, particularly African Americans and Latinos. These beliefs have created a sometimes volatile mix of resentment that erupts into violence, as the Korean merchants learned in the Los Angeles riots of 1992.

Institutionalized Discrimination against Asian Americans

The model minority stereotype traditionally has obscured the issue of discrimination against Asian Americans. This stereotype, as with so many other stereotypes, runs counter to the facts. For without doubt, prejudice and discrimination have been very much a part of one Asian experience in America.

Legal Discrimination

Legalized discrimination against Asian Americans is best exemplified by immigration legislation, most of which was designed to exclude Asian immigrants from competing with white Europeans and, at the same time, to perpetuate negative stereotypes about Asians.

Chinese Immigration. In 1848, the arrival of two men and one woman from China began a flow of Chinese immigrants that spanned three decades (Zo, 1978). The majority of Chinese immigrants were recruited as labor for the mine industry in the western United States, and later for the building of railroads that would connect the West and East coasts. This massive immigration, however, produced a series of efforts to constrain social mobility and occupational opportunity (McKenzie, 1928; Miller, 1969):

- In 1855, California passed a law placing a fifty-five-dollar head tax on every Chinese immigrant. In 1858, a law was passed forbidding Chinese immigration into the state. In 1876 the U.S. Supreme Court ruled both laws unconstitutional.
- The U.S. Congress passed the Chinese Exclusion Act of 1882. The act suspended the immigration of Chinese laborers to the United States for ten years and prohibited persons of Chinese ancestry residing in the United States from obtaining U.S. citizenship after the effective date of the act. An 1888 amendment to the act applied the exclusion to all Chinese immigrants except merchants, students, teachers, tourists, and government officials. The act was extended for ten years in 1892, for two years in 1902, and indefinitely in 1904. The act was repealed in 1943 by Congress and replaced by a legislative agenda that established a quota system for Chinese immigrants.

Chinese immigrants in San Francisco during the late 1890s.

Japanese Immigration. The Japanese began arriving in the United States, especially on the West Coast, at the turn of the twentieth century. Immediately upon their arrival, they were accused of taking jobs away from U.S. citizens, of working for very low wages, and of displacing white domestic and factory workers. Anti-Japanese sentiment quickly gained supporters from participants in the Chinese exclusion movement (Penrose, 1973; Fukuda, 1980). As the number of Japanese immigrants grew, the demand for a national policy restricting Japanese immigration increased. The United States tried to avoid enacting immigration legislation against the Japanese by reaching an accord with Japan called the "Gentleman's Agreement of 1907." Under this compact, Japan agreed not to issue passports to skilled or unskilled workers, except for those already in the United States, or to wives or children of these workers. However, the agreement did not stem the tide of anti-Japanese sentiment:

- The 1917 Immigration Act was enacted in order to stop Japanese immigration as well as immigration from other Asian countries. The act barred admission of any person from "islands not possessed by the United States adjacent to the Continent of Asia" or the continent of Asia (excluding Persia and parts of Afghanistan and Russia).
- The 1924 National Origins Act was passed in order to stop the flow of Japanese immigrants. The act barred the immigration of Japanese wives even if their husbands were U.S. citizens, and prohibited the immigration of Japanese aliens ineligible for U.S. citizenship. The act reinforced the legal decision in *Ozawa v. United States* (1922) that persons of Japanese ancestry could not become naturalized citizens.

Filipino and Korean Immigration. While immigration from Japan and China accounted for the bulk of Asian immigration to the United States prior to the 1920s, other Asian groups came in smaller numbers. Two of these groups were Filipinos and Koreans. Since the Philippine Islands were a territory of the United States in the 1920s, they were exempt from the 1917 Immigration Act and the 1924 National Origins Act. As a result, Filipinos were free to immigrate to the United States; they are now the second largest Asian ethnic population in the United States. Filipinos were recruited to work on sugar plantations in Hawaii and as field laborers in the California agricultural industry (Knoll, 1982; Kitano, 1980). However, as the number of Filipinos grew in California, riots between Filipinos and white Americans took place. The white rioters saw the Filipinos as another part of the "Asian horde" attempting to enter the United States. Partly in response to tensions between Filipinos and white Americans on the West Coast, the U.S. Congress passed, in 1934, an act granting deferred independence to the Philippine Islands and imposing an annual quota of fifty Filipino immigrants to the U.S. mainland per year.

As early as 1885, Korean political exiles came to the United States (Kitano and Daniels, 1988). The first sizable wave of Korean immigrants went to Hawaii; between 1903 and 1905, approximately seven thousand Koreans immigrated there (Choy, 1979). By 1905, one thousand Koreans were living in California. These immigrants expected to find better working and living conditions; instead, they found low wages and substandard housing. In an attempt to protect its citizens, the Korean government banned the entry of Koreans to the United States; as a consequence, Korean immigration did not reach noticeable proportions again until the passage of the Immigration and Naturalization Act of 1965.

The Internment of Japanese Americans. Besides the use of immigration legislation to both exclude and control Asian immigrants to and within the United States, the U.S. government manipulated the legal system to discriminate against Japanese Americans by placing them in internment camps after the bombing of Pearl Harbor on December 7, 1941. Immediately after the bombing, the FBI rounded up over two thousand Japanese Americans suspected of aiding Japan's war effort. Not satisfied with the small numbers of incarcerated Japanese Americans, the Hearst press, through the column of Henry McLemore, rallied the cry of "Japs Must Go" (cited in Kitano, 1980:216):

> I am for the immediate removal of every Japanese on the West Coast to a point deep in the interior . . . let 'em be pinched, hurt, and hungry. Personally, I hate Japanese. And that goes for all of them.

The identifiability of Asians has made it easy for white persons to exclude them from their neighborhoods.

Responding to mounting demands for anti-Japanese legislation, on February 19, 1942, President Franklin D. Roosevelt signed Executive Order 9066, which established restricted military areas and authorized the building of relocation camps. These camps were located in California, Arizona, Idaho, Wyoming, Colorado, Utah, and Arkansas. Interestingly, even though Executive Order 9066 did not specify that it applied to persons of Japanese descent, it was applied to them exclusively. The U.S. government argued that the relocation camps were vital to the national security of the United States.

The movement of Japanese Americans to the relocation camps began in March 1942. Anyone at least one-eighth Japanese was relocated. Of the approximately 127,000 Americans of Japanese descent living in the United States in 1940, 110,000 were placed in relocation camps (Peterson, 1971; Tsuchida, 1990). Japanese Americans were forced to sell property and businesses at a fraction of their value—usually 5 cents on the dollar—and were allowed to bring to the camps only what they could carry. The relocation of Japanese Americans to the camps was generally smooth as a result of Japanese American cooperation; they responded to posted notices, gathered at designated departure areas, and boarded trains or buses for the trip to the camps.

Although things may have looked calm on the surface, there was turbulence underneath. Japanese Americans regarded the relocation camps as concentration camps (Daniels, 1971). At some camps, there were riots; at others, there were periods of silence between the Japanese Americans and the white guards; and in some camps anti-American slogans were painted on banners and buildings. In the cases of *Korematsu v. United States* (1944) and *Hirabayashi v. United States* (1943), Japanese Americans used the U.S. court system to question the legal status of the relocation camps. The U.S. Supreme Court upheld Executive Order 9066 in both cases (Bell, 1973).

Japanese Americans were officially released from the relocation camps on January 2, 1945. As might be expected, they wanted to know how the United States was going to redress their losses. According to the Commission on Wartime Relocation and Internment of Civilians (1983), the losses suffered by Japanese Americans interned in the camps—personal wealth, residences, businesses, and farms—were between $185 million and $400 million. In 1948, the U.S. Congress passed the Japanese American Evacuation Claims Act, which limited claims to a maximum amount of $2,500, with all claims to be submitted within eighteen months of the act's passage. The $131 million Congress appropriated for the act paid ten cents for every dollar of actual loss. It took the federal government seventeen years to process all the claims submitted; in the end, the federal government paid out $38 million (in 1942 dollars, without interest) of the $131 million allocated by Congress.

In 1976, President Gerald Ford issued Presidential Proclamation 4417, which rescinded Executive Order 9066 and apologized to the Japanese American community. This proclamation created a new concern that victimization of Japanese Americans was being perpetuated by the government's failure to fully redress their losses during the internment period. In 1980, Congress created the Commission on Wartime Relocation and Internment of Civilians (1983) in order to examine the issue of uncompensated loss of income and property to Japanese Americans during the internment period. In 1983, the commission made the following recommendations:

1. The U.S. government must offer an "official apology" to Japanese Americans.
2. The U.S. government should pardon Japanese Americans convicted of violating Executive Order 9066.
3. The U.S. government should establish a $1.5 billion fund, from which $20,000 would be paid to each of the approximately 60,000 survivors of the relocation camps.

Prompted by the commission's recommendation, Congress passed the Civil Liberties Act of 1988, authorizing the $20,000 compensation payment for living survivors of the relocation camps.

The internment itself and the reluctance in its aftermath to apologize for suspending Americans' civil rights and to compensate for obvious damages afterward sent a clear message to all Asians: This can happen to you. Though this seemed implausible, it remained a subtle threat. More significantly, the willingness to suspend Asians' (but not Germans') civil rights reflected, and at the same time contributed to, a willingness to use the law to restrict Asian immigration and to threaten those who are already here with deportation or harassment. This legal threat persists today; although it is not as blatant as the one faced by Latinos, it is just as real, especially in a period where economic tensions between the United States and its Asian trading partners are high.

Economic Discrimination

Legal discrimination against Asian immigrants limits their economic opportunities. The driving force behind anti-Asian sentiment and negative beliefs is, and has been, fear that Asian immigrants would displace white workers. The ability of Asian immigrants to create economic opportunities for themselves through small business activities was curtailed in the early decades of this century by stereotypes portraying them as dirty, immoral, unassimilable, sly, sneaky, and cheap. Such negative beliefs are typically applied to middleman minority groups, but they have been particularly intense when applied to Asian Americans because many white Americans, African Americans, and Latinos sense that Asians want their jobs (Takaki, 1989).

These fears became codified in a set of social beliefs portraying Asians as a threat to the social and economic fabric of U.S. society. For example, according to the U.S. Commission on Civil Rights (1992), even though Asian Americans are represented in greater numbers than other ethnic minorities in white-collar occupations in the United States, they suffer from discrimination that limits their mobility within these occupations. They

Box 7.3

Asian Gangs and Legal Discrimination

Gangs are a part of the organizational structure of many Asian societies, being linked to their version of organized crime (trafficking narcotics, prostitution, gambling, extortion, loan sharking, and other illegal activities). Elements of this activity have been imported into the United States and adapted to ghetto life. Among the Chinese, for example, violent street gangs are linked to *tongs,* fraternal societies (sometimes called "clans") that control much of the internal activity in large urban Chinese enclaves in order to secure large profits from illegal activities. The gangs control territories, typically for one of the tongs.

The result of this gang activity is that all citizens in the affected areas feel threatened by gang violence. Many complain bitterly that the police do not attack this problem with the same zeal as they attack, say, Mafia activities in other ethnic enclaves. Few federal resources—FBI and special investigators and prosecutors—or local resources—organized crime units or drug enforcement units—are devoted to Asian ghettos, where it is presumed that residents "can take care of themselves." Inattention to gangs and organized crime in Asian communities represents a form of legal discrimination against the model minority.

eventually confront the glass ceiling: They are in, but they can go only so far. The glass ceiling is partially attributed to stereotypical notions of Asian Americans—unaggressive, poor communicators in English, and unassimilated. Asian Americans in white-collar, especially management, occupations express their concerns as follows (U.S. Commission on Civil Rights, 1992:132):

- I am of the opinion that most Asian Americans are facing an insurmountable glass wall in the corporate world. As a matter of fact, most of us have given up hope of advancing up the corporate ladder. The more we think about it, the more frustrated, discouraged, and depressed we become. . . .
- I suspect that the minds of many corporate managers and the senior staff members who have direct control . . . are still in the 1960s. As a consequence, for most of them we Asians are a suspect class, and we usually have to prove that we are better in order to be equal. . . .
- Most of us have proved our technical capability. However, many major corporations tend to overlook the non-technical side of many Asian Americans. Corporations pick pigeon holes for us. And what is worse, they believe that we are quite content staying in those technologically airtight pigeon holes.

Many Asian Americans perceive the glass ceiling as the product of attitudes held by white Americans. In a survey of Asian American professionals and managers in the San Francisco Bay area, Cabezas et al. (1989) found that respondents regarded prejudice as the factor that limited their upward mobility. In particular, Asian respondents blamed prejudicial attitudes for excluding them from corporate network structures, creating an environment of management insensitivity, and inhibiting mentoring opportunities for them within the corporate organization. One economic result of these attitudes is income inequality for Asian American professionals and managers (see Box 7.1) due to limited upward mobility (Cabezas and Kawaguchi, 1990).

How real is the glass ceiling for Asian Americans? According to the U.S. Commission on Civil Rights (1988), Asian American men are less likely to be in management positions than white men with the same qualifications. In a study of the aerospace industry, the U.S. General Accounting Office (1989) found that Asian Americans were less successful in moving from professional to managerial positions than were either white Americans or other ethnic minority groups. A study of Asian American engineers found that they were less likely to be in management positions or to be promoted to management positions than were white engineers with the same qualifications (Tang, 1991). An analysis of managers in the aerospace industry also showed that while Asian Americans constituted a higher percentage of aerospace professionals than either African Americans or Latinos, they constituted the lowest percentage of managers (Chiu, 1994). A study of San Francisco's civil service found that because Asian Americans lacked opportunities for promotion, they tended to cluster in technical jobs (Der and Lye, 1989). Not only are Asian Americans clustered in some jobs in San Francisco's civil service, they are also underrepresented (13 percent) in the civil service relative to their number (28 percent) in San Francisco's population (Moore and Gunnison, 1994). This evidence affirms the existence of a glass ceiling for Asian Americans.

One result of the glass ceiling is that Asian Americans who have white-collar management and professional positions earn less than white Americans in similar positions (Cabezas and Kawaguchi, 1988). Limited upward mobility becomes a subtle but widespread form of economic discrimination, which reflects and reinforces negative beliefs held by top-level management in American corporations.

Political Discrimination

Despite their increasing numbers in the last two decades, Asian Americans are relatively absent from political offices and activities. For example, outside of the state of Hawaii, few Asian Americans have been elected to political office. According to the U.S. Commission on Civil Rights (1992), 10 percent of the California population is Asian American; yet, only two Asian Americans serve in Congress, only one has been elected to a state position, and currently, no Asian American serves in the California legislature. Political offices at the local level have also evaded Asian Americans (Tamayo, Toma, and Koh, 1991; Karnow, 1992). For example, in Daly City, California, where Asian Americans constitute over 42 percent of the population, no Asian American has ever been elected to the city council; in New York City, with an Asian American population of over a half million, no Asian American has ever been elected to the city council; and in Los Angeles, only recently has one Asian American been elected to the city council (he lost in his bid to become mayor). The relative absence of Asian Americans from the political scene has resulted in some embarrassing moments. For example, Daniel Inouye was born in the United States and was a decorated soldier, having earned the Distinguished Service Cross during World War II. During the Iran-Contra hearings, however, he became the target of telephone calls and telegrams, often containing racial slurs, that told him to return to Japan.

The political underrepresentation of the Asian American population is largely the result of discriminatory political practices. Bai (1991:733–734) has identified the model minority stereotype as contributing to the political underrepresentation of the Asian American population:

> This popular preconception of Asian Pacific Americans as a politically silent "model minority" is just one of the many barriers facing Asian Pacific Americans who desire to enter the political process . . . . Obscured by the popular type which labels them as the "successful" minority, however, Asian Pacific Americans are viewed either as not warranting special protection from official discriminatory practices or as already participating greatly in the political process.

What are some of the other barriers to the political participation and representation of Asian Americans? They are discussed below.

Apportionment Policies. Similar to the political power of other ethnic populations in the United States, that of Asian Americans has been diluted by gerrymandering policies that split the population into several districts. In a study of how apportionment policies affect the political power of the Asian American population, Tamayo, Toma, and Koh (1991) have noted that Senate district boundaries split the Asian American community in San Francisco; and in Los Angeles, Koreatown, Chinatown, and Filipinotown are each split into several city council districts. As a result of gerrymandering, Asian Americans are not able to elect representatives from their own ranks because their voting power has been diluted.

Bilingual Election Materials. According to a provision of the Voting Rights Act of 1982, if 5 percent of a district's voting-age population is identifiable as a "single-language minority," then bilingual voting materials (that is, ballots) must be made available in the language of that minority. The linguistic diversity among Asian American populations and their lack of residential concentration prevent them from constituting 5 percent of a district's voting-age population (U.S. Commission on Civil Rights, 1992). As a result, the unavailability of bilingual election materials makes limited proficiency in English a barrier to the political participation of Asian Americans. For example, in 1980 over a hundred thousand Chinese Americans

Box 7.4

Does a Glass Ceiling Exist for Asian Americans?

- An Asian American sales professional with an MBA in marketing and sales had worked with the same Fortune 500 company for well over a decade and received many sales achievement awards when he was promoted to be the regional sales manager for the San Francisco Bay area. He had been working in that position for three years when a new management group came in. His new boss frequently used racial slurs against him. For instance, one time, when he was speaking to his boss, his boss said, "Slow down, I cannot write as fast as a Chinaman." Eventually he was demoted and transferred to a sales territory. When he asked his boss why he had been demoted, his boss told him that it was his "gut feeling" that he [the sales professional] was not a good manager and that he did not exhibit leadership qualities. The man subsequently filed a discrimination suit against his employer at the California Fair Employment and Housing Commission and was issued a right-to-sue letter. The suit was eventually settled out of court. He still works for the same company, but he has not been reinstated to his old position.
- A woman of Asian Indian descent was hired as the personnel manager for a midwestern city. She was the first woman and the first minority ever to be hired in a managerial position by that city. As soon as she arrived at her job, she began encountering resistance from her staff, and when she brought their behavior to the attention of her boss, he told her that her staff was insubordinate because she was a woman of color. Almost a year after she started the job, despite receiving an above-average performance appraisal, she was abruptly fired without severance pay. A subsequent investigation by the city's human relations commission found that "substantial evidence exists to show that the Complainant was discriminated against because of her sex, female, and her face, Asian; her national origin, India; and her

were of voting age in New York City, but the size of New York's population prevented this number from constituting the necessary 5 percent cutoff point for bilingual election materials. In an effort to incorporate Chinese Americans into the electoral process, federal legislation was passed in 1992 requiring bilingual ballots for Chinese American voters in parts of Manhattan, Brooklyn, and Queens (Dunn, 1994). However, two problems emerged in the effort to provide bilingual ballots: It is difficult to provide a transliteration of English names in Chinese characters, and ballot slots on voting machines are not big enough to accommodate both Chinese and English characters on the same ballot. Margaret Fung, executive director of the Asian American Legal Defense and Education Fund (quoted in U.S. Commission on Civil Rights, 1992:161), notes that:

> In Chinatown, four out of five voters have language difficulties. These voters stated . . . that they would vote more often if bilingual assistance were

color, non-white, in the manner in which she was terminated/suspended and in the conditions under which she performed her job." Despite the human relations commission finding, the city did nothing to rectify the situation. In fact, city employees repeatedly told the woman's professional colleagues and others who called that she was under suspension for not performing up to par. As a result, the woman could not find another comparable job, suffered considerable mental anguish, and did not have the financial resources necessary to pursue her case in court.

- In early 1988, Angelo Tom, a fifth-generation Chinese American who had worked at the U.S. Department of Housing and Urban Development's (HUD) San Francisco Regional office for nine years and become nationally recognized as the leading community planning and development analyst in the bay area, was turned down for promotion to the position of supervisor of his unit. The woman chosen to fill the job had less experience than Mr. Tom. At the time of Mr. Tom's rejection there were only three Asian Americans in middle-management positions at HUD's San Francisco office and none in upper management, and several qualified Asian Americans had repeatedly been rejected for management positions. After Mr. Tom filed a complaint, a HUD investigation found that he had been rejected for the position because he did not have leadership or interpersonal skills and was too technical for the job. Mr. Tom then requested and received a formal hearing in front of the U.S. Equal Employment Opportunity Commission (EEOC). At that hearing, witnesses refuted the HUD contention that he had poor leadership and interpersonal skills, and the EEOC administrative law judge agreed. He also held that a white man who was highly technically skilled would have been promoted with the confidence that he could develop the general outlook necessary to perform the management job. Mr. Tom was awarded back pay, a retroactive promotion, and attorney's fees.

Source: U.S. Commission on Civil Rights, 1992, pp. 134–135.

provided. Similarly in Queens, four out of every five limited-English proficient Asian American voters indicated that they would vote more if bilingual assistance were provided.

Political Party Snobbery. Both the Democratic and Republican parties have ignored the Asian American population, creating a lack of political party identification among Asian Americans (Bai, 1991). In turn, Asian American candidates for political office have encountered difficulties in attracting support from the major political parties. In addition, these parties have failed to create agendas that incorporate Asian American concerns. For example, in a 1989 *Washington Post* article, Joel Kotkin and Bill Bradley (1989) chastised the Democratic party for not creating a political agenda that responds to Asian American concerns and for promoting anti-Asian political rhetoric: "Yet to date, the Democrats have been remarkably resistant . . . to the idea of a less Eurocentric foreign policy. Perhaps the most ominous is the increasingly anti-Asian tone of Democratic rhetoric, all too clearly demonstrated in the 'Japan-bashing' and 'Korean-bashing' campaign ads." As preparation for the 1992 presidential election, Republicans established an outreach office in GOP national headquarters that targeted the recruitment of voters in the Asian American community (Awanohara, 1990). Republicans used the themes of anticommunism, antiwelfarism, and entrepreneurship to appeal to Asian American voters.

Educational Discrimination

The high levels of educational attainment by Asian Americans are often interpreted to mean that this ethnic group does not experience discrimination in education (Peng, 1990; Hsia, 1988; and Wang, 1988). Yet, considerable amounts of discrimination exist, especially in institutions of higher education. The higher level of Asian American enrollment in colleges and universities has resulted in strong anti-Asian sentiments (Chiu, 1994:1093):

> White college students rework college acronyms into biting commentary on Asian American presence. MIT becomes "Made in Taiwan," UCLA becomes "University of Caucasians Living Among Asians," and U.C. Irvine (UCI) becomes "University of Chinese Immigrants."

Let us review a couple of prominent cases that highlight the problem.

Brown University. Between 1980 and 1983 the Asian American admission rate at Brown University fell below the overall admission rate, even though the admission rate of Asian Americans had been historically higher than the overall admission rates. As a result, the Asian American Student Association of Brown University produced a report; its analysis of admission rates between 1979 and 1983 found the following:

- The Asian American admission rate dropped from 46 percent to 26 percent, while the overall admission rate declined from 27 percent to 24 percent.
- An analysis of academic qualifications between Asian American and white American applicants did not show significant changes for Asian Americans that would justify the decrease in their admission rate.
- The acceptance of the model minority stereotype by the university administration and admissions office resulted in reduced efforts to recruit Asian American students.

Brown University responded to the report's findings by establishing the Brown University Corporation Committee on Minority Affairs. After a review of the Asian American Student Association report, this committee admitted that Asian American applicants had been treated unfairly in the admissions process. The committee recommended that in order to rectify injustices against Asian American applicants, and minority applicants in general, the admission rate of minority applicants with academic qualifications comparable to those of nonminority applicants should be equal to the admission rate of nonminority applicants.

Berkeley. The Asian American Task Force on University of California Admissions was formed in 1984 to examine a decline in Asian American freshman enrollment. In particular, the task force was concerned about the fact that as the pool of Asian American applicants grew between 1979 and 1984, the proportion of Asian American freshmen declined (Takagi, 1990). As the controversy intensified and attracted the attention of the California legislature, the auditor general of California (1987) completed a review of freshman admissions policies at Berkeley. The auditor general's report concluded that Asian American freshman applicants had been admitted at a lower rate than white American applicants despite a larger increase in the grade point average (GPA) of Asian American applicants than of white American applicants.

In 1989, the academic senate at Berkeley moved to examine the controversy surrounding Asian American freshman admissions by forming the Special Committee on Asian American Admissions. The committee reviewed admission policies, interviewed admissions personnel, and read application files. After its lengthy investigation, the committee produced a report that listed three factors responsible for the drop in Asian American freshman admissions:

1. The university's decision not to guarantee admission to applicants under the Educational Opportunity Program (EOP), and to exclude them from affirmative action initiatives (that is, applicants from economically disadvantaged backgrounds but who are not members of underrepresented groups), had a significant effect on Asian American freshman admissions because the majority (90 percent) of EOP applicants were found to be Asian Americans.
2. In the fall of 1984 the College of Letters and Science decided to raise the minimum GPA for admission but not the minimum scores on college entrance exams (for example, SATs). Applicants to Berkeley, at the time, could meet either the minimum GPA or the minimum test score for admission. Since Asian American applicants were more likely to gain admission to Berkeley on the basis of their GPA and white students on the basis of their test scores, the change in the minimum GPA discriminated against Asian American applicants. That is, Asian American applicants had to meet higher standards than white applicants.
3. The Office of Admissions and Records announced on December 28, 1983, that applicants of "permanent alien" status not meeting a minimum SAT verbal score would be redirected to another UC campus. Even though this decision was reversed ten days later, the admissions office established a minimum score of 400 on the verbal part of the SAT for immigrant applicants only. The implementation of a minimum SAT verbal score was an obstacle to Asian American immigrant applicants.

Harvard. In 1988 the U.S. Office for Civil Rights, in response to concerns raised by the Asian American community at Harvard University, initiated a review of undergraduate admissions there. After two years of investigating undergraduate admissions, the Office for Civil Rights did not find discriminatory policies or procedures regarding Asian American applicants. Although the Office for Civil Rights cleared Harvard of discrimination charges, the review of applicant folders uncovered practices that some would deem discriminatory. In its review of applicant folders, the Office for Civil Rights found:

- Inequitable use of "ethnic readers" for Asian American applicant folders. Members of ethnic groups were used in the undergraduate admissions process to control for special cultural or ethnic factors. The Office for Civil Rights found that only a small number of Asian American applicant folders were read by Asian Americans. Consequently, it was possible that special cultural or ethnic factors were overlooked regarding Asian American applicants.
- Written comments stereotyping Asian American applicants. Some of these comments were: soft-spoken, math oriented, English-speaking difficulty, shy, and reserved. The Office for Civil Rights suggested that while the comments did not affect negatively the admission rate of Asian American applicants, they did reflect the operation of stereotypical beliefs about Asian Americans.

Housing Discrimination

A 1980 poll of white American attitudes toward Asian Americans found that the majority of white respondents (1) were against Asians moving into their neighborhoods, (2) believed that there were "too many" Asians in the United States, and (3) felt that Asians should have settled in other Asian countries (U.S. Commission on Civil Rights, 1986). At that time, in 1980, many white residents did not welcome Asian Americans into their neighborhoods, a situation that persists today. The U.S. Commission on Civil Rights (1986) documented the following examples of acts by white Americans who sought to discourage Asian Americans from living in their predominantly white neighborhoods:

- In San Francisco, white neighbors painted anti-Asian graffiti on the car of the only Asian American resident in the neighborhood.
- In Seattle, Washington, white neighbors fired gunshots at a home occupied by an Asian American family while the family was in the house.
- In Providence, Rhode Island, white neighbors painted "No Nips" on a house the day after an Asian family moved in.
- In 1987, anti-Asian flyers were distributed to mailboxes in the Bensonhurst and Gravesend neighborhoods of Brooklyn. These flyers urged the boycotting of Asian businesses and demanded that real estate agents not sell property to Asians in the neighborhoods. As a result of the flyers, Asian businesses and real estate offices that had sold property to Asians were vandalized (Giordano, 1987a and b).
- In 1981, a Cambodian family that bought a home in a white neighborhood in Maine was the target of racial bigotry. As the father played with

his children in the snow, one of his white neighbors threw a snowball at him, a snowball containing a rock. The Cambodian man approached his neighbors, blood streaming down his face, to ask why they had hurt him. His neighbors responded: "Go back where ya came from, gook" (U.S. Commission on Civil Rights, 1989).

- In Massachusetts, arsonists set fire to an apartment building that left thirty-one Cambodians homeless (Yen, 1988).

Thus, the popular belief that Asians prefer to live "with their own kind" is weakened by the discrimination Asian Americans experience when entering non-Asian neighborhoods.

Typically, the model minority does not protest as loudly as others to discriminatory treatment, but this treatment is a fact of life for Asian Americans today, over one hundred years since they began immigrating to the United States. Chinatowns, Little Tokyos, Koreatowns, Little Manilas, and similar Asian enclaves exist for reasons other than the desire to live with "their own kind."

STRATIFICATION OF ASIAN AMERICANS

White American workers regarded early Asian immigrants as a threat to their jobs. In contrast, large-scale employers in agriculture and in the railroad industry viewed Asians as an inexpensive source of productive labor. Nevertheless, despite employers' views, when a majority of the working population sees a minority as a threat, negative beliefs are codified which, ironically, intensify the sense of threat. Such beliefs also legitimize discrimination. In the case of Asian immigrants, acts of violence and legal restrictions initially prevented them from fully realizing economic opportunities and gaining political power. Ghettoization ensued as a response to hostility in the host society. Yet, Asian Americans made significant gains in education, which, in turn, opened opportunities in jobs, especially after the early fears of the "yellow peril" faded and the panic of Pearl Harbor abated with the victory over Japan in World War II. Education credentials coupled with middleman entrepreneurial skills enabled the descendants of these early immigrants to enter the middle classes but with restrictions on where they could live and how high on the corporate ladder they could climb. More recent tensions with Asian trading partners, along with a new wave of Asian immigrants, have rekindled old fears, intensified negative beliefs, and generated sporadic acts of discrimination against both newly arrived and established Asian American groups.

All these factors have sustained the subtle restrictions on this disproportionately middle-class minority. In time, these restrictions may diminish, but as long as Asian Americans remain readily identifiable in tight domestic job markets and in tension-filled international trade with Asian nations, the potential for sustaining or even increasing barriers to full economic and political participation remains.

Box 7.5

Violence against Asian Americans

Two murders of Asian Americans in the 1980s have been etched into the national consciousness as examples of the potential intensity of discrimination against Asian Americans: the murder of Vincent Chin in 1982 and the murder of Jim (Ming Hai) Loo in 1989. These killings are prominent examples, but they are not isolated incidents. Violence against Asians leading to injury and sometimes *death* occurs with disturbing frequency across the country and affects many different Asian groups.

VINCENT CHIN

The racially motivated murder of Vincent Chin and the inability of the American judicial system to bring his murderers to justice became a vivid symbol and source of outrage during the mid-1980s. The facts of the case are as follows.

On the evening of June 19, 1982, Vincent Chin, a 27-year-old Chinese American, met with some friends in a Detroit bar to celebrate his upcoming wedding. He was accosted by Ronald Ebens and Michael Nitz, two white automobile factory workers, who reportedly called him a "Jap" and blamed him for the loss of jobs in the automobile industry. Ebens and Nitz chased Chin out of the bar, and, when they caught up with him, Nitz held Chin while Ebens beat him "numerous times in the knee, the chest, and the head" with a baseball bat. Chin died of his injuries four days later.

Ebens and Nitz were initially charged with second-degree murder but subsequently were allowed to plead guilty to manslaughter. In March 1983 the defendants were each sentenced to three years' probation and fined $3,780 by Wayne Circuit County Judge Charles Kaufman, who reasoned that the defendants had no previous history of violence and were unlikely to violate probation.

The U.S. Department of Justice brought federal civil rights charges against Ebens and Nitz to a federal grand jury, which indicted them on November 2, 1982. On June 18, 1984, Ebens was found guilty of interfering with Chin's civil rights, and on September 18, 1984, he was sentenced to twenty-five years in prison. However, Nitz was acquitted of the federal civil rights charges.

Ebens's conviction was overturned by the Sixth Circuit Court of Appeals in September 1986 for technical reasons, including issues pertaining to the admissibility of audiotapes and prosecutorial misconduct (overzealousness) in preparing witnesses. When Ebens came up for retrial in the Eastern District of Michigan, the defense moved for a change of venue on the grounds that Ebens could not get a fair trial in Detroit. The defense motion was granted, and the trial was moved to Cincinnati. The case was retried during the month of April 1987, and this time Ebens was acquitted.

The acquittal of Ebens in the second federal trial means that neither Ebens nor Nitz ever went to prison for Vincent Chin's killing. Some have speculated that the main reason the Cincinnati jury acquitted Ebens is that the jury could not comprehend the reality of anti-Asian bias. Whereas Detroit in the early 1980s was the scene of a massive media campaign against foreign imports, especially those from Japan, a campaign that inflamed anti-Asian sentiments in that city, there had not been the same type of campaign in Cincinnati. Also, there were very few Asians in Cincinnati, and anti-Asian sentiments were not widespread.

Others contend that the Cincinnati jury's acquittal of Ebens reflects a fundamental problem with current federal civil rights laws. Ebens was charged under federal criminal civil rights law Section 245(b), which prohibits (among other things) the racially motivated interference by force or threat of force with a person's use of public facilities, such as restaurants and bars. Some experts argue that the jury may have been confused about what had to be shown for there to be a civil rights violation under Section 245(b); even though the jury may have felt that the attack was indeed racially motivated, it might not have thought that Ebens specifically intended to interfere with Chin's use of a public facility (the bar).

JIM (MING HAI) LOO

Seven years after Vincent Chin's killing, another Chinese American was killed in Raleigh, North Carolina, under similar circumstances. Jim (Ming Hai) Loo, 24, had immigrated to the United States from China thirteen years before, was working in a Chinese restaurant, and was saving money so that he could attend college. On the evening of Saturday, July 29, 1989, during an altercation that began in a nearby pool hall, Loo was hit on the back of the head by a handgun held by Robert Piche. He fell into a broken beer bottle, which pierced his eye and caused a bone fragment to enter his brain, resulting in his death on July 31.

Loo and several Vietnamese friends had been playing pool in the pool hall, when Robert Piche, 35, and his brother, Lloyd Piche, 29, began calling them "gooks" and "chinks" and blaming them for American deaths in Vietnam. Lloyd Piche said, "I don't like you because you're Vietnamese. Our brothers went over to Vietnam, and they never came back," and "I'm gonna finish you tonight." Although the manager forced the Piche brothers to leave the pool hall, they waited outside for Loo and his friends, and attacked them as they left the pool hall. Robert Piche and his brother first attacked one of Loo's friends, Lahn Tang, with a shotgun, but when Tang escaped, Robert swung a pistol at another of Loo's friends, Jim Ta. He missed his intended victim and hit Loo on the head instead.

Although Lloyd Piche made most of the racial remarks, he did not strike the fatal blow. He was sentenced to six months in prison for disorderly conduct and simple assault (on Tang), both of which are misdemeanors. In March 1990, Robert Piche was found guilty of second-degree murder and assault with a deadly weapon and sentenced to a total of thirty-seven years in prison. He will be eligible for parole after serving four and one-half years. Although Judge Howard E. Manning, Jr., gave Piche a stiff lecture, the sentence was less than he could have meted out: Under North Carolina law, Piche could have been given life in prison.

Many Asian American community leaders, struck by the similarities between Loo's murder and Chin's, pressed the U.S. Department of Justice to bring federal civil rights charges against Robert and Lloyd Piche. They were particularly anxious to see a prosecution of Lloyd Piche, who received a minimal sen-

Box 7.5

Violence against Asian Americans (continued)

tence despite being the chief instigator of the incident. After a lengthy investigation, the Justice Department announced on March 29, 1991, that it had indicted Lloyd Piche on federal civil rights charges, but it did not indict Robert Piche.

Lloyd Piche was indicted on eight counts of violating federal civil rights laws. On July 15, 1991, in a federal district court in Wilmington, North Carolina, Lloyd Piche was found guilty on all eight counts. On October 15, 1991, Lloyd Piche was sentenced to four years in prison and ordered to pay over $28,000 in restitution to the Loo family. Although the Justice Department had sought the maximum sentence under federal sentencing guidelines, Piche's sentence was less than the minimum sentence (six to seven and one-half years) under federal guidelines.

There are many similarities between the Loo and the Chin murders. In each case, the victim was a young man spending an evening relaxing with friends in a public facility (a bar in Chin's case, a pool hall in Loo's). In each case, an altercation began inside the public facility, and violence leading to murder erupted outside of the facility. In each case, the victim was killed after being mistaken for or associated with Asians of other nationalities. In Chin's case, his killers were venting hostility against foreign Japanese, and in Loo's case, his murderers apparently mistook him for a Vietnamese. Thus, both Chin and Loo became victims simply because they were of Asian descent.

Together, the Chin and Loo murders underscore the harsh reality of ethnically motivated violence against Asians. They also signal in different ways the general public's lack of awareness of and to some extent indifference toward anti-Asian discrimination. The three-year probation and almost nominal fines imposed by Judge Kaufman on Chin's murderers are suggestive of very little value being placed on an Asian American life. The ultimate failure of the American justice system to convict Ebens of civil rights charges, perhaps partly because of the Cincinnati jury's difficulty in believing in the existence of anti-Asian hatred, also implies that many Americans view racial hatred purely as a black–white problem and are unaware that Asian Americans are also frequently targets of hate crimes. Finally, neither murder was given much national prominence. Chin's killing did receive some national attention, but Loo's killing (in stark contrast to the murder of a young black man in Bensonhurst that occurred at roughly the same time) was hardly covered by the national media and raised no national sense of outrage.

Unlike the Vincent Chin case, Loo's murder resulted in a successful federal prosecution—the first ever successful federal civil rights prosecution where the victim was Asian American. If given sufficient attention, the federal civil rights trial of Lloyd Piche could do much to highlight the racial aspect of Loo's killing and would send a message that anti-Asian racism will not be tolerated by the U.S. government.

Source: U.S. Commission on Civil Rights, 1992, pp. 25–28.

RESPONDING TO DISCRIMINATION

The Asian populations discussed in this chapter—Chinese, Japanese, Korean, and Filipino—are much more successful economically than the ethnic populations explored in other chapters of this text, except perhaps Cuban Americans. A much higher percentage of Asian Americans are middle class and white collar than these other populations; as a consequence, their "success" has made Asian Americans the model minority. However, the success of these established Asian immigrant groups has not been fully matched by newer immigrants. The hostility toward these new migrants creates a climate of prejudice and antagonism for the Asian American community as a whole.

Historically Asians have not mounted highly visible or violent protests against those who discriminate against them. Indeed, part of the reason why Asian Americans are considered the model minority is, no doubt, their relatively low-key protests against discrimination. For example, the internment of Japanese Americans did not generate confrontation, except in the court system. Earlier laws that restricted the rights of Chinese and Japanese Americans were often accepted, and only later challenged in court. Asian American middleman minorities in inner-city neighborhoods have countered violence with civil protests (marches and court actions) but not confrontation. The harassment and, at times, violence against Asian Americans who enter white neighborhoods usually are uncontested. The clear discrimination in college admissions patterns has been challenged, in a quiet and legal way.

The lack of effective political organization in many Asian American communities has also hindered protests against discrimination. Indeed, not until 1986 was a pan-Asian organization—the Asian-American Voters Coalition—formed to consolidate diverse Asian subpopulations into an effective voting bloc. Potentially this bloc could affect elections in states like California, Texas, New York, and Illinois, where significant numbers of Asian Americans reside, but at this time, there is little evidence to indicate the influence of this bloc.

The subtlety of much discrimination—for example, college admissions practices, corporate glass ceilings, and gerrymandering of voting districts—coupled with the sporadic nature of acts of violence against Asian Americans by angry whites and disadvantaged minorities makes it difficult to mount a concerted corrective effort, especially by a largely politically passive model minority that is not perceived to have problems. Especially as we approach the twenty-first century when considerable effort has been made by governmental and legal agencies to be more conscious of, and to correct for, past and present discrimination against African Americans, Latinos, and Native Americans, comparatively little effort has been made on behalf of, or by, Asian Americans. Without protests and political mobilization by Asians, it is not likely that much will be done in the future—another cost of being the quiet, model minority.

THE PRECARIOUS SITUATION FOR ASIAN AMERICANS

Are Asian Americans really the model minority in the United States? On the surface, one could argue that their educational, occupational, and economic status is an indicator of success, especially in light of efforts to limit Asian American presence in, and assimilation into, mainstream American society. Asian Americans thus fit the model minority stereotype because many have overcome the odds and succeeded. Beneath the surface, however, the model minority image has negative repercussions for not only Asian Americans but other ethnic groups as well. For other ethnics, Hurk and Kim (1989:530) have noted that:

> The dominant group's stereotype of Asian Americans as a model minority also affects negatively other minorities. Since the Asian Americans' "success" may be considered by the dominant group as a proof of openness in the American opportunity structure, there is a constant danger that other less successful minorities could be regarded as "inferior" and/or "lazy." These less achieving minorities may be blamed for their own failure and become victims of scapegoating ("Japanese have made it. Why can't they?").

The dominant group (that is, white society) can thus use the model minority image of Asian Americans as an ideological tool to maintain a pattern of unequal access to valued resources. To overstate the case in order to emphasize our point: Asian Americans succeed because they represent a small (though growing) percentage of the total population and, hence, pose less of a threat to the majority; other minority populations, such as African Americans and Latinos, are much larger and consequently pose more of a threat, which leads to more intense discrimination (Blumstein, 1982; Aguirre and Baker, 1988). With the model minority as a basis for comparison, these larger populations appear less successful—an unfair comparison because of the greater degree of discrimination experienced by these larger minority groups. Members of larger minority groups grow to resent Asian Americans whose success is used to highlight their failure. As the success of the model minority stereotype is used by white society to illustrate the "openness" of the American opportunity structure, other minority populations, which have experienced far more discrimination, will be blamed for their inability to take advantage of imagined opportunities. Yu (1980) has noted that many African Americans and Latinos resent Asian Americans because they believe that Asian Americans are the first to receive assistance in the United States. Similarly, Thornton and Taylor (1988) have found that many African Americans feel distant from Asian American populations and do not perceive Asian Americans as a minority group.

The model minority stereotype creates problems for Asian Americans as well, perpetuating the perception that poverty, homelessness, mental illness, crime, and other social problems do not exist among Asian Americans. As Crystal (1989:406) has noted:

> Rather than the "yellow peril" of the past, Asian Americans are currently viewed as an exemplary group of honest and hardworking citizens with low

Box 7.6

The Model Minority under Attack

Asian and Pacific Islanders have made great strides in U.S. society. There is no question that they have made impressive economic and education gains. But, have these gains shielded the Asian and Pacific Islander population from racist attacks?

According to the Washington-based civil rights group, The National Asian Pacific American Legal consortium, anti-Asian violence was up 37 percent between 1994 and 1995. In 1995, there were 458 reported incidents of racial attack or harassment against Asians in the United States. The consortium stated that Asians in the United States are subject to racist attacks because they are viewed by Americans as "perpetual foreigners, making them especially vulnerable to xenophobic attacks." Twenty-five percent of the anti-Asian incidents in 1995 occurred in California. Los Angeles leads all counties in the state with a recorded 53 incidents. New York was second behind California, 61 incidents, in the number of anti-Asian incidents.

Source: National Asian Pacific American Legal Consortium 1996.

> rates of juvenile delinquency and divorce. They are perceived as having few, if any, mental health problems and are thought to live in homogeneous communities composed of stable, close-knit families that "take care of their own" with little need of outside social services.

In reality, the lower rates of return on education, especially at the postsecondary level, and the existence of a glass ceiling in the job sector indicate that Asian Americans do indeed experience institutionalized discrimination and prejudice.

SUMMARY

The first Asians came to America beginning in the 1850s and were instrumental in the development of the commercial, industrial, and agricultural infrastructure of the West. For many years, Asian immigration was restricted, but over the last decade these restrictions have been relaxed, and the Asian population has doubled in size since 1980, although it is still quite small compared to the African American and Latino populations.

Asian Americans match or exceed white Americans in terms of average family income, educational attainment, incumbency in managerial and professional occupations, and life span. Yet, the signs of discrimination are evident along a number of fronts: Asian poverty rates exceed those of whites; returns on education to Asians are less than those for whites; and many Asians still remain segregated from non-Asians.

Asians are readily identifiable because of their distinctive eye fold and, to a lesser extent, color tones of their skin; hence, they are easy targets of discrimination. Although their success gives them the title of a "model minority" that has succeeded in spite of obstacles, lurking beneath the surface of this portrayal is a more sinister revival of the old "yellow peril" stereotype in which Asians are seen as foreigners who take jobs, admission slots in higher education, and business opportunities away from non-Asians. In the past, such perceived threats and their codification into negative stereotypes have propagated considerable violence against Asians, but more significant has been the long legacy of open legal and political discrimination against Asians, which has abated only over the last few decades. Yet, Asians still are subject to considerable violence against them from other minorities and whites. As the Asian population has increased over the last decade, many more subtle forms of discrimination have been evident: Asians frequently run up against a glass ceiling, keeping their careers in check despite obvious performance and other qualifications. Asians rarely get elected to political office because of gerrymandering of their neighborhoods and because non-Asians are reluctant to vote for Asians. Asians are underrepresented in governmental appointments despite the fact that their educational credentials qualify them for these appointments in disproportionate numbers. Asians have been subjected to a quota system by elite colleges and universities, thereby denying opportunity to many qualified Asian students. And informal housing discrimination, often punctuated with white violence, is still evident in many communities. Historically, Asians have not been prone to visible protests, but in more recent years, legal and political challenges to all of these discriminatory practices have been mounted, indicating that Asians will no longer passively accept discrimination.

POINTS OF DEBATE

Asian Americans are caught in a difficult bind: Their success engenders white hostility and, at the same time, is also used to condemn less successful minorities, thereby arousing increased hostility from disadvantaged minorities. Asians are caught in the middle of all manner of ethnic hostility, and as the percentage of Asians in the population increases, many intensely debated issues will surface:

1. Since they are so successful, especially relative to other large minorities, should Asian complaints about subtle forms of discrimination limiting their further success be given the same attention as those from more disadvantaged minorities? Should programs to help Asians be of the same intensity as those to help less successful minorities? Should efforts at reducing ethnic discrimination be calibrated along a sliding scale, with those who are worse off getting most of the attention? The law would say no as an answer to all of these questions, but the policies of government always involve interpretations and selective implemen-

tations of the law. Is this desirable? Necessary? Inevitable in light of political realities?

2. As the Asian population grows in size and occupies many economic niches desired not only by whites but more significantly by other minorities, can hostility toward Asians be reduced, or will this tension, as manifested in the hostility of African Americans and Latinos toward Asian-owned businesses in their communities, become a chronic feature of the American landscape? If so, what is to be done to reduce this hostility?
3. Is American society in danger of hardening the lines of hostility among Asians, whites, Latinos, and blacks? If all are competing for the same scarce resources—jobs, income, education, housing—how is the tension to be mitigated? Or is America on the path toward tension-provoking ethnic pluralism with each subpopulation viewing the other with considerable hostility? Is this what most Americans want? If not, what is to be done?

CHAPTER 8

White Ethnic Americans

It is often noted that America is a land of immigrants. The largest waves of immigration occurred in the nineteenth century when vast numbers of non-Protestant white Europeans successively began to enter the United States. The southern Irish were the first non-Protestants to enter in significant numbers in the early 1800s. In the final decades of the nineteenth century and the first two decades of the twentieth century, additional waves of Catholic Italians and Poles as well as Jews immigrated. This influx posed a threat to the Anglo-Saxon Protestant core, setting in motion the dynamics of discrimination.

These white ethnic populations eventually overcame Anglo-Saxon Protestant discrimination and moved up the socioeconomic ladder, and their success—which is often used to condemn Native Americans, African Americans, and Latinos for not doing as well—has contributed to present-day negative stereotypes about other ethnic groups and to persistent patterns of discrimination. Although the history of these white subpopulations does provide an example of what is possible for other ethnic groups, the greater identifiability of the currently unassimilated makes them targets of prejudice and discrimination that typically inhibit full movement into the American mainstream.

RESOURCE SHARES OF WHITE ETHNIC GROUPS

Table 8.1 lists the occupations of prominent European-origin ethnics in 1980 and, then again, in 1990. At the bottom of the table, the occupations of non-European ethnic subpopulations are presented as a basis for comparison. By reading down the table, the percentage of each ethnic subpopulation in the various occupations listed across the top of the table is reported. In a rough sense, the occupations on the left of the table generate higher incomes and prestige than those on the right side of the table.

Families await processing at Ellis Island, through which most European immigrants of the last century and early part of the 20th century had to pass.

A person's occupation can say a great deal about access to scarce resources; and while we might also like to have income data for this detailed list of white ethnics, the only data available from the census bureau (and these data had to be hand-calculated from the raw census figures) are on the occupations of European-origin ethnics. Thus, we will simply have to assume that the occupations listed across the top of the table are a reasonable proxy for resource shares. Since occupation is related to educational credentials, to income, and, hence, to living standards, the inferences to be drawn from these data are appropriate.

What, then, do these data say? European-origin white ethnics are more likely to be in managerial and professional occupations than African Americans, Latinos, Native Americans, and, to somewhat varying degrees, Asians. Except for Russians who have the highest percentage in managerial and professional occupations (and those listed under Russian are predominately Jewish immigrants) and for Irish who lag slightly behind some white ethnics, the British Isle–origin ethnics occupy more favored occupations than non-British Isle ethnics. And if we compare 1980 and 1990, we can see that the gap between British Isle–origin ethnics and other Europeans has not closed.

By following any particular white ethnic's percentages across the table, it is evident that all the European-origin ethnics do better than all other non-European ethnics, except Asians who do the best among non-Europeans in securing managerial and professional positions but not as well as

TABLE 8.1. Occupations of Prominent Ethnic Groups, 1980 and 1990

Ethnic Subpopulations by Ancestry	*Percentage in Managerial and Professional Specialty Occupations*		*Percentage in Technical, Sales, and Administrative Support Occupations*		*Percentage in Service Occupations*		*Percentage in Precision Production, Craft and Repair Occupations*		*Percentage in Operators, Fabricators, and Laborers*		*Percentage in Farming, Forestry, and Fishing Occupations*	
	1980	1990	1980	1990	1980	1990	1980	1990	1980	1990	1980	1990
European ethnic groups												
British Isles												
English	30	40	32	36	10	7	12	7	14	8	2	2
Irish	28	33	33	39	11	9	12	8	14	10	2	1
Scottish	35	43	34	34	9	7	10	7	10	7	2	2
Welsh	36	43	33	34	8	7	11	8	10	7	2	1
German	28	33	32	37	10	9	12	9	15	10	3	2
Italian	27	33	36	41	11	9	12	8	13	8	1	1

Polish	28	35	34	39	10	8	12	8	14	9	2	1
Dutch	24	31	30	37	12	9	13	10	18	11	3	2
French	26	31	33	39	11	10	13	9	15	10	2	1
Swedish	31	38	33	37	10	8	12	7	11	8	3	3
Norwegian	30	36	32	36	10	9	11	8	12	8	5	3
Russian	46	57	36	33	5	4	6	3	6	3	1	*
Czech	30	35	34	36	9	8	12	9	11	9	4	3
Hungarian	32	40	34	37	9	7	11	8	13	7	1	1
Danish	32	39	33	36	9	8	11	7	11	7	4	3
Portuguese	22	23	31	36	12	11	12	11	20	16	3	3
Non-European ethnic groups												
African Americans	15	20	21	30	23	19	10	9	28	21	3	1
Latinos	16	14	27	26	16	17	13	14	25	23	3	6
Native Americans	17	20	26	29	15	17	16	15	23	15	3	4
Asians	28	31	31	33	14	14	11	8	13	13	3	1

* < 1 percent.

Source: U.S. Bureau of the Census, 1983e, 1993c.

most white ethnics. Yet, except for Latinos, all ethnics appear to have been somewhat upwardly mobile in securing managerial and professional occupations (the Latino drop between 1980 and 1990 can be attributed to the massive immigration of the poor and uneducated Latinos, coupled with very high dropout rates from high school among Latinos).

Reading down the second column of the table where percentages of ethnics in technical, sales, and administrative support occupations are listed, all ethnic subpopulations have improved their representation in these types of occupations, again except for Latinos who reveal about the same percentage as in 1980. Much of this shift is the result of changes in the occupational structure of the society toward white-collar occupations, but some of this change is due to real improvement in living standards.

The service occupations listed in the middle of the table represent a good indicator of mobility patterns; those ethnics who see their percentage decline in service occupations will generally experience an increase in their percentage in managerial, professional, technical, sales, and administrative positions. At the same time that their numbers increase in these higher-paying jobs, their percentages in the manual occupations on the right side of the table decline. Indeed, all ethnics see their percentage in manual occupations decline, or remain about the same—again, signaling the shift of the broader occupational structure away from manual jobs. Yet, some ethnics see a greater decline in their percentages in manual occupations than others, which is another indicator of upward mobility among ethnics between the 1980s and 1990s.

Thus, in a very rough sense, as we can see from the percentages of various ethnic groups in basic types of occupations (as reported by the census bureau), European-origin ethnics do well in securing occupations that bring income and prestige. In Table 8.2, we pull from the census figures another basis for comparing the resource shares of white ethnics as a whole to Latinos, Asians, blacks, and Native Americans. By education, median earnings, poverty status, labor force participation, and, once again, occupations, it is clear that white ethnics do better than all other ethnics, except Asians who evidence a higher percentage of college graduates than whites and, as a result, have higher median incomes than all other ethnics.

Thus, on some measures of success, Asian Americans have achieved parity with, or exceeded, white Europeans in access to particular resources. Yet Asian American poverty rates are higher than those for white ethnics (indicating that not all Asian Americans are succeeding, as the model minority stereotype would suggest). Compared to white ethnic Americans and Asian Americans, other ethnic groups are about twice as likely to be unemployed. With respect to occupational distribution, white ethnic groups and Asian Americans are far more likely to have higher-income jobs than other ethnic groups. In 1990, as in 1980, white ethnic groups as a whole had greater access to resources than African Americans, Latinos, and Native Americans. The only significant change between 1980 and 1990 is the improved quality of life for Asian Americans.

TABLE 8.2. Resource Shares of Prominent Ethnic Groups, 1990

	White Americans	African Americans	Latinos	Asian Americans	Native Americans
Education (25 years old and older)					
Less than 9th grade	8.9%	13.8%	30.7%	12.9%	14.0%
Four years or more of high school	88.8%	77.5%	50.8%	80.4%	49.5%
Four years or more of college	28.5%	16.7%	9.2%	44.0%	9.3%
Median earnings					
Persons 25 years old and older	$20,233	$15,764	$11,954	$25,193	$14,428
Poverty status					
Families below poverty level	7.8%	27.8%	23.4%	10.8%	36.1%
Persons below poverty level	10.0%	30.7%	26.2%	12.8%	38.7%
Labor force participation					
Employed	67.2%	63.9%	66.5%	66.3%	52.3%
Unemployed	4.7%	11.3%	8.2%	4.2%	8.8%
Occupations					
Managerial and professional	27.5%	16.1%	10.7%	27.9%	16.9%
Technical and sales	45.6%	28.2%	14.7%	43.3%	25.3%
Service	16.1%	22.3%	16.2%	15.7%	16.2%
Operators, fabricators, and laborers	10.0%	22.7%	29.9%	7.6%	19.9%
Farming, forestry, and fishing	1.1%	1.6%	8.0%	0.2%	3.6%

Sources: 1990 Census Detailed Occupation Characteristics from the EEO File; 1990 Census of Population and Housing Summary Table File 3c.

These tables show that successive waves of white European immigrants and their descendants have been able to overcome the effects of initial discrimination. To understand how white ethnic groups have assimilated with the Anglo-Saxon core of American society, we should examine particular European-origin subpopulations in more detail. What is true for these illustrative cases has been, in general, true for other white ethnics who migrated to America.

IRISH AMERICANS

Irish Americans constitute approximately 18 percent of the population in the United States, which makes them the third largest ethnic group behind the English and Germans (Lieberson and Waters, 1988:34). The first major wave of Irish immigrants arrived in the 1700s, but the exact national heritage of these immigrants is a subject of debate. Most were Protestant Scots-Irish, who had immigrated to northern Ireland after the British conquest of Ireland (Leyburn, 1962), but many southern and Catholic Irish also immigrated—perhaps as many as a third of the total in this first large influx (Dickson, 1966:60–70). Because of prejudice against "Papists," many of these Catholics were forced to convert to some form of Protestantism in order to avoid persecution. By the end of the Revolutionary War, 10 percent of the colonial population was Irish (signaling that the American legacy of the Irish coincided with American society at its founding).

The next wave of immigration began in the 1830s owing to several factors (Shrier, 1958): the potato famine of the 1840s, persistent British persecution of poor Irish, and British encouragement of emigration as a solution to their "Irish problem." Unlike the earlier wave of immigrants who came in search of more opportunities, many of these southern and Catholic migrants saw themselves as banished to America by the British, which perhaps accounts for their intense loyalty to their homeland (Miller, 1985).

As the first of the non-Protestant white ethnic groups to immigrate to America in large numbers, the Irish were targets of vicious prejudice and sustained discrimination. Two generations later, however, most Irish Americans had overcome these disadvantages.

Identifiability of Irish Americans

As with all white ethnic groups, the identifiability of the Irish could be made only in terms of distinctive cultural, behavioral, and organizational patterns. In the nineteenth century, very conscious efforts were undertaken to portray mainly southern Catholic Irish as a distinct "race," thereby imputing biological differences where none existed. During this time "Scots-Irish" became a popular label, as Protestant northern Irish sought to distance themselves from southern Catholics. Before the efforts to identify southern Catholics, Scots-Irish simply had considered themselves Irish, but with the emerging hostility toward the southern Irish, these northerners sought to differentiate themselves in order to avoid discrimination.

Underlying prejudicial stereotypes of the southern Irish were objections to their Catholicism, their poverty, and their willingness to work for wages lower than those accepted by earlier immigrants. Prejudicial stereotypes perpetuated the perception of the southern Irish as identifiably different and, hence, legitimate targets of discrimination.

Negative Beliefs about Irish Americans

As early as the eighteenth century, southern Irish were subject to negative stereotyping because of their Catholicism. These stereotypes were the basis on which some questioned Irish American political loyalty. Indeed, the suspicion that an Irish American politician would be governed by the Pope was articulated as recently as 1960 when John F. Kennedy—an Irish Catholic—ran for president.

The most vicious stereotypes, however, emerged with the large-scale immigrations of the nineteenth century. Fueled by the threat of so many non-Protestant, low-wage workers, white Protestants stereotyped the Irish as immoral and unintelligent, and Irish Catholics in particular as wicked, ignorant, and temperamental (Knobel, 1986:27). All subsequent waves of Catholic white ethnic groups were similarly stereotyped, especially those, such as the Italians and Poles, who immigrated in large numbers to the United States.

Far more vicious were stereotypes of the Irish as less than human. English prejudice against the Irish was imported to America and intensified; and in the context of evolutionary theories and the plight of African Americans, the English prejudice against the Irish was imported to America and amplified into vicious stereotypes of the Irish as subhuman. Some stereotypes portrayed the Irish as apelike, drunk, hostile, and immoral (Curtis, 1971). Even more disparaging were portrayals of the Irish population as a "missing link" between apes, Africans, and the English. Today these extreme stereotypes have diminished, but at times the Irish are viewed as tending toward drunkenness, pugnaciousness, and corruption. Thus, although the Irish have largely overcome prejudice and discrimination, muted forms of the old stereotypes persist.

The Dynamics of Discrimination against Irish Americans

Economic Discrimination

As with most white non-Protestant ethnic groups who migrated to the United States in the nineteenth century, the Catholic Irish were forced to take low-wage jobs. Earlier Protestant Irish, most of whom were "Scots-Irish," had penetrated business and professional positions, but those who came later were less educated and skilled; as a result, they began their experience in America with jobs in manufacturing, mining, construction (of railroads, canals), textiles, and domestic service. Because many women immigrated alone, domestic service offered these women a place to live. Earlier pre-Revolutionary northern Irish had also done much of the menial and domestic labor, often as indentured servants, but by the 1830s and 1840s, when the southern Irish began to come in large numbers, the Scots-Irish had begun to be economically mobile.

What made for economic discrimination was the exclusion of these migrating Catholic Irish workers from anything but unskilled work by Protestant employers, a tactic that was legitimated by beliefs in their "racial" inferiority, low intelligence, general pugnaciousness, and unreliability. Aggravating this situation was the use of even lower wage black workers to threaten the job security of Irish workers, generating black-Irish tension that persists to this day in many northeastern cities (Roediger, 1991; Bonacich, 1976). Moreover, because Irish children were forced to go to work early in life, the second generation frequently did not acquire the educational credentials necessary for mobility out of low-wage jobs.

By the turn of the century, however, both the northern and southern Irish were becoming economically mobile (Dinnerstein and Reimers, 1988). The industrial expansion in the East and Midwest created new opportunities for more skilled workers, and since the Irish had arrived several decades before the large influx of Italians, Poles, and other white ethnic groups, they were more assimilated and advantaged. Economic mobility also came through political success. In many cities, Irish Americans created and controlled the "big-city political machine." For all its corruption, political machines could provide government jobs to individuals and contracts to Irish-owned businesses. During this time, many Irish American workers overcame discrimination by unionizing; their efforts were so successful that they dominated many local unions, especially in mining, construction, and dock work. Although Irish Americans remained dramatically underrepresented in high-skill and professional jobs, they were establishing a more secure economic base from which subsequent generations could move into higher-skill blue-collar jobs, white-collar positions, and an expanding array of professions. Today many Irish Americans have overcome earlier discrimination as revealed by their higher incomes, jobs, and educational credentials (Lieberson and Waters, 1988).

Political Discrimination

One of the enduring stereotypes about Irish Americans is their involvement in corrupt big-city political machines. Political machines in large cities had, of course, emerged and prospered before the Irish were able to penetrate them, but the massive immigration of southern Catholic Irish to the cities created a new constituency for these corrupt political machines. Large pools of poor, ill-housed, and unemployed individuals sustained the machines, and despite the graft and corruption, the machines provided food, jobs, and housing to people in desperate straits in a national political and economic climate where the role of the federal government in addressing urban problems was minimal.

Not only did the political machines provide needed services, but they became an early path to upward mobility for many Irish Americans as well as for large numbers of Italian, Polish, and Jewish immigrants. The corrupt letting of city contracts to private businesses created jobs in a government-supported private sector. Moreover, the machines generated networks of ties among political, business, religious, and philanthropic leaders who, in turn, controlled vast arrays of employment opportunities for poor immigrants. Although the machines in Brooklyn, New York, Boston, New Haven, Philadelphia, Chicago, and various smaller cities in the Northeast and upper Midwest often extracted a high price in misuse of tax revenues and in subsidies for unneeded or inefficient workers, early generations of white immigrants would have suffered even more without them.

Big political machines could not endure forever, since their corruption and inefficiency were all too obvious. As white ethnic groups became more secure, the need for these corrupt networks diminished, leading to a series of reform movements that established new structures of city government. However, it was not until the 1970s that the Chicago political machine began to fall apart, which shows how a network of power can exist long past the time it serves useful functions.

Success at the local level of politics did not translate into positions of power for Irish Americans at the national level, however. Prejudicial attitudes toward Catholics in an Anglo-Saxon Protestant society excluded Irish Americans from appointments in the judiciary and executive branches of government, and limited their success in statewide and national electoral politics. Only in the 1920s did the Catholic Irish begin to enjoy some success in national politics when Alfred E. Smith became the Democratic candidate for president. It was not until the administration of President Roosevelt in the 1930s that Irish Americans were appointed to visible positions in the judiciary, the White House, and other executive branches of government. President Truman continued Roosevelt's pattern of appointing Irish Americans to powerful government positions. When John F. Kennedy ran for president in the 1960s, many of the old fears about "Papists" were revived, although Kennedy's subsequent election appears to have broken the last discriminatory barriers to full political participation by Irish Americans. Today, the fact that a political candidate is Catholic or Irish is not important, unless it influences that candidate's views on such emotionally charged issues as abortion.

Educational Discrimination

Irish Americans have educational achievement scores above the national average. Most Irish American children are educated in Catholic schools, many of which were created in the mid-1800s to retain Irish ethnicity in the face of intense efforts of the public schools to "Americanize" Irish Catholics. A vast system of Catholic primary and secondary schools, Catholic universities, hospitals, charities, and community service organizations emerged as a result.

Today the educational component of Catholic parochial schools serves many non-Irish Catholics, such as Mexican Americans, Italian Americans, and significant numbers of African Americans. These schools are no longer sustained by discrimination in public schools, as in the 1880s, but by the desire to maintain religious affiliation and, simultaneously, to avoid the problems of the decaying public school systems in many urban areas. Thus, the Catholic school system enabled early generations of Irish (and eventually other Catholic immigrants like Italians and Poles) to overcome discrimination against all non-Protestants in the public schools and to sustain important elements of their ethnicity. As this system of education has evolved, it has provided opportunities for Irish Americans to acquire credentials that have facilitated the movement of the last two generations of Irish Americans into higher economic, political, social, and educational positions.

The Stratification of Irish Americans

Because the Irish were the first non-Protestant population to immigrate to Protestant America, conflict with the Anglo-Saxon core was inevitable. Large numbers of very poor Catholics, willing to work for low wages and settling in cities where their numbers upset old balances of power and social mores, were threatening to indigenous, Protestant residents. The resulting conflict occurred on several fronts: between higher-wage English workers and lower-wage Irish, between Anglo-Saxon employers in industry who tried to destroy unions and Irish workers who sought the protection of unions, between Anglo-Saxon incumbents in political machines and Irish aspirants to power, and between residents of Anglo-Saxon Protestant neighborhoods and Irish Catholics who desperately needed housing. Conflict led to discrimination; education levels, employment profiles, and residence patterns of the first two generations of Irish Catholics indicate that this discrimination was effective (Lieberson and Waters, 1988). For these early immigrants, poor housing, low-wage employment, and low levels of education were typical.

When Irish Americans gained local political power, as the Catholic system of schools and service organizations developed, and as patronage jobs to workers and contracts to Irish-run businesses increased, Irish Americans began to move forward economically, educationally, and socially by the turn of the century. Today, Irish Americans are highly assimilated, retaining their ethnicity through Saint Patrick's Day celebrations, expressions of loyalty toward their homeland, and vestiges of their old neighborhoods and local political power.

When Irish Americans moved up the socioeconomic ladder, they came into conflict with more recent white immigrants and with African Americans as they migrated northward in the first two decades of this century. These new immigrants began to pose a threat not only to the Anglo-Saxon core but also to the more established Irish Americans. In particular, African Americans were viewed as a threat because industrialists used them as strikebreakers in efforts to destroy the unions of the Irish and other white ethnic groups. Today, African Americans still suffer from the legacy of this hostility (Bonacich, 1976).

Because they are white, those Irish who immigrated to the United States were more easily assimilated into the mainstream of American society. Today, Irish Americans are virtually indistinguishable from the descendants of the Anglo-Saxon core in terms of their place in the American socioeconomic hierarchy.

ITALIAN AMERICANS

In the early decades of the nineteenth century, some northern Italians began to migrate to South and North America in a steady trickle that continued for the rest of the century (Schiavo, 1934; U.S. Bureau of the Census, 1975). The large-scale immigration of southern Italians began in the 1860s and peaked in the first decade of the twentieth century. In contrast to earlier northern Italians, who tended to be more educated, affluent, and able to enter professions and small businesses, the southern Italians were more likely to be poor, uneducated, and agrarian peasants. Moreover, southern Italians tended to sojourn: staying for short periods, making some money, and returning to Italy. Indeed, perhaps as many as one-third of these later Italian immigrants did return to their homeland, a rate of repatriation that far surpasses any other ethnic group during this period (Learsi, 1954). In all, some four million Italian migrants poured into the United States between 1880 and 1920, with close to 90 percent coming from southern Italy or the island of Sicily (U.S. Bureau of the Census, 1975). These peasant immigrants were fleeing poverty, low wages, unemployment, economic and political domination by elites, governmental neglect, and declining agricultural productivity (Lopreato, 1970). Soon after entering the United States, they formed "Little Italys" in various cities, primarily in the Northeast but also in the Midwest and somewhat later in the West. From these locations they sought relatively unskilled jobs in public works projects, such as canals, sewer systems, and roadways, and in similar labor-intensive sectors of the economy.

Identifiability of Italian Americans

As with the Irish, southern Europeans were portrayed as a distinct "race" that was inferior intellectually and morally. Both the media and intellectuals depicted Italians as incapable of assimilating into Anglo-Saxon society. Fear of intermarriage with Anglo-Saxons was expressed routinely. Underlying these attitudes were Protestant prejudices against Catholics, as well as other cultural differences between northern and southern European ethnic groups (Gambino, 1974; Higham, 1963). Moreover, because Mediterranean Italians have somewhat darker skin tones than northern Europeans, their identifiability by skin color made them seem like a different "race" to northern Europeans.

Negative Beliefs about Italian Americans

The early use of intelligence tests was particularly harmful to Italian Americans because the tests were highly biased against people who were unacculturated and uneducated (Tomasi and Engel, 1970). Italian American schoolchildren (and other newly arrived white ethnic children as well) and enlisted personnel in the army tended to score poorly on these tests, which was used as "scientific proof" of Italians' inferior intellect (Kamin, 1974:1–20). When a group is portrayed as inferior in any way, discrimination follows.

Along with early portrayals of intellectual inferiority came a more persistent "mafia" stereotype portraying Italians as people involved with crime and having little integrity. Up to the prohibition period, Irish and Jewish Americans controlled most organized criminal syndicates. When a number of visible and infamous Italians moved into these criminal syndicates, the Italian gangster stereotype emerged and stuck. For Italian Americans, crime was a means toward upward mobility in a hostile society, but the general crime rates for Italians during this period were actually low (Lopreato, 1970:124–126). The mafia stereotype remains today in American culture—defined, and perhaps perpetuated, by movies such as *The Godfather* trilogy, *The Untouchables,* and *Prizzi's Honor.*

Perhaps even more pernicious are media portrayals of Italian males as somewhat ingratiating but tough, dim-witted, and oversexed womanizers (as portrayals of "The Fonz" in television reruns of *Happy Days* testify). Today, Italian jokes are uttered with relative impunity, along with ethnic labels such as "dago" and "wop." Images of Italian Americans as overly emotional, jealous, oversexed when young, fat mammas when old, physical, tough, and racist hard hats still exist (Gambino, 1974:352). Thus, far more than the Irish and Poles, Italian Americans still suffer from negative stereotyping, despite their success in fighting the effects of economic, political, and educational discrimination for over two generations.

The Dynamics of Discrimination against Italian Americans

Economic Discrimination

Today, Italian Americans have incomes and employment histories approximating those for other whites. Yet, despite the high visibility of a few individuals, Italians are still underrepresented in top administrative positions of government and private industry, even as Italian American workers occupy rank-and-file positions proportionate to their numbers in the general population. Italian Americans are thus just beginning to reach full economic mobility, as their levels of educational attainment and income have surpassed national averages.

The previous one hundred years have seen considerable economic discrimination against Italians. From the beginning, many came as indentured workers to bosses who provided low-wage work, overpriced food, and expensive slum housing. Under such a system it was difficult for migrants to escape poverty, but eventually this system began to collapse. Even under less oppressive conditions, early Italian immigrants faced a number of barriers: language, few vocational skills, little education, and isolation in Italian ghettoes away from job networks. Blatant discrimination also hindered upward mobility for these immigrants who were paid lower wages and excluded from unions. These practices subsided by the turn of the century; and in fact, Italian Americans became very active in the union movement.

Southern Italian immigrants became upwardly mobile during the first decades of this century. Union involvement provided jobs of increasing skill; the sons of many unskilled and semiskilled workers moved into higher-skill craft occupations; and entrepreneurial activity among Italian businessmen increased, with many achieving considerable economic success. The great depression curtailed some of this progress, but the post–World War II period saw continued Italian American upward mobility into white-collar jobs, professions, and businesses (Greeley, 1977). Some scholars predict that fourth-generation Italians may achieve parity with British and German ethnic groups in levels of education, income, and employment (Alba, 1985).

Political Discrimination

Early Italian immigrants had relatively low voter participation rates, a pattern attributed to the distrust that many southern Italians felt toward government and to the dampening effects of low socioeconomic status on political activity (Lopreato, 1970). Coupled with more general anti-Catholic prejudices among the broader population, these attitudes prevented Italian Americans from holding national political office. For example, it was not until 1950 that an Italian American was elected to the Senate. As late as the 1940s, fewer than a dozen Italian Americans served in the House of Representatives. And, only in 1962 did an Italian American hold a cabinet post in the federal government. The first Italian American vice presidential candidate was nominated in 1984; two years later the first Italian American was appointed to the Supreme Court.

At the local political level, Italian Americans have fared somewhat better, becoming allied with the Democratic political machines in northeastern and midwestern cities. Although the Protestant reform movements that curtailed the activities of big-city political machines temporarily loosened the Italian American foothold in the halls of local power, upward mobility and a declining distrust of government increased Italian American voter participation to a point where many cities with significant Italian American communities elected Italian mayors and city council members. Thus, even before World War II Italian Americans exhibited a significant presence in local politics, despite the fact that anti-Catholic prejudice prevented Protestant voters from voting for Italian Americans as state and national candidates.

By the 1970s, the political barriers to state and national politics were rapidly coming down. Italian mayors, governors, congressional representatives, and senators became increasingly common. Today, Italian Americans hold office in local, state, and congressional political arenas in numbers approximately proportionate to their numbers in the general population. Third- and fourth-generation Italian Americans have moved rapidly into politics, proving that they have overcome anti-Italian and anti-Catholic prejudice and discrimination.

Educational Discrimination

The first wave of southern Italian migrants to the United States tended to be illiterate and impoverished. Their children went to school for short periods of time in order to acquire basic skills, then dropped out to help support the family. The high dropout rates were also due to the pervasive culture in the public schools, which sought to "Americanize" Italians. Children were put under enormous pressure to change their look, their speech, their dress, and their demeanor to conform with a more Anglo-Saxon profile.

The Catholic school system was not a readily available alternative to the first waves of southern Italian immigrants because of conflict with Irish Americans, who dominated this system, and because of their inability to pay for tuition and books. As a consequence, Italian youth either endured the public schools or dropped out. These high dropout rates hindered the second generation's economic mobility.

By the 1920s, Italian Americans began to make significant progress in education, a trend that has continued into the 1990s. Today, the average number of years of education completed by Italian Americans surpasses that of many other white ethnic groups, and that of the white population as a whole. Thus, third and fourth generations of Italian American immigrants have overcome the effects of discrimination against the first and second generations; as levels of education have increased, upward economic and political mobility has ensued.

Legal Discrimination

The passage of the Immigration Act of 1924 limited immigration to the United States, especially for eastern and southern Europeans. The quota set for Italians was over ten times lower than the quota for the British and five times lower than the quota for Germans. Clearly the intent was to favor Anglo-Saxons and northern Europeans over all other ethnic groups, with the result that many Italians were prevented from immigrating to the United States. Although the laws were changed several times, only the new Immigration Law of 1965 enabled more Italians to immigrate by using the unfilled quotas of other ethnic groups from northern Europe. However, the earlier restrictions on immigration sent a not-too-subtle message to Italian Americans: You are inferior and undesirable. Such messages supported existing negative beliefs about Italians in the United States and, no doubt, perpetuated discriminatory practices up to World War II.

Stratification of Italian Americans

As the second largest Catholic population to enter the United States, Italian immigrants threatened the Anglo-Saxon Protestant core. This threat was reinforced by other large influxes of Catholic Poles and Jews. Nativist sentiments ran high within the Protestant white community. Much like the Irish, Italians were portrayed as an inferior "race" that could potentially "mongrelize" America through intermarriage. Italians constituted the first wave of immigrants from southern Europe to the United States, which made them seem doubly different and, hence, threatening.

In addition to white Protestant hostility, Italians faced, at least initially, Irish fears about the presence of yet another disadvantaged immigrant population. Such fears were aggravated when employers used Italians as strikebreakers against unions heavily populated by Irish workers. The problems that Italians initially had in enrolling their children in Catholic schools attest to the tension between Irish and Italians—a tension that was aggravated by the wave of poor Catholic Polish immigrants.

The lack of education and job skills, coupled with Protestant and Irish discrimination, ensured that first- and most second-generation Italian Americans would be at the bottom of the socioeconomic ladder. Similar to all white ethnic groups, however, Italians had some distinct advantages: They were white and possessed organizational resources in family and church; over time these resources could be used to penetrate unions, skilled workplaces, white-collar jobs, professions, and schools. By the third generation, rapid upward mobility was occurring. Today, Italian Americans are above the national average in educational attainment and income. Lingering stereotypes and informal discrimination against Italian Americans persist, however. The final phase of assimilation is yet to be completed, although it is imminent.

JEWISH AMERICANS

Jews have been the most persistently persecuted minority group in history. Massacres of Jews have occurred since Rome's occupation of present-day Israel in the period before and after the birth of Christ. The intensity of this persecution is etched in the modern conscience by the death camps of Nazi Germany. Indeed, many American Jews are the descendants of those who sought refuge from more recent forms of persecution. The first Jewish immigrants to the United States, the Sephardic Jews, arrived in the 1640s to escape massacres and expulsion from Spain and Portugal; their numbers did not exceed a few thousand. The second group of Jewish immigrants began to enter the United States in the 1840s in an effort to escape the widening scale of persecution in Europe. Most of these immigrants came from what is now Germany and settled in the Midwest, causing the Jewish population to grow from 15,000 to more than 250,000 in the early 1880s (Herberg, 1960:176). The third wave of immigration, beginning in the 1880s and lasting until the 1920s, led to the significant presence of Jews in America. Coming from areas of eastern Europe controlled by the Russian Czar (and later the communists of the former Soviet Union), some two million Jews settled in the United States, primarily in urban areas of the Northeast (Lestschinsky, 1955:56). While many sought refuge from persecution, the vast majority came voluntarily in search of opportunities in a new land (Sklare, 1971; Learsi, 1954). Yet, even as the Immigration Act of 1924 curtailed the mass immigration of all ethnic groups to the United States, some 400,000 more Jews immigrated, in most cases to escape Nazi persecution. By the eve of World War II, however, immigration policy had become so strict that many hundreds of thousands of Jews who desperately sought refuge in America were forced to stay and suffer the consequences of Hitler's death camps. Some 150,000 were able to enter the United States as political refugees; among these were many of the great scientists and intellectuals of modern times—Albert Einstein, Edward Teller, Eric Fromm, Herbert Marcuse, and Bruno Bettelheim.

In more recent decades, immigration statistics for the American Jewish population are inaccurate because the Immigration and Naturalization Service no longer identifies immigrants by religion; estimates run as high as 500,000 recent immigrants. Today, around six million Jews live in America, a figure that comes close to 50 percent of the world's Jewish population. The rest live primarily in Israel, the recently independent states of the former Soviet Union, and various European and South American countries. The majority of Jewish Americans live in the Northeast, although the number (as with the rest of the population) residing in the West and South is increasing rapidly—mirroring the trend in the general population. Jewish Americans represent about 3 percent of the American population; yet their massive immigration in the 1880s activated the same dynamics of discrimination experienced by other white ethnic groups, such as the Irish, Italians, and Poles.

Identifiability of Jews

Throughout history, Jews have been considered a "race," but the basis for this designation is social and cultural, not biological. Those who have persecuted Jews in the United States and around the world have used the spurious belief that Jews are biologically different as the basis for extreme forms of discrimination. In reality, there is no distinguishing physical trait that makes it easy to designate someone as a "Jew."

Jews are defined by their religious beliefs, which are based on the texts

The Jewish community strives to maintain its identifiability in U.S. society.

of the Torah, or the first five books of the Bible. Orthodox Jews adhere to the Torah in strict terms—ritual, food preparation and consumption, and synagogue attendance. About one-fifth of all American Jews are Orthodox. At the other extreme are Reform Jews, who represent perhaps one-third of the American Jewish population and who have modernized and secularized their religious activity. Between these extremes are Conservative Jews, who represent from one-third to one-half of all American Jews.

Being Jewish in a Protestant society makes one different, but many Jews are not outwardly religious. Moreover, synagogue attendance rates tend to be low, rendering this particular indicator of religious affiliation relatively useless (except for some Orthodox Jews, who may be easily identified by dress, demeanor, and ritual practices). Thus, religion does not outwardly distinguish Jews from gentiles.

In many respects, the source of Jewish identifiability is the awareness of a shared history of persecution and the sense among Jews that they constitute a community with a unique set of traditions. Because Jews have historically been treated as a distinct community rather than as a nationality, they have developed organizations, networks, and shared beliefs that have provided them with a sense of identity and that, during historical episodes of extreme discrimination, have allowed them to survive in hostile environments. Thus, unlike other white ethnic groups living in the United States whose identity is tied to their country of origin, Jews have maintained a sense of being a community that has sustained itself within many countries. Consequently, Jews have been able to mobilize resources—primarily organizational but also economic and educational—that make them somewhat distinguishable, *to themselves,* and that enable them to rank high in terms of education and income in America (Goldschneider, 1986).

Negative Beliefs about Jews

Because Jews have persisted as a cohesive and successful community within hostile societies, negative beliefs about them have evolved over time and, under conditions of extreme persecution, have intensified. These beliefs have been reinforced by the "middleman minority" positions Jews have historically occupied; as we noted in Chapter 2, middleman minority groups are traditionally targets of hostility.

From the Middle Ages to the present, Jews have been the subjects of persistent prejudicial beliefs and stereotypes. Although Christ was crucified by the Romans, some people believe that Jews were the culprits. In a Christian society like the United States, this belief undergirds hostility toward Jews. In fact, some Catholic and Protestant ministers have in the past promoted this idea, conveniently ignoring all the pertinent historical facts. Jews are also stereotyped as shrewd, crafty, cheap, money-grubbing, materialistic, and sly (Glock and Stark, 1966; Gordon, 1988). Another set of beliefs are based on the "Jewish conspiracy." In the 1920s and 1930s in America, people such as Henry Ford actively propagated the idea that Jews were involved in an international conspiracy to control all governments. The Ku Klux Klan, the German-American Bund, media personalities such as the Catholic priest Charles E. Coughlin, and even Charles Lindbergh saw Jews as conspiring to control the world. Even as late as the 1970s, a member of the Joint Chiefs of Staff could be heard arguing that Jews "own, you know, the banks in the country, the newspapers" (Selzer, 1972). More recent debates over the threat of Zionism and the "Jewish lobby" in Congress have revived elements of the Jewish conspiracy theory.

Most surveys and polls report dramatic drops in negative stereotypes about Jews over the last sixty years (Lipset, 1987). In fact, many Americans hold very positive views of Jews as intelligent, educated, and industrious. Yet, often lurking beneath the surface are subtle condemnations of Jews as being *too* bright, hardworking, and ambitious. However, many of the older stereotypes—from "Christ killers" to "money grubbers"—still prevail. People know that it is unacceptable in most public situations, including surveys and polls, to utter these negative beliefs, but the recent increase in acts of vandalism in Jewish cemeteries and synagogues indicates that below the polite surface lurk powerful prejudices against Jews. These beliefs often legitimate discriminatory practices against Jews in America.

The Dynamics of Discrimination against Jewish Americans

The comparatively high incomes and levels of education among Jewish Americans is a tribute to their ability to overcome open discrimination in jobs, politics, housing, and education, as well as more covert discrimination in clubs, fraternal organizations, and other social groups. Yet, despite a record of economic and academic success, Jews are underrepresented in many occupations, professions, and high-level positions of power.

Economic Discrimination

Early Jewish immigrants assumed middleman minority positions. Although most Jews of German origin arrived with little money, they had entrepreneurial skills that enabled them to start small businesses (primarily in the garment, jewelry, meat, and leather trades) as well as trading and financial positions. By the 1890s, census data report that almost 60 percent of Jews were in trade and finance, 20 percent were in office work, and only 6 percent were in the professions. With centuries of experience in finding economic niches in the hostile environments of Europe, Jews were able to find such niches in the United States (Glazer, 1957).

The eastern European Jews who began to immigrate to the United States in the 1880s tended to be less educated and skilled than earlier German immigrants; as a result, they established an economic foothold in unskilled manufacturing jobs, as did other white immigrants. Men and women worked long hours for low wages in sweatshops; many women did sewing and laundry in the home to help make ends meet. Those eastern European immigrants who had small-business experience were able to find middleman minority niches, as had earlier German migrants. Because education and study have always been highly valued in the Jewish community, considerable upward mobility was possible for the sons and daughters of these Jewish immigrants. For example, by the early 1900s, Jews in the Northeast were moving into law, medicine, and other professions, while assuming middle-level clerical positions in businesses and government.

Immigration was cut off in the 1920s, and those who had made it to the United States continued their economic mobility. When the great depression hit in the 1930s, however, this mobility was curtailed by economic discrimination. The success of Jewish Americans was now intensely resented in a tightening job market; signs reading "No Jews need apply" were common. Jews were excluded from many professional positions in banking, teaching, medicine, law, and engineering, as well as more skilled blue-collar and clerical jobs. Jews began to experience systematic, institutionalized discrimination, which forced them to find economic opportunities in risky sectors such as media and small business, and in professional and clerical jobs for which they were overqualified. The legacy of economic discrimination remains today, for Jews are underrepresented in high-level positions in banking, in management positions at savings and loans, utilities, and insurance companies, and the top levels of management in almost all industries. The two exceptions to this pattern are the media and plastics, in which Jews took the early risks.

On average, Jewish Americans are wealthier than non-Jews. This wealth is the result of taking risks in a narrow range of businesses such as clothing, mass communications, jewelry, and merchandising, while overcoming quotas and outright bans in professions such as law and medicine. Jewish Americans exist in what is termed a "golden ghetto," but it is nonetheless a ghetto. In the 1990s, however, the pattern of informal exclusion appears to be diminishing; it is likely that Jewish Americans will move into a broader range of management positions commensurate with their education and skill.

Open exclusion (or token representation) of Jews in country clubs, some fraternal and community organizations, and many elite social circles indicates that informal discrimination and quotas persist even today at the close of the twentieth century. Because these organizational affiliations are often crucial to the development of informal contacts and networks necessary for economic success and mobility, Jewish Americans will continue to feel the effects of this form of exclusion.

Political Discrimination

Unlike many minority groups who have established themselves in economic middlemen positions, Jewish Americans have been politically active, voting in large numbers and engaging in volunteer political activity. Yet, despite their economic and academic success, this involvement has not translated into significant political power until recent decades. Jews have become governors of a few northeastern states over the years, and they have been successful in local politics where there is a substantial community of Jewish Americans. Yet, Jewish Americans did not gain access to higher-level administrative positions in the federal government until the 1930s; they have had only a handful of Supreme Court appointments, despite the fact that a high proportion of lawyers and law professors are Jewish Americans, and they reached proportionate representation in Congress only in the 1970s. Jewish Americans are now overrepresented in Congress, holding 8 percent of Senate seats and constituting 7 percent of the House membership.

Although Jewish Americans have become increasingly prominent in politics, their underrepresentation in top management positions in industry and manufacturing limits their ability to use informal economic power to secure top-level appointments in those governmental posts where experience as a corporate manager is considered important (Zweigenhaft and Domhoff, 1982; Alba and Moore, 1982). Yet, 90 percent of Americans say that they would vote for a qualified Jewish presidential candidate, whereas less than 50 percent would have done so five decades ago (Marger, 1991:204). Such shifts in attitudes indicate that Jewish Americans will become increasingly assimilated in the political arena.

Legal Discrimination

Unlike many other societies, the United States never legally institutionalized anti-Semitism. Before the signing of the Constitution, most states had established "Christian-only" restrictions for public office. Indeed, it is possible that some signatories to the Constitution were anti-Semitic (or anti-non-

Christian); yet these prejudices are not reflected in law or in government policy. The closest instances approaching legal discrimination against Jews have been the *blue laws* of many communities that require businesses to close on Sunday—a day when many Jewish businesses could remain open.

Discrimination against Jewish Americans has been largely informal. Jews have had to overcome informal restrictive quotas in jobs and education, informal restrictive housing practices, and informal restrictive memberships in clubs and social organizations. The law has rarely supported these practices, except in the area of housing, where written restrictive covenants were enforced until the 1960s. Yet, legal tolerance of informal discrimination is, in fact, a form of legalized discrimination. Indeed, until passage of the various civil rights acts in the 1960s, the legal system did not attack the injustices of such informal practices of discrimination.

Educational Discrimination

It may seem absurd, on the surface, to consider educational discrimination against the most educated ethnic subpopulation in the United States. The long tradition of respect for learning and education in the Jewish community is so powerful that it has been possible to overcome clear patterns of discrimination. One of these patterns was established at the turn of the century, when Jewish American children were segregated in many of the public schools in the Northeast. Despite this segregation, however, Jewish students completed high school in much higher numbers than did non-Jews. Another discriminatory pattern was the informal, but often articulated, quota system for Jewish American high school graduates in American colleges and universities. Particularly in private schools, this system of limiting Jewish enrollment existed well into the 1960s. Also, on college campuses, discrimination in membership to fraternities and sororities was, and is, rampant. Jewish students have responded by forming their own fraternities and sororities. In private elite schools, the informal contacts and networks formed socially can be crucial to future occupational placement in mainstream corporate America; in this respect, many Jewish Americans are at a disadvantage. However, the magnitude of Jewish academic achievement in a society valuing educational credentials has enabled Jewish Americans to find business and professional niches and, increasingly in recent decades, to penetrate large, elite corporations. Despite their obvious economic success, Jewish graduates still encounter invisible barriers and must endure the subtle favoritism given to less educated and skilled non-Jews.

The Stratification of Jewish Americans

Because many Jewish Americans have been enormously successful, the fact that many Jews live below the poverty line (but in low percentages compared to the rest of the population) is often overlooked. Success has come despite sometimes intense informal discrimination, legitimized by prejudicial beliefs. Such discrimination has been fueled by perceptions of threat from non-Jews. All immigrants once competed for industrial jobs, especially when the depression diminished the job market. Jewish American skill in running small businesses, in education, and in the professions posed a threat to gentiles. Coupled with long-standing and inaccurate European beliefs that Jews are shrewd and conspiratorial, this sense of threat increased and, in turn, intensified informal discrimination.

Jewish Americans are concentrated in the middle and upper middle strata, and are underrepresented in both lower socioeconomic positions and elite political and economic spheres. However, because movement into more elite positions has become increasingly possible, Jewish Americans are likely to penetrate and achieve parity in this sphere.

SUMMARY

The one hundred years from the early nineteenth century to the first decades of the twentieth century are the bookends for the mass immigration of non-Protestant Europeans to America. Their religion and eagerness to work threatened the existing Anglo-Saxon core. The non-Protestant southern Irish came in the early years of the last century, followed in the second half of the century by large influxes of Italians, Poles, and Jews. Because these migrants were white and European, their early experiences with discrimination were more readily overcome than those who are more readily identified by surface biological features.

The advantages of white skin in overcoming discrimination in America can be found in the resource shares of white ethnics today. They secure better jobs, earn more money, attain more education, and live in less segregated neighborhoods than most non-European ethnics. Thus, while the legacy of negative stereotyping persists and discrimination is still evident, these forces have not prevented white ethnic groups from gaining their share of the resources available in America.

The Irish, who today represent the third largest ethnic population behind those from the British mainland and Germany, were the first of the white ethnics to come to America after the Anglo-Saxon core. The Protestant Irish had arrived in the 1700s, but it was the Catholic Irish immigration beginning in the 1830s that escalated discrimination against the Irish. These non-Protestant migrants came from the heart of rural impoverishment and were desperate for any work—thereby representing a threat not only to Protestantism as the dominant religion but to the wages and economic security of those already settled in America. These perceived threats fueled prejudicial stereotypes labeling the Irish Catholics as a distinct "race" who are wicked, ignorant, and less than human. Efforts to exclude them from better jobs, centers of political power, public schools, and adequate housing were, in the long run, unsuccessful as the Catholic Irish worked their way up the occupational system. They captured or created the big-city political machines, utilized the Catholic school system to overcome discrimination in public schools, and used their financial and political clout to move into better neighborhoods. This mobility threatened other whites, but it also led to considerable assimilation of the Catholic Irish into the societal mainstream, which reduced the threat experienced by the descendants of earlier immigrants. Indeed, the more successful Catholic Irish became, the more they began to fear the new waves of European immigrants who would threaten their hard-won gains.

Small numbers of northern Italians immigrated to the United States during the early decades of the nineteenth century, but beginning in 1860 large numbers of poor, less educated, rural southern Italians entered the country. As with the Irish, systematic efforts were made to identify these Italians as a separate "race" because of their Catholicism, southern European ways, and Mediterranean skin tones. These characteristics made them different from the Anglo-Saxon core and subject to prejudicial beliefs and blatant discrimination. Initial negative stereotypes of Italian Americans branded them as lacking intelligence and, somewhat later, as having loose morals and a propensity toward violence as well as crime. More recent stereotyping focuses on the presumed emotionality, sexuality, bigotry, and hotheadedness of Italian Americans. Such negative stereotyping was initially used to bolster discrimination in jobs, schools, and politics. Even the law began to restrict immigration from southern Europe. Yet, as with other white ethnics, their white skin, strong family structures, commitment to church, and effective use of unions enabled second- and third-generation Italians to move up the stratification system so that today they are above most other ethnics in the shares of resources. Still, there are lingering stereotypes about Italians, often highlighted in the media. These may still serve to support informal patterns of discrimination.

Jews have been persecuted all over the world. As their numbers increased during the 1840s in America and especially when immigration accelerated in the 1880s, discrimination became as obvious here as elsewhere in the world. Later, in the years preceding and during World War II, more Jews came to escape the ravages of Nazism. Today, a steady stream of Jews still migrates to America, making the United States the place of residence for almost half of the world's Jewish population. Like other white ethnic minorities, Jews were distinguished as a peculiar "race," which made them just "different" enough to justify discrimination. Negative stereotypes could be brutal, such as those portraying Jews as "Christ killers" (an impossible charge since the Romans performed the actual execution). But more subtle and age-old stereotypes of Jews as cheap with money, sly, and clannish, coupled with more blatant and rather paranoid visions of a world Jewish conspiracy, still haunt Jewish Americans, as well as Jews all over the world. Out of necessity, Jews have had to sustain a strong sense of ethnic identity, hence their need to establish a viable set of institutions in a discriminating world. As they did so, they developed the organizational and financial resources to succeed in educational attainment, business, and professional activity. Yet, this success is circumscribed by the exclusionary practices in almost all spheres of American life. Ordinary jobs, many professions, business opportunities, and top management positions still remain somewhat closed to the Jewish population. Significant inroads into politics and government jobs have been made by Jews only in recent decades, but informal discrimination persists in housing, social clubs, and non-Jewish businesses.

For all white ethnics—Jews, Italians, Irish, and many others—their white skin has made a big difference in their overcoming discrimination. By simply adopting the culture, speech, values, and other characteristics of the Anglo-Saxon core, white ethnics could blend with the general population and move up the educational and occupational ladder. They have realized the "American dream." Many of the descendants of these white ethnic immigrants who blazed this upwardly mobile trail have, at times, lost awareness of the legacy of discrimination communicated in words like "wop," "Paddy," or "Pollack." In fact, the descendants of the white ethnic immigrants are often the perpetuators of bigotry and discrimination against people of color.

The tenuous nature of their own economic standing may account for the tradition of racism among white ethnics. Discrimination against African Americans emerged full-blown in the early decades of the twentieth century when black workers were used as strikebreakers (Bonacich, 1976; Olzak, 1992). Early Asian immigrants experienced considerable resistance when they were perceived as a threat to the hard-won gains of white ethnics. And Latinos were also viewed as a potential labor pool that would take away the jobs of white ethnic laborers. Recent patterns of increased immigration by Latinos and Asians, coupled with old prejudices against African Americans, sustain the sense of threat among white ethnics over their jobs and culture. Such threats are magnified by global corporate systems that pull jobs overseas. As we have seen, threat is the fuel behind prejudice and discrimination. Hence, competition with empowered people of color makes the success of some white ethnics seem tenuous. The movement of manual labor into the world economy, coupled with the proportional decline of members of the original Anglo-Saxon core and their white converts, has increased ethnic tensions in America and now represents a major problem for peaceful ethnic relations in the next century.

POINTS OF DEBATE

Caucasians with European-looking features are at an advantage in American society. They are able to overcome discrimination by simply assimilating into the Anglo-Saxon core, while retaining a few of their old ethnic traditions that do not threaten this core. By contrast, people of color and those with non-European features must face constant reminders from others about their "distinctiveness." Even with social assimilation into much of the core, they still stand out physically. The unwillingness of white ethnics to accept the efforts at social mobility by members of other ethnic groups in realizing the American dream makes for many points of debate:

1. How is it possible for white people to understand what it is like to "stand out" and to be vulnerable to the imposition of prejudicial beliefs and acts of discrimination in various encounters with whites? Can whites recognize the enormous psychic costs of this situation for members of readily identifiable minority populations? What can be done about this situation? Should current efforts to impose a "political correctness" ideology on all others be allowed to continue? If so, who is to decide what is correct? Or, alternatively, is the introduction of sensitivity training in the workplace, school, or community a better path? If so, who decides what will be taught, from what perspective, and *by* whom *to* whom? Or is it best to let the forces involved take a natural course? If so, should a society that values equal opportunity allow the inevitable discrimination that results from a "hands-off" policy to continue?
2. Can white Americans fully understand that the playing field has not been, and is not today, equal in a society that values equality of opportunity? The legacy of slavery, Jim Crow, conquest and annexation, reservation life, and many other patterns of discrimination makes it difficult for many, though not all, to have the same chance in the society as whites. White Americans tend to be fixated on, and angry over, the reverse discrimination that inevitably accompanies efforts at inclusive affirmative action. Must white Americans suffer the same frustration and anger that many members of minorities have endured over the decades? Is it the same? Or, is it possible for white Americans to accept a certain amount of reverse discrimination in order to compensate for past discrimination against specific ethnics? If not, then what is to be done by white America to curb the pathologies inherent in decades, if not centuries, of discrimination—the pathologies of racism, violence, crime, drug use, welfare dependency, and other problems that accompany long-term discrimination?

CHAPTER 9

The Future of Ethnicity in America

THE NEW IMMIGRANTS

With the exception of Native Americans, who were already here, and African Americans, who were brought as slaves, the population of the United States has been built by immigrants. The ever-changing ethnic makeup of the United States—past, present, and future—is the result of immigration patterns and relative birthrates among immigrant populations (Portes and Rumbaut, 1990). Figure 9.1 delineates the trends in legal immigration from 1900 to 1993. Legal immigration steadily increased after World War II, then dramatically escalated to a peak of 1,827,167 in 1991. Of course, this figure accounts for only legal immigration; a considerable amount of illegal immigration has occurred, primarily from Latin America. By 1993, legal immigration rates had fallen to 904,300 under the impact of the 1990 Immigration Act (discussed shortly); however, this drop probably was more than compensated for by illegal immigration rates (Vernez and McCarthy, 1990; Fernandez and Robinson, 1994).

Countries of Origin

Table 9.1 reports the area of origin of those who immigrated to the United States between 1951 and 1993; the post–World War II period of escalating immigration saw a dramatic change in the national origins of immigrants (Rolph, 1992; U.S. Department of Justice, 1991a). In 1951, almost 68 percent of immigrants came from Europe and Canada, slightly over 6 percent from Asia, and about 25 percent from Latin America and the Caribbean. Over the last three decades, however, the percentage of immigrants from Europe and Canada has dropped dramatically, while the Asian and the combined Latin American and Caribbean percentages have increased. As of 1993, almost 50 percent of all legal immigrants came from Latin American

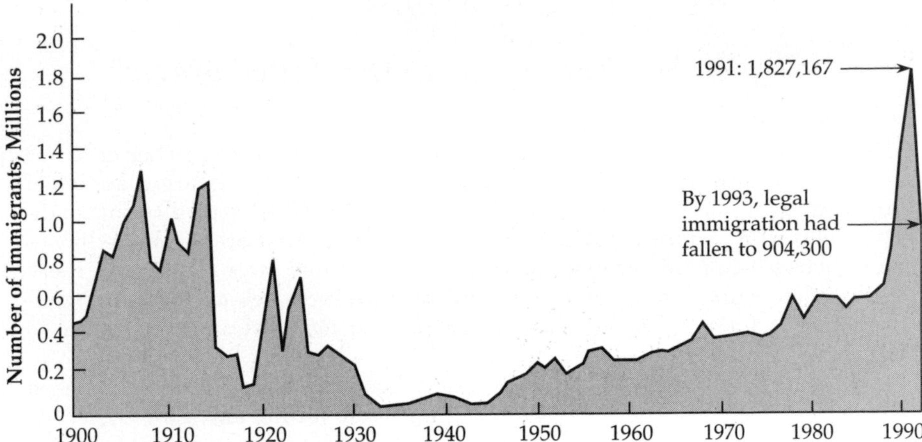

FIGURE 9.1. Legal immigration in the twentieth century.
Source: U.S. Bureau of the Census, 1995.

or Caribbean countries and 30 percent from Asian countries. If illegal immigrants could be counted, of course, these percentages would be much higher.

An Immigration and Naturalization Service (INS) report offers a more complete breakdown of the area of origin of immigrants from 1983 to 1993. In Figure 9.1 one can note that legal immigration peaked in 1991, but has been declining since then. Figure 9.2 shows that the majority of legal immigrants came from Mexico, the next largest number came from Asia, then the Caribbean, followed by Europe, Central America, South America, Africa, and the former Soviet Union. Because immigrants from Mexico, Central America, and South America constitute the Latino population in the United States, they are by far the largest ethnic group (Mozo and Vasquez, 1988). Since a significant portion of the Caribbean immigrant population is black, the combined African and Caribbean figure exceeds the white European figure by almost a 1.5-to-1 margin (see Figure 9.2).

TABLE 9.1. The Shifting Profile of Immigrants to the United States, 1951 through 1993

Area of Origin	1951–60	1961–70	1971–80	1981–90	1991–93
Europe and Canada	67.7%	46.3%	21.6%	12.5%	13.1%
Asia	6.1	12.9	35.5	37.5	30.0
Latin America and the Caribbean	24.6	39.2	40.3	47.1	49.9

Sources: Elizabeth Rolph, *Immigration Policies: Legacy from the 1980s and Issues for the 1990s* (Santa Monica, CA: The RAND Corporation, 1992); U.S. Department of Justice, 1991a; U.S. Bureau of the Census, 1995.

Box 9.1

Why Do Mexicans Come to the United States?

Why do Mexicans come to the United States? Is it the promise of riches or fame? Is it the perception of the United States as a paradise? The historical survey of Mexican immigration to the United States in Chapter 6 identified social conditions in Mexico and the need for cheap labor in the United States as the "push-pull" factors behind Mexican immigration to the United States. Although these socioeconomic indicators may explain the circumstances behind Mexican immigration, do we know what reasons Mexicans offer for Mexican immigration to the United States?

In a study conducted by Aguirre (1993) regarding the association between English-language and U.S.-origin communication media and how Mexicans perceive Mexican social issues, he found that Mexicans have definite perceptions as to why Mexicans immigrate to the United States. By order of decreasing importance, Aguirre found that Mexicans believe that Mexicans immigrate to the United States for the following reasons:

1. There is no employment in Mexico (59 percent).
2. Mexicans want to earn more money (38 percent).
3. The standard of living is higher in the United States (36 percent).
4. There are better employers in the United States (32 percent).
5. Mexicans like adventure (28 percent).

Source: A. Aguirre, "Communication Media and Mexican Social Issues: A Focus on English Language and U.S.-Origin Communication Media," *International Journal of Comparative Sociology* 34: 231–243 (1993).

Consequences of the New Immigration Patterns

The most recent census data on immigration trends, coupled with past immigration rates and birthrates, form the ethnic profile of America reported in Table 9.2. Today, 75 percent of the U.S. population is white, 12 percent is black, 9 percent is Latino, close to 3 percent is Asian–Pacific Islander, and less than 1 percent is Native American (U.S. Bureau of the Census, 1992b). According to the U.S. Census Bureau (1992b), however, these numbers are expected to change dramatically if current patterns of immigration, fertility rates, and age distribution of various ethnic subpopulations persist. By the year 2050, the white population will decrease to a slight majority—from 52 to 53 percent. Latinos will make up 21 to 24 percent of the population, blacks 13 to 16 percent, Asians (including Pacific Islanders) 11 to 13 percent, and Native Americans less than 1 percent. We can, of course, see these trends around us each day in terms of whom we encounter in school, work, neighborhood, and public places. For a comparison of native-born and immigrant persons in the United States, see Box 9.2.

Ethnic diversity coupled with rapid shifts in the relative numbers of

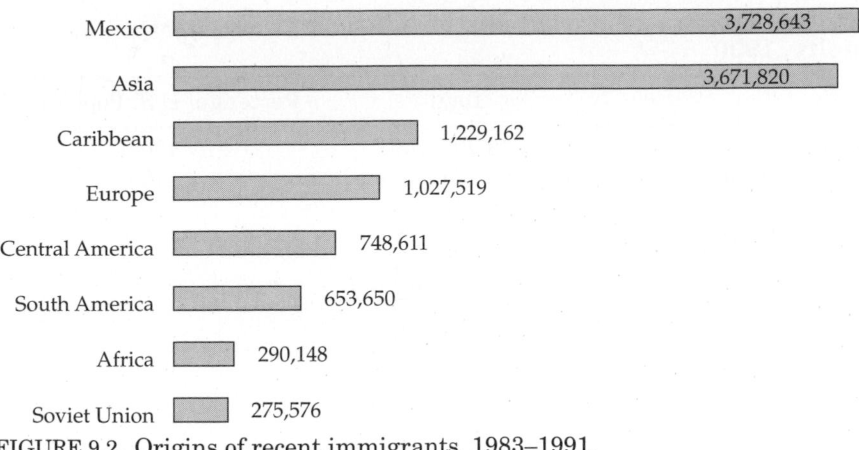

FIGURE 9.2. Origins of recent immigrants, 1983–1991.
Source: U.S. Bureau of the Census, 1992b, 1995.

different ethnic subpopulations makes ethnicity a salient issue and, for many, an unsettling one. Members of all ethnic populations must accommodate one another, a task that may prove difficult and, when unsuccessful, may create the same dynamic of discrimination experienced by past generations of immigrants.

Reasons for the Shift in Immigration Patterns

This shift in immigration patterns is, to a great extent, the result of changes in immigration laws over the last three decades. Rolph (1992) has suggested that much of the shift is due to the Immigration Act of 1965, which eliminated country-specific quotas that had favored European countries and, simultaneously, allowed immediate family members of U.S. citizens the opportunity to enter the country without numerical restriction. In addition, prior to 1965, immigrants from European countries had entered the United States largely through a program that gave visas to persons in professions and occupations that were in short supply. The Immigration Act of 1965 placed a 20 percent ceiling on these visas. Thus, as Rolph (1992:10) notes: "Removal of country-specific quotas and the new preference system designed to facilitate family reunification had been . . . responsible for substantial changes in the ethnic composition and skill level of the immigrant pool over the years."

The growth of immigrant populations from Asia and combined Latin American and Caribbean countries between 1981 and the present is related to two additional pieces of immigration legislation. The first, the Refugee Act of 1980, encouraged immigration from Asian countries—especially from Vietnam, Laos, and Cambodia. In the aftermath of the Vietnam War, Congress enacted the Refugee Act in an attempt to regulate the flow and number of refugees that qualified for admission to the United States. A *refugee*

TABLE 9.2. Summary Characteristics of the U.S. Population by Ethnicity, 1990

Ethnicity	Total	Percent of U.S. Population
All persons	248,709,873	100.0
White non-Latino	188,128,296	75.6
Black	29,986,060	12.1
American Indian*	1,959,234	0.8
Asian	6,908,638	2.8
Chinese	1,645,472	
Filipino	1,406,770	
Japanese	847,562	
Asian Indian	815,447	
Korean	798,849	
Vietnamese	614,547	
Cambodian	147,411	
Hmong	90,082	
Laotian	149,014	
Thai	91,275	
Other Asian	302,209	0.1
Bangladeshi	11,838	
Burmese	6,177	
Indonesian	29,252	
Malasian	12,243	
Okinawan	2,247	
Pakistani	81,371	
Sri Lankan	10,970	
All other Asian	148,111	
Pacific Islander	365,024	.01
Hawaiian	211,014	
Samoan	62,964	
Guamanian	49,345	
Other Pacific Islander	41,701	
Tongan	17,606	
Tahitian	944	
Northern Mariana Islander	960	
Pelauan	1,439	
Fijian	7,036	
All other Pacific Islander	13,716	
Latino origin	22,354,059	9.0
Mexican	13,495,938	
Puerto Rican	2,727,754	
Cuban	1,043,932	
Other†	5,086,435	

*Includes Eskimo and Aleut.

†Includes persons from El Salvador, Guatemala, Honduras, Nicaragua, and Costa Rica.

Source: U.S. Bureau of the Census, 1992b.

Box 9.2

Native-Born and Immigrant Persons in the United States

Table 9.3 summarizes selected characteristics of the U.S. population by ethnicity and immigration status. One can make the following derivations from Table 9.3.

EDUCATIONAL ATTAINMENT

- Black immigrants and Asian immigrants have a higher rate of college completion than their counterparts in the native-born population. In contrast, white and Latino native-born persons have a higher rate of college completion than their counterparts in the immigrant population.

HOUSING

- In general, immigrants live in renter-occupied housing. However, of the immigrant populations in the table, only Asians have a majority of persons that live in owner-occupied housing.

POVERTY STATUS

- With the exception of black immigrants, immigrants have higher poverty rates than native-born persons. Asian and Latino immigrants are more likely to receive AFDC than their native-born counterparts. In contrast, native-born white and black persons are more likely to receive AFDC than their immigrant counterparts. Comparatively speaking, black immigrants are less likely to receive welfare assistance than other immigrant groups.

INCOME

- With the exception of Asian native-born persons, the majority of both native-born and immigrant persons earn less than $20,000. Native-born persons are more likely than immigrants to earn $35,000 or more. However, with the exception of white persons, the number of persons that earn $50,000 or more in the black, Asian, and Latino populations is almost the same for native-born and immigrant persons.

UNEMPLOYMENT

- White and Asian immigrants have a higher unemployment rate than their counterparts in the native-born population. Only black immigrants have a lower unemployment rate than their counterparts in the native-born population. Latino native-born and immigrant persons have the same unemployment rate.

TABLE 9.3. Selected Characteristics of the Native-Born and Immigrant Population in the United States, 1994

	Population, %							
	White		*Blacks*		*Hispanics*		*Asians*	
Characteristic	Native-Born	Immigrant	Native-Born	Immigrant	Native-Born	Immigrant	Native-Born	Immigrant
Educational attainment								
Not a high school graduate	16	42	27	23	10	17	34	57
High school graduate or some college	61	40	61	56	58	40	56	34
College graduate	15	11	9	14	23	30	7	6
Graduate/professional degree	8	7	3	7	9	13	3	3
Housing								
Owner-occupied unit	72	47	47	30	69	51	48	35
Renter-occupied unit	28	53	53	70	31	49	52	65
Poverty status								
In poverty	11	24	34	23	11	18	30	32
Receiving AFDC only	10	2	16	14	5	9	10	11
Other welfare only	3	4	3	2	4	6	2	3
AFDC and other welfare	*	*	*	*	*	*	*	*
Income								
Less than $10,000	32	43	45	36	28	35	44	47
$10,000–$19,999	24	29	25	33	21	23	25	32
$20,000–$34,999	23	16	19	21	27	21	20	14
$35,000–$49,999	11	6	7	6	13	10	7	4
$50,000 or more	10	6	4	4	11	11	4	3
Employment status								
Unemployed	6	9	13	12	5	7	11	11

* < 1 percent.

Source: March 1994 CPS: The Foreign-Born Population: 1994.

was defined as anyone who held a "well-founded fear of persecution in their home country." At the same time, *asylees* (persons who petition for legal status in the United States because they fear persecution in their country of origin) were given the same statutory recognition as a refugee. The Refugee Act of 1980 resulted in the arrival of large numbers of immigrants from Vietnam, Laos, and Cambodia as either refugees or asylees.

The second piece of legislation, the Immigration Reform and Control Act (IRCA) of 1986, targeted two immigrant groups: *long-term undocumented residents* (LTUR) and *special categories of agricultural workers* (SCAW) who had entered the United States illegally. While the primary purpose of the IRCA was to curb undocumented immigration, it also sought to protect those persons already in the United States from being uprooted and deported. The implementation component of the IRCA was an amnesty program that offered legal status to (1) persons who had resided continuously in the United States since January 1, 1982, and (2) persons who could demonstrate that they had worked ninety days or more in designated agricultural labor between May 1985 and May 1986. Since the vast majority of immigrants from Latin America were most likely to enter the agricultural labor force in the United States, the IRCA resulted in an increase of immigration from Latin America in the 1986 to 1990 period (Hollmann, 1992; Vernez, 1990).

The effects of immigration policy on the ethnic composition of the U.S. population are summarized in Table 9.4. The majority of immigrants entering the United States under the IRCA were from Latin America and the Caribbean. In contrast, the majority of immigrants entering under the refugee and asylee programs were from Asia.

In response to public pressure and to a mixture of lobbying interests, the 1990 Immigration Act allowed immigration to increase substantially—hence, the peak reported in Figure 9.1 in the year after its passage. The act encouraged immigration of more skilled workers and those from Europe, but it also sought to limit numbers of immigrants in the future. The full effect of this law is hard to estimate, but, as reported above, the reality for the next half century is that the U.S. population will include more Latinos and more Asians because of the continued effects of the 1965 and 1986 acts.

TABLE 9.4. Ethnic Composition of Immigrant Population under the IRCA and Refugee Programs, 1981 through 1990

	Asia, %	Latin America*/Caribbean, %
IRCA applicants	4.9	88.2
Refugees and asylees	70.0	12.0

*Includes immigrants from Mexico and Central America.
Source: Rolph, 1992.

TABLE 9.5. Patterns of Immigrant Settlement by State and Metropolitan Area, 1990

	Refugees and Asylees, %	IRCA Applicants, %
State		
California	33	54
Florida	11	5
Illinois	5	5
New Jersey	2	2
New York	6	6
Texas	6	15
*Metropolitan area**		
Los Angeles–Long Beach	17	27
New York	11	5
Chicago	3	5
Anaheim–Santa Ana	4	5
Houston	1	4
Miami	7	2

*Metropolitan statistical area.
Source: U.S. Department of Justice, 1991a.

Settlement Patterns of the New Immigrants

Where do recent immigrants live? Table 9.5 reports where refugees and asylees and IRCA applicants have settled, by state and region. California is the state most heavily populated by these refugees and asylees and IRCA applicants; in 1990, 87 percent of the refugees and asylees and IRCA applicants settled there, especially in southern California along the Long Beach–Los Angeles and Anaheim–Santa Ana metropolitan corridors. Currently, states where immigrants locate are forced to carry the financial burden of managing these immigrants' transition into U.S. society (Vernez and McCarthy, 1996).

Other Characteristics of the New Immigrants

Table 9.6 summarizes some of the characteristics of the immigrants who came to the United States after 1983. Regarding educational attainment, several differences are evident. First, a noticeable proportion of Latinos have not graduated from high school. Second, on average, almost one-third of Europeans have completed four years of high school. Third, slightly more than one-third of the Asian population has completed four years or more of college. In 1994, the college completion rate of the Asian population was almost six times that of the Latino population and more than twice that of the European population. In general, Asian and Latino immigrants in the United States have high educational aspirations and outcomes (Gray et al., 1996; Vernez and Abrahamse, 1996).

TABLE 9.6. Characteristics of Foreign-Born Persons* in the United States, 1983 through 1994

	Asian, %				*Latino, %*				*European, %*			
Characteristics	1983	1986	1988	1994	1983	1986	1988	1994	1983	1986	1988	1994
Educational attainment												
Not high school graduate	26.5	26.6	23.9	12.9	60.1	58.0	58.8	40.9	40.2	33.3	30.5	33.0
4 years of high school	20.5	23.6	21.5	30.8	22.8	23.4	23.6	24.3	31.7	34.1	35.3	31.4
4 years or more of college	36.6	34.7	36.3	34.0	7.8	7.8	6.7	6.1	15.2	18.3	19.1	13.6
Labor force status												
Employed	55.2	56.4	60.7	53.6	54.0	60.9	63.4	52.2	44.7	48.9	49.9	50.6
Unemployed	5.7	4.9	3.1	4.0	10.1	6.3	4.5	6.4	4.0	2.3	1.5	5.2
Residence												
In poverty area	7.2	10.5	16.5	18.0	18.8	27.5	37.0	31.7	5.5	4.0	6.0	24.1
Not in poverty area	92.8	89.5	83.6	82.0	81.2	72.5	62.9	68.3	94.5	96.0	94.0	75.9
Citizenship status												
Naturalized	39.3	41.2	45.4	51.7	30.0	29.7	31.4	38.3	71.1	65.1	66.4	69.2
Not a citizen	58.7	57.6	52.1	48.3	68.3	67.6	66.2	61.7	27.0	31.7	31.4	30.8

*Persons 14 years old and older.

Source: U.S. Bureau of the Census, 1991d; March 1994 CPS: *The Foreign-born Population: 1994.*

In general, Asians, Latinos, and Europeans tend to be employed in the United States. Interestingly, both Asians and Latinos have higher employment rates than Europeans. Latinos tend to have a higher unemployment rate, followed by Asians and Europeans, respectively. The vast majority of Asians, Latinos, and Europeans live in nonpoverty areas. Latinos have a higher rate of living in poverty areas than either Asians or Europeans.

Finally, among the three populations, the group born in Europe has generally had the highest naturalization rate. This statistic is consistent with Rolph's (1992) suggestion that U.S. immigration policies have historically favored persons of European origins. The larger proportion of noncitizens among the Asian and especially the Latino populations may suggest something about their accommodation in U.S. society. Asians and Latinos tend to locate within residential or geographical areas where they are the majority population. For example, many settle in areas where their native language is dominant—in the neighborhood, the workplace, and the home (Wilson and Portes, 1980; Portes and Rumbaut, 1990; and Wallace, 1989). Settlement within areas of shared ethnic identity may curtail interest in becoming naturalized citizens (see Chavez, Flores, and Lopez-Garza, 1990; Greenwell, DeVanzo, and Valdez, 1993; and Jaret, 1991). In a sense, the structural accommodation of Asians and Latinos in the United States may facilitate their participation in, but not their absorption into, mainstream social institutions (see Box 9.3 on the economic progress of immigrants).

THE IMMIGRATION DILEMMA

Despite the fact that most Americans are the descendants of immigrants, recent immigrants are not welcomed by a majority of the American public (Morganthau, 1993). These immigrants have sparked debate over such questions as who can come; how many can come; who is to pay for their needs; how can institutions, like the schools, and the economy absorb them; and will they adopt the tenets of the Anglo-Saxon core culture (Trueba, 1989; Valdez et al., 1993; and Vernez, 1993). Table 9.8 illustrates the changes in public opinion concerning immigration, to the United States in general and to heavily populated states such as California and Florida in particular. Two-thirds of Americans—up from one-third in 1965—now want immigration reduced; the number of those who want immigration to remain "about the same" has dropped ten percentage points in the last decade; the percentage of those who have "no opinion" dropped by 50 percent. These data indicate that immigration is now a priority issue on the American agenda. Indeed, it became a major issue in the presidential election in 1996.

Part of the reason for this hardening of public opinion is, no doubt, the result of the recent shift in composition of the immigrant population: from mostly European to mostly Latin American, Caribbean, and Asian. This shift has aroused the suspicion and fears not only of those of European ancestry but also among those of Latino ancestry. The Latino National Political Survey—the most extensive effort to date to measure Latino attitudes—found considerable hostility toward new immigrants, who represent economic competition for those already here (de la Garza et al., 1992). Perhaps the growing sentiment against immigrants extends to many ethnic subpopulations who perceive the same threat.

Much of the energy and vitality of the United States lies in its immigrant subpopulations. If the American public now wants to close the borders, will such restrictions damage the engine that has driven America? In some respects this question is rhetorical because, legally or illegally, immigrants will continue to arrive in the United States.

The dilemma is this: Will the inevitable influx of immigrants set in motion a dynamic of discrimination and ethnic antagonism that will undermine the structure and integrity of American society? Could this relatively recent broad-based resentment of non-European immigrants escalate the intensity of the dynamic to a new, disintegrative level? As we close our review of American ethnicity, these questions are worth consideration, especially in light of the disintegrative effects of ethnic conflict in the societies examined in Chapter 10 on ethnicity in world context.

THE FUTURE DYNAMIC OF DISCRIMINATION

The shift in the ethnic composition of American society over the next fifty years will increase the Latino, Asian, and African American subpopulations. Most of the Latino population will consist of Mexican Americans, with significant numbers of Puerto Ricans, Central and South Americans, and Spanish-speaking Caribbean Islanders (Mahler, 1995; Pessar, 1995). The Asian population will be of diverse origins; Filipinos are likely to be the most numerous, followed by Chinese, Vietnamese, Koreans, and Asian Indians (Lessinger, 1995; Freeman, 1995). The predominant segment of the African American population will be the descendants of slaves, supplemented by some recent Caribbean and African immigrants.

If we refer to the theoretical model presented in Chapter 2 and delineated in Figures 2.1 and 2.2 on pages 35 and 39, we can make some predictions about the future of ethnic relations in the United States. The key variables in the model are the following:

1. The size of an ethnic population
2. The entrepreneurial and educational resources of a population
3. The distinctiveness and identifiability of a population
4. The sense of threat experienced by other ethnic groups, especially the dominant ethnic subpopulations
5. The intensity of negative and prejudicial stereotypes
6. The degree of discrimination against a subpopulation
7. The resource shares of a subpopulation
8. The level of stratification, or confinement to a particular social class
9. The salience of egalitarian values and beliefs

Box 9.3

Economic Progress of Immigrants

How do immigrants fare in the economic marketplace? How has the economic progress of immigrants changed between 1970 and 1990? The data presented in Table 9.7 are helpful in answering these two questions. Table 9.7 compares the median weekly earnings of immigrant workers with those of native-born workers in order to derive a measure of how immigrant workers fare relative to native-born workers. For example, in 1970, early arrivals in the United States from Mexico earned 63 percent of the median weekly earnings of native-born workers. Some of the more salient characteristics of the data in Table 9.7 are the following:

MEXICO

- Early arrivals have done better than late arrivals in narrowing the earning gap between immigrants and native-born workers.
- Regardless of arrival date, the earning gap between immigrants and native-born workers has widened between 1970 and 1990.

EUROPE

- The earning gap between immigrant and native-born workers has exceeded parity.
- Regardless of arrival date, immigrants reach or exceed parity in earnings within the first ten years.

ASIA

- Early arrivals have made greater gains than late arrivals in narrowing the earning gap between immigrant and native-born workers.
- Similar to European immigrant workers, Asians have reached or exceeded parity with the earnings of native-born workers within ten years.

We have seen how these variables have structured the lives of ethnic groups discussed in Chapters 4 through 8; let us now assess how these variables will influence the lives of recent immigrants within these groups.

Latinos and the American Future

As the largest minority in the future, Latinos will not be able to fill middleman minority niches and positions. The sheer size of this subpopulation, along with its average lower levels of education, job skills, and financial resources, will continue to limit the entrepreneurial opportunities for most Latinos. The sense of threat generated by the growing size of the Latino population will increase and generate considerable negative stereotyping. The movement of many Latinos back and forth to their country of origin

TABLE 9.7. Relative Median Weekly Earnings of Immigrant and Native-Born Workers for Earlier versus More Recent Arrivals by Country of Origin, 1970 to 1990

Date of Arrival	Country of Origin, 1970, %	1980, %	1990, %
Mexico			
Early arrivals: 1965–1969	63	61	57
Late arrivals: 1975–1979	—	52	50
Europe			
Early arrivals: 1965–1969	94	101	105
Late arrivals: 1975–1979	—	90	110
Asia			
Early arrivals: 1965–1969	74	120	141
Late arrivals: 1975–1979	—	78	115

Source: Schoeni et al., 1996.

In general, the data in Table 9.7 suggest that, given the earning gap, immigrant workers from Mexico are not assimilating to the U.S. labor market. If Mexican immigrant workers were assimilating to the U.S. labor market, then the earning gap between them and native-born workers would have narrowed between 1970 and 1990. In contrast, immigrant workers from Europe and Asia have reached or exceeded parity in earnings with native-born workers because they have assimilated successfully to the U.S. labor market. In addition, the widening earning gap for Mexican immigrant workers between 1970 and 1990 suggests that they may be disproportionately segmented in low-skill and low-wage jobs in the United States.

will ensure the survival of barrios, patterns of intragroup marriage and reproduction, native language use, and other cultural traditions. These cultural ties will not only sustain identifiability but also increase the sense of threat to a diminishing white majority and an African American population who will have to compete with Latinos for jobs.

These negative effects of increasing numbers and low socioeconomic position eventually will be neutralized by a number of factors: (1) Most Latinos are less physically identifiable than either Asian Americans or African Americans; (2) Latinos are likely to intermarry with other ethnic groups in relatively large numbers because of their physical and cultural similarities with the white population; (3) the Latino population will continue to concentrate in the Southwest and, by virtue of their numbers, will acquire access to political power; (4) Latinos will obtain academic credentials in sig-

TABLE 9.8. Public Opinion on Appropriate Levels of Immigration to the United States

	Immigration levels should be:			
Survey Year and Scope	Increased, %	Kept the Same, %	Reduced, %	No Opinion, %
1965 (U.S.)[a]	8	39	33	20
1977 (U.S.)[b]	7	37	42	14
1982 (Calif.)[c]	5	31	62	2
1984 (U.S.)[d]	8	38	40	14
1987 (Calif.)[e]	8	38	40	14
1988 (Fla.)[f]	6	24	67	3
1990 (U.S.)[g]	9	29	48	14
1992 (U.S.)[h]	5	28	59	8
1992 (Calif.)[h]	8	18	63	11

[a]George H. Gallup, *The Gallup Poll: Public Opinion, 1935–1971*, vol. 3 (New York: Random House, 1972), p. 1953.
[b]George H. Gallup, *The Gallup Poll: Public Opinion, 1972–1977*, vol. 2 (Wilmington, DE: Scholarly Resources, Inc., 1979), p. 1050.
[c]California Opinion Index, "Immigration" (mimeo), Field Institute, San Francisco, June 1982.
[d]Jonathan Alter and Joseph Contreras, "Closing the Door?" *Newsweek*, June 25, 1984, p. 18. Average of responses to immigration level.
[e]California Opinion Index, "Immigration" (mimeo), Field Institute, San Francisco, October 1987.
[f]*Atlanta Journal*, January 31, 1988.
[g]*Los Angeles Times*, June 5, 1990, p. A23 (Roper Organization poll).
[h]*American Attitudes toward Immigration* (New York: The Roper Organization, April 1992).
Source: Thomas Muller, *Immigrants and the American City* (New York: New York University Press, 1993).

nificant numbers and, hence, will have access to nonmenial jobs and higher incomes. Coupled with these factors are the effects of civil rights laws, which can, and will, be used to redress many of the law enforcement abuses of the past. Moreover, affirmative action extensions of these laws—or those that survive current efforts to eliminate them—will also be used to facilitate educational attainment and job placement. These large numbers of Latinos will continue to infiltrate the Anglo mainstream, even as a large mass remains ghettoized in barrios.

Despite these mitigating factors, the large size of the Latino population and its concentration in the Southwest, as well as in the larger cities of the Northeast and south Florida, will continue to fuel the hostility and resentment of white Americans who believe that their majority status is threatened and who feel forced to accommodate a "foreign culture" in ways never before experienced in America. Such hostility will translate into discrimination. If economic pressures continue to limit the number of available jobs and the flow of tax revenues to schools and other institutional structures, then considerable conflict and antagonism will ensue. The flash points will be symbolic issues such as bilingual education, and language use in general, or highly visible stratification issues such as gang violence. The underlying tension will emanate from the threat that a large Latino population poses to the integrity of white American culture, job security, education, public services, and control of political power. As we saw in Chapter 6, the antagonism has been great as Latinos approached 8 percent of the U.S. population; as the Latino surpasses 20 percent of the general population and over 50 percent in much of the Southwest, the antagonism will increase.

Asian Americans in the Future

The Asian population is highly diverse, immigrating from many different societies and cultures. As reported in Table 9.2, currently the largest Asian American population is the Chinese (1.6 million), followed by Filipinos (1.5 million), the Japanese (0.84 million), Asian Indians (0.81 million), Koreans (0.79 million), and the Vietnamese (0.61 million). Except for the Japanese, these populations have been growing rapidly over the last decade. Individually, no Asian subpopulation will ever constitute more than 1 to 1.5 percent of the total population, but as a whole and adding Cambodians, Hmong, Laotians, Thailanders, Indonesians, Malaysians, Okinawans, Pakistanis, Sri Lankans, and a dozen or so Pacific Islander subpopulations to this list, Asians may constitute as much as 11 to 12 percent of the U.S. population.

This increase in the aggregate numbers of Asian Americans may pose an increased threat to white Americans, especially if world competition with Japan and emerging Asian economic powers creates economic hardships for non-Asian workers. Most Asian Americans are likely to move into middleman minority and professional niches because many bring with them education (or an education ethic), entrepreneurial skills, and systems for pooling capital. Different Asian ethnic groups may seek somewhat different middleman minority niches, although considerable competition among Asians may occur in certain metropolitan areas (Whitmore, Trautmann, and Caplan, 1989). Equally likely, younger Asians will secure those academic credentials that will place them in middle- and upper-middle-class professions and occupations. Their growing numbers in higher education and occupations formerly dominated by white Americans will cause considerable hostility and discrimination. Moreover, Latinos and African Americans will resent Asians who take advantage of opportunities in small business, higher education, and middle-class professions and positions. As a result, negative stereotypes about Asians will be propagated and used to justify discrimination, primarily of the informal and subtle kind that Asian Americans experience today (see Chapter 7).

Mitigating these discriminatory forces are counterforces: (1) Significant numbers of Asian Americans will intermarry with white Americans, thereby blurring the lines of physical distinction; (2) Asian American communities will continue to use their resources to promote success in business and education, two arenas where positive interaction with white Americans frequently occurs; (3) large numbers of Asian Americans living in the metropolitan areas will use their financial resources to mobilize political and legal resources to combat discrimination; and (4) young Asian Americans will use their academic credentials to penetrate all types of middle-class economic positions, thereby breaking the cycle of Asian confinement to middleman minority activity.

Asian American success will generate hostility among those who are less successful. Asian Americans who do not have academic credentials or other resources will remain in menial jobs within Asian ghettos or will enter the labor market and compete with Latinos and African Americans in a declining pool of lower-skilled and semiskilled jobs.

It is likely that Asian Americans will continue to use their resources to overcome discrimination. History has shown that when broad-based anti-Asian sentiments emerge, Asian Americans tend to come out of their "cultural shell" and fight discrimination aggressively. Yet, we predict that within the next fifty years, relatively peaceful relations will prevail among diverse Asian subpopulations and mainstream America.

African Americans in the Future

As African Americans approach 16 percent of the population in the future, many of the problems that confront this population today will persist. The size of the population prevents it from filling only middleman minority niches, unless Asian Americans abandon these niches because of African American and, to a lesser extent, Latino hostility and violence. Negative stereotypes will perpetuate hostility from as well as toward African Americans. Moreover, as poorer African Americans and Latinos compete for the decreasing number of low-skilled and semiskilled jobs, tensions, mutual stereotyping, and hostility between these populations may increase (Graham, 1990).

The economic future of the African American population will be both bitter and sweet. As a result of affirmative action and other programs, many African Americans have escaped poverty, and the proportion of African Americans in the middle class will continue to increase. African Americans have increased their average years of education, violent crime in slums has decreased, literacy skills have increased, and drug use has declined (Jencks, 1991:5). However, the drop in male college enrollment may hinder further upward mobility for many males. Also, trends toward a dramatically expanded black middle class will emphasize the socioeconomic differences within the black population. Many poor black families are headed by single mothers and their relatives; these caretakers must raise children without benefit of a father at home, often in substandard housing located in violent and crime-infested neighborhoods. Under these conditions, the jobless rate for young males has increased; many have simply withdrawn from the labor market and some have drifted into gangs. Those who do not join the expanding middle class are likely to find it harder to rise above poverty, and their offspring will carry the legacy of poverty into adulthood. This scenario will become reality if the national economy does not improve and if the American public does not address the social problems with dollars from both the public and private sectors. In the future,

African Americans will be overrepresented in the lowest socioeconomic strata without enough resources to correct this imbalance. Tension between poor African Americans and other ethnic groups will persist as a result of a combination of factors: competition for jobs and government resources, resentment over long-term poverty and discrimination, and the incursion of other ethnic groups into entry-level, menial jobs.

Although black culture and its icons—celebrities in sports, music, movies, and television—will continue to penetrate the Anglo-Saxon cultural core, the general population of blacks will experience discrimination owing to skin color and other cultural differences. In most cases this discrimination will be informal and subtle, but very real. Moreover, despite a growing African American middle class becoming more integrated with white and Asian Americans in jobs, housing, and education—with a concomitant reduction in the intensity of established stereotypes and blatant forms of discrimination—the problems of those left behind will foster new levels of threat, new negative stereotypes, and new forms of discrimination.

These predictions are based on attributes shown in the discrimination model, which apply to African Americans living in poverty: large in number, easy to identify, threatening to other populations, negatively stereotyped, low on the socioeconomic ladder, lacking in resources, and persistent targets of discrimination. The white Americans' sense of threat that affirmative action programs as well as government aid programs diminish their own well-being will discourage many from making resources available to the black community and, thereby, from redressing this long-standing American dilemma.

CONCLUSION: THE PROBLEMATIC NATURE OF A MULTICULTURAL AMERICA

No large-scale society has ever successfully integrated all of its ethnic subpopulations, nor has any ever eliminated the tensions among ethnic populations. The United States has done better than most societies along these lines, primarily because it was created through immigration to a land where genocide had been practiced on the indigenous population (Takaki, 1993). The most enduring problems are the plight of African Americans who cannot escape the legacy of slavery and Native Americans who have not overcome the effects of their conquest and attempted genocide. The most visible new problem in the future is the growth of the Latino population and the challenges this poses to the Anglo-Saxon cultural core.

As our speculative scenario has emphasized, the enduring problems of a large black population and the explosive growth of the Latino population ensure tension in the future. Added to these two fault lines are the growth of diverse Asian ethnics, the continued plight of Native Americans, and the declining size of white ethnics relative to other ethnic subpopulations. Just how these points of cleavage will play out cannot be known for sure, but the salience of ethnicity will increase in the next decades.

Box 9.4

People of Color Express Their Resentment of White Americans

How do people of color feel about white Americans? A Harris poll of minority groups suggests that minority groups may be tired of white American perceptions that things in America are better for minorities. According to the Harris poll, two in three minority group members agreed with assertions that white people are insensitive to other people, have a long history of bigotry, and believe they can boss other people around. Some of the more interesting findings of the Harris poll were the following:

	Percent Agreeing with Statement		
Statement	Blacks	Latinos	Asians
"Whites are insensitive to other people and have a long history of bigotry and prejudice."	76	56	54
"Whites believe they are superior, can boss other people around."	79	52	45
"Whites control power and wealth in America and do not want to share it with nonwhites."	76	52	34
"Whites founded the most democratic society on . . . earth."	49	62	46

The Harris poll results suggest that there is much room for change in people's perceptions before one may be able to speak of a "multicultural" America. It may be that white Americans need to reassess their perceptions of how well things really are in America for minority persons. The responses of minority persons in the Harris poll identify several areas upon which white Americans can focus their attention.

Source: The National Conference; poll of 3,000 conducted by Louis Harris in the summer and fall of 1993.

Some celebrate ethnic diversity, but it should be noted that no large-scale society with highly diverse and entrenched ethnic subpopulations has been stable (Gold, 1995). As we will see in the next chapter, ethnic tensions have torn societies apart. For example, the collapse of the Soviet empire along roughly ethnic lines, the brutality of hostility in what was once Yugoslavia, the festering conflicts in the "United" Kingdom over Northern Ireland, the ethnic hostilities among diverse Muslim sects in most countries of the Middle East, the state of tension between Indians and Pakistanis, and the "wars" of ethnic liberation all over the world today illustrate that when ethnicity runs deep, conflict becomes intense.

Thus, ethnic pluralism must revolve around relatively weak ethnic identification, or otherwise it becomes a focal point for societal disintegration (Trueba, 1993). It is now politically *in*correct to question pluralism or, worse, to extol the virtues of integration of ethnics into an Anglo-Saxon cultural core—at least within academia. But if there is no cultural core to which each wave of immigrants adjusts, or if ethnic populations of any size refuse or cannot adjust, then societal integration will be tenuous. It is for this reason that discrimination is such a harmful force: It often forces ethnics to sustain deep-seated ethnic patterns at odds with the cultural core. Discrimination is, of course, inevitable when some feel threatened by the presence of other ethnics, but if the discrimination can be only temporary and, in fact, serve to decrease differences between ethnics as its victims seek to reduce their identifiability and, hence, their vulnerability to discrimination, then something positive comes of discrimination. But when discrimination is intense, long-term, and inhibits assimilation, then it creates cleavages along ethnic lines, and such cleavages are among the most volatile forces of human organization. And so, if discrimination over the next decades prevents African Americans, Latinos, and Asian-Americans from adopting the cultural core and from fully participating in the society, and at the same time heightens their ethnic identity, it will increase the level of ethnic tension in America, perhaps to the point of societal disintegration.

Such is not likely to be the case because of powerful values and beliefs emphasizing equality and because these cultural tenets have been codified into laws and enforcement procedures. These can be used to mitigate discrimination and to weaken the intensity of people's diverse ethnic identities. At the same time, the reality of a declining proportion of the population from Anglo-Saxon European stock can, perhaps, force some changes in the Anglo-Saxon cultural core, not to the point of its destruction, which would only deepen ethnic boundaries, but to the point of inclusion of new cultural elements from African, Latino, and Asian cultures. Such inclusion has always occurred, but the ethnics involved were white and European. In particular, just whether the same inclusion can occur for the descendants of black slaves and the returning descendants of those who were pushed off their land in the Southwest is the real problem of the future. These are the most volatile cleavages; others also exist but the populations involved are too small to disintegrate the society. If these points of antagonism among whites, blacks, and browns in America can be reduced in the next century, then the United States will have been unique in the history of the world.

POINTS OF DEBATE

As the United States becomes more pluralistic, and as lines of ethnic distinction harden, tensions will escalate. Such tensions and the conflicts that they generate will force all Americans to think seriously about a number of debatable issues:

1. Can any society remain integrated when ethnic identifications are strong, when the cultural core has eroded, and when ethnic conflicts are frequent? No society has yet to do so; hence, all Americans need to consider whether America is on the road to permanent partitions and the conflicts that these divisions generate. Liberal ideologies preach the virtues of diversity, conveniently ignoring the conflictive reality that they cause, whereas conservative ideologies demand rigid conformity to the cultural core and propose tension-producing, repressive means to ensure this conformity. Is there not some middle way—as exemplified by the case of past immigrants—to open the avenues of opportunity to the new immigrants, absorb portions of the immigrant culture into the cultural core, and eventually generate a revised core of old and new citizens? If this seems politically incorrect, or naive, or impossible, then what is the fate of America? Are we locked into an inexorable and destructive path of ethnic conflict?
2. Can illegal immigration be stopped? This is the immigration that bothers and threatens Americans the most. Most discussions of this problem involve political and ideological posturing rather than concrete solutions to the problem. Thus far, simply adding border patrol agents, using new high-tech means of detection, massive deportations, and other procedures have not been particularly effective. Do we try more of the same thing? Do we dare entertain solutions that, historically, have proved effective, such as shooting those who cross a border? Or do we admit that repressive means are unacceptable to society and seek alternatives, such as the economic development of Mexico, Latin American, and the Caribbean, thus reducing incentives to immigrate? If the latter, how do we pay for such actions?
3. In a society where the unskilled, entry-level jobs are fast disappearing to labor markets overseas and to labor-reducing technologies, how are the new poor and unskilled immigrants to find work and to become part of the American mainstream? If there is no clear track for the unskilled to make it in America—as their predecessors in the past—then what is to be done? Who will support them? How are the pathologies of despair—crime, drug use, gangs, welfare dependency—to be avoided?
4. Can the United States cut off immigration without destroying its ultimate source of energy and vitality? Can it encourage limited and selective immigration in the face of rampant illegal immigration? If the answer is no to both questions, then what does this mean for America's future?

CHAPTER 10

American Ethnic Tensions in Global Perspective

In virtually every part of the world, tensions among ethnic subpopulations can be found. Bombings, mass killings, armed mobilization of ethnic armies, coup d'états from ethnically aligned military leaders, and many other forms of conflict are now common (Hoffman, 1992). Some of these events make the news in America because of their violence, brutality, and human suffering—as has been the case in Rwanda, Bosnia, Checkestan, and other places. Media images of mass graves, loose flesh over frail skeletons, and seemingly irrational hatreds have now become a part of Americans' daily consumption of the news. Indeed, America's ethnic tensions can, at times, seem rather muted compared to what appear to be age-old antagonisms among many peoples of the world. Yet, even this media barrage does not communicate the full extent of ethnic conflict in the world today (Gurr, 1993; Williams, 1994). Ethnic killing in Sri Lanka, India, Pakistan, South America, Iraq, Africa, Asia and Southeast Asia, and just about every part of the globe go unreported to American audiences. In 1995 alone, there were forty-nine ethnopolitical conflicts; and there were two hundred and fifty-eight subpopulations—roughly one-sixth of the world's population—at risk for armed ethnopolitical conflict (Gurr and Moore, 1996). Thus, the tensions that exist in America are not unique; if anything, they are less intense than those in many other parts of the world.

FORCES INCREASING WORLD ETHNIC CONFLICT

It could be argued that conflict among ethnic groups has increased over the last fifty years. Ethnic warfare and even genocide are now frequent events (Horowitz, 1992), as are internal revolts and coup d'états based upon ethnic lines. This escalation of ethnic conflict has occurred under the influence of several interrelated forces. One force has been the retreat since the 1960s of former seagoing colonial powers or, as was the case in the Soviet Union, the collapse of a land-based empire (Batur-VanderLippe, 1996; Williams, 1994). In either case, these former powers have turned governance of many societies back to the indigenous population. On the positive side, this retreat has reduced some of the highly exploitive economic practices of the colonial powers, but on the negative side, the capacity to maintain peace among ethnic groupings has also been reduced or, even worse, turned over to one ethnic group which then has persecuted its rivals, thereby engendering escalated hatreds. Since old ethnic enemies were often thrown together in arbitrary geographical boundaries created by the colonial powers—indeed, boundaries that rarely corresponded to precolonial territories among populations—many old intersocietal conflicts have now been turned into intrasocietal ethnic conflicts. Such intrasocietal conflicts have also been aggravated by internal migrations of hostile ethnics into each other's territory during the period when colonial and empire control could regulate hostilities; now with traditional enemies inside each other's territories, conflict takes on a new intensity and brutality. Postcolonialism has thus produced many multiethnic societies in which people can now vent long-standing hatreds toward each other.

Another force is population growth, which puts strains on the capacity of a society to produce sufficient resources to support itself and on the ability of government to meet the needs of its people. As a result, competition for scarce resources escalates, inevitably increasing inequality and poverty. If divisions in wealth, income, and prestige become associated with ethnicity, then conflict potential is dramatically escalated.

Yet another force is the world market in weapons, which enables ethnic subpopulations to become as well armed as the governments trying to control ethnic conflict. When all protagonists can buy automatic weapons, antitank technology, missiles, and cannon power, ethnic conflicts escalate into deadly warfare; and once large numbers of conflicting ethnic groups are killed with modern weaponry, their respective hatreds deepen and their ability to reach compromises declines.

Still another force is international migration patterns, as a combination of economic desperation, war, political persecution, and perceived economic opportunities all encourage people to move out of their homelands to other countries (Williams, 1994). As these migrants enter new countries, they are inevitably resented, and they are seen as a threat to the indigenous population, especially as their numbers grow from higher birthrates or from continued migrations of their kind into the society. What Americans perceive as the "Mexican problem" of illegal immigration is, in fact, experienced by many other societies around the world.

CONTEXTUAL FACTORS IN ETHNIC CONFLICT

At the core of all ethnic conflicts is competition for scarce resources, whether economic, political, cultural, or territorial (Williams, 1994:64; Banton, 1983). When this competition is viewed as ethnic—that is, ethnic subpopulations perceive that their principal competitor is another ethnic group—then ethnics see each other as a threat and set off the dynamics of discrimination analyzed for major American ethnic subpopulations in the previous chapters. But the context of such threat and discrimination often determines just how the competition and conflict will be played out.

One important factor is the capacity of the state to control competition and conflict; weak states will have difficulty keeping ethnic conflict under control. A related factor is the degree of political democratization in a society; coercive states can keep a lid on conflict for a time, but when the conflict emerges, the accumulated hostilities often make the conflict violent (as is evident in the old Yugoslavia today), whereas more democratic states can often allow less intense forms of conflict to become part of the political process of accommodation and compromise (Zimmermann, 1980; Gurr and Moore, 1996), although if the conflict becomes too violent (as was the case in Los Angeles in the early 1990s), even a democratic state will suspend civil liberties and use its coercive powers. An additional political factor is use of ethnic issues by self-interested political leaders who trade on ethnic fears and escalate them for their own political purposes (Brown, 1996).

The productivity of the economy is also a critical variable; a low-productivity economy will not be able to expand in ways that keep ethnic competition from becoming a zero-sum game where one group gets resources to the detriment of others. For even under conditions of inequality, an expanding economy creates a bigger resource base, which can often cut down on conflicts among groups competing for these resources.

History is always a contextual consideration in ethnic tensions. A long-term pattern of domination of one ethnic group by another will often make it difficult to compromise and resolve differences because the ethnic hatred has been passed down from generation to generation.

The international setting always becomes important in ethnic conflict. When ethnic groups in competition or even open conflict have allies in other societies who are willing to supply weapons, money, and technology expertise to one or more of the combatants, the conflict will be more violent and difficult to stop. A related geographical factor is the effect of contagion, as successful ethnic mobilization in one region inspires other ethnics in the same or different societies to mobilize for conflict. Another contextual factor in the international arena is the degree to which great powers have interest in the territory where ethnic conflict occurs; when the United States or another major power has economic, strategic-military, political, and cultural interests in a territory, it will often intervene into ethnic conflict, sometimes seeking to mitigate its intensity but, equally often, taking sides.

The resources over which the conflict occurs are an important contextual factor. Ethnic conflicts will take on somewhat different patterns depending upon whether the conflict is over land and territory, access to economic opportunities and power, civil liberties, or cultural issues such as rights to use a language or practice a religion.

Box 10.1

What Fuels the Fires of Ethnic Tension?

In a study of thirty-four major internal ethnic conflicts since World War II, Michael E. Brown of Harvard's Center for Science and International Affairs argues that twenty-three of these major ethnic conflicts have been "consciously and deliberately triggered and engineered by political leaders inside the countries involved" (Brown, 1996). Thus, the typical explanation for ethnic conflicts—long-standing historical tensions between ethnic subpopulations that suddenly burst to the surface—needs some qualification. True, there may be tensions among ethnics, but these do not spontaneously emerge into heated conflict. Rather, the parties involved need to be inflamed by political leaders seeking attention and power. People have to be stirred up to kill each other, and this can come only with their mobilization by political leaders. Humans generally do not spontaneously kill each other on a massive scale; they must be mobilized—ideologically, emotionally, and organizationally—to do so. American ethnic relations do not reveal the same level of violence as in many other countries around the world, but we can see very close to home what is involved. Today, political leaders, especially in an election year in America, play upon citizens' fears and diffuse sense of threat over issues like affirmative action and illegal immigration. They do not just respond to people's concerns; they create this concern in order to get votes. In so doing, they fan the fires of ethnic tension beyond what it would have otherwise been. This is not to say that people do not possess a sense of threat on their own, but this sense becomes heightened, intensified, and focused by virtue of the often irresponsible and self-serving actions of political leaders.

Demography almost always plays a role in ethnic conflict. The relative size of the antagonistic ethnic groupings is especially important; size differentials among ethnic groups and relative rates of population growth will change the nature of the threat that fuels ethnic conflict.

These contextual factors do not, however, change the underlying dynamic of ethnic antagonism. As we have seen for the American case, ethnic discrimination of a dominant ethnic subpopulation is fueled by perceived threats from another identifiable ethnic subpopulation. Such threats are used to generate negative stereotypes about the ethnic group which, in turn, legitimate discrimination. When discrimination becomes institutionalized in economic, legal, political, educational, and housing patterns, it generates differential resource shares among ethnic subpopulations. These differentials can, when persisting over generations, produce a system of ethnic stratification in which ethnicity and social class position become correlated. Such stratification sustains the identifiability of ethnic groups, which then perpetuates the cycle of threat, negative stereotyping, and discrimination. In democratic societies with egalitarian values, such ethnic stratification becomes a political issue as people compare the values of the society with the reality of ethnic discrimination. Indeed, within and outside the political arena, such values become a resource in the mobilization of ethnics to pursue their interest in decreasing discrimination. In less democratic societies, however, mobilization for violence can become more likely when ethnics perceive that there are few channels for redressing grievances.

We can see these basic dynamics of ethnic antagonism in just about any part of the world, although they are altered by the aggravating forces and contextual factors discussed above. To appreciate fully the global dimension of ethnic tensions, we should selectively review ethnic conflict in various parts of the globe. In this way, we can place into a more historical and comparative context the dynamics of discrimination in America. It would be impossible to review all ethnic conflict in the world, but we can select cases that give us a sense for the range of ethnic tensions that currently prevail. We will begin close to home, first in Canada, and then move to the southern hemisphere and examine Brazil which, like the United States, also imported African slaves and subjugated its aboriginal populations. Next, we move to Europe, examining the long-standing conflict in Northern Ireland which, despite recent movement toward peace, continues to inspire terrorist bombings. We then move across the English Channel to find new conflicts all over continental Europe, especially in societies like Germany where migration by Turks and other Muslims into the society has dramatically increased the ethnic diversity and tension. To the east of western Europe stands the remnants of the old Soviet Union and the eastern bloc, which is rapidly splintering into nation-states along ethnic lines and which, in some cases like the old Yugoslavia, is a new arena for genocide. To the east, where the Mediterranean meets Israel and opens to the Middle East, the conflict between Jews-Israelis and Palestinians-Arabs presents another example of a long-term conflict that continues to spark violence, despite recent efforts at accommodation. Across the Mediterranean and into Africa, we can see many cases where old colonial areas have become the new nations of Africa, but nations with intense ethnic tension and potential for violence. Rwanda is an example of a small and poor former colony that erupted into violence and efforts at genocide, whereas South Africa is a much larger and wealthier country which, somewhat miraculously, avoided a full-scale revolution but which now faces problems of overcoming the legacy of apartheid. These cases can thus help us put into perspective American ethnic relations.

CANADA

In America, we often forget that Canada is not only a distinct nation with its own heritage but also a country with mounting ethnic tensions (Bolaria and Li, 1985). These tensions are most evident between the French-speaking population (often termed *Francophones*) and the English-speaking population (*Anglophones*). Because 80 percent of the French-speaking portion of Canada is located in the province of Quebec, the tension between Quebec and the rest of Canada revolves around how to maintain French culture within a predominately Anglophone society. This English-French split can, however, obscure other fault lines of tension. One is between the dominant French and English charter groups who founded Canada, on the one side, and the other non-British and non-French ethnic groups that have also settled in Canada—groups such as Dutch, Germans, Ukrainians, Jews, Poles, Greeks, Portuguese, Chinese, Indians and Pakistanis, West Indians, Italians, American whites and blacks, and Caribbeans, Africans, and others (Herberg, 1989). In addition to this diversity is the relationship between all other ethnics and the original aboriginal peoples who constitute about 5 percent of the Canadian population (Waldman, 1985). These aboriginals are grouped into several categories (Schaefer, 1966:467–468): *Indians* composed of members of the over six hundred officially recognized tribes or bands, the majority of whom live on reserves and reservations much like those in the United States; *Intuit* or those people, often termed *Eskimos,* who live at the very northern edge of Canada; *Métis* or Canadians of mixed ancestry between aboriginal and other ethnic populations; and *Non-status Indians* who have been denied the right by government to register as Indians (Friders, 1990).

All of this diversity creates tensions (Hiller, 1991). The aboriginal peoples face most of the problems of American Indians, such as ambiguity in their citizenship and nationhood status, abject poverty, high rates of infant mortality, low high school graduation rates, and government welfare dependency. The tensions between the dominant French and British, on the one side, and more recent immigrant ethnics, on the other, similarly reflect the American scene. Those who are white and European-looking and who learn French and/or English can assimilate, whereas those who are identifiable by virtue of skin color or facial features have encountered many of the same problems as American ethnics who are physically identifiable. Blacks and Asians account for about 10 percent of the population in Canada, but their presence is more noticeable because of their concentration in the urban areas of three provinces—Ontario where Toronto is located, Quebec where Montreal is found, and British Columbia where Vancouver is the dominant city. And like America, much of the black population is descended from the early slave population, although slavery was a less viable institution in Canada and was discontinued in 1833 (as it was throughout the whole British Empire in 1834). Asians in Canada are often the descendants of early immigrants who came to Canada about the same time as they did to the United States and, like their counterparts in America, experienced efforts to limit their immigration.

The many new immigrants from all parts of the world, coupled with the continued visibility of distinct subpopulations from earlier times, have created a sense of threat on the part of those who feel vulnerable to competition from these ethnics. Indeed, even though Canada is a sparsely populated society, at least relative to its land mass, legislation enacted in the late 1970s has restricted immigration, especially nonwhite immigrants. The major fault line in Canada, however, is between Quebec and the rest of the country (McRoberts, 1988). The only equivalent situation in the United States was, perhaps, the desire of the South to secede from the Union before the Civil War. In essence, two nations have evolved in Canada—one from the original French settlers and another from the British who in 1759 defeated the French and thereby ended France's colonial adventure in Canada but who did not defeat the desire of New France (Quebec) to sustain its culture. Today, about one-quarter of the Canadian population is French-speaking, and this proportion controls about a quarter of the nation's wealth.

Yet, the legacy of the past continues to haunt Canada. The British had made Quebec part of the British Empire but had granted the French in Canada certain rights: the use of French civil law, the maintenance of French as an official language, and the practice of Catholicism. Still, the French-speaking population was a minority surrounded by an English-speaking North America. After the American Revolutionary War, thousands of Anglophones entered Canada, giving New France its first sizable British-origin population. There were immediate conflicts, with the result that Canada was split into lower and upper provinces—Ontario and Quebec, respectively. In 1867, all of the Canadian provinces were linked together, a situation that further isolated Quebec as a French-speaking population surrounded by Anglophones. Even within Quebec, the British-origin population began to gain control of commerce and finance; and from there, they created their own system of schools, neighborhoods, businesses, churches, and other institutions. The French-origin population began to feel like all colonized peoples, and as a consequence, a new nationalism emerged in the early decades of this century. Through the middle of this century, the provincial government of Quebec, along with activism by the Catholic church, quietly assumed control of the economic and educational systems, often leading to the out-migration of Anglophone companies, people, and capital. Much of this effort appeared to operate as a moderating position, making Quebec a viable society within Canada, but over the last several decades the nationalist *Parti Québécois* began to pursue aggressively the separation of Quebec from Canada.

By 1976, the Parti Québécois had won control of the government of Quebec, sending shock waves throughout Canada. This control of government led to many new policies, especially with respect to French as the official language of Quebec. Since this time, the issue of separation has surfaced several times, most recently in 1995 when the referendum to separate Quebec from the rest of Canada lost by half of a percentage point, 50.6 percent against separation and 49.4 percent in favor. Passage of the referendum was impeded by several forces. One was the status of the aboriginal peoples, many of whom argued that if Quebec can secede from Canada, so could they secede from Quebec. Another force was the large influx of immigrants over the last decades; and in fact, they provided the votes to defeat the referendum. Currently, Quebec faces continued immigration of non-French ethnics into Montreal, a fact that increases the French-speaking population's sense of threat because these immigrants are often reluctant to lose the umbrella of protection that they perceive the larger Canadian government will provide. Thus, in the future, the nationalism of the French-speaking population will come into conflict with Anglophones as well as the interests of new immigrants from other parts of the world.

The future of Canada is, in fact, rather precarious in light of the intense French nationalism in Quebec. If Quebec were to pass a referendum to secede, what would happen (Banting, 1992)? How would issues of citizenship be decided? Would people and capital flow out of Quebec? If so, to what degree? Would the Anglophone portion of Canada intervene militarily? If not, then would other provinces begin to secede or even apply to the United States for statehood? When ethnic populations are attached to a territory, they often attempt to gain autonomy from the larger society; and if this occurs just north of the American border, what does this event mean for the configuration of both Canada and the United States in the twenty-first century?

BRAZIL

Brazil is the largest country in Latin America, in terms of both its territory and population size. Its history parallels that of the United States in many important respects (Burns, 1993): It was originally colonized by Europeans—in the case of Brazil, the Portuguese. These colonizers overwhelmed the aboriginal peoples and, unlike similar efforts in the United States, successfully enslaved many of the native Indians (although many more died

Box 10.2

Separatists Taken to Court

In mid-1996, a new chapter unfolded in the issue of Quebec's secession from Canada: The central government in Ottawa intervened with a lawsuit, challenging the separatists' doctrine that Quebec voters alone can determine the independence of Quebec from the rest of Canada. There has always been considerable ambiguity over the legal right of Quebec to withdraw from the broader Canadian union; most legal scholars believe that the Canadian Constitution would have to be modified to permit secession. The modification would have to be approved by the other provinces in Canada, an unlikely possibility. Whatever the outcome of the lawsuit, it will keep the issue of separation in the public's mind, both inside and outside of Quebec. Moreover, whatever the decision, it must be enforced, and it can be asked: Enforced by what means?

because of their lack of resistance to European diseases, as was also the case in the United States). The colonizers also imported African slaves on a large scale, and in fact, they imported eight times as many slaves as the slave states in America—although at the peak of slavery the two countries had about the same number of slaves, between four and five million (Knight, 1974). In the late nineteenth century, a large influx of European immigrants—primarily Italian but also significant numbers of Germans, Spanish, and Portuguese—occurred as the original colonizers lifted what had been severe restrictions on immigration. Yet, despite these similarities, ethnic relations in Brazil took a somewhat divergent path from those in the United States, especially with regard to the white–black tensions that prevail in North America (Smith, 1974; Freyre, 1963).

Explanations for the differences between American and Brazilian ethnic relations typically begin with the differences in the way slavery was structured in the two countries (Elkins, 1959; Freyre, 1956). One difference is that Brazil was much more dependent upon its slave population to sustain a viable economy. An outcome of this difference is that the slave population was much larger relative to those of European (mostly Portuguese) origin; and in fact, by the end of the last century, the black population outnumbered whites—a situation that led the white-controlled government to lift previous restrictions on European immigration. Another difference between the United States and Brazil was the relative harshness of the two systems of slavery. The Brazilian system clearly recognized that black slaves were humans, and as a result, slaves were given (at least on paper) legal rights, although slave masters could generally deal with their slaves in any manner they chose with virtual impunity (Boxer, 1962). Along with this recognition of slaves as humans came other attitudes: Slaves were in their position by virtue of a fate that had worked against them, and they were not seen in the harsh religious terms of Protestants in America (Tannenbaum, 1946). Still, the question over whether slavery was more benign in Brazil or America is debated, although there appear to have been differences in at least the harshness of attitudes and stereotypes about blacks.

Perhaps reflecting these less harsh stereotypes about the African-origin population were the comparatively high rates of *manumission,* or the freeing of slaves, in Brazil. While much of this manumission represented a strategy on the part of slave holders to rid themselves of the injured, sick, weak, and old (Degler, 1971), it had the effect of creating a very large nonslave population of blacks who could pursue jobs and occupations outside of the plantation and who could demonstrate that freed slaves would not represent threats to whites (Marger, 1994:438). With high rates of manumission, the transition from a slave-based to a nonslave economy occurred over a longer period of time (in fact, slavery was not officially abolished in Brazil until 1888, over two decades after the American Civil War); as a consequence, the transition to a nonslave economy was not the result of a cataclysmic and violent event but a more gradual evolution that even the slave holders recognized as inevitable.

Also in contrast to the United States were much higher rates of interbreeding between European and African-origin peoples, creating a large mulatto sector that today constitutes over 40 percent of the entire Brazilian population (Degler, 1971; Marger, 1994:443–444). The interpretations for this rate of interbreeding vary: Some argue that it occurred because whites had more sympathetic attitudes toward blacks, while others (perhaps more correctly) argue that the below-parity sex ratio of the early colonizers created a dramatic shortage of European women which, in turn, led to high rates of white male sexual relations with African-origin women. Whatever the precise reason, the result has been for Brazilians to see black–white differences in very different terms than Americans: Black and white are not dichotomous; there are many shades of skin color, and as a result, Brazilians have fewer concerns about defining an individual as either black or white. In fact, social class position appears to be more important than skin color; and as Brazilians often say, social mobility up the class ladder "whitens" darker-skinned ethnics, whereas movement down the class ladder will "darken" lighter-skinned ethnics, including European-origin individuals.

Today, Brazilians are committed at an ideological level to assimilation of all members of the population which, it is hoped, will break down all distinct physical and cultural differences. In the United States, the assimilationist ideology generally applied only to whites and perhaps Asians, but rarely to African-origin ethnics who were expected to assimilate culturally but not physically. And presently, because of the patterns of discrimination documented in Chapter 4 and the response of blacks to this discrimination, the idea of interethnic breeding of American blacks and whites as a way to reduce ethnic tensions is viewed suspiciously by whites and often defined as "genocide" by blacks. In contrast, Brazilians see blending as an ideal, although this ideal is often more ideological than real. The ideology of assimilation is reflected in the laws of the legal system in Brazil, but much like such laws in America, there are informal practices of discrimination, and as a consequence, a system of ethnic stratification persists.

This system of ethnic stratification is sustained by high levels of residential segregation in terms of skin color (Telles, 1992). And, at the institutional level, whites hold the higher economic and political positions; and although blacks are overrepresented in the lower economic and political positions, whites can be found in these lower positions as well. Mulattos can be seen at all social class levels, and they constitute a majority of middle classes and represent a significant though minority proportion of upper classes. Though disproportionately in the lower classes, blacks do occupy some portion of middle class, but very few blacks hold upper-class positions (Andrews, 1992). This class system does not parallel that in the United States, it must be emphasized, because the traditional land-holding elite along with successful merchants and professionals control the upper classes, while the middle class is small and the lower class is huge compared to their respective counterparts in the United States.

This system of stratification has produced far fewer conflicts than in

America, perhaps because of the large mulatto population that can penetrate the middle and upper classes. Indeed, the cultural ideal is to undergo a "whitening" (a) by intermarriage with lighter-skinned Brazilians and (b) by upward mobility that apparently reduces, in people's minds, at least to a degree, the salience of darker skin. Yet, there is considerable prejudice against darker-skinned individuals; and while whites advocate an ideology that skin color should not influence opportunities, they also express a desire to maintain social distance and to avoid marriage to darker-skinned individuals (Andrews, 1991). In turn, these more subtle prejudicial attitudes reinforce informal practices of discrimination in job placements, in schools, and in access to integrated housing (Telles, 1992). Much of this discrimination is defined in terms of class position—that is, people are desirable or undesirable in terms of their social class more than their skin color—and there is probably a greater recognition of class basis as opposed to ethnic basis of prejudice and discrimination in Brazil than in the United States. Still, skin color is also an independent force in people's perceptions and actions toward each other in Brazil; and in fact, there are signs that increased job competition, coupled with the disadvantages of blacks in such competition, will increase ethnic tensions. Such is especially likely to be the case as blacks press for their legally defined civil rights, and whites experience an escalated sense of threat in the economic, political, and social arenas.

It is unlikely, however, that these tensions will erupt into American-style conflict between blacks and whites, for at least two reasons: (1) the ideological emphasis on equality of opportunity and on ethnic amalgamation and (2) the recent recognition by government that it must respond to the persistence of ethnic inequality which, in the past, had been defined solely in terms of class inequalities (Andrews, 1991).

Aside from these ideological and governmental forces, there are additional reasons that widespread white–black violence is less likely than in the United States. First, the economic interdependence between blacks and whites has always been greater in Brazil than in the United States, primarily because African-origin individuals were needed in not only the plantation economy but also the industrial and trades portions of the economy as well. Although the dropping of immigration barriers to Europeans in the late nineteenth century was designed to secure more white industrial and trade labor to lower this dependence on blacks, there still remains an economic interdependence among whites, blacks, and mulattos. Second, more of the culture of the African-origin population has been retained in Brazil. Because many more slaves were imported into Brazil over a somewhat longer period of time than the United States, they brought a constant renewal of the African culture; and as a consequence, the respective class positions of blacks, mulattos, and whites were not so highly correlated with linguistic, religious, and ideological differences, thereby making conflicts more class based than cultural. Indeed, opposition among ethnic groups is not so much over collective goods such as language, religion, civil rights, and political liberties which, on paper at least, are available to all, but more on access to employment, educational, and housing opportunities, which tend to be defined as class problems rather than as purely the product of ethnic discrimination by one ethnic group on another (Williams, 1994). This subtle difference in emphasis—from ethnicity to class—mitigates against ethnic polarization and violent conflict. Finally, mobility is possible in Brazil, especially as the middle class expands. Moreover, the salience of skin color recedes with such mobility, and coupled with the large proportion of mulattos in the middle classes, the class system may prove capable of reducing further the correlation between skin color and class position.

Yet, there remain potential dangers in Brazil. One danger is the geographical distribution of the population by skin color and ethnicity: The agrarian northeast is predominately black and mulatto; the industrial, commercial, urban, and wealthy southeast is mostly European, as is the south; and the extreme north and interior, especially the Amazon basin, are populated by aboriginals. When distinct populations occupy clear territories, they often seek sovereignty, although at present, the high migration rates of blacks and mulattos to the more affluent southeast have undermined some of the correlation between skin color and region. Another danger point is the vast class and ethnic inequalities that persist in Brazil, coupled with what is often a weak state, especially in terms of its finances. As the state must respond to high demands for welfare, assistance, and services, its financial ability to control ethnic tensions may be reduced. And, should widespread violence erupt, new ethnic hatreds and antagonisms will emerge, and older ones will be given voice, thereby increasing the level of ethnic tension and the potential for future violence.

NORTHERN IRELAND

A very small population of 1.5 million people has captured considerable media attention in America. At first, it seems implausible that fellow Christians—500,000 Catholics and 1 million Protestants—should want to kill one another, but religion is only a surface marker of a much deeper ethnic conflict over the distribution of power which, in turn, determines people's access to jobs, education, residence, leisure activities, and just about all aspects of social life (Smith and Chambers, 1991). But if we only remember the response of Protestant Americans to the immigration of Irish Catholics to our shores, it is clear that fellow Christians can often perceive each other as threats and, thereby, set off vicious cycles of ethnic antagonism (Terchek, 1977).

In the case of Northern Ireland, the long history of the conflict is important in understanding present tensions (Rose, 1971). In the 1600s, Scots and British embarked on the colonization of Ireland, and in the north, this effort is sometimes referred to as the "plantation of Ulster" (which comprises the six counties of what was perceived by the Catholics as an Irish province). This colonization involved the displacement of Irish Catholics from their land by Protestants, a process that initiated a series of revolts by Catholics and countermassacres by the Protestant English.

The conflict in Ireland also became involved in the geopolitics between England and the Netherlands when the king of the Netherlands, William of Orange, defeated the last Catholic monarch in England in 1690; from this point on, Protestants asserted their dominant position in the northern part of Ireland. The *Order of Orange* was then established as a fraternal organization to combine military, political, religious, and economic interests in the cause of Protestant control and domination of Ulster, or Northern Ireland. The penal laws that enabled this domination to be implemented were, in fact, so severe that many of the "Scotch-Irish," who had been part of the early colonization, left Ireland and migrated to America in the 1700s, as we noted in Chapter 8. But the Order of Orange, along with various political organizations that were to emerge in the next three hundred years, was designed to maintain the domination of Protestants in Ulster.

A further geopolitical involvement concerned the status of Ireland as a whole. The Irish had long resented British control of Ireland, and in 1914 a limited version of home rule for the Irish was granted. By 1925, Britain, Ireland, and Northern Ireland had accepted the division of Ireland into two states, the Catholic south and the Protestant-dominated north. Yet, the signs of potential violence were evident back then, as the Irish Republican Army (IRA) refused to accept the partitioning of Ireland and as various Protestant militants worried that release from Britain was a prelude to a takeover by Catholics in southern Ireland.

Yet, for many decades into the 1960s, violence and conflict appeared to wane, as efforts were made to resolve differences (Marger, 1991:511). In the post–World War II era, economic growth had created opportunities for Catholics, and as the Protestant-dominated Parliament sought to stimulate economic growth, educational opportunities for Catholics expanded (McAllister, 1977). As a result, a new Catholic middle class emerged, as did political leaders determined to change the political inequalities in Ulster. They modeled their efforts along the lines of the civil rights movement for African Americans in the United States, staging peaceful protests, marches, sit-ins, and even adopting much of the ideology of the American civil rights movement. The goal of both Catholic leaders and Protestant sympathizers was to end discrimination in voting, employment, and housing—much as the American civil rights movement had sought to do. What is especially significant is that the movement focused on the problems of discrimination in Northern Ireland, per se; and unlike previous protests, the movement downplayed the issue of unification of northern and southern Ireland. The Protestant prime minister in Northern Ireland supported these efforts, and by the late 1960s, the ethnic tensions between Protestant and Catholics appeared to be easing (Rose, 1971).

Protestant extremists feared this movement, however, and they organized a countermovement that rapidly led to Protestant violence against the civil rights marchers, the resignation of the sympathetic prime minister, and the mobilization of the provisional IRA to protect Catholics from Protestant violence (this defensive role soon turned into offensive measures such as the bombings that have been portrayed in the world media). The violence brought the British back into Northern Ireland, suspending the Parliament and, in essence, taking control of Ulster—a situation that was initially welcomed by both sides but soon made the Catholic minority feel as if they had been taken over by an invading army. By 1972, the situation had hardened Catholic attitudes, escalated Protestant fears about Catholics, and created the current situation of an uneasy standoff between the Protestant majority, the Catholic minority, and the reluctant British army and government in the middle (Rose, 1990).

The present situation is fueled by the sense of threat that Protestants feel for their potential loss of power should the south and north ever be united and by the intense resentment of Catholics over discrimination in politics, housing, jobs, and education. Since Protestants and Catholics in Northern Ireland look alike, identifiability becomes problematic; and as a result, cultural symbols, interpersonal gestures, names, accents, dress, demeanor, use of words, and other subtle cues are used to distinguish who is Protestant and who is Catholic. Difficult as it may be, Protestants and Catholics often perceive each other as "looking different" at a more biological level, but these perceptions are only fueled by fears and resentments (Marger, 1994:518). Protestants often perceive Catholicism to be a coherent world-level conspiracy that would suppress their religious freedoms. Moreover, they see unification of Ireland as not only increasing the power of world Catholicism but also isolating them from Britain as they suddenly become a minority. Protestants sustain their fears by negative beliefs about Catholics as "lazy," "dirty," "ignorant," "shiftless," and other characteristics that dominant populations typically construct when they fear a minority (recall the stereotypes about the Irish, enumerated in Chapter 8, when they first migrated to America and threatened Protestants). Catholics, on the other hand, appear to have few fears about Protestantism as a religion, per se, but only resentments—elaborated into negative stereotypes—over the discriminatory use of political and economic power by Protestants.

These negative beliefs and stereotypes have created a somewhat ironic pattern of discrimination. As tensions mounted and as episodic violence ensued, Protestants and Catholics migrated to their own districts within the large cities, especially Belfast (500,000) and Londonderry (90,000), but this residential segregation into separate communities was only a modern manifestation of less intense segregation patterns that were initiated during the Scots-British colonization. Yet, the residential divisions—often involving walls and barricades between Protestant and Catholic districts—have created opportunities for Catholics in many institutional spheres. When only Catholics sell goods and services to Catholics, when Catholic schools teach only Catholics, when other institutional activities are so segregated, new opportunities for Catholics to move into the middle classes have emerged (Osborne and Cormack, 1991). Thus, on the surface, the society-wide distribution of Catholics and Protestants across social classes looks much the same, but the converging distribution is an artifact of the high degree of residential and institutional segregation of Catholic and Protestant communities. Still, many Catholics have been given professional, educational, and economic opportunities as a result of this segregation.

At the more macro level, however, Protestants still dominate politics (through the Unionist party and the Order of Orange) or will continue to do so when the current British occupation ends. Catholic unemployment rates are much higher than those for Protestants. And, while the universities are more integrated than the rest of the society, Protestants dominate the system now and will do so to a greater degree when the British occupation ends.

Thus, Northern Ireland illustrates that when religion becomes part of the ideology around which ethnic identity is sustained, the potential for violence escalates. Economic and political issues become transformed into moral questions that arouse emotions and intensify conflict. Each party to the conflict also has external allies—the Protestants have the British on the mainland (however, reluctantly), and the Catholics have the Republic of Ireland to the south and the large Irish Catholic population in America. The existence of these allies assures that both parties will be well financed and armed in those conflicts that emerge.

What, then, is to be the solution to the standoff in Northern Ireland? There are several possible options in reducing tensions and conflict: One is power sharing between Protestants and Catholics in their own government, a solution that seemed within grasp in the 1960s but that now appears to be a remote possibility given the anger and hatreds created by three decades of separation and episodic violence. Another solution is further partitioning of Northern Ireland into Catholic and Protestant territories, with each to decide if they will remain sovereign states or merge with either The Republic of Ireland or the United Kingdom. This solution seems difficult in light of the logistical problems and high costs of moving, once again, the population into their separate territories—although this may be in the long run the only viable solution. Another solution is to sustain the status quo where, after decades of violence and movement into their own segregated spheres, Catholics and Protestants are able to sustain daily routines. In a sense, the antagonists have learned to live with the tension and conflict. Yet, the potential for escalated violence always remains as long as extremist groups on both sides—the IRA, on the one side, and the right-wing Protestant militia groups, on the other—seek to change the status quo toward alignment of the north with Ireland or, alternatively, with England.

The fragile peace between Catholics and Protestants was broken in mid-1996, when "peace talks" among the various parties in Northern Ireland and the United Kingdom did not include *Sinn Fein,* the political wing of the Irish Republican Army. As the major political organization among Catholics, barring Sinn Fein from participation probably assured that the fragile peace would not endure, although hopes were high that some kind of settlement could be reached. Soon a bombing in London occurred. Then, the

Order of Orange sought to organize a march through Catholic districts in Belfast, which led to rioting and shootings. The peace process, which had some hope of succeeding in 1994 when the IRA announced a cessation of terrorism, is now back where it was before: tenuous, unstable, and likely to erupt into violence at any time.

WESTERN EUROPE

The western nations of Europe have, over the last several decades, experienced a dramatic increase in immigration from outside their respective borders (Castles, Booth, and Wallace, 1984). In the aftermath of World War II, Germany in particular opened its borders to immigrants—as partial compensation for the atrocities of the genocide committed against the Jews (Castles, 1992). But all countries had comparatively open immigration policies because many needed "guest workers"—much as has been the case in the United States with workers from Mexico and Latin America.

One pattern of immigration has been movement of those in the southern part of Europe or along the Mediterranean into the more industrial and affluent countries such as Germany, France, Switzerland, and the Netherlands. Thus, workers from comparatively poor and overpopulated countries like Portugal, Greece, Spain, Turkey, and what used to be Yugoslavia began to move into the ethnically more homogeneous countries of industrial Europe. The pace of this immigration accelerated in the 1960s, reaching even northern European nations like Sweden and Norway.

Another pattern of immigration has been the movement of people from the former colonies of the old colonial powers, especially Britain which began to absorb migrants from Jamaica, India, and Pakistan. But all of the old colonial powers have immigration of their former colonists, such as Indonesians in the Netherlands, Algerians in France, and central Africans in Germany and Belgium.

As has been the case in the United States, these immigrants began to pose threats to the indigenous populations, particularly as their numbers increased and their proportion of the population grew. Those who came as temporary workers often stayed, and now several generations of Turks, Greeks, Algerians, Yugoslavs, and other ethnics live in European nations without full citizenship and without much desire or hope for returning home. Whether as unskilled labor or small-time entrepreneurial business operators, most came with the idea of returning to their homeland, but as is often the case with sojourners, their intent on going home has kept them from fully integrating into their host society, while their continued presence and ethnic distinctiveness escalates the sense of threat that they pose to the mainstream ethnic population. As differences between the indigenous ethnics and minorities are sustained through residential segregation and economic specialization in certain types of labor and small-business activity, negative stereotypes have been propagated by the dominant ethnics which, in turn, escalate their sense of fear as well as their acts of discrimination. These immigrations are particularly stressful because most European countries have in recent history remained relatively homogeneous, and hence, they have little experience with large numbers of immigrants. Now, people who look different, who practice a different religion, who speak a foreign language, and who remain in their ethnic communities can be found in all European societies in large numbers, escalating the sense of threat of the indigenous population. Even southern countries like Italy, which in the past has been an exporter of immigrants to other countries, reveal new immigrant population that has increased the sense of threat.

In Germany, which in essence had an open-door policy after World War II, the rate of immigration has been very high; and the resurgence of German nationalism, especially in its extreme form of Nazi-oriented skin-head youth, is but one marker of the sense of threat activated by the several million Turks and other non-Christian immigrants to Germany. Most of these Muslim migrants do not have citizenship; and while Germany has until recently had extremely generous welfare policies, these ethnics experience discrimination in housing, schooling, and job opportunities—all of which force them to remain within their ethnic communities and thereby retain their distinctiveness (Castles, 1992). These immigrants are but part of the problem in Germany, which has had to absorb immigrants from what used to be East Germany, while undertaking massive economic and infrastructural reconstruction of the east. Moreover, the breakup of the Soviet Union, coupled with the independence of the old Soviet bloc countries like Poland, Hungary, and Yugoslavia, has increased immigration into all of western Europe, but Germany in particular.

Thus, the dynamics of discrimination as they have operated in America are being repeated in western Europe, as these countries seek to absorb ethnically distinct migrants. The same processes of threat, negative stereotyping, discrimination, and ethnic stratification should, therefore, be expected—although these processes can be counteracted somewhat by the egalitarian values of the advanced industrial nations of Europe. Yet, since European nations are much smaller than the United States, both in terms of land mass and population size, the sense of threat posed by immigrants is perceived to be greater, especially since the indigenous ethnics often have very low birthrates compared to the new immigrant populations. Much as Americans in the Southwest fear for the loss of Anglo culture and their majority status as Latino immigrants outbreed the native born, so many in Europe have the same fears but without the experience of America as a nation of immigrants. As a result, even as western Europe seeks to develop a common market and sense of "European society," nationalism has reemerged as a response to the threats perceived to be posed by immigrants (Walsh, 1992).

THE COLLAPSE OF THE SOVIET EMPIRE

Beginning in the 1600s, Russia began to expand to the west and south, setting into motion what would eventually evolve into the Soviet Union (Collins, 1986:186–191). This expansion occurred first in Ukraine and other Slavic lands where control of fellow Slavs and Christians was relatively easy, especially as the nobility of these lands could be bought off by favors from the Russian elite. But eventually, the empire moved into the Caucasus and Central Asia, which are populated by Muslims and which, culturally, were very different from the areas previously conquered by the growing empire. Early conquest was in the name of pan-Slavism and the glory of Russia as well as the Christian Orthodox Church (Kohn, 1960), but after the Communist revolution in 1917, pan-Slavism was abandoned in favor of a broader Russian nationalism revolving around communism and the Communist party.

During the cold war in the aftermath of World War II, the Soviet Union encompassed well over one hundred nationalities and ethnic subpopulations, such as Russians, "white" Russians, Estonians, Jews, Slovenians, Ukrainians, Moldavians, Kurds, Chechens, Azerbaijanis, Latvians, and many others; and the empire had control over satellite societies of the Soviet bloc, including Hungary, Poland, Czechoslovakia, Romania, Bulgaria, and Yugoslavia (Dixon, 1990; Knippenberg, 1991).

This association of territory with land presented a problem of social integration for the central government in Moscow, since each ethnic population viewed the land as its territory and the Russian invaders as colonists. Thus, during the occupation by Russians, the ethnic identity of most non-Russians and even Slavs in the empire remained much as it had been before the conquest. Russians migrated into these new territories, and very serious efforts were made to create—whether by military force, school indoctrination, economic cooptation, encouragement of atheism, or oppressive political administration—a broader Russian-dominated culture of communism. Conversely, non-Slavs moved toward Moscow, especially Muslims, who now experience very severe discrimination. The breakup of the Soviet Union in the late 1980s and early 1990s, along with the violent aftermath of this collapse, indicates the extent to which territorial-based ethnic identities had remained in place during the Russian occupation, despite the internal movements of ethnics around the empire (Duttler, 1990).

Not only did the empire break up along ethnic lines, with the Baltic states first to leave, but even fellow Slavs such as "white" Russians, Ukrainians, and Serbs in Yugoslavia sought their own national identity. Asian and Muslim regions have also sought to break away, with varying degrees of success, but in the long run, it is likely that all of the Caucasus and Central Asian sections of the old Soviet Union will form new societal boundaries based along ethnic lines. Even existing societies within the Soviet bloc began to break apart along ethnic lines, as occurred in Czechoslovakia when it split into the Czech Republic and Slovakia and as is now tragically occurring in what used to be Yugoslavia.

Within what is now Russia, ethnic tensions are very high. As territory of the empire has been lost and as the defeat in the cold war with the west undermines Russian pride, old ethnic tensions between Russians, on the one side, and Jews and Muslims, on the other, have become open. Prejudice and discrimination have always existed against Jews and Muslims (of various ethnic origins); and as the difficulties—price inflation, loss of employment, and organized crime, for example—of modernizing along capitalist lines have escalated in Russia, these old tensions have become intensified as many Russians blame their fate on Jews and Muslims inside Russia as well as other ethnics outside in its former territories. Right-wing politicians in Russia exploit this sense of anger, emphasizing the threat that non-Russian and non-Slavic ethnic groups pose to Russia; and the most extreme advocates argue for the rebuilding of the empire through coercive means. Yet, it is not likely that the empire can be re-created because Russia is simply not sufficiently wealthy to do so, because the newly freed ethnics would fight back and force the Russians to fight a many-front war, and because the west would directly or indirectly (through arms sales) support those who resisted renewed Russian imperialism. Yet, the humiliation of their defeat in the cold war, the collapse of their empire, the dislocations involved in trying to jump-start a communist system into free-enterprise capitalism, and the many other forces of change in Russia have created such economic and political dislocation that ethnicity becomes, once again, a way to vent anger and to define insecurities in terms of ethnic threats. The result will be, no doubt, further ethnic conflict in Russia, especially if the fragile political system now in place collapses in these last years of the twentieth century.

BOSNIA, CROATIA, AND SERBIA

The Balkans have, for many centuries, been at the forefront of conflicts within Europe. The root of the problem probably goes back to the 1400s when the Ottoman Empire expanded into Bosnia, creating a Muslim presence within Christendom. Croatia was primarily Catholic and Slavic, while Serbia was Orthodox Christian and Slavic. Most Bosnian Slavs, however, converted to Islam, thereby increasing the sense of threat perceived by Christians in Europe, especially because of justified fears that the Ottoman Empire would seek to expand further into Christian Europe. In a very real sense, these fears have persisted in transmuted form to the present day, and as we have seen over the last few years, these accumulated hatreds and fears have erupted into intense ethnic conflict.

Yet, even as the buildup to the present conflict occurred, the split was not purely along Christian–Muslim lines. During most of this century, the Serbians gradually became the more dominant subpopulation and had used this dominance in both obvious and subtle ways to discriminate against other subpopulations, creating a considerable amount of anti-Serbian sentiment. This anti-Serbian sentiment was so intense that Croats sided with Adolf Hitler in World War II, participating with the Germans in the killing of many Serbs and Muslims as well as Jews.

Thus, in 1945, when the six Slavic populations were united under communism, there were centuries of animosity among subpopulations in the new Yugoslavia. By the 1990s, 40 percent of Yugoslavia was composed of Serbs who shared commitment to Orthodox Christianity and who had also shared a similar World War II experience with Russia, 23 percent were Croats who had been allies with Germany in World War II, and 9 percent were Bosnians who, as Muslims, had no European allies. As the Soviet Empire began to collapse and as the central control of the Yugoslavian state weakened with the death of its most forceful post–World War II leader, old ethnic tensions began to resurface among these populations, tensions fueled by fears from the distant past and from more recent experiences during World War II and its aftermath. In particular, even as surface daily life in Yugoslavia seemed to be peaceful, the salience of religion had remained a point of deep division—or at least a symbol of past conflicts. As each of these three ethnic populations sought to carve out a territory for its own nation, conflicts over boundaries were inevitable, as were conflicts within boundaries among those who lived inside their enemy's cities, towns, and villages. Thus, as the conflict erupted, it involved more than armies mutually invading each other's territory; it turned neighbors, who had lived in relative peace, against each other. In particular, Serbs living in what Muslims saw as their land, Bosnia-Herzegovina, began to seek control of Muslim cities and territories. When war broke out, therefore, it was inevitably going to be bloody, although the atrocities committed by Serbs within Bosnia—mass killings, rape of women, and deliberate starvation of prisoners and citizens—far exceed what might have been expected or tolerated in the modern world.

The war has been complicated by the geopolitical situation outside the areas of battle. Most European nations do not want to side with the Muslims in Bosnia-Herzegovina, presumably because non-Serbian Bosnians are not Christians (Cohen, 1994). Yet it is the Christian Serbs who are committing the most violent acts. Ironically, in light of past conflicts with Muslims in the Middle East, the United States is the strongest supporter of the Bosnian Muslims and has worked the hardest to broker a peace in the region. Yet, until the arms embargo on Bosnia was lifted by the United States (and United Nations) in 1994, the battle was very one-sided, enabling the Serbs to commit true war crimes similar to those perpetrated by Nazi Germans. Only when Croatia briefly entered the war to protect its boundaries against Serbia did the tide of the warfare shift to the point that the United States became willing to commit ground troops to the area, along with reluctant troops from other countries in Europe.

The war has, of course, intensified existing ethnic hatreds; and it has made refugees of many Muslims and Serbs who had once resided in their enemy's newly claimed territory. And in Bosnia, the creation of separate Serbian and Bosnian cities is an invitation to further conflict, especially when the foreign troops imposing this inviable solution leave the area. And so, far into the future it can be expected that the mutual fears and hatreds will persist among the antagonists in this part of the world, with each viewing the other as a source of threat and with each portraying the other population in highly negative terms. The end result will be more violence, unless external powers like the United States and key European nations remain in the area to maintain the peace (a most unlikely event in the long run).

PALESTINIANS AND ISRAELIS

One of the most contentious ethnic battlegrounds in the world is the Middle East, where historically Judaism, Christianity, and Islam are interwoven—all ultimately deriving their religion from the book of Abraham—and where Jews and Muslims now stand in conflict over a territory known for several centuries as "Palestine." The present conflict between Israelis and Palestinians can be traced back at least two thousand years, when Jews were exiled from Palestine; and as a result, they began to settle in Europe and other parts of the Middle East where they experienced considerable prejudice and discrimination. The birth of Christ in Bethlehem and his death in Jerusalem, but more significantly some fifty years after Christ's death, Paul's use of the Roman infrastructure (markets and trade routes) to preach Christianity, eventually led to the conversion of the Roman Empire to Christianity (Mann, 1986), which, in turn, made Jerusalem a destination for many Christian pilgrimages. In the seventh century, Palestine slowly came under Muslim control with the spread of Islam all over the Middle East. By the beginning of the twentieth century, Palestine had become a part of the Ottoman Empire of the Turks, and though this control by a Muslim-dominated empire increased the presence of Islam in Palestine, some migrations of Jews back to Palestine were tolerated.

During World War I, the Turks were driven out of Palestine when the British expanded their colonial empire into the Middle East, particularly Egypt but Palestine as well. It is this British occupation that initiated the current problems because the British endorsed creating a Jewish homeland in Palestine. *Zionism* or the desire to create a Jewish nation in its biblical homeland—that is, Palestine—had existed for a long time, but the British endorsement of this desire encouraged more Jews to immigrate to Palestine from Russia and the rest of Europe as well as the northern part of Africa and other portions of the Middle East (the latter often referred to as "Oriental Jews" who are, culturally, very different from those Jews who have come from Europe).

Still, at the end of World War I, only about 15 percent of the population in Palestine was Jewish (Schaefer, 1996:477); the rest was, for the most part, Arab. But, the migrations posed a threat to Arabs who felt that Zionism would destroy their way of life (a perception which was not without foundation), and during the next two decades, tension between Arabs and Jews increased, erupting into riots on the part of Muslims who demanded that Jewish immigration be stopped by Britain. In the end, the British acceded to these demands, despite the fact that many Jews from Germany desperately needed to come to Palestine in order to escape persecution in Nazi Germany. Instead, many Jews came to America when their first destination of choice had been what was eventually to become Israel.

In the aftermath of World War II, and especially as the atrocities against Jews in Germany and Poland became evident to the world, Zionism intensified, with the inevitable result that the Arabs' sense of threat escalated. The British, who by now felt caught in the middle of an unresolvable conflict, gave the new United Nations its first major test. In 1948, under the United Nations, the state of Israel was created, and the British withdrew (Lesch, 1983). Conflict was almost immediate as the surrounding Arab nations—particularly, Egypt, Syria, Jordan, Iraq, and Lebanon—mobilized to return control of Palestine to Palestinians who are a distinct ethnic subpopulation within the Arab world. The *Palestine Liberation Organization* (or PLO) emerged as the most important conduit for foreign support of Palestinians and for political efforts to return Israel, or Palestine, to Palestinian ethnics.

In this hostile environment, Israel sought to defend its borders, and at the same time, well over a million Arabs fled or were expelled from Israel, giving the PLO many new recruits. These Arabs fled to neighboring countries, creating a refugee population outside the borders of the newly formed state and, among those within the borders of Israel, a restless sense of being a refugee in what Palestinians and other Arabs perceived as their own land (although the Israeli government has always been willing to provide social, educational, and other forms of assistance to residents within the borders of Israel). To counter the threat posed by these internal and external refugees and by the simple fact of being surrounded by nations that refused to recognize the legitimacy of Israel, the government encouraged a large-scale immigration to Israel under the ideological banner of Zionism. Every Jew in the world was given the right to become an Israeli citizen, and in light of the long history of persecution of Jews in Europe and Russia, rates of immigration to Israel escalated dramatically. The city of Jerusalem remained split, however, between a Jewish half aligned with Israel and a Muslim half as part of Jordan.

In 1967, Egypt and Syria once again sought to take control of Israel and, in what was known as the Six Day War, were defeated by the Israeli army. Israel not only repelled the attacks but also took what had been Arab territory—the Golan Heights in the north where Syria, Lebanon, and Israel meet, the West Bank which includes Jerusalem and Bethlehem along the middle portion of the border with Jordan, the Gaza Strip along the Mediterranean south of Israel, and, most humiliatingly, the Sinai of Egypt north of the Suez Canal. Subsequent attacks by Arab nations on Israel reinforced the simple fact of Israeli military superiority; and as a result, the Palestinian ethnic minority within Israel and its newly acquired territories would have to mobilize for itself, receiving aid from Arab nations but not being liberated by invading Arab armies (Said et al., 1988). In 1979, in a brokered agreement between Egypt and Israel, half of the Sinai was returned to Egypt in exchange for Egypt's recognition that Israel had a right to exist (something which, at the time, no Arab state had done).

The occupied territories acquired in the Six Day War of 1967 were viewed initially as a buffer zone by the Israeli government—as a kind of strategic advantage against any further attacks from Arab nations. In the 1980s, however, Jewish settlements were being created in these territories, thereby escalating the sense of threat among Arabs and Palestinians living in these areas. Palestinians saw that their hopes for their own homeland were quickly vanishing; and as a consequence, their fears and prejudices against Israel erupted in what is termed the *Intifada,* or uprising against Israelis in occupied territories. Strikes, boycotts, bombings, hit-and-run attacks against soldiers, and other acts of disobedience to Israeli authority became chronic and intense. Much of this uprising occurred outside the structure of the PLO, mobilizing a wide spectrum of the Palestinian population against the Israeli occupation of their territories or, at least, what had been their lands before the Six Day War. Later the PLO encouraged these protests, and organizations, such as *Hamas,* grew and mobilized resources (both domestic and foreign) for social services as well as for revolt and terrorism. The Intifada and its aftermath are the direct result of over two million Palestinians (there are about six million all together) living under the control of Israel, either within the original borders of Israel or the territories acquired during the Six Day War (Roudi, 1993). In response to terrorist attacks on Israeli soldiers, settlements, and towns, Israel has continued to throw suspected Palestinian activists in jails or to remove them from the country—a tactic that appears only to have polarized sentiments of Israelis and Palestinians against each other.

Remarkably in 1994, an agreement between the government of Israel and PLO was signed by their respective leaders. This accord was to end the state of war between Palestinians and Israelis and to create a self-governing territory in the Gaza Strip and the West Bank for Palestinians. The transformation of the PLO and other militant groups inside and outside of the PLO into the Palestinian Authority and the movement of Israeli troops out of Gaza have begun the process of creating a new nation. Yet, the economic problems of the emerging Palestinian state are enormous; basically, they have no core economy except providing services for each other and appealing for aid from abroad. Moreover, the brokered peace agreement is in a constant state of potential collapse, as the assassination of the Israeli Prime Minister in 1995 by a militant wing of Hamas and as the subsequent shelling by Israel of terrorist (and, unfortunately, civilian as well) camps in Lebanon in 1996 document. Indeed, the question as to whether or not the newly emerging state of Palestine and Israel can sustain the peace accord in a still hostile Arab world—especially in Syria, Iraq, and Iran but also Palestinians living in all parts of the Middle East—is unclear at the present moment.

In addition to this fragile situation between the new Palestine and Israel are remaining problems that can erupt into ethnic violence. One is the pace by which the Palestinian Authority will be able to move to a true, independent state that is completely separated from Israel; if this pace is too slow, then more violence can be expected. Another difficult problem is the city of Jerusalem which is the Israeli capital but, at the same time, viewed by Muslims as a holy city. Another problem is the continued existence of the Israeli settlements in Gaza and the West Bank, coupled with the fanaticism of Jews in these settlements (mixed with the fanaticism of various Palestinian groups). Still another vexing problem is what to do with the Palestinian refugees who live outside Israel, the West Bank, and Gaza in other parts of the Arab world; as long as this large refugee population exists, it will pose problems to each of the Arab governments where Palestinians reside while creating logistical problems of integrating this population into the new Palestinian homeland. These problems all assure that Israeli-Palestinian tensions will persist well into the twenty-first century.

Indeed, the elections of a conservative Israeli prime minister in 1996 ensure that the peace process will be even more fragile. The current prime minister campaigned against full Palestinian autonomy in Gaza as a separate nation, against returning land taken in the Six Day War in exchange for peace agreements, against cessation of construction of Jewish settlements on conquered territory, and against splitting of Jerusalem into self-governing districts. Under these conditions, ethnic conflict will inevitably escalate, unless the United States can apply pressure to moderate these proposed policies of the new Israeli government.

RWANDA AND BURUNDI

Central Africa has had some of the most brutal ethnic and political conflicts of the century. The basic problem in this region, as in much of colonial Africa, is that the boundaries created by colonial powers—mostly German, Belgium, and French—incorporated often antagonistic populations. In a divide-and-conquer strategy of administration, colonial rule generally favored one ethnic population over others within the artificial territorial boundaries imposed by a European power. The result was that hatreds among ethnic subpopulations would inevitably intensify. In the postcolonial phase of nation-building in central Africa, political regimes have tended to be oppressive and, when necessary, violent. Many thousands of individuals have been killed by armies of the government and rebellious factions who are often financed and supported by neighboring societies and, at times, even old colonial powers. These conflicts between repressive political regimes and rebellious factions of the population have often occurred along what are perceived to be ethnic differences, often elaborated into perceptions of "racial" differences; and as the killings have continued, the intensity of the hatreds has grown. Nowhere are these tragic dynamics more evident than in the areas of Rwanda and Burundi, which during the 1990s endured mass killings as ethnic antagonisms between the two major ethnic subpopulations, the Hutus and the Tutsis, led to massacres that can be labeled only as genocidal.

The tensions between the Hutus and Tutsis go back to the fifteenth century. In the eleventh century, the agrarian Hutus settled the region now known as Rwanda and Burundi, driving off or killing the hunter-gatherers of the area. In the 1400s, the cattle-herding Tutsis began to move into the area that had been controlled by the Hutus for over three hundred years; and gradually, the Tutsis were to gain control of the territory, despite the fact that they were far outnumbered by the Hutus. Whatever conflicts had occurred before European colonization had nonetheless resulted in a certain degree of amalgamation of the two populations who, by the nineteenth century, spoke virtually the same language. Still, because the Tutsis dominated politically, there remained considerable tension between the Tutsis and Hutus. This tension was reinforced by the distinctiveness of the two populations: The Tutsis tend to be tall and thin with more European-looking facial features, while the Hutus are shorter and stockier with wider noses. As a result, each was identifiable (at least in the minds of Tutsis and Hutus), which, in turn, facilitated the development of negative stereotypes that only fueled the mutual sense of threat. Thus, upon European contact and colonial control, the two groups were distinctive ethnic subpopulations, who saw each other in negative terms and as mutual threats. The dominant Tutsis were threatened by the overwhelming numbers of Hutus, whereas the Hutus resented the control exercised by the Tutsi minority over their lives.

In the late nineteenth century, German colonizers established the first form of European influence over the region, making what is now Rwanda and Burundi a German "protectorate" in 1884 and utilizing the Tutsi-dominated political system as a means for exerting indirect administrative control (Louis, 1963). In essence, the Germans gave the Tutsi elite favors in exchange for their continued control over the Hutus who constituted most of the population and who performed much of the labor on the coffee plantations that the Germans exploited. During World War I, Belgium took over the area and began to incorporate Hutus into the colonial administration, a tactic that only intensified the tensions between the two populations. They did so by turning over administration of outlying governments to the Hutus, while allowing the Tutsis to maintain their domination in the larger cities and in the central government. This split only intensified the mutual sense of threat and the negative stereotyping between the two populations; and in particular, it gave the Hutus a political and territorial base from which they could mobilize opposition to their domination by the Tutsis in the cities and central government.

By the late 1950s, the tensions between the Hutus and Tutsis had escalated to ever more frequent killing, and in the last year of the decade, Hutus killed many thousands of Tutsis and forced many more to flee Rwanda. The Hutus were also able to win the election of 1959; and in 1961, they petitioned the world community for nationhood status. In response the United Nations voted to separate the area into two nations, Rwanda dominated by the Hutus and Burundi controlled by the Tutsis (Fegley, 1993). This situation was not, however, stable as the Tutsis in Burundi sought to invade Rwanda, causing the Hutus to kill many thousands of Tutsis within Rwanda and forcing many more to flee to Burundi and other neighboring nations. Independence of the two nations thus only intensified the conflict, with each seeing the other as a territory to be invaded by their respective armies, which were supported by external powers. By 1990, it was clear that Uganda tended to support the Tutsis, presumably because the president's parents had been Tutsi immigrants to Uganda, while France sought to consolidate its influence in the region by bringing Hutu-controlled Rwanda into the French-dominated economic alliance among central African nations.

In 1990, Tutsi exiles invaded Rwanda to overthrow the Hutu government, and a new round of intense and violent conflict began. Both sides were well armed by external governments, and while the Hutu population vastly outnumbered the Tutsis, the respective armies were more equally matched. In 1994, the battle escalated after the apparent assassination of the Hutu president (the Burundi president had been assassinated the year before); and suddenly, Hutu civilians and soldiers began mass killings of Tutsis within Rwanda. It is estimated that these massacres killed half of the Tutsi population in Rwanda (a figure approaching perhaps as much as three hundred thousand people), a portrait of killing that can be described only as genocide. The Tutsi army in Burundi responded by taking control of the capital of Rwanda, after a series of major victories against the Hutu army, which was not as well organized as that of the Tutsis. As a result, two million Hutus fled Rwanda, fearing retaliation by the Tutsis; similarly, many Tutsis moved outside of Rwanda and Burundi in an effort to escape cross-fire between the armies and potential retaliation by Hutus (who comprise over 85 percent of the region's population). Thus, millions of refugees now reside outside of Rwanda and Burundi in poor nations which can ill-afford to support them without foreign aid.

By 1995, armed conflict continued in both Rwanda and Burundi as Hutus mobilized to take back their nation dominated once again by Tutsis; and in fact, they even went so far as to strike at the capital of Burundi. By the end of 1996, a brokered cease fire and period of relative peace had led to a Hutu becoming president of Burundi. But in July of 1996, the Tutsi-dominated army had executed a coup and installed a former Tutsi president as the new leader of Burundi. The reasons for the coup are obscure, but the United Nations had revealed considerable evidence of mass killings on both sides before the coup. The new president has sought to create a cabinet of both Hutus and Tutsis in an effort at national reconciliation, but given the

In Rwanda, massacres have been common in recent years. Piles of dead bodies are a common sight in the ethnic killing, creating problems of disposal and potential disease for the already weakened populations of this region.

recent past of mass killings, it is questionable whether this fragile peace can be sustained through the rest of the 1990s.

Thus, as the century nears its close, the problems of the region are far from resolved, although a certain degree of peace exists because the United Nations and key nation members, such as the United States and France, have helped to impose some order in the region. Yet, a conflict that began in the fifteenth century as the Tutsi herders moved into Hutu farming areas has persisted and, indeed, intensified by various forms of colonization by European powers—German, then Belgium, and lastly, France. The ethnic hatreds have grown, as each group (quite correctly) sees the other as a threat to their life. As a consequence, it is unlikely that this conflict will be resolved in the foreseeable future.

SOUTH AFRICA

For the whole of the twentieth century, the most ethnically stratified society of the modern world has been South Africa; indeed, as other societies were making efforts to lower barriers among ethnic subpopulations, South Africa was constructing them. And, in the post–World War II period, full-scale *apartheid,* or the institutionalization of separateness among ethnics, was in place. Even today, with the dramatic changes in the political system as the black numerical majority has assumed control of much of this political system, changes must confront not only the last fifty years of deliberate segregation but in fact a three-hundred-year historical legacy of ethnic discrimination (Thompson, 1990).

The history of South Africa is tied to the east and Asia, where all the European powers sought trade routes to India. In 1652, the Dutch East India Company established a colony in Cape Town at the southern end of the African continent in order to facilitate the movement of vessels and their valuable cargo around the Cape of Good Hope (which, before the Suez Canal, was the only shipping route for trade with much of Asia). The indigenous peoples, the San Bushmen and Khoikhoi or Hottentots, were both insufficient in number to perform the menial labor of the new colony; and so, the Dutch along with some French Huguenots and German settlers began to import slaves from further up the African continent. As the colony became larger, many of these settlers moved into the interior of the country in order to set up plantations. These *Boers,* which is a Dutch word for "farmers," were to continue their movement inland; and as they did so, they confronted the indigenous populations of *Bantu-speaking peoples* who, today, constitute the vast majority of the South African population. The conflicts of the Boers and various populations of Bantu-speakers were intense and lasted many decades, each viewing the other (quite correctly) as a threat to their way of life. During this period from the late 1600s to the beginning of the nineteenth century, the Boers developed a distinct culture built upon isolation from the European influences on whites in Cape Town on the coast and upon intensely negative beliefs about black Africans (Fredrickson, 1981). Indeed, the isolation was so great that the Boers developed their own language—*Afrikaans*—which is distinct from Dutch (Thompson, 1990); and more importantly, they developed a culture emphasizing that (1) the Boars were the "true white tribe" of South Africa (ignoring the fact that they were displacing or subordinating blacks who had been on the land for thousands of years), (2) the Boars were superior to blacks who were perceived to be less than human, and (3) the Boars were given the right by God to subordinate the indigenous populations and to take their lands (Thompson, 1985). If one could combine the most negative stereotypes that whites had for black slaves in the American South before 1860 and for Native Americans whose land was taken by the 1850s, then one can get a sense for the intensity of the prejudicial stereotypes that Boers had toward those they sought to conquer and oppress. In fact, the Boers began to call themselves *Afrikaners;* and it is the descendants of these Afrikaners who in the second half of the twentieth century were to take power and formalize apartheid.

The Afrikaners' assumption of political power, however, must be viewed in the context of the British takeover of Cape Town in 1806. Like the Dutch East India Company, the British wanted to secure trade routes to India, doing so by militarily taking control of the key servicing point on the Cape. The British also sought to settle the areas around Cape Town, and so immigration was encouraged. The result was the outmigration from Cape Town of Afrikaners, with the British in pursuit. When diamonds and then gold were discovered in the second half of the nineteenth century in the interior of what was to become South Africa, British interests in control of the interior increased; and thus, the second half of the three-hundred-year history of the area was to be marked not just by Afrikaner–African conflict but also by Afrikaner–British tensions as the latter sought to extend their colonial empire.

During the nineteenth century, as the Afrikaners sought to carve out their own territories, they fought both British and Bantu-speaking Zulus. As they defeated the Africans and fought off the British, at least for a time, they used forced labor, slavery, and violence to assure that the labor for their plantations and emerging mining operations was not only available but pliant. As they defeated the Zulu, they established the Republic of Natal in 1838, and as they moved further north, the Orange Free State and Transvaal were created. By the beginning of this century, however, the British had won the Boer Wars and were in control of all these territories. In the process of taking Afrikaner territory, the British had abolished slavery (throughout the British Empire in 1834), which hurt the plantation economy built by Afrikaners, and they had begun to annex not just territories but the mining industry as well.

In 1910, the Cape, Natal, the Orange Free State, and Transvaal were merged in the Union of South Africa, later the Republic of South Africa. For the next forty years, moderate Afrikaners and British were able to win national elections, keeping the more radical *Afrikaner National party* from imposing what was to become formalized apartheid. The resulting system was not, however, particularly benign: Ethnic distinctions among categories of people were made—black, whites, coloured (mixed ancestry), and later Asians (mostly Indian); only whites had rights to vote because of property and other restrictions on nonwhites; occupational segregation was highly correlated with color designation so that whites had all of the key economic positions and blacks all of the menial and subordinate positions (Asians and coloureds were eventually able to occupy middleman minority positions and other less menial occupational tracks); residential segregation was enforced between blacks and white, and, to somewhat lesser extent, among coloureds and Asians as well; nonwhites were very limited in their rights to own land, which, in turn, was used as a criterion for voting rights; blacks were sent to inferior and segregated schools, which were soon to become even more inferior when the state took over education from the missionaries.

As bad as this level of discrimination was, the victory of the Afrikaner National party in 1948 was to make things worse. For, it is at this juncture that apartheid was formalized into a system of ethnic stratification along the lines of color. For the next four decades, the Afrikaner National party would control the political arena, while the British-origin settlers would exert control over the key industries of South Africa. The party began its rule by creating four official categories—whites, coloureds, Asians, and Africans—as the basis for laws that segregated the society along ethnic lines; and in fact, subcategories of these basic ones were often used to micromanage apartheid at the town and neighborhood level. A series of laws, coercively enforced, became the backbone of apartheid: The Population Registration Act required all members of the population to register by color or "racial" designation; the Group Areas Act prohibited black Africans from residing outside of designated areas; the Bantu Self-Government Act pushed much of the black population into territories or "homelands"; and a series of acts gave the police ever more power to suspend civil rights and to use violence where necessary to maintain apartheid along every dimension of social life (Thompson, 1990).

Even under these oppressive conditions, there was opposition to apartheid. Many moderate British, especially those involved in the world economy (mining and trade), voiced moderate protests either on moral grounds or, more likely, on the grounds that it was bad for business, especially as the world community began to impose economic, social, and political sanctions on South Africa. Liberal academics also opposed apartheid, as did various civil rights activists. But most importantly, black Africans began to organize politically into two major parties (Meli, 1988), the *African National Congress* (the ANC) and the *Pan-African Congress* (PAC). These two parties were often engaged in bitter rivalry, but they both posed threats to the whites who imposed apartheid; and as a result, these parties and other political organizations were banned and their leaders, such as Nelson Mandella (of the ANC), were thrown into prison. But the opposition did not stop; and the activities of the parties and other political organizations were evident in the territories and townships inhabited by black Africans. Demonstrations by blacks near large urban centers led to government suspension of even more civil rights and to the use of violence against Africans, but in the end, the government had to allow nonwhites to organize into labor unions (on a restricted basis) and into multiethnic parties. By the mid-1980s, Asians and coloureds were allowed limited participation in politics; and soon, black South Africans were to be allowed to vote, thereby changing the nature of South Africa as it moves into the twenty-first century.

The key events began in 1990 when the South African prime minister, F. W. DeKlerk, reinstated previously banned black organizations, freeing Nelson Mandella who, as leader of the banned ANC, had been in jail for close to three decades. A year later, a "Peace Accord" was signed by DeKlerk and African leaders who all pledged to develop a multiparty democracy. In 1992, DeKlerk called for a national referendum in which whites were to choose whether they favored the legal dismantling of apartheid, a referendum in which close to 70 percent of whites voted in favor of ending apartheid and writing a new constitution. In 1994, South Africa held its first national election in which all members of the society could vote, giving Nelson Mandella a five-year term as president. And in 1996, a new constitution was written, guaranteeing freedom from discrimination.

The future of South Africa is, however, filled with both promise and problems. To dismantle apartheid requires more than changes in law and political elites. Housing and territorial segregation needs to be reduced; and new economic opportunities need to be provided in an economy that has been built around the exploitive use of cheap black labor. In a government strapped for money and in a society with a three-hundred-year history of mutual threats among ethnic subpopulations, with a long legacy of intensely prejudicial stereotypes and beliefs, and with formal and informal discrimination down to the neighborhood level, the complete dismantling of apartheid will be difficult. If we only consider the legacy of slavery as it continues to fuel ethnic antagonism in the United States, then perhaps the magnitude of the problems ahead in South Africa can be appreciated. The major difference is that blacks constitute 75 percent of the population, a figure that is projected to increase to almost 80 percent by the beginning of the next century (Marger, 1996:404), whereas whites are only 13 percent of the population—figures that are just about the reverse of those in America (if we include Latinos in the count of whites). But the economy is owned by whites, whereas the polity will increasingly be controlled by blacks. Therein resides many of the problems and dilemmas for South Africa in the future as it seeks to break down its system of ethnic stratification.

CONCLUSION

If we look around the world, then, it is clear that ethnic conflict is pervasive. The driving forces of ethnic discrimination—mutual fears, negative stereotyping and prejudice, competition and conflict over resources, inequality and stratification—can be found everywhere. In this sense, the American situation is hardly unique, although there are several significant differences between the United States and many other places in the world. First, the northern European invasion of what was to become the United States was conducted by a vastly superior military force in a sparsely populated land. Hence, once the aboriginal population was killed—through disease, murder, and war—the fault line of antagonism diminished the threat from those whose territory had been taken. Only in the Southwest and Mexico, where the descendants of the Spanish and original natives live, has significant ethnic conflict stemming from the initial conquest and expansion of the territory been evident. A second difference is that the United States is a land of immigrants with each successive wave being absorbed, to varying degrees, into the sociocultural mainstream. Only the descendants of African slaves and, perhaps, the remaining descendants of Native Americans confront overwhelming barriers to integration into the society's mainstream. A third difference between America and other places on the globe is that the association of distinct territory with ethnicity exists only in the Southwest, and even here the connection is not as intense as that in other parts of the world, and as a result, a major source of ethnic tension is mitigated. Fourth, the territory of the nation is very large, allowing movement of peoples in ways that can release tensions as much as inflame them. Fifth, economic growth has encouraged the immigration of ethnics to America, while at the same time, this growth has been driven by the hard work of immigrants; and as a result, ethnic conflicts have revolved more around economic competition in an expanding economy capable of providing some resources to most people. Sixth, political democracy coupled with egalitarian values has operated to diffuse many potential conflicts by virtue of offering avenues for political protest and ameliorative actions. Seventh, recent ethnic conflicts in America have for the most part been confined to economic, political, and social justice questions rather than differences in religious and high-intensity moral questions that only inflame ethnic conflict.

Yet, ethnic conflict still persists in America, and indeed, it may accelerate, but if we view such conflict in global context, it does not seem as volatile as in many other parts of the world. Such escalation of conflict in America is most likely when ethnic populations perceive each other as threats, thereby setting off another round of negative stereotyping, discrimination, inequality, and ethnic stratification. The critical question for Americans is: Can the persisting pattern of ethnic stratification be reduced so that social class position is not highly correlated with ethnic identity? Inequalities in large-scale societies are inevitable, and they will always be a source of tension and conflict; but when class divisions become intertwined with ethnic divisions, the volatility of the conflict increases. If we look at the most violent or potentially violent ethnic conflicts in the world today, they always reveal this connection between resource distribution and ethnicity. And if we add to this connection additional fuel—such as the association of ethnicity with territory, ethnicity with religion, ethnicity with political oppression, ethnicity with long-term historical conflicts, ethnicity with external allies driven by economic or religious interests, and other factors that intensify the conflict—then it is not hard to see why ethnic conflict is not only so pervasive in the world but so violent. The United States can avoid most of these intensifying factors, but resolving ethnic tensions in America must begin with programs and policies designed to reduce the correlation between economic well-being and ethnicity.

References

Acuña, Rodolfo. 1981. *Occupied America: A History of Chicanos,* 2d edition. New York: Harper & Row.

Adams, Karen, and Daniel Brink (eds.). 1990. *Perspectives on Official English: The Campaign for English as the Official Language of the USA.* Berlin: Mouton de Gruyter.

Aguirre, Adalberto, Jr. 1973. "Communication Media and Mexican Social Issues: A Focus on English-language and U.S.-origin Communication Media." *International Journal of Comparative Sociology* 34:231–243.

———. 1980. "The Sociolinguistic Situation of Chicano Adolescents in a California Border Town." *AZTLAN: International Journal of Chicano Studies Research* 10:55–67.

———. 1982. "The Political Economy Context of Language in Social Service Delivery for Hispanics." In *Ethnicity and Public Policy,* edited by Winston Van Horne, pp. 89–104. Madison: University of Wisconsin Press.

———. 1984. "Language Use in Bilingual Mexican American Households." *Social Science Quarterly* 65:565–572.

———. 1988. "Language Use and Media Orientations in Bilingual Mexican-Origin Households in Southern California." *Mexican Studies/Estudios Mexicanos* 4:115–130.

———. 1990. "Poverty in the United States: Race, Ethnic, and Gender Differentials." In *Income and Status Differences Between White and Minority Americans: A Persistent Inequality,* edited by Sucheng Chan, pp. 101–112. Lewiston, NY: Edwin Mellen Press.

———. 1993. "Communication Media and Mexican Social Issues: A Focus on English-language and U.S.-origin Communication Media." *International Journal of Comparative Sociology* 34:231–243.

———. 1995a. "Nativist Feeling and Immigrant Workers: An Interpretive Note." *Latino Studies Journal* 6:48–62.

———. 1995b. "Ethnolinguistic Populations in California: A Focus on LEP Students and Public Education." *The Journal of Educational Issues of Language Minority Students* 15:77–91.

Aguirre, Adalberto, Jr., and David Baker. 1988. "A Descriptive Profile of the Hispanic Penal Population: Conceptual and Reliability Limitations in Public Use Data." *The Justice Professional* 3:189–200.

———. 1989. "The Execution of Mexican American Prisoners in the Southwest." *Social Justice* 16:150–161.

———. 1991. *Race, Racism and the Death Penalty in the United States.* Berrien Spring, MI: Vande Vere Publishing.

———. 1993. "Racial Prejudice and the Death Penalty: A Research Note." *Social Justice* 20:150–155.

———. 1994. *Perspectives on Race and Ethnicity in American Criminal Justice.* New York: West Publishing Company.

———. 1996. *Black Slave Executions in the United States from 1641 to 1865.* Unpublished manuscript.

Aguirre, Adalberto, Jr., and Ruben Martinez. 1984. "Hispanics and the U.S. Occupational Structure: A Focus on Vocational Education." *The International Journal of Sociology and Social Policy* 4:50–59.

———. 1993. *Chicanos In Higher Education: Issues and Dilemmas for the 21st Century.* ASHE-ERIC Higher Education Report No. 3. Washington, DC: The George Washington University, School of Education and Human Development.

Ainsworth, Robert. 1989. *An Overview of the Labor Market Problems of Indians and Native Americans.* Washington, DC: National Commission for Employment Policy Research Report No. 89-02.

Alba, Richard. 1985. *Italian Americans: Into the Twilight of Ethnicity.* Englewood Cliffs, NJ: Prentice-Hall.

Alba, Richard, and Gwen Moore. 1982. "Ethnicity in the American Elite." *American Sociological Review* 47:373–383.

Almaguer, Tomas. 1994. *Racial Fault Lines: The Historical Origins of White Supremacy in California.* Berkeley: University of California Press.

Ambler, Marjane. 1990. *Breaking the Iron Bonds: Indian Control of Energy Development.* Lawrence, KS: University Press of Kansas.

American Council of Learned Societies. 1932. *Report of the Committee of Linguistic and National Stocks in the Population of the United States.* Washington, DC: American Council of Learned Societies.

American Historical Association. 1932. *Annual Report on Proceedings, Volume 1.* Washington, DC: U.S. Government Printing Office.

American Jewish Committee. 1991. *American Jewish Yearbook.* New York: American Jewish Committee.

Anderson, Terry (ed.). 1992. *Property Rights and Indian Economics.* Landham, MD: Rowman Littlefield Publishers.

Andrews, George. 1992. "Racial Inequality in Brazil and the United States: A Statistical Comparison." *Journal of Social History* 26:233–248.

Andrews, George Reid. 1991. *Blacks and Whites in Sao Paulo, Brazil 1888–1988.* Madison, WI: University of Wisconsin Press.

Andrews, William. 1994. "The Black Male in American Literature." In *The American Black Male,* edited by Richard Majors and Jacob Gordon, pp. 59–68. Chicago: Nelson-Hall Publishers.

Aponte, Robert. 1991. "Urban Hispanic Poverty: Disaggregations and Explanations." *Social Problems* 38:516–528.

Auditor General of California. 1987. *A Review of First-Year Admissions of Asians and Caucasians at the University of California at Berkeley.* Sacramento, CA: Auditor General's Office.

Auletta, Ken. 1982. *The Underclass.* New York: Random House.

Awanohara, Susumu. 1990. "Spicier Melting Pot: Asian Americans Come of Age Politically." *Far Eastern Economic Review* (Nov. 22): 30, 32–36.

Ayala, Cesar. 1996. "The Decline of the Plantation Economy and the Puerto Rican Migration of the 1950s." *Latino Studies Journal* 7:62–90.

Bach, Robert. 1980. "The New Cuban Immigrants: Their Background and Prospects." *Monthly Labor Review* 103:39–46.

Bai, Su. 1991. "Affirmative Pursuit of Political Equality for Asian Pacific Americans: Reclaiming the Voting Rights Act." *University of Pennsylvania Law Review* 139:731–767.

Banting, Keith G. 1992. "If Quebec Separates: Restructuring Northern North America." In *The Collapse of Canada?* edited by R. K. Weaver. Washington, DC: The Brookings Institution.

Banton, Michael. 1983. *Racial and Ethnic Competition.* Cambridge: Cambridge University Press.

Barrera, Mario. 1979. *Race and Class in the Southwest: A Theory of Racial Inequality.* South Bend, IN: University of Notre Dame Press.

———. 1985. "The Historical Evolution of Chicano Ethnic Goals: A Bibliographic Essay." *Sage Race Relations Abstracts* 10:1–48.

Barringer, Herbert, Robert Gardner, and Michael Lewis. 1993. *Asian and Pacific Islanders in the United States.* New York: Russell Sage Foundation.

Bartelt, H. Guillermo. 1992. "Boarding School Language Policy and the Spread of English among Indians of the American Southwest." In *Native Americans and Public Policy,* edited by Fremont J. Lyden and Lyman H. Legters, pp. 137–146. Pittsburgh: University of Pittsburgh Press.

Baver, S. 1984. "Puerto Rican Politics in New York City: The Post–World War II Period." In *Puerto Rican Politics in Urban America,* edited by James Jennings and Monte Rivera, pp. 43–60. New York: Greenwood Press.

Bayes, Jane. 1982. *Minority Politics and Ideologies in the United States.* Novato, CA: Chandler Sharp Publishers.

Bean, Frank, Barry Edmonston, and Jeffery Passel (eds.). 1990. *Undocumented Migration to the United States: IRCA and the Experience of the 1980s.* Santa Monica, CA: RAND and the Urban Institute.

Bean, Frank, and Marta Tienda. 1987. *The Hispanic Population of the United States.* New York: Russell Sage Foundation.

Bean Frank, Georges Vernez, and Charles Keeley. 1989. *Opening and Closing the Doors: Evaluating Immigration Reform and Control.* Santa Monica, CA: RAND and the Urban Institute.

Becerra, Jose, Carol Hogue, Hani Atrash, and Nilsa Perez. 1991. "Infant Mortality among Hispanics: A Portrait of Heterogeneity." *Journal of the American Medical Association* 265:217–221.

Bell, Derrick, Jr. 1973. *Race, Racism and American Law.* Boston: Little, Brown and Company.

Bell-Fialkoff, Andrew. 1993. "A Brief History of Ethnic Cleansing." *Foreign Affairs* 3:115–117.

Benavides, Alfredo. 1981. "Education and the Environment: Pesticide Contamination and Children's Learning." *Social Studies Teacher* 2:5, 13.

Bieder, Robert. 1980. "Scientific Attitudes Toward Indian Mixed-Bloods in Early Nineteenth Century America." *Journal of Ethnic Studies* 8:17–30.

Bishop, Herbert. 1917. "The Mission as a Frontier Institution in the Spanish-American Colonies." *American Historical Review* 23:42–61.

Blalock, Hubert M., Jr. 1967. *Toward a Theory of Minority-Group Relations.* New York: Wiley.

Blauner, Robert. 1969. "Internal Colonialism and Ghetto Revolt." *Social Problems* 16:393–408.

———. 1972. *Racial Oppression in America.* New York: Harper and Row.

———. 1989. *Black Lives, White Lives: Three Decades of Race Relations in America.* Berkeley: University of California Press.

Blumstein, Alfred. 1982. "On the Racial Disproportionality of United States' Prison Populations." *Journal of Criminal Law & Criminology* 73:1259–1281.

Bolaria, G. Singh, and Peter S. Ki. 1985. *Racial Oppression in Canada.* Toronto, Canada: Garamond Press.

Bonacich, Edna. 1972. "A Theory of Ethnic Antagonism: The Split Labor Market." *American Sociological Review* 37:547–559.

———. 1973. "A Theory of Middleman Minorities." *American Sociological Review* 38:583–594.

———. 1976. "Advanced Capitalism and Black-White Race Relations in the United States: A Split Labor Market Interpretation." *American Sociological Review* 41:34–51.

Boozer, Michael, Alan Krueger, and Shari Wolkon. 1992. "Race and School Quality Since *Brown v. Board of Education.*" In *Brookings Papers in Economic Activity: Microeconomics 1992,* edited by Martin Baily and Clifford Winston, pp. 169–326. Washington, DC: Brookings Institution.

Boskin, Joseph. 1986. *Sambo: The Rise and Demise of an American Jester.* New York: Oxford University Press.

Boswell, Thomas. 1985. "The Cuban Americans." In *Ethnicity in Contemporary America: A Geographical Appraisal,* edited by Jesse McKee, pp. 95–116. Dubuque, IA: Kendall/Hunt.

Boxer, Charles R. 1962. *The Golden Age of Brazil.* Berkeley, CA: University of California Press.

Brown, Dee. 1970. *Bury My Heart at Wounded Knee: An Indian History of the American West.* New York: Holt, Rinehart and Winston.

Brown, Michael E., et al. 1996. *The International Dimensions of Internal Conflict.* Cambridge, MA: MIT Press.

Bryce-Laporte, Roy. 1982. "The New Immigration: Its Origin, Visibility, and Implications for Public Policy." In *Ethnicity and Public Policy,* edited by Winston Van Horne, pp. 62–88. Madison: University of Wisconsin Press.

Bullard, Robert. 1991. "Housing Problems and Prospects for Blacks in Houston." *Review of Black Political Economy* 19:175–194.

———. 1993. "Race and Environmental Justice in the United States." *The Yale Journal of International Law* 18:319–335.

Bullock, Henry A. 1967. *A History of Negro Education in the South.* New York: Praeger.

Bunzel, John, and Jeffrey Au. 1987. "Diversity or Discrimination?—Asian Americans in College." *The Public Interest* 87:49–62.

Burns, E. Bradford. 1993. *A History of Brazil,* 3rd edition. New York: Cornell University Press.

Cabezas, Amado, and Gary Kawaguchi. 1988. "Empirical Evidence for Continuing Asian American Income Inequality." In *Reflections on Shattered Windows: Promises and Prospects for Asian American Studies,* edited by Gary Okihiro, Shirley Hume, Arthur Hansen, and John Liu, pp. 144–164. Pullman, WA: Washington State University Press.

———. 1990. "Industrial Sectorization in California in 1980: The Continuing Significance of Race/Ethnicity, Gender, and Nativity." In *Income and Status Differences Between White and Minority Americans: A Persistent Inequality,* edited by Sucheny Chan, pp. 57–99. Lewiston, NY: Edwin Mellen Press.

Cabezas, Amado, Larry Shinagawa, and Gary Kawaguchi. 1986–1987. "New Inquiries into the Socioeconomic Status of Filipino Americans in California." *Amerasia Journal* 13:1–21.

———. 1990. "Income Differentials Between Asian Americans and White Americans in California, 1980." In *Income and Status Differences Between White and Minority Americans: A Persistent Inequality,* edited by Sucheny Chan, pp. 181–201. Lewiston, NY: Edwin Mellen Press.

Cabezas, Amado, Tse Tam, Brenda Lowe, Anna Wong, and Kathy Turner. 1989. "Empirical Study of Barriers to Upward Mobility of Asian Americans in the San Francisco Bay Area." In *Frontiers of Asian American Studies: Writing, Research and Commentary,* edited by Gail Nomura, Russell Endo, Stephen Sumida, and Russell Leong, pp. 93–115. Pullman, WA: Washington State University Press.

Califa, Antonio. 1989. "Declaring English the Official Language: Prejudice Spoken Here." *Harvard Civil Rights—Civil Liberties Law Review* 24:293–348.

Calmore, John. 1993. "Spatial Equality and the Kerner Commission Report: A Back-to-the-Future Essay." *North Carolina Law Review* 71:1487–1518.

Caputo, Richard. 1993. "Family, Poverty, Unemployment Rates, and AFDC Payments: Trends among Black and Whites." *Families in Society: The Journal of Contemporary Human Services* 74:515–526.

Carro, John. 1980. "Impact of the Criminal Justice System on Hispanics." In *National Conference on Law Enforcement and Criminal Justice,* pp. 361–382. Washington, DC: U.S. Department of Justice Law Enforcement Assistance Administration.

Cash, W. J. 1941. *The Mind of the South.* New York: Vintage Books.

Castles, Stephen. 1992. "Migrants and Minorities in Post-Keynesian Capitalism: The German Case." In *Ethnic Minorities and Industrial Change in Europe and North America,* edited by M. Cross. Cambridge: Cambridge University Press.

Castro, Max, Margaret Haun, and Ana Roca. 1990. "The Official English Movement in Florida." In *Perspectives on Official English: The Campaign for English as the Official Language of the USA,* edited by Karen Adams and Daniel Brink, pp.150–160. New York: Mouton de Gruyter.

Cella, John. 1982. *The Highest Stage of White Supremacy: The Origins of Segregation in the South.* New York: Cambridge University Press.

Chang, Robert. 1993. "Toward an Asian American Legal Scholarship: Critical Race Theory, Post-Structuralism, and Narrative Space." *California Law Review* 81:1243–1323.

Chapa, Jorge, and Richard R. Valencia. 1993. "Latino Population Growth, Demographic Characteristics, and Educational Stagnation: An Examination of Recent Trends." *Hispanic Journal of Behavioral Sciences* 15:165–187.

Chavez, Leo, Estevan Flores, and Marta Lopez-Garza. 1990. "Here Today, Gone Tomorrow? Undocumented Settlers and Immigration Reform." *Human Organization* 49:193–205.

Chavira, Ricardo. 1977. "A Case Study: Reporting of Mexican Emigration and Deportation." *Journalism History* 4:59–61.

Chiu, Daina. 1994. "The Cultural Defense: Beyond Exclusion, Assimilation, and Guilty Liberalism." *California Law Review* 82(4):1053–1125.

Choy, Bong-youn. 1979. *Koreans in America.* Chicago: Nelson-Hall.

Chun, Ki-Taek. 1980. "The Myth of Asian American Success and Its Educational Ramifications." *IRCO Bulletin* 15:1–12.

Churchill, Ward. 1992. *Fantasies of the Master Race: Literature, Cinema, and the Colonization of American Indians.* Marroe, ME: Common Courage Press.

———. 1993. "Crimes Against Humanity." *Z Magazine* (March):43–47.

Churchill, Ward, and Winona LaDuke. 1992. "Native North America: The Political

Economy of Radioactive Colonialism." In *The State of Native America: Genocide, Colonization, and Resistance,* edited by M. Annette Jaimes, pp. 241–266. Boston: South End Press.

Churchill, Ward, and Glenn Morris. 1992. "Key Indian Laws and Cases." In *The State of Native America: Genocide, Colonization, and Resistance,* edited by M. Annette Jaimes, pp. 13–21. Boston: South End Press.

Clifton, James (ed.). 1989. *Being and Becoming Indian: Biographical Studies of North American Frontiers.* Chicago: Dorsey.

Cohen, Roger. 1994. "West Fears Bosnia." *The New York Times,* March 13.

Commission on Wartime Relocation and Internment of Civilians. 1983. *Personal Justice Denied.* Washington, DC: U.S. Government Printing Office.

Coughlin, Ellen. 1994. "Returning Indian Remains." *The Chronicle of Higher Education* (Mar. 16), pp. A8, A9, A16.

Cox, Oliver. 1948. *Caste, Class, and Race.* Garden City, NY: Doubleday.

Crosby, Alfred. 1976. "Virgin Soil Epidemics as a Factor in Aboriginal Depopulation in America." *William and Mary Quarterly* 33:289–299.

Cruz, Wilfredo. 1995. "Police Brutality in African American and Latino Communities." *Latino Studies Journal* 6:30–47.

Crystal, David. 1989. "Asian Americans and the Myth of the Model Minority." *Social Casework* 70:405–413.

Curtis, Lewis P. 1971. *Apes and Angels: The Irish Victorian Caricature.* Washington, DC: Smithsonian Institution Press.

Daniel, Pete. 1973. *The Shadow of Slavery: Peonage in the South 1901–1969.* London: Oxford University Press.

Daniels, Roger. 1971. *Concentration Camps USA: Japanese Americans and World War II.* Hinsdale, IL: Dryden Press.

Darby, John. 1976. *Conflict in Northern Ireland: The Development of a Polarized Community.* Dublin: Gill and Macmillan.

Degler, Carl. 1971. *Neither Black nor White: Slavery and Race Relations in Brazil and the United States.* New York: Macmillan.

de la Garza, Rodolfo O., Louis DeSipio, F. Chris Garcia, John Garcia, and Angelo Falcon. 1992. *Latino Voices: Mexican, Puerto Rican, and Cuban Perspectives on American Politics.* Boulder, CO: Westview Press.

Delgado, Richard, and Jean Stefancic. 1992. "Images of the Outsider in American Law and Culture: Can Free Expression Remedy Systemic Social Ills?" *Cornell Law Review* 77:1258–1297.

Deloria, Vine, Jr. 1969. *Custer Died for Your Sins.* New York: Macmillan.

———. 1976. "The Place of Indians in Contemporary Education." *American Indian Journal* 2:2.

———. 1992. "Trouble in High Places: Erosion of American Indian Rights to Religious Freedom in the United States." In *The State of Native America: Genocide, Colonization, and Resistance,* edited by M. Annette Jaimes, pp. 267–290. Boston: South End Press.

Deloria, Vine, Jr., and Clifford Lytle. 1983. *American Indians, American Justice.* Austin: University of Texas Press.

Denber, Rachel (ed.). 1992. *The Soviet Nationality Reader: The Disintegration in Context.* Boulder, CO: Westview Press.

Der, Henry, and Colleen Lye. 1989. *The Broken Ladder '89: Asian Americans in City Government.* San Francisco: Chinese for Affirmative Action.

Díaz-Cotto, Juanita. 1996. *Gender, Ethnicity, and the State: Latina and Latino Prison Politics.* Albany, NY: SUNY Press.

Dickson, Robert J. 1966. *Ulster Immigration to Colonial America, 1718–1773.* London: Routledge & Kegan Paul.

Dinnerstein, Leonard, and David M. Reimers. 1988. *Ethnic Americans: A History of Immigration,* 3d edition. New York: Harper & Row.

Domenech, Emmanuel. 1860. *Seven Years Residence in the Great Deserts of North America.* London: Longmans.

Drinan, Robert. 1991. "Civil Rights and the Thousand Days of the Bush Administration." *America* 164:624–626.

Duleep, Harriet, and Seth Sanders. 1992. "Discrimination at the Top: American-born Asian and White Men." *Industrial Relations* 31:416–432.

Dunn, Ashley. 1994. "Bilingual Ballot Law Fails to Help Chinese American Voters." *The New York Times* (August 14):34.

Duran, Livie, and H. Russel Bernard (eds.). 1973. *Introduction to Chicano Studies.* New York: Macmillan.

Durham, Jimmie. 1992. "Cowboys and Notes on Art, Literature, and American Indians in the Modern American Mind." In *The State of Native America: Genocide, Colonization, and Resistance,* edited by M. Annette Jaimes, pp. 423–438. Boston: South End Press.

Dutter, L. E. 1990. "Theoretical Perspectives on Ethnic Political Behavior in the Soviet Union." *Journal of Conflict Resolution* 34:11–34.

Dyste, Connie. 1990. "The Popularity of California's Proposition 63: An Analysis." In *Perspectives on Official English: The Campaign for English as the Official Language of the USA,* edited by Karen Adams and Daniel Brink, pp. 141–150. New York: Mouton de Gruyter.

Eagle, Adam. 1992. *Alcatraz! Alcatraz!: The Indian Occupation of 1969–1971.* Berkeley: Heyday Books.

Edmunds, R. David. 1983. "Tecumseh, the Shawnee Prophet, and American History: A Reassessment." *Western Historical Quarterly* 14:261–276.

Eggers, Mitchell, and Douglas Massey. 1992. "A Longitudinal Analysis of Urban Poverty: Blacks in U.S. Metropolitan Areas between 1970 and 1980." *Social Science Research* 21:175–203.

Elkins, Stanley. 1959. *Slavery: A Problem in American Institutional and Intellectual Life.* Chicago, IL: University of Chicago Press.

Equal Employment Opportunity Commission. 1985. *Equal Employment Opportunity Report—1983: Job Patterns of Minorities and Women in Private Industry.* Washington, DC: U.S. Government Printing Office.

Estrada, Leo, F. Chris Garcia, Reynaldo Macias, and Lionel Maldonado. 1988. "Chicanos in the United States: A History of Exploitation and Resistance." In *Latinos and the Political System,* edited by F. Chris Garcia, pp. 28–64. Notre Dame, IN: University of Notre Dame Press.

Fainstein, Norman. 1993. "Race, Class and Segregation: Discourses about African Americans." *International Journal of Urban and Regional Research* 17: 384–403.

Falcon, Angelo. 1984. "Puerto Rican Politics in New York City: 1860s to 1945." In *Puerto Rican Politics in Urban America,* edited by James Jennings and Monte Rivera, pp. 15–42. New York: Greenwood Press.

———. 1988. "Black and Latino Politics: Race and Ethnicity in a Changing Urban Context." In *Latinos and the Political System,* edited by F. Chris Garcia, pp. 171–194. Notre Dame, IN: University of Notre Dame Press.

Falcon, Priscilla, and Patricia J. Campbell. 1991. "The Politics of Language and the Mexican American: The English Only Movement and Bilingual Education." In

Racism and the Underclass: State Policy and Discrimination Against Minorities, edited by George W. Shepherd, Jr., and David Penna, pp. 145–158. New York: Greenwood Press.

Farley, John. 1987. "Disproportionate Black and Hispanic Unemployment in U.S. Metropolitan Areas: The Roles of Racial Inequality, Segregation and Discrimination and Male Joblessness." *American Journal of Economics and Sociology* 46:129–150.

———. 1995. "Race Still Matters: The Minimal Role of Income and Housing Cost As Causes of Housing Segregation in St. Louis, 1990." *Urban Affairs Review* 31:244–254.

Farley, Reynolds. 1990. "Blacks, Hispanics, and White Ethnic Groups: Are Blacks Uniquely Disadvantaged?" *American Economic Review* 80:237–241.

Farley, Reynolds, and Walter R. Allen. 1987. *The Color Line and the Quality of Life in America.* New York: Russell Sage.

Farley, Reynolds, and William H. Frey. 1994. "Changes in the Segregation of Whites from Blacks During the 1980s: Small Steps Towards a More Integrated Society." *American Sociological Review* 59:23–45.

Feagin, Joe R. 1989. *Racial and Ethnic Relations,* 3d edition. Englewood Cliffs, NJ: Prentice-Hall.

———. 1991. "The Continuing Significance of Race: Antiblack Discrimination in Public Places." *American Sociological Review* 56:101–116.

Feagins, Ken. 1990. "Affirmative Action or the Same Sin?" *Denver University Law Review* 67:442–451.

Fegley, Randall. 1993. *Rwanda.* Oxford: Clio Press.

Fernandez, Edward, and J. Gregory Robinson. 1994. *Illustrative Ranges of the Distribution of Undocumented Immigrants by State* (Technical Working Paper No. 8). Washington, DC: U.S. Bureau of the Census.

Fitzpatrick, Joseph. 1987. *Puerto Rican Americans: The Meaning of Migration to the Mainland,* 2d edition. Englewood Cliffs, NJ: Prentice-Hall.

Fix, Michael, and Paul Hill. 1990. *Enforcing Employer Sanctions: Challenges and Strategies.* Santa Monica, CA: The RAND Corporation.

Fogel, Robert, and Stanley Engerman. 1974. *Time on the Cross.* Boston: Little, Brown.

Fost, Dan. 1991. "American Indians in the 1990s." *American Demographics* (Dec.):26–34.

Fredrickson, George M. 1971. *The Black Image in the White Mind.* New York: Harper & Row.

———. 1981. *White Supremacy: A Comparative Study in American and South African History.* New York: Oxford University Press.

———. 1988. *The Arrogance of Race.* Middletown, CT: Wesleyan University Press.

Freeman, James. 1995. *Changing Identities: Vietnamese Americans 1975–1995.* Boston: Allyn and Bacon.

Freyre, Gilberto. 1956. *The Masters and the Slaves.* New York: Knopf.

———. 1963. *New World in the Tropics.* New York: Vintage.

Frideres, James S. 1983. *Native People in Canada,* 2nd edition. Scarborough, Ontario: Prentice-Hall of Canada.

———. 1990. "Policies on Indian People in Canada." In *Race and Ethnic Relations in Canada,* edited by P. S. Li. Toronto: Oxford University Press.

Fukuda, Moritoshi. 1980. *Legal Problems of Japanese Americans.* Tokyo: Keio Tsushin Company.

Gabriel, Paul E., Donald R. Williams, and Susanne Schmitz. 1990. "The Relative Occupational Attainment of Young Blacks, Whites, and Hispanics." *Southern Economic Journal* 57:35–46.

Gambino, Richard. 1974. *Blood of My Blood: The Dilemma of Italian-Americans.* Garden City, NY: Doubleday.

Garcia, F. Chris, and Rodolfo de la Garza. 1977. *The Chicano Political Experience: Three Perspectives.* North Scituate, MA: Duxbury Press.

Garcia, Ignacio. 1996. "Backwards from Aztlan: Politics in the Age of Hispanics." In *Chicanas and Chicanos in Contemporary Society,* edited by Robert M. De Anda, pp. 191–204. Boston: Allyn and Bacon.

Garcia, Juan. 1980. *Operation Wetback.* Westport, CT: Greenwood Press.

Gee, Harry. 1993. "Employment Issues for Asians in Texas." In *Meeting the Challenge: Critical Issues in Education, Health, and Employment in Texas,* pp. 39–46. College Station, TX: Texas A&M University Institute for Race and Ethnic Studies.

Genovese, Eugene D. 1965. *The Political Economy of Slavery.* New York: Vintage Books.

Geshwender, James, and Rita Carroll-Seguin. 1990. "Exploding the Myth of African-American Progress." *Signs* 15:285–299.

Ginzberg, Eli. 1991. "Access to Health Care for Hispanics." *Journal of the American Medical Association* 265:238–241.

Giordano, Rita. 1987a. "Anti-Asian Fliers' Origin a Mystery." *Newsday* (Nov. 4).

———. 1987b. "Bensonhurst: Anti-Asian Bias Linked to Incidents." *Newsday,* (Dec. 15).

Glazer, Nathan. 1957. *American Judaism.* Chicago: University of Chicago Press.

Glazer, Nathan, and Daniel P. Moynihan. 1970. *Beyond the Melting Pot,* 2nd edition. Cambridge: MIT Press.

Glock, Charles Y., and Rodney Stark. 1966. *Christian Beliefs and Anti-Semitism.* New York: Harper & Row.

Gold, Steven. 1995. *From the Workers' State to the Golden State: Jews from the Former Soviet Union in California.* Boston: Allyn and Bacon.

Goldschneider, Calvin. 1986. *Jewish Continuity and Change: Emerging Patterns in America.* Bloomington: Indiana University Press.

Gomes, Ralph C., and Linda Faye Williams. 1990. "Race and Crime: The Role of the Media in Perpetuating Racism and Classism in America." *The Urban League Review* 14:57–69.

Gordon, Milton. 1964. *Assimilation in American Life: The Role of Race, Religion, and National Origins.* New York: Oxford University Press.

———. 1981. "Models of Pluralism: The New American Dilemma." *Annals of the American Academy of Political and Social Science* 454:178–188.

Graham, Hugh D. 1990. "Race, Language, and Social Policy: Comparing the Black and Hispanic Experience in the U.S." *Population and Environment* 12:43–58.

Gray, Maryann, Elizabeth Rolph, and Elan Melamid. 1996. *Immigration and Higher Education: Institutional Responses to Changing Demographics.* Santa Monica: RAND.

Grebler, Leo, Joan Moore, and Ralph Guzman. 1970. *The Mexican-American People: The Nation's Second Largest Minority.* New York: Free Press.

Greeley, Andrew M. 1971. *Why Can't They Be Like Us?* New York: Dutton.

———. 1974. *Ethnicity in the United States: A Preliminary Reconnaissance.* New York: Wiley.

———. 1977. *The American Catholic: A Social Portrait.* New York: Harper and Row.

———. 1981. *The Irish Americans.* New York: Harper and Row.

Greenwell, Lisa, Julie DaVanzo, and R. Burciage Valdez. 1993. "Social Ties, Wages, and Gender among Salvadorean and Filipino Immigrants in Los Angeles." Santa Monica, CA: RAND Program for Research on Immigration Policy DRU-213-PRIP.

Grove, John, and Jiping Wu. 1991. "Who Benefitted from the Gains of Asian-Americans, 1940–1980?" In *Racism and the Underclass: State Policy and Discrimination Against Minorities,* edited by George Shepherd and David Penna, pp. 99–117. New York: Greenwood Press.

Gurr, Robert Ted and Will H Moore. 1997. "Ethnopolitical Rebellion: A Cross-sectional Analysis of the 1980s with Risk Assessment for the 1990s." *American Journal of Political Science* 41: forthcoming.

Gurr, Ted R. 1993. "Why Minorities Rebel: A Global Analysis of Communal Mobilization and Conflict Since 1945." *International Political Studies* 6:135–169.

Hamilton, Horace C. 1964. "The Negro Leaves the South." *Demography* 1:273–295.

Hardy-Fanta, Carol. 1993. *Latina Politics, Latino Politics: Gender, Culture, and Political Participation in Boston.* Philadelphia: Temple University Press.

Harmon, Alexandra. 1990. "When Is an Indian Not an Indian? 'Friends of the Indian' and the Problems of Indian Identity." *Journal of Ethnic Studies* 18:95–123.

Harrison, Roderick J., and Daniel H. Weinberg. 1992. "Changes in Racial and Ethic Residential Segregation, 1980–1990." Paper presented at the American Statistical Association Meeting, Boston, August.

Hawkins, Chuck. 1993. "Denny's: The Stain That Isn't Coming Out." *Business Week* (June 28):98–99.

Herberg, Edward H. 1989. *Ethnic Groups in Canada: Adaptations and Transitions.* Scarborough, Ontario: Nelson Canada.

Herberg, Will. 1960. *Protestant-Catholic-Jew.* Garden City, NY: Doubleday.

Hernandez-Chavez, Eduardo, Andrew Cohen, and Anthony Beltramo (eds.). 1975. *El Lenguaje de los Chicanos: Regional and Social Characteristics of Language Used by Mexican Americans.* Arlington, VA: Center for Applied Linguistics.

Hero, Rodney. 1990. "Hispanics in Urban Government and Politics: Some Findings, Comparisons and Implications." *Western Political Quarterly* 43:403–414.

———. 1992. *Latinos and the U.S. Political System: Two-Tiered Pluralism.* Philadelphia: Temple University Press.

Hietala, Thomas. 1985. *Manifest Density: Anxious Aggrandizement in Late Jacksonian America.* Ithaca, NY: Cornell University Press.

Higham, John. 1963. *Strangers in the Land: Patterns of American Nativism 1860–1925,* 2nd edition. New York: Atheneum.

Hillard, David, and Lewis Cole. 1993. *This Side of Glory: The Autobiography of David Hillard and the Story of the Black Panther Party.* New York: Little, Brown and Company.

Hilliard, Asa G. 1988. "Conceptual Confusion and the Persistence of Group Oppression through Education." *Equity and Excellence* 24:36–43.

Hiller, Harry H. 1991. *Canadian Society: A Macro Analysis.* 2nd edition. Scarborough, Ontario: Prentice-Hall of Canada.

Hing, Bill Ong. 1993. *Making and Remaking Asian America Through Immigration Policy 1850–1990.* Stanford, CA: Stanford University Press.

Hoffman, Abraham. 1974. *Unwanted Mexican Americans in the Great Depression: Repatriation Pressures, 1929–1939.* Tucson: University of Arizona Press.

Hoffman, B. 1992. "Current Research on Terrorism and Low-Intensity Conflict." *Studies of Conflict Terrorism* 15:25–37.

Hollmann, Frederick. 1992. "National Population Trends." In *Population Trends in the 1980's,* pp. 1–11. Washington, DC: U.S. Bureau of the Census Special Studies P-23-No. 175.

Horowitz, Harold, and Kenneth Karit. 1969. *Law, Lawyers and Social Change: Cases and Materials on the Abolition of Slavery, Racial Segregation and Inequality of Educational Opportunity.* New York: The Bobbs-Merrill Company.

Horowitz, Irving Louis. 1992. *Taking Lives: Genocide and State Power,* 3d edition. New Brunswick, NJ: Transaction Press.

Hosokawa, Bill. 1982. "Accentuating the American in Japanese American." *Perspectives: The Civil Rights Quarterly* 14:40–44.

House Committee on Indian Affairs. 1934. U.S. Department of the Interior Hearings on HR7902, 73rd Congress, 2d Session. Washington, DC: U.S. Government Printing Office.

Hsia, Jayjia. 1988. *Asian Americans in Higher Education and at Work.* Hillsdale, NJ: Lawrence Erlbaum Associates.

Hu, Arthur. 1989. "Asian Americans: Model Minority or Double Minority?" *AMERASIA* 15:243–257.

Hughes, Mark, and Janice Madden. 1991. "Residential Segregation and the Economic Status of Black Workers: New Evidence for an Old Debate." *Journal of Urban Economics* 29:28–49.

Humphrey, Norman. 1941. "Mexican Repatriation from Michigan: Public Assistance in Historical Perspective." *Social Service Review* 15:497–513.

Hunnington, Samuel P. 1966. "Political Modernization: America vs. Europe." *World Politics* 18:147–148.

Hurk, Won, and Kwang Kim. 1989. "The 'Success' Image of Asian Americans: Its Validity, and Its Practical and Theoretical Implications." *Ethnic and Racial Studies* 12:512–538.

Hurtado, Albert. 1982. "Hardly a Farm House—A Kitchen without Them: Indian and White Households on the California Borderland Frontier in 1860." *Western Historical Quarterly* 13:245–270.

Hurtado, Albert, and Peter Iverson (eds.). 1994. *Major Problems in American Indian History: Documents and Essays.* Lexington, MA: D.C. Heath and Company.

Huskisson, Gregory. 1988. "Enough Is Enough: Blacks Protest Redlining." *Black Enterprise* (October):22.

Imhoff, Gary. 1990. "The Position of U.S. English on Bilingual Education." *The Annals* 508:48–61.

Jackson, Aurora. 1993. "Black, Single, Working Mothers in Poverty: Preferences for Employment, Well-Being, and Perceptions of Preschool-age Children." *Social Work* 38:26–35.

Jaffe, A., Ruth Cullen, and Thomas Boswell. 1980. *The Changing Demography of Spanish Americans.* New York: Academic Press.

Jaimes, M. Annette. 1992. "Federal Indian Identification Policy: A Usurpation of Indigenous Sovereignty in North America." In *Native Americans and Public Policy,* edited by Fremont Lyden and Lyman Legters, pp. 113–135. Pittsburgh: University of Pittsburgh Press.

Jaret, Charles. 1991. "Recent Structural Change and U.S. Urban Ethnic Minorities." *Journal of Urban Affairs* 13:307–336.

Jarvenpa, Robert. 1985. "The Political Economy and Political Ethnicity of American Indian Adaptations and Identities." In *Ethnicity and Race in the U.S.A.: Toward the Twenty-First Century,* edited by Richard D. Alba, pp. 29–48. New York: Routledge.

Jaynes, Gerald David, and Robin Williams (eds.). 1989. *A Common Destiny: Blacks and American Society.* Washington, DC: National Academy Press.

Jencks, Christopher. 1991. "Is the American Underclass Growing?" In *The Urban Underclass,* edited by C. Jencks and P. E. Peterson, pp. 28–102. Washington, DC: The Brookings Institution.

Jones-Correa, Michael and David Leal. 1996. "Becoming 'Hispanic': Secondary Panethnic Identification Among Latin American-Origin Populations in the United States." *Hispanic Journal of Behavioral Sciences* 18:214–254.

Jones, Eugene. 1988. *Native Americans as Shown on the Stage, 1753–1916.* Metuchen, NJ: Scarecrow Press.

Jordon, Winthrop D. 1962. "Modern Tensions and the Origins of American Slavery." *Journal of Southern History* 28:18–30.

———. 1968. *White Over Black: American Attitudes Toward the Negro, 1550–1812.* Chapel Hill: University of North Carolina Press.

Juarez, José. 1995. "The American Tradition of Language Rights: The Forgotten Right to Government in a 'Known Tongue.'" *Law and Inequality* 13:443–642.

Kamin, Leon J. 1974. *The Science and Politics of I.Q.* New York: Wiley.

Kang, Jerry. 1996. "Negative Action Against Asian Americans: The Internal Instability of Dworkin's Defense of Affirmative Action." *Harvard Civil Rights–Civil Liberties Law Review* 31:1–47.

Karnow, Stanley. 1992. *Asian Americans in Transition.* New York: Asia Society.

Keller, Gary. 1985. "The Image of the Chicano in Mexican, United States, and Chicano Cinema: An Overview." In *Chicano Cinema: Research, Reviews and Resources,* edited by Gary Keller, pp. 13–58. Binghamton, NY: Bilingual Review Press.

Keller, Gary (ed.). 1985. *Chicano Cinema: Research, Reviews, and Resources.* Binghamton, NY: Bilingual Review Press.

Kelly, Lawrence. 1975. "The Indian Reorganization Act: The Dream and the Reality." *Pacific Historical Review* 44:291–312.

Kinder, Donald, and Lynn Sanders. 1990. "Mimicking Political Debate with Survey Questions: The Case of White Opinion on Affirmative Action for Blacks." *Social Cognition* 8:73–103.

Kitano, Harry. 1980. *Race Relations.* Englewood Cliffs, NJ: Prentice-Hall.

Kitano, Harry, and Roger Daniels. 1988. *Asian Americans: Emerging Minorities.* Englewood Cliffs, NJ: Prentice-Hall.

Kluegel, James R., and Lawrence Bobo. 1993. "Opposition to Race-Targeting: Self-Interest, Stratification Ideology, or Racial Attitudes?" *American Sociological Review* 58:443–464.

Kluegel, James R., and Eliot R. Smith. 1986. *Beliefs about Inequality in America.* Hawthorne, NY: Aldine de Gruyter.

Kluger, Richard. 1975. *Simple Justice: The History of Brown v. Board of Education and Black America's Struggle for Equality.* New York: Vintage Books.

Knight, Franklin W. 1974. *The African Dimension in Latin American Societies.* New York: Macmillan.

Knippenberg, Hans. 1991. "The Nationalities Question in the Soviet Union." In *States and Nations: The Rebirth of the Nationalities Question in Europe,* edited by H. van Amersfoort and H. Koppenberg. Amsterdam: KNAG.

Knobel, Dale T. 1986. *Paddy and the Republic.* Middletown, CT: Wesleyan University Press.

Knoll, Tricia. 1982. *Becoming Americans: Asian Sojourners, Immigrants, and Refugees in the Western United States.* Portland, OR: Coast to Coast Books.

Kohn, Hans. 1960. *Pan-Slavism: Its History and Ideology.* New York: Vintage Books.

Kotkin, Joel, and Bill Bradley. 1989. "Democrats and Demographics; Asians, Hispanics and Small Business Are the Party's Future." *Washington Post,* February 26.

Kousser, J. Morgan. 1974. *The Shaping of Southern Politics: Suffrage Restrictions and the Establishment of the One-Party South, 1880–1910.* New Haven, CT: Yale University Press.

Kunitz, Stephen. 1971. "The Social Philosophy of John Collier." *Ethnohistory* 18:213–239.

LaDuke, Winona. 1981. "Indian Land Claims and Treaty Areas of North America: Succeeding into Native North America." *CoEvolution Quarterly* 32:64–65.

Lander, Ernest McPherson. 1969. *The Textile Industry in Antebellum South Carolina.* Baton Rouge: Louisiana State University Press.

Langberg, Mark, and Reynolds Farley. 1985. "Residential Segregation of Asian Americans in 1980." *Sociology and Social Research* 70:71–75.

Langley, Lester. 1988. *MexAmerica: Two Countries, One Future.* New York: Crown.

La Piere, Richard T. 1934. "Attitudes vs. Actions." *Social Forces* 13:230–237.

Learsi, Rufus. 1954. *The Jews in America: A History.* Cleveland, OH: World Publishing.

Lee, Moon. 1993. "Asian Americans Don't Fit Their Monochrome Image." *The Christian Science Monitor* (July 27):9, 10.

Lesch, Ann M. 1983. "Palestine: Land and People." In *Occupation: Israel Over Palestine,* edited by N. H. Aruri. Belmont, MA: Association of Arab-American University Graduates.

Lessinger, Johanna. 1995. *From the Ganges to the Hudson: Indian Immigrants in New York City.* Boston: Allyn and Bacon.

Lestschinsky, Jacob. 1955. "Economic Development of American Jewry." In *The Jewish People,* vol. 4, pp. 131–156. New York: Jewish Encyclopedic Handbooks.

Lewis, Ronald L. 1979. *Coal, Iron and Slaves: Industrial Slavery in Maryland and Virginia 1715–1865.* Westport, CT: Greenwood Press.

———. 1989. *Black Workers: A Documentary History from Colonial Times to the Present,* edited by Philip S. Foner and R. L. Lewis. Philadelphia, PA: Temple University Press.

Leyburn, James G. 1962. *The Scotch-Irish.* Chapel Hill: University of North Carolina Press.

Li, Peter S. (ed.). 1990. *Race and Ethnic Relations in Canada.* Toronto: Oxford University Press.

Lieberson, Stanley, and Mary C. Waters. 1988. *From Many Strands: Racial and Ethnic Groups in Contemporary America.* New York: Russell Sage.

Lipset, Seymour Martin. 1987. "Blacks and Jews: How Much Bias?" *Public Opinion* 10 (July/August):4–5, 57–58.

Litwack, Leon F. 1961. *North of Slavery: The Negro in the Free States, 1790–1860.* Chicago: University of Chicago Press.

Lopez, Alfred. 1973. *The Puerto Rican Papers.* Indianapolis, IN: Bobbs-Merrill.

Lopez, Manuel. 1986. "Su Casa No Es Mi Casa: Hispanic Housing Conditions in Contemporary America, 1949–1980." In *Race, Ethnicity, and Minority Housing in the United States,* edited by Jamshid Momeni, pp. 127–145. New York: Greenwood Press.

Lopreato, Joseph. 1970. *Italian Americans.* New York: Random House.

Louis, W. Roger. 1963. *Ruanda-Urundi, 1884–1919.* Oxford: Clarendon Press.

Lummins, Charles. 1968. *Bullying the Hopi.* Prescott, AZ: Prescott College Press.

Lyman, Stanford. 1986. *Chinatown and Little Tokyo: Power, Conflict, and Community among Chinese and Japanese Immigrants in America.* Milwood, NY: Associated Faculty Press.

———. 1990. "Race, Sex, and Servitude: Images of Blacks in American Cinema." *International Journal of Politics, Culture and Society* 4:49–77.

Macias, Reynaldo. 1993. "Language and Ethnic Classification of Language Minorities: Chicano and Latino Students in the 1990s." *Hispanic Journal of Behavioral Sciences* 15:230–257.

Mahler, Sarah. 1995. *Salvadorans in Suburbia: Symbiosis and Conflict.* Boston: Allyn and Bacon.

Maldonado, Rita. 1976. "Why Puerto Ricans Migrated to the United States in 1947–1973." *Monthly Labor Review* 9:7–18.

Maldonado-Denis, Manuel. 1972. *Puerto Rico, A Socio-historic Interpretation,* translated by E. Vialo. New York: Random House.

Marger, Martin N. 1991. *Race and Ethnic Relations in America: American and Global Perspectives.* Belmont, CA: Wadsworth.

Marquez, Benjamin. 1993. *LULAC: The Evolution of a Mexican American Political Organization.* Austin: University of Texas Press.

Martinez, Ramiro, Jr. 1996. "Latinos and Lethal Violence: The Impact of Poverty and Inequality." *Social Problems* 43:131–146.

Martinez, Tomás. 1969. "Advertising and Racism: The Case of Mexican Americans." *El Grito* 2 (Summer):13–31.

Massey, Douglas. 1983. *The Demographic and Economic Position of Hispanics in the United States: The Decade of the 1970s.* Washington, DC: National Commission for Employment Policy.

Matthaei, Julie, and Teresa Amott. 1990. "Race, Gender, Work: The History of Asian and Asian-American Women." *Race and Class* 31:61–80.

Mazon, Mauricio. 1984. *The Zoot-Suit Riots: The Psychology of Symbolic Annihilation.* Austin: University of Texas Press.

McAdam, Doug. 1982. *Political Processes and the Development of Black Insurgency, 1930–1970.* Chicago: University of Chicago Press.

———. 1988. *Freedom Summer.* New York: Oxford University Press.

McAllister, Ian. 1977. *The Northern Ireland Social Democratic and Labour Party.* London: Macmillan.

McCarthy, Cameron. 1990. *Race and Curriculum.* New York: The Falmer Press.

McCarthy, Kevin, and R. Valdez. 1986. *Current and Future Effects of Mexican Immigration in California.* Santa Monica, CA: The RAND Corporation.

McDonnell, Janet. 1991. *The Dispossession of the American Indian 1887–1934.* Bloomington, IN: Indiana University Press.

McKenzie, R. 1928. *Oriental Exclusion.* Chicago: University of Chicago Press.

McKinney, Scott, and Ann B. Schnare. 1989. "Trends in Residential Segregation by Race: 1960–1980." *Journal of Urban Economics* 26:269–280.

McQueen, Michel. 1991. "Voters' Responses to Poll Disclose Huge Chasm Between Social Attitudes of Blacks." *Wall Street Journal,* May 17, p. A16.

McRoberts, Kenneth. 1988. *Quebec: Social Change and Political Crisis,* 3d edition. Toronto: McClelland and Stewart.

McWilliams, Carey. 1968. *North from Mexico: The Spanish-Speaking People of the United States.* New York: Greenwood Press.

Medina, Marcell, Jr. 1988. "Hispanic Apartheid in American Public Education." *Educational Administration Quarterly* 24:336–349.

Meli, Francis. 1988. *South Africa Belongs to Us: A History of the ANC.* Bloomington: Indiana University Press.

Mendoza Report. 1978. *Access of Non or Limited English Speaking Persons of Hispanic Origin to the New York City Department of Social Services.* Washington, DC: U.S. Department of Health, Education, and Welfare.

Merrell, James. 1984. "The Indians' New World: The Catawba Experience." *William and Mary Quarterly* 41:537–565.

Merton, Robert K. 1949. "Discrimination and the American Creed." In *Discrimination and National Welfare,* edited by R. H. MacIver, pp. 99–126. New York: Harper and Row.

Meyer, Doris. 1978. "Early Mexican-American Responses to Negative Stereotyping." *New Mexico Historical Review* 53:75–91.

Meyer, Melissa. 1991. " 'We Can Not Get a Living As We Used To': Dispossession and the White Earth Anishinaabeg, 1889–1920." *American Historical Review* 96:386–394.

Miller, Kerby A. 1985. *Emigrants and Exiles.* New York: Oxford University Press.

Miller, Stuart. 1969. *The Unwelcome Immigrant: The American Image of the Chinese, 1785–1882.* Berkeley: University of California Press.

Minerbrook, Scott. 1993. "Blacks Locked Out of the American Dream." *Business and Society Review* 87:23–28.

Montero, Darrel. 1981. "The Japanese Americans: Changing Patterns of Assimilation Over Three Generations." *American Sociological Review* 46:829–839.

Mooney, James. 1928. *The Aboriginal Population of America North of Mexico.* Washington, DC: Smithsonian Institution Miscellaneous Collections, vol. 80, no. 7.

Moore, Theresa, and Robert Gunnison. 1994. "Blacks and Asians Say the System Is Insensitive." *San Francisco Chronicle* (Mar. 3):A4.

Morales, Armando. 1972. *Ando Sangrando (I am Bleeding): A Study of Mexican American-Police Conflict.* La Puente, CA: Perspectiva Publications.

———. 1973. "Police Deployment Theories." In *Voices: Readings from El Grito,* edited by V. Octavio I. Romano, pp. 167–180. Berkeley, CA: Quinto Sol Publications.

Morales, Julio. 1986. *Puerto Rican Poverty and Migration: We Just Had to Try Elsewhere.* New York: Praeger.

Morganthau, Tom. 1993. "America: Still a Melting Pot?" *Newsweek* (Aug. 9), pp. 16–23.

Morris, Glenn. 1992. "International Law and Politics: Toward a Right to Self-Determination for Indigenous People." In *The State of Native America: Genocide, Colonization, and Resistance,* edited by M. Annette Jaimes, pp. 55–86. Boston: South End Press.

Moses, Marion. 1993. "Farmworkers and Pesticides." In *Confronting Environmental Racism: Voices From The Grassroots,* edited by Robert Bullard, pp. 161–178. Boston: South End Press.

Mozo, S. Montes, and J. Garcia Vasquez. 1988. *Salvadorian Migration to the United States: An Exploratory Study.* Washington, DC: Georgetown University Center for Immigration Policy and Refugee Assistance.

Muller, Thomas. 1993. *Immigrants and the American City.* New York: New York University Press.

Mulvey, Sister Mary. 1936. *French Catholic Missionaries in the Present United States, 1604–1791.* Washington, DC: Catholic University of America Press.

Munoz, Carlos, Jr. 1989. *Youth, Identity, Power: The Chicano Movement.* New York: Verso.

Murguia, Edward. 1975. *Assimilation, Colonialism, and the Mexican American People.* Austin: University of Texas at Austin Center for Mexican American Studies Monograph Series No. 1.

Nakanishi, Don. 1988. "Asian Pacific Americans and Selective Undergraduate Admissions." *Journal of College Admissions* 118:17–26.

National Center for Health Statistics. 1991. *Health: United States, 1990.* Hyattsville, MD: Public Health Service.

National Puerto Rican Coalition. 1985. *Puerto Ricans in the Mid '80s: An American Challenge.* Washington, DC: National Puerto Rican Coalition.

Nelson, Candace, and Marta Tienda. 1985. "The Structuring of Hispanic Ethnicity: Historical and Contemporary Perspectives." *Ethnic and Racial Studies* 8:49–74.

Newbury, C. 1988. *The Cohesion of Oppression: Clientship and Ethnicity in Rwanda, 1860–1960.* New York: Columbia University Press.

Newton, James E., and R. L. Lewis (eds.). 1978. *The Other Slaves: Mechanics, Artisans and Craftsmen.* Boston: G.K. Hall.

Nguyen, Beatrice Bich-Dao. 1993. "Accent Discrimination and the Test of Spoken English: A Call for an Objective Assessment of the Comprehensibility of Nonnative Speakers." *California Law Review* 81:1325–1361.

Noriega, Jorge. 1992. "American Indian Education in the United States: Indoctrination for Subordination to Colonialism." In *The State of Native America: Genocide, Colonization, and Resistance,* edited by M. Annette Jaimes, pp. 371–402. Boston: South End Press.

O'Connor, John. 1980. *The Hollywood Indian: Stereotypes of Native Americans in Film.* Trenton, NJ: New Jersey State Museum.

O'Hare, W., and J. Felt. 1991. *Asian Americans: America's Fastest Growing Minority Group.* Washington, DC: Population Reference Bureau Report No. 19.

Olzak, Susan. 1986. "A Competition Model of Collective Action in American Cities." In *Competitive Ethnic Relations,* edited by S. Olzak and J. Nagel, pp. 17–46. Orlando, FL: Academic Press.

———. 1992. *The Dynamics of Ethnic Competition and Conflict.* Stanford, CA: Stanford University Press.

Ortego, Philip D. 1973. "The Chicano Renaissance." In *Introduction to Chicano Studies,* edited by L. I. Duran and H. R. Bernard, pp. 568–584. New York: Macmillan.

Osako, Masako. 1984. "Japanese-Americans: Melting into the All-American Pot?" In *Ethnic Chicago,* edited by Melvin Holli and Peter Jones, pp. 69–76. Grand Rapids, MI: William B. Eerdmans Publishing.

Osborne, R. D. 1990. "Northern Ireland: the Irreducible Conflict." In *Conflict and Peacemaking in Multiethnic Societies,* edited by J. V. Montville. Lexington, MA: Lexington Books.

Osborne, Robert, and Robert Cormack. 1991. "Religion and Labour Market: Patterns and Profiles." In *Discrimination and Public Policy in Northern Ireland,* edited by R. J. Cormack and R. D. Osborne. Oxford: Clarendon Press.

Osborne, Stephen. 1989. *Indian-Hating in American Literature, 1682–1857.* Unpublished doctoral dissertation, University of Michigan, Ann Arbor.

Padilla, Felix. 1987. *Puerto Rican Chicago.* Indiana: University of Notre Dame Press.

Padilla, Raymond, and Alfredo Beravides (eds.). 1992. *Critical Perspectives on Bilingual Education Research.* Tempe, AZ: Bilingual Press/Editorial Bilingue.

Page, Bryan. 1980. "The Children of Exile: Relationships Between the Acculturation Process and Drug Use among Cuban Youth." *Youth and Society* 11:431–447.

Paisano, Edna. 1992. "Selected Social and Economic Characteristics for the American Indian, Eskimo, and Aleut Population for Selected Areas: 1990." Presented at the Meeting for the Census Advisory Committees on the American Indian and Alaska Native, Asian and Pacific Islander, Black and Hispanic Population for the 1990 Census, November 5–6, Phoenix, Arizona.

Palm, Risa. 1985. "Ethnic Segmentation of Real Estate Agent Practice in the Urban Housing Market." *Annals of the Association of American Geographers* 75:58–68.

Paredes, Raymond. 1977. "The Mexican Image in American Travel Literature, 1831–1869." *New Mexico Historical Review* 52:5–29.

Park, Robert E. 1916. "The City: Suggestions for the Investigation of Human Behavior in an Urban Environment." *American Journal of Sociology* 20:577–612.

———. 1950. *Race and Culture.* Glencoe, IL: Free Press.

Park, Robert E., and Ernest W. Burgess. 1924. *Introduction to the Science of Sociology.* Chicago: University of Chicago Press.

Parker, Linda. 1989. *Native American Estate: The Struggle Over Indian and Hawaiian Lands.* Honolulu: University of Hawaii Press.

Passel, Jeffrey. 1976. "Provisional Evaluation of the 1970 Census Count of American Indians." *Demography* 13:397–409.

———. 1993. "Discussion: Racial Identity/Classification and Its Effect on the Undercount." In *Proceedings of the Bureau of the Census 1993 Research Conference on Undercounted Ethnic Populations,* pp. 345–353. Washington, DC: U.S. Bureau of the Census.

Passel, Jeffrey, and Patricia Berman. 1986. "Quality of 1980 Census Data for American Indians." *Social Biology* 33:163–182.

Pedraza-Bailey, Silvia, and Teresa Sullivan. 1979. "Bilingual Education in the Reception of Political Immigrants: The Case of Cubans in Miami, Florida." In *Bilingual Education and Public Policy in the United States,* edited by Raymond Padilla, pp. 376–394. Ypsilanti: Eastern Michigan University Department of Foreign Languages and Bilingual Studies.

Peng, Samuel. 1990. "Attainment Status of Asian Americans in Higher Education." In *Contemporary Perspectives on Asian and Pacific American Education,* edited by Russell Endo, Virgie Chattergy, Sally Chou, and Nobuya Tsuchida, pp. 56–77. South El Monte, CA: Pacific Asia Press.

Penrose, Eldon. 1973. *California Nativism: Organized Opposition to the Japanese, 1890–1913.* San Francisco: R & E Research Associates.

Perez, Lisandro. 1980. "Cubans." In *Harvard Encyclopedia of American Ethnic Groups,* edited by Stephan Ternstrom, pp. 256–261. Cambridge, MA: Belknap Press.

———. 1986. "Immigrant Economic Adjustment and Family Organization: The Cuban Success Story Re-Examined." *International Migration Review* 20:4–20.

Pessar, Patricia. 1995. *A Visa for a Dream: Dominicans in the United States.* Boston: Allyn and Bacon.

Peterson, William. 1971. *Japanese Americans: Oppression and Success.* New York: Random House.

Pinkney, Alphonso. 1969. *Black Americans.* Englewood Cliffs, NJ: Prentice-Hall.

———. 1984. *The Myth of Black Progress.* New York: Cambridge University Press.

Pitt, Leonard. 1966. *The Decline of the Californios.* Berkeley: University of California Press.

Pohlmann, Marcus D. 1990. *Black Politics in Conservative America.* New York: Longmans.

Portes, Alejandro. 1990. "From South of the Border: Hispanic Minorities in the United States." In *Immigration Reconsidered: History, Sociology, and Politics,* edited by V. Yans-McLaughlin, pp. 160–184. New York: Oxford University Press.

Portes, Alejandro, and Dag MacLeod. 1996. "What Shall I Call Myself? Hispanic Identity Formation in the Second Generation." *Ethnic and Racial Studies* 19:523–547.

Portes, Alejandro, and Ruben Rumbaut. 1990. *Immigrant America: A Portrait.* Berkeley: University of California Press.

President's Commission on Mental Health. 1978. *Report of the Special Populations Subpanel on the Mental Health of Asian/Pacific Americans,* vol. 3. Washington, DC: U.S. Government Printing Office.

Price, John. 1978. *Native Studies: American and Canadian Indians.* New York: McGraw-Hill/Ryerson Limited.

Rable, George C. 1984. *But There Was No Peace: The Role of Violence in the Politics of Reconstruction.* Athens: University of Georgia Press.

Reed, Ishmael. 1993. *Airing Dirty Laundry.* Reading, MA: Addison-Wesley.

Reed, Wornie. 1990. "Racism and Health: The Case of Black Infant Mortality." In *The Sociology of Health and Illness: Critical Perspectives,* 3d edition, edited by P. Conrad and R. Kern, pp. 34–44. New York: St. Martins Press.

Reisler, Mark. 1996. "Always the Laborer, Never the Citizen: Anglo Perceptions of the Mexican Immigrant During the 1920s." In *Between Two Worlds: Mexican Immigrants in the United States,* edited by David G. Gutierrez, pp. 23–43. Wilmington, DE: Scholarly Resources.

Ricketts, Erol R., and Isabel Sawhill. 1988. "Defining and Measuring the Underclass." *Journal of Policy Analysis and Management* 7:316–325.

Robbins, Rebecca. 1992. "Self-Determination and Subordination: The Past, Present, and Future of American Indian Governance." In *The State of Native America: Genocide, Colonization, and Resistance,* edited by M. Annette Jaimes, pp. 87–121. Boston: South End Press.

Robinson, Cecil. 1963. *With the Ears of Strangers: The Mexican in American Literature.* Tucson: University of Arizona Press.

Rodriguez, Havidan. 1992. "Population, Economic Mobility and Income Inequality: A Portrait of Latinos in the United States, 1970–1991." *Latino Studies Journal* 3:55–86.

Rodriquez, Nestor. 1987. "Undocumented Central Americans in Houston: Diverse Populations." *International Migration Review* 21:4–26.

Roediger, David R. 1991. *The Wages of Whiteness: Race and the Making of the American Working Class.* New York: Verso.

Rogg, Eleanor. 1974. *The Assimilation of Cuban Exiles: The Role of Community and Class.* New York: Academic Press.

Rolison, Gary. 1993. "Nonemployment of Black Men in Major Metropolitan Areas." *Sociological Inquiry* 63:328–329.

Rolph, Elizabeth. 1992. *Immigration Policies: Legacy from the 1980s and Issues for the 1990s.* Santa Monica, CA: The RAND Corporation.

Romo, Ricardo. 1989. "The Urbanization of Southwestern Chicanos in the Early Twentieth Century." In *Race and Culture in America,* edited by Carl Jackson and Emory Tolbert, pp. 235–249. Edina, MN: Burgess International Group.

Rose, Richard. 1971. *Governing Without Consensus: An Irish Perspective.* Boston: Beacon Press.

———. 1990. "Northern Ireland: The Irreducible Conflict." In *Conflict and Peacemaking in Multiethnic Societies,* edited by J. V. Montville. Lexington, MA: Lexington Books.

Ross, Thomas. 1990. "Innocence and Affirmative Action." *Vanderbilt Law Review* 43:297–336.

Roudi, Nazy. 1993. "The Palestinians." *Population Today* 21(1):8–14.

Rowan, Carl T. 1993. *Dream Makers, Dream Breakers: The World of Justice Thurgood Marshall.* New York: Little, Brown and Company.

Rubel, Arthur. 1966. *Across the Tracks.* Austin: University of Texas Press.

Russell, James. 1994. *After the Fifth Sun: Class and Race in North America.* Englewood Cliffs, NJ: Prentice-Hall.

Said, Edward W., et al. 1988. "A Profile of the Palestinian People." In *Blaming the Victims,* edited by E. W. Said and C. Hitchens. London: Verso.

San Miguel, Guadalupe, Jr. 1987. *"Let All of Them Take Heed": Mexican Americans and the Campaign for Educational Equality in Texas, 1910–1981.* Austin: University of Texas Press.

Sanchez, George. 1951. *Concerning Segregation of Spanish-Speaking Children in the Public Schools.* (Inter-American Education Occasional Paper No. 9.) Austin: University of Texas Press.

Santiago, Anne M., and Margaret G. Wilder. 1991. "Residential Segregation and Links to Minority Poverty: The Case of Latinos in the United States." *Social Problems* 38:492–515.

Schaefer, Richard T. 1990. *Racial and Ethnic Groups,* 4th edition. Glenview, IL: Scott Foresman/Little, Brown.

Schafer, Daniel. 1993. "A Class of People Neither Freemen nor Slaves: From Spanish to American Race Relations in Florida, 1821–1861." *Journal of Social History* 26:587–609.

Schiavo, Giovanni. 1934. *The Italian in America Before the Civil War.* New York: Vigo Press.

Schick, Frank, and Renee Schick. 1991. *Statistical Handbook on U.S. Hispanics.* New York: Oryx Press.

Schneider, Mark, and Thomas Phelan. 1990. "Blacks and Jobs: Never the Twain Shall Meet?" *Urban Affairs Quarterly* 26:299–313.

Schoeni, Robert, Kevin McCarthy, and Georges Vernez. 1996. *The Mixed Economic Progress of Immigrants.* Santa Monica: RAND.

Schrieke, B. 1936. *Alien Americans: A Study of Race Relations.* New York: The Viking Press.

Schuman, Howard, Charlotte Steeh, and Lawrence Bobo. 1985. *Racial Attitudes in America: Trends and Interpretations.* Cambridge, MA: Harvard University Press.

Select Committee on Aging. 1992. "Farmworkers' High Mortality: Government Neglect?" Washington, DC: U.S. Government Printing Office.

Selzer, Michael. 1972. *"Kike"—Anti-Semitism in America.* New York: Meridian Press.

Serwer, Andrew. 1993. "What to Do When Race Charges Fly." *Fortune* 128:95–96.

Shively, J. 1992. "Cowboys and Indians: Perceptions of Western Films among American Indians and Anglos." *American Sociological Review* 57:725–734.

Shorris, Earl. 1992. *Latinos: A Biography of the People.* New York: Avon Books.

Shrier, Arnold. 1958. *Ireland and the American Emigration, 1850–1900.* Minneapolis: University of Minnesota Press.

Simmons, Ozzie G. 1973. "The Mutual Images and Expectations of Anglo-Americans and Mexican Americans." In *Introduction to Chicano Studies,* edited by Livie Duran and H. Russell Bernard, pp. 112–120. New York: Macmillan.

Singleton, Royce, and Jonathan H. Turner. 1975. "Racism: White Oppression of Blacks in America." In *Understanding Social Problems,* edited by D. Zimmerman and L. Weider, pp. 130–160. New York: Praeger.

Sissons, Peter. 1979. *The Hispanic Experience of Criminal Justice.* New York: Hispanic Research Center at Fordham University.

Sklare, Marshall. 1971. *American Jews.* New York: Random House.

Smith, David J., and Gerald Changers. 1991. *Inequality in Northern Ireland.* Oxford: Clarendon Press.

Smith, Geoffrey. 1992. "There's No Whites Only Sign But . . ." *Business Week* (Oct. 26):78.

Smith, Grahm (ed.), *The Nationalities Question in the Soviet Union.* London: Longman, 1990.

Smith, T. Lynn. 1974. *Brazilian Society.* Albuquerque, NM: University of New Mexico Press.

Smits, David. 1991. "Squaw Men, Half Breeds, and Amalgamators: Late 19th Century Anglo-American Attitudes Toward Indian-White Race-Mixing." *American Indian Culture and Research Journal* 15:29–61.

Snipp, C. Matthew. 1986. "The Changing Political and Economic Status of the American Indians: From Captive Nations to Internal Colonies." *American Journal of Economics and Sociology* 45:145–157.

———. 1989. *American Indians: The First of This Land.* New York: Russell Sage.

Sowsky, Gorgi, Edward Lai, and Barbara Plake. 1991. "Moderating Effects of Sociocultural Variables on Acculturation Attitudes of Hispanics and Asian Americans." *Journal of Counseling & Development* 70:194–204.

Spinden, Herbert. 1928. "The Population of Ancient America." *Geographical Review* 18:640–660.

Stampp, Kenneth M. 1956. *The Peculiar Institution: Slavery in the Ante-Bellum South.* New York: Vintage Books.

Staples, Robert. 1975. "White Racism, Black Crime, and American Justice: An Application of the Colonial Model to Explain Crime and Race." *Phylon* 36:14–22.

Starobin, Robert S. 1970. *Industrial Slavery in the Old South.* London: Oxford University Press.

Stedman, Raymond. 1982. *Shadows of the Indian: Stereotypes in American Culture.* Norman: University of Oklahoma Press.

Steele, Shelby. 1990. *The Content of Our Character.* New York: St. Martins.

Stephan, Walter, and Cookie Stephan. 1989. "Antecedents of Intergroup Anxiety in Asian-Americans and Hispanic-Americans." *Journal of Intercultural Relations* 13:203–219.

Stewart, Omer. 1987. *Peyote Religion: A History.* Norman, OK: University of Oklahoma Press.

Stoddard, Ellwyn R. 1973. *Mexican Americans.* New York: Random House.

Strong, Edward. 1934. *The Second-Generation Japanese Problem.* Stanford, CA: Stanford University Press.

Sue, Stanley, Nolan Zane, and Derald Sue. 1985. "Where Are the Asian American Leaders and Top Executives?" *PLAAMARC Research Review* 4:13–15.

Suzuki, Bob. 1989. "Asians." In *Shaping Higher Education's Future: Demographic Realities and Opportunities, 1990–2000,* edited by Arthur Levine and Associates, pp. 87–115. San Francisco: Jossey-Bass.

Swinton, David. 1989. "The Economic Status of Black Americans." In *The State of Black America,* pp. 9–39. New York: National Urban League.

Takagi, Dana. 1990. "From Discrimination to Affirmative Action: Facts in the Asian American Admissions Controversy." *Social Problems* 37:578–592.

Takaki, Ronald (ed.). 1987. *From Different Shores: Perspectives on Race and Ethnicity in America.* New York: Oxford University Press.

———. 1989. *Strangers from a Different Shore: A History of Asian Americans.* Boston: Little, Brown.

———. 1993. *A Different Mirror: A History of Multicultural America.* Boston: Little, Brown.

———. 1996. "The Myth of the 'Model Minority.'" In *Taking Sides: Clashing Views on Controversial Issues in Race and Ethnicity,"* 2d edition, edited by Richard Monk, pp. 41-47. Guilford, CT: Dushkin.

Tamayo, William, Robin Toma, and Stewart Koh. 1991. *The Voting Rights of Asian Pacific Americans.* Los Angeles: University of California at Los Angeles Asian American Studies Center.

Tambiah, S. J. 1986. *Sri Lanka: Ethnic Fratricide and the Dismantling of Democracy.* Chicago, IL: University of Chicago Press.

Tang, Joyce. 1991. *Asian American Engineers: Earnings, Occupational Status, and Promotions.* Paper presented at the Annual Meeting of the American Sociological Association, Cincinnati, OH.

Taylor, Ronald. 1973. *Sweatshops in the Sun—Child Labor on the Farm.* San Francisco: Earthwork.

Telles, Edward E. 1992. "Residential Segregation by Skin Color in Brazil." *American Sociological Review* 57:186–197.

Thomas, Gail. 1995. "Notes on Asian American Employment." In *Race and Ethnicity in America: Meeting the Challenge in the 21st Century,* edited by Gail Thomas, pp. 265–268. Washington, DC: Taylor & Francis.

Thomas, R. Roosevelt, Jr. 1990. "From Affirming Action to Affirming Diversity." *Harvard Business Review* 68:107–117.

Thompson, Laura, and Alice Joseph. 1944. *The Hopi Way.* Ann Arbor: University of Michigan Press.

Thompson, Leonard. 1964. "The South African Dilemma." In *The Founding of New Societies,* edited by L. Hartz. New York: Harcourt Brace and World.

———. 1985. *The Political Mythology of Apartheid.* New Haven, CT: Yale University Press.

———. 1990. *A History of South Africa.* New Haven, CT: Yale University Press.

Thornton, Michael, and Robert Taylor. 1988. "Intergroup Attitudes: Black American Perceptions of Asian Americans." *Ethnic and Racial Studies* 11:474–488.

Tinker, George, and Loring Bush. 1991. "Native American Unemployment: Statistical Games and Coverups." In *Racism and the Underclass: State Policy and Discrimination Against Minorities,* edited by George W. Shepherd, Jr., and David Penna, pp. 119–144. New York: Greenwood Press.

Titiev, Misha. 1944. "Old Oraibi" (Papers of the Peabody Museum of American Archaeology and Ethnology, vol. 22, no. 1). Cambridge, MA: Harvard University Press.

Tolnay, Stewart E., and E. M. Beck. 1992. "Racial Violence and Black Migration in the American South, 1910–1930." *American Sociological Review* 57:103–116.

Tomasi, Silvano, and Madeline Engel (eds.). 1970. *The Italian Experience in the United States.* New York: Center for Migration Studies.

Torres, Maria de los Angeles. 1988. "From Exiles to Minorities: The Politics of Cuban Americans." In *Latinos and the Political System,* edited by F. Chris Garcia, pp. 81–98. Notre Dame, IN: University of Notre Dame Press.

Trennert, Robert. 1982. "Educating Indian Girls at Nonreservation Boarding Schools, 1878–1920." *Western Historical Quarterly* 13:271–290.

Trevino, Fernando, M. Moyer, R. Valdez, and Christine Stroup-Benham. 1991. "Health Insurance Coverage and Utilization of Health Services by Mexican Americans, Mainland Puerto Ricans, and Cuban Americans." *Journal of the American Medical Association* 265:233–237.

Trueba, Henry. 1986. *Success or Failure? Learning and the Language Minority Student.* New York: Newbury House.

———. 1989. *Raising Silent Voices: Educating the Linguistic Minorities for the 21st Century.* New York: Newbury House.

———. 1993. "Race and Ethnicity: The Role of Universities in Healing Multicultural America." *Educational Theory* 43:41–54.

Tsuchida, Nobuya. 1990. "The Evacuation and Internment of Japanese Americans during World War II: An Invaluable Lesson on the American Judicial System." In *Contemporary Perspectives on Asian and Pacific American Education,* edited by Russell Endo, Virgie Chattergy, Sally Chou, and Nobuya Tsuchida, pp. 160–191. South El Monte, CA: Pacific Asia Press.

Turner, Jonathan H. 1992. "Inequality and Poverty." In *Social Problems in America,* edited by G. Ritzer and C. Calhoun, pp. 73–138. New York: McGraw-Hill.

Turner, Jonathan H., and Edna Bonacich. 1980. "Toward a Composite Theory of Middleman Minorities." *Ethnicity* 7:144–158.

Turner, Jonathan H., and Alexandra Maryanski. 1993. "The Biology of Human Organization." *Human Ecology* 3:1–36.

Turner, Jonathan H., and Royce Singleton. 1978. "A Theory of Ethnic Oppression." *Social Forces* 56:1001–1008.

Turner, Jonathan H., Royce Singleton, and David Musick. 1984. *Oppression: A Sociohistory of Black-White Relations in America.* Chicago: Nelson-Hall.

U.S. Bureau of the Census. 1963. *U.S. Census of Population: 1960 (PC2–1B).* Washington, DC: U.S. Government Printing Office.

———. 1972. *The Excluded Student (Report III): Educational Practices Affecting Mexican Americans in the Southwest.* Washington, DC: U.S. Government Printing Office.

———. 1973a. *U.S. Census of Population: 1970 (PC2-1D).* Washington, DC: U.S. Government Printing Office.

———. 1973b. *1970 Census of Housing and Population (Subject Report PC2-1F).* Washington, DC: U.S. Government Printing Office.

———. 1975a. *Historical Statistics of the United States: Colonial Times to 1970.* Washington, DC: U.S. Government Printing Office.

———. 1975b. *The Navajo Nation: An American Colony.* Washington, DC: U.S. Government Printing Office.

———. 1976. *Puerto Ricans in the Continental United States: An Uncertain Future.* Washington, DC: U.S. Government Printing Office.

———. 1979a. *The Social and Economic Status of the Black Population in the United States: An Historical Overview, 1790–1978 (P-23-No. 80).* Washington, DC: U.S. Government Printing Office.

———. 1979b. *Civil Rights Issues and Asian and Pacific Americans: Myths and Realities.* Washington, DC: U.S. Government Printing Office.

———. 1980. *Success of Asian Americans: Fact or Fiction?* Washington, DC: U.S. Government Printing Office.

———. 1981. *Persons of Spanish Origin in the United States: March 1980 (P-20-No. 361).* Washington, DC: U.S. Government Printing Office.

———. 1983a. *U.S. Census of Population: 1970 (PC80-1).* Washington, DC: U.S. Government Printing Office.

———. 1983b. *1980 Census of Population (PC80-51-10).* Washington, DC: U.S. Government Printing Office.

———. 1983c. *Asian and Pacific Islander Population by State: 1980 (PC80-51-12).* Washington, DC: U.S. Government Printing Office.

———. 1983d. *America's Black Population: 1970 to 1982, A Statistical View (PIO/POP-83-1).* Washington, DC: U.S. Government Printing Office.

———. 1983e. *Ancestry of the Population by State: 1980.* Washington, DC: U.S. Government Printing Office.

———. 1985. *1980 Census of Population (Subject Report PC80-2-10).* Washington, DC: U.S. Government Printing Office.

———. 1986. *Recent Activities Against Citizens and Residents of Asian Descent.* Washington, DC: U.S. Government Printing Office.

———. 1988. *The Economic Status of Americans of Asian Descent: An Exploratory Investigation.* Washington, DC: U.S. Government Printing Office.

———. 1989a. *Money, Income and Poverty Status in the United States: 1987 (P-60-No. 161).* Washington, DC: U.S. Government Printing Office.

———. 1989b. *Civil Rights Issues in Maine.* Washington, DC: U.S. Government Printing Office.

———. 1991a. *Current Population Reports, The Hispanic Population of the U.S. Southwest Borderland (P-23-No. 172).* Washington, DC: U.S. Government Printing Office.

———. 1991b. *Current Population Reports, The Hispanic Population in the United States: March 1990 (P-20-No. 449).* Washington, DC: U.S. Government Printing Office.

———. 1991c. *The Black Population in the United States: March 1990 and 1989 (P-20-No. 448).* Washington, DC: U.S. Government Printing Office.

———. 1991d. *Studies in American Fertility (P-23-No. 176).* Washington, DC: U.S. Government Printing Office.

———. 1992a. *The Asian and Pacific Islander Population in the United States: March 1991 and 1990 (P-20-459).* Washington, DC: U.S. Government Printing Office.

———. 1992b. *Population Trends in the 1980's (P-23-No. 175).* Washington, DC: U.S. Government Printing Office.

———. 1992c. *Civil Rights Issues Facing Asian Americans in the 1990s.* Washington, DC: U.S. Government Printing Office.

———. 1993a. *1990 Census of Housing—Detailed Housing Characteristics: American Indian and Alaska Native Areas (1990 Ch-2-1A).* Washington, DC: U.S. Government Printing Office.

———. 1993b. *Statistical Abstract of the United States: 1993.* Washington, DC: U.S. Government Printing Office.

———. 1993c. *Ancestry of the Population in the United States: 1990.* Washington, DC: U.S. Government Printing Office.

———. 1994a. *The Hispanic Population in the United States: March 1993* (Series P20-475). Washington, DC: U.S. Government Printing Office.

———. 1994b. *Characteristics of American Indians by Tribe and Language: 1990.* Washington, DC: U.S. Government Printing Office.

———. 1995. *Statistical Abstract of the United States 1995.* Washington, DC: U.S. Government Printing Office.

U.S. Commission on Civil Rights. 1970. *Mexican Americans and the Administration of Justice in the Southwest.* Washington, DC: U.S. Government Printing Office.

———. 1996. *Briefing on Efforts to End Discrimination in Mortgage Lending: Executive Summary.* Washington, D.C.: U.S. Commission on Civil Rights.

U.S. Department of Commerce. 1989. *Poverty in the United States, 1987.* Series P-60, No. 163. Washington, DC: U.S. Government Printing Office.

U.S. Department of Health, Education and Welfare. 1976. *A Statistical Portrait of the American Indian.* Washington, DC: U.S. Government Printing Office.

U.S. Department of Health and Human Services. 1993. *Health United States 1992 and Healthy People 2000 Review.* Washington, DC: U.S. Department of Health and Human Services Pub. No. 93-1232.

U.S. Department of Housing and Urban Development. 1991. *Housing Discrimination Study.* Washington, DC: U.S. Department of Housing and Urban Development.

U.S. Department of Justice. 1980. *National Hispanic Conference on Law Enforcement and Criminal Justice.* Washington, DC: U.S. Department of Justice Law Enforcement Assistance Administration.

———. 1991a. *1990 Statistical Yearbook of the Immigration and Naturalization Service.* Washington, DC: U.S. Government Printing Office.

———. 1991b. *Teenage Victims: A National Crime Survey Report.* Washington, DC: U.S. Government Printing Office.

———. 1991c. *School Crime: A National Crime Victimization Survey Report.* Washington, DC: U.S. Government Printing Office.

———. 1995. *Bureau of Justice Statistics Sourcebook of Criminal Justice Statistics—1994.* Washington, DC: U.S. Government Printing Office.

U.S. Department of Labor. 1989. *Monthly Review* 112. Washington, DC: U.S. Government Printing Office.

———. 1991. *Preliminary Report on Discrimination in the Workplace and the Existence of the "Glass Ceiling."* Washington, DC: U.S. Government Printing Office.

U.S. General Accounting Office. 1989. *Equal Employment Opportunity: Women and Minority Aerospace Managers and Professionals.* Washington, DC: U.S. Government Printing Office.

Valdez, R. Burciaga, Julie DaVanzo, Georges Vernez, and Mitchell Wade. 1993. "Immigration: Getting the Facts." RAND Issue, Paper #1. Santa Monica, CA: The RAND Corporation.

van den Berghe, Pierre. 1978. *Race and Racism: A Comparative Perspective,* 2nd edition. New York: Wiley.

——— 1981. *The Ethnic Phenomenon.* New York: Elsevier.

Verdun, Vincene. 1993. "If the Shoe Fits, Wear It: An Analysis of Reparations to African Americans." *Tulane Law Review* 67:597–668.

Vernez, Georges. 1990. *Immigration and International Relations: Proceedings of a Conference on the International Effects of the 1986 Immigration Reform and Control Act (IRCA).* Santa Monica, CA: RAND and the Urban Institute.

———. 1993. *Needed: A Federal Role in Helping Communities Cope with Immigration.* Santa Monica, CA: Program for Research on Immigration Policy RP-177.

Vernez, Georges, and Allan Abrahamse. 1996. *How Immigrants Fare in U.S. Education.* Santa Monica, CA: RAND.

Vernez, Georges, and Kevin McCarthy. 1990. *Meeting the Economy's Labor Needs Through Immigration: Rationales and Challenges.* Santa Monica, CA: RAND.

———. 1996. *The Costs of Immigration to Taxpayers: Analytical and Policy Issues.* Santa Monica, CA: RAND.

Villareal, Roberto. 1988. "The Politics of Mexican-American Empowerment." In *Latino Empowerment: Progress, Problems, and Prospects,* edited by Roberto Villareal, Norma Hernandez, and Howard Neighbor, pp. 1–9. New York: Greenwood Press.

Wagenheim, Kal (ed.). 1973. *Puerto Ricans: A Documentary History.* Garden City, NY: Doubleday, Anchor.

Wallace, Steven P. 1989. "The New Urban Latinos: Central Americans in a Mexican Immigrant Environment." *Urban Affairs Quarterly* 25:239–264.

———. 1990. "Race Versus Class in the Health Care of African-American Elderly." *Social Problems* 37:517–534.

Walsh, James H. 1992. "Migration and European Nationalism." *Migration World* 20:19–22.

Wang, L. Ling-chi. 1988. "Meritocracy and Diversity in Higher Education: Discrimination Against Asian Americans in the Post-Bakke Era." *The Urban Review* 20:183–209.

Warner, W. Lloyd. 1941. "Introduction." In *Deep South,* edited by Allison Davis, Burleigh Gardner, and Mary Gardner, pp. 1–6. Chicago: University of Chicago Press.

Warner, W. Lloyd, and Leo Srole. 1945. *The Social Systems of American Ethnic Groups.* New Haven, CT: Yale University Press.

Weber, Max. 1905–1906 [1930]. *The Protestant Ethic and the Spirit of Capitalism,* translated by T. Parsons. New York: Scribner and Sons.

Weinberg, Meyer. 1977. *A Chance to Learn: The History of Race and Education in the United States.* New York: Cambridge University Press.

Welch, Susan. 1990. "The Impact of At-Large Elections on the Representation of Blacks and Hispanics." *Journal of Politics* 52:1050–1076.

Welch, Susan, J. Gruhl, and C. Spohn. 1984. "Dismissal, Conviction, and Incarceration of Hispanic Defendants: A Comparison with Anglos and Blacks." *Social Science Quarterly* 65:257–264.

Whetstone, Muriel. 1993. "The Story Behind the Explosive Statistics: Why Blacks Are Losing Ground in the Workforce." *Ebony* (Dec.):102–104.

White, John. 1985. *Black Leadership in America: From Booker T. Washington to Jesse Jackson.* New York: Longmans.

Whitmore, John, Marcella Trautmann, and Nathan Caplan. 1989. "The Socio-Cultural Basis for the Economic and Educational Success of Southeast Asian Refugees (1978–1982 Arrivals)." In *Refugees as Immigrants: Cambodians, Laotians, and Vietnamese in America,* edited by David W. Haines, pp. 121–137. Totowa, NJ: Rowman & Littlefield.

Wildavsky, Ben. 1990. "Tilting at Billboards: Butts (et al.) vs. Poutts." *New Republic* (Aug. 20):19–20.

Williams, Robert. 1990. *The American Indian in Western Legal Thought: The Discourses of Conquest.* New York: Oxford University Press.

Williams, Robin M., Jr. 1994. "The sociology of Ethnic Conflicts: Comparative and International Perspectives." *Annual Review of Sociology* 20:49–79.

Williamson, Joel. 1984. *The Crucible of Race: Black/White Relations in the American South Since Emancipation.* New York: Oxford University Press.

Wilson, Kenneth, and Alejandro Portes. 1980. "Immigrant Enclaves: An Analysis of the Labor Market Experience of Cubans in Miami." *American Journal of Sociology* 86:295–319.

Wilson, William J. 1987. *The Truly Disadvantaged.* Chicago: University of Chicago Press.

Wirth, Louis. 1945. "The Problem of Minority Groups." In *The Science of Man in the World Crisis,* edited by R. Linton, pp. 347–372. New York: Columbia University Press.

Wong, Bernard. 1976. "Social Stratification, Adaptive Strategies and the Chinese Community of New York." *Urban Life* 5:33–52.

Wong, Eugene. 1978. *On Visual Media Racism: Asians in the American Motion Pictures.* New York: Arno.

Woodward, C. Vann. 1966. *The Strange Career of Jim Crow,* 2nd edition. New York: Oxford University Press.

Wright, Bobby, and William Tierney. 1991. "American Indians in Higher Education: A History of Cultural Conflict." *Change* 23:11–18.

Yen, Earl. 1988. "Flames Leave Massachusetts Cambodian Families Homeless." *Asian Week,* Dec. 2.

Yu, Jin. 1980. *The Korean Merchants in the Black Community.* Elkins Park, PA: Philip Jaisohn Foundation.

Zimmermann, Ekkart. 1980. "Macro-comparative Research on Political Protest." In *Handbook of Political Conflict: Theory and Research,* edited by Ted Robert Gurr. New York: Free Press.

Zinn, Maxine Baca. 1989. "Family, Race, and Poverty in the Eighties." *Signs: Journal of Women in Culture and Society* 14:856–874.

Zo, Kil. 1978. *Chinese Emigration into the United States, 1850–1880.* New York: Arno.

Zweigenhaft, Richard L., and G. William Domhoff. 1982. *Jews in the Protestant Establishment.* New York: Praeger.

Photo Credits

9 The New York Historical Society; **16** Mark Chester/Photo Researchers; **52** Jack Spratt/The Image Works; **76** Corbis/Bettmann; **83** M. Rosenthal/The Image Works; **98** UPI-Corbis/Bettmann; **112** Larry Mangino/The Image Works; **130** UPI-Corbis/Bettmann; **148** Glen Korengold/Stock, Boston; **161** Margaret Granitsas/The Image Works; **180** California Historical Society Library; **182** UPI-Corbis/Bettmann; **203** Library of Congress; **219** Barbara Alper/Stock, Boston; and **275** Michel Euler/AP/Wide World.

Index

American Ethnicity

The Dynamics and Consequences of Discrimination